Parliament in British Politics

Second Edition

Philip Norton

palgrave
macmillan

07/25 2
328.41 NOR
POLITICS
PARLIAMENT
BRITAIN POLITICS
UK

First edition 2005
Second edition 2013

Published by
PALGRAVE MACMILLAN

Palgrave Macmillan in the UK is an imprint of Macmillan Publishers Limited, registered in England, company number 785998, of Houndmills, Basingstoke, Hampshire RG21 6XS.

Palgrave Macmillan in the US is a division of St Martin's Press LLC, 175 Fifth Avenue, New York, NY 10010.

Palgrave Macmillan is the global academic imprint of the above companies and has companies and representatives throughout the world.

Palgrave® and Macmillan® are registered trademarks in the United States, the United Kingdom, Europe and other countries

ISBN 978-0-230-29192-8 hardback
ISBN 978-0-230-29193-5 paperback

This book is printed on paper suitable for recycling and made from fully managed and sustained forest sources. Logging, pulping and manufacturing processes are expected to conform to the environmental regulations of the country of origin.

A catalogue record for this book is available from the British Library.

A catalog record for this book is available from the Library of Congress.

10   9   8   7   6   5   4   3   2   1
22 21 20 19 18 17 16 15 14 13

Printed in China

Contents

PART 1   PARLIAMENT AND GOVERNMENT

List of Figures and Tables

Preface

The purpose of this book is embodied in the title. First, it seeks to provide a rich description of the institution of Parliament. It is a distinct and institutionalized body, with its own members, practices and procedures. Though many claim to have an interest in politics, few admit to knowing a great deal about Parliament and how it works. This book provides an introduction to the workings of Parliament in the twenty-first century.

Second, it explains how Parliament serves as key body within British politics. Parliament does not exist in a vacuum. From serving as a largely closed institution, with little opportunity for people to observe or to influence, in a relatively small political community, it has become a much more open institution in what is becoming an increasingly crowded political environment. It has a relationship with a number of bodies that are responsible for making decisions that impact upon the lives of citizens. The principal and most enduring relationship is with government. Much of the literature on Parliament focuses on that relationship. This work encompasses that relationship but goes beyond it. Parliament has a long but increasingly close and demanding relationship with the citizen. My earlier work, *Does Parliament Matter?*, published in 1993, examined how Parliament related both to government and the people. This work extends that study, putting it not only in a more explicit theoretical framework but also within the context of what has been termed the hollowing out of the state.

The determination of public policy is no longer confined to the core executive in the United Kingdom, in other words to the Prime Minister and Cabinet in London. Policy-making powers have become more dispersed, some passing to the institutions of the European Community, now the European Union, some to devolved institutions in Scotland, Wales and Northern Ireland, and some in effect to the courts. This fragmentation of policy-making has created significant challenges for Parliament. This volume seeks to locate Parliament's place within the British polity in the light of what is a dynamic constitutional milieu and to identify how it has responded to the challenges posed by these developments.

The challenges are not confined to those deriving from constitutional change. Parliament has had to cope with a growing volume of legislation and more demands made of Members of Parliament by constituents. Since the first edition of this book was published in 2005, it has had to contend with public opprobrium as a result of the expenses' scandal. The unauthorized publication in 2009 of MPs' expense claim forms revealed inappropriate and in some cases illegal claims; the House of Lords also faced a similar scandal over peers' expenses claims. This came in an era of mistrust and lingering public perceptions of MPs serving not the public interest, but their own.

Parliament has variously sought to adapt to the demands made of it and the changing constitutional and political landscape. It has sough to strengthen itself in its relationship with government, exhibiting a continuing tension between the needs of government to get its business done and the need for members to call government to account. It has attempted to mould its procedures to enable it to respond to the fragmentation of policy-making power, not least in relation to membership of the EU, to devolution, and to the incorporation into UK law of most provisions of the European Convention on Human Rights. The courts have begun to occupy territory that was previously the principal or exclusive preserve of Parliament.

Parliament has undergone significant changes as a result. The first edition sought to draw out those changes. This edition has proved necessary, not least because of what has happened since its publication. The extent of change is significant, but is often not seen beyond the confines of Westminster and Whitehall. It is masked to some degree by the continuing ceremony that retains symbolic importance, such as the State Opening of Parliament. Stories about the House of Lords are regularly accompanied by pictures of peers in robes at State Opening, an abiding image for many but one that conveys nothing about the work of the House as an integral part of Parliament. Both Houses are among the busiest legislative chambers in the world, but few appreciate how each works and its role in the polity.

This volume, then, seeks to make sense of where Parliament is today within the nation's constitutional and political framework and how it got to where it is. It concludes by looking at the debate as to where it should be going, or rather where each House should be going. Parliament is one legal entity, but comprises of two distinct Houses. It thus distinguishes the role of each.

In writing this new edition, I have retained the basic framework of the original, but adapted it to take account of recent changes. In particular, greater space and emphasis is given to how Parliament has sought to adapt to the hollowing out of the state. I have utilized a mix of quantitative and qualitative sources and drawn as far as possible on the most recently available data. I have also utilized my position as a participant-observer to inform the analysis. I have tried to ensure that, within the overall coherence of the work, each chapter is as self-contained as possible in order to enhance the utility of the work, enabling readers to look independently at particular aspects of Parliament and students to utilize chapters as appropriate for class assignments.

In preparing this new edition, I have incurred various debts, not least to Steven Kennedy of Palgrave Macmillan, whose gentle reminders that a new edition was necessary ensured that the work was completed. I have benefited greatly, as will be apparent from the text, from the data produced by Parliament, not least the library of each House. I have also appreciated greatly the willingness of parliamentary colleagues – both members and officials – to share with me their knowledge and experience.

As always, responsibility for any errors, omissions or distorted interpretations rests solely with me. I am always pleased to receive comments from readers. My work has variously been informed by feedback from my students and from less captive audiences.

PHILIP NORTON

University of Hull

The author and publishers would like to thank the following who have kindly given permission for the use of copyright material: The Hansard Society for Figure 11.1; Robert Worcester for Figure 11.2; and Crown copyright material is reproduced under the terms of the Open Government License v1.0.

1

Parliament in Perspective

It is common for a country to have a legislature – a body created to approve measures that will form the law of the land. Legislatures exist under a variety of names, of which National Assembly is the most popular (Loewenberg 2011, p. 18). Some use the term Congress, Parliament or Legislative Assembly. Others use terms specific to their language. In the United Kingdom, and in Commonwealth countries influenced by British experience, Parliament is preferred.

Two assumptions inform contemporary perceptions of legislatures (Norton 1990a, pp. 3–5). One is long-standing: that is, that legislatures exist to make law. The second, deriving from the late nineteenth century, is that legislatures are in decline.

The first perception derives from the very name *legislature*. *Legis* is the genitive of *lex,* meaning law; *lator* means carrier or proposer. A *legislator* was therefore someone who carried law. Legislatures have thus, by definition, been treated as bodies for carrying, or making, law. 'The legislative' declared John Locke in his *Second Treatise on Government* in 1689, 'is no otherwise legislative of the society but by the right it has to make laws for all parts and for every member of society, prescribing rules for their actions, and giving power of execution where they are transgressed' (Locke 1960). Baron de Montesquieu, in *The Spirit of Laws* published in 1748, a work that was to have a powerful influence in America, similarly defined legislative power as that of enacting temporary or perpetual laws, and the amending or abrogating of those already made (Montesquieu 1949). Law was thus created by legislatures. It was the very task that gave them their name and justified their existence.

The second assumption has existed for more than a century. Various nineteenth-century scholars, such as the English journalist Walter Bagehot (1867) and the American academic A. Lawrence Lowell (1896), identified the likely consequences for legislatures of the growth of party. However, it was to be a twentieth-century work by the scholar-statesman Lord Bryce that popularized the perception of decline. In *Modern*

1

Democracies, published in 1921, Bryce titled Chapter 58 'The Decline of Legislatures'. In the following chapter, he identified five 'chronic ailments' that had undermined representative assemblies, with party as the principal ailment. Though Bryce qualified his assertion, the notion of decline became associated with his work. It is one that has found a resonance in the subsequent study of legislatures.

The decline of legislatures

That there should be a perception of decline is not surprising. In the nineteenth century, legislatures grew in number and political significance. This growth in significance was not uniform, however; some countries, such as Germany, witnessed no 'golden age' of parliament. However, such countries were exceptional. Parliamentarianism was a feature of the century (Sontheimer 1984). Yet no sooner had this condition been reached than it began to deteriorate. Legislatures were unable to withstand the various pressures favouring executive dominance in the formulation and determination of public policy.

Industrialization generated an increasingly urban population with no political voice. Pressure for such a voice was to result in the widening of the franchise and the growth of political parties. In Britain, for example, the 1867 Reform Act – which increased the size of the electorate by almost 90 per cent – spurred the creation of mass-membership parties. Parties served to aggregate the demands of an electorate that lacked the willingness and the sophistication to consider the merits of individual candidates. Parties were beholden to electors for their success, and successful candidates owed their position to the party label. Continued party success came to depend on parties being able to implement promises made to the electorate. Implementation of such promises depended on party loyalty in the legislature. Scope for independent action by the elected members was squeezed out.

The party thus came to dominate the electoral and parliamentary processes. The party chose the candidates, raised the money to fight elections, and set the agenda. Party leaders occupied the central positions of government and decided what measures were to be laid before the legislature for approval. Party thus ensured that the site of policy-making – of crafting coherent measures of public policy – was the executive, not the legislature.

Industrialization had a further effect. Not only did it generate a mass franchise, it also resulted in a more specialized society. Interests became more differentiated – and more organized. In Britain, trade associations grew in number in the first half of the nineteenth century, and various professional and employers' organizations were established. These organizations began to compete to protect their own interests. What was notable in the first half of the century became more pronounced in the second half. Organized groups became more extensive in number and more national in structure. Trade unions, legalized in the 1870s, began to organize. The greater and more specialized the demands made of government by these groups, the greater the specificity of government policy (Richardson and Jordan 1979, pp. 44–5). The more specialized government policy became, the more government relied on groups for advice, information and co-operation in implementing policy.

The support of the party could usually be taken for granted by government: that of interest groups could not. Increasingly, groups were drawn into the policy-making process. In Britain, a number of groups were effectively co-opted into that process and given statutory representation on advisory bodies. The National Health Insurance Act of 1924, for example, gave the medical profession representation on bodies set up to administer the system of social insurance. Co-option was extended in succeeding decades, and groups continued to grow in number. Government itself became more specialized and increasingly dependent on a growing bureaucracy. Contact with government departments became frequent and institutionalized (Norton 2001a, ch. 7). By the 1970s, the links were extensive.

Hence, in the process of making law, legislatures came to be seen as increasingly marginalized. Party – or parties – dominate in the legislature. As Hibbing (2002, p. 35) has noted, 'most objective observers would concede that party norms usually trump legislative norms – in the U.K. and in most other countries'. The thrust of public policy is determined by party and confirmed by the electorate at periodic elections. The specific measures of public policy are formulated by government departments following consultation with affected interests, and those measures are subsequently presented to the legislature for approval. The legislature will usually lack the political will to challenge them; a partisan majority will exist to pass them. It may also lack the resources to challenge them: if presented with a measure that has the support of the different groups affected by it, it may have no alternative source of information or advice to challenge the agreed package. Consequently, the measures are passed.

The paradox of legislatures

The position of legislatures, on the basis of this analysis, thus appears to be straightforward. They are marginal bodies in policy-making. Yet legislatures present us with a seeming paradox.

On the one hand, legislatures are in decline, yet on the other, they are ubiquitous. They span the globe. In 2011, according to the Inter-Parliamentary Union (IPU), there were no less than 189 countries where national parliaments existed. This means that only a handful of nations do not have a legislature. (The United Nations has 193 member nations.) They exist in large, populous countries and in small island states. Many have existed for decades; some for centuries. Furthermore, they show no signs of diminishing in number. As military regimes have been toppled or have handed over power, so legislatures have been established. Following periods of military rule, countries such as Brazil and Greece have reverted to elected legislatures. As the Soviet Union fell apart, the legislatures of central and eastern European states gave way to new democratic legislatures. Legislatures are appearing in countries of the Middle East, which have little or no history of creating such bodies. The creation of legislatures is seen clearly as being important.

The significance of legislatures is recognized by political leaders; indeed, to them, legislatures are considered to be necessary. Their importance is also acknowledged frequently by citizens, and is reflected in attitudes and in action. Although politicians may be distrusted, there is recognition of the significance to the nation of the parliament. Citizens often petition their national legislature or spend time meeting or writing to members of the legislature. In some countries, members of the parliament will often find citizens coming to their local offices to seek their assistance. Pressure groups will often develop links with parties in parliament or lobby parliamentarians. The media will variously cover what goes on within a parliament. One of the events regularly covered by the British media, for example, is Prime Minister's Question Time in the House of Commons.

If legislatures are so marginal, why are there so many of them – notable not only for their number but also their resilience – and why do citizens attach importance to them? The paradox is resolved by fact that there is more to legislatures than law-making. Those who bemoan the decline of legislatures are adopting a narrow focus. This can be demonstrated by looking at legislatures in terms of power and the functions they fulfil.

The power of legislatures

Power is a contested concept. It is normally defined as A getting B to do what B would not otherwise do. In fact, there are different views of power (Lukes 2004). Three principal views can be characterized as the *pluralist*, the *elitist* and the *institutional* (Norton 2004a). Each has a utility in helping to explain the relevance of a legislature within the political system.

The *pluralist* defines power it in terms of the resolution of disputes once an issue has come on to the political agenda. Whoever achieves the outcome they desire has exerted power. Power in pluralist terms takes two forms: coercion and persuasion. The former exists where someone achieves a desired outcome by acting in such a way that others feel they have no option but to comply. In other words, there is no choice. People may comply with the instructions of a police officer because the officer is seen as having the authority, morally or legally, to issue such instructions. Such coercion is thus viewed as a legitimate action. If someone points a gun at an innocent bystander and orders them to hand over their money, the bystander is likely to feel compelled to comply. This is seen as an illegitimate action, having no moral or legal base (quite the reverse). In neither case does the person who complies feel that they can do otherwise but comply. If a beggar approaches a passer-by and asks for money, the passer-by may or may not give them money: there is an element of choice. If they hand over the money, then they have been persuaded to do so. Sometimes the dividing line between coercion and persuasion is a thin one, and the threat or prospect of coercion may accompany an attempt at persuasion, but the distinction is important.

It is a relevant distinction for the purpose of analysing legislatures. Legislatures have a coercive capacity through their ability legitimately to say 'no' to government. They can kill a measure by voting it down. Political bodies that have the capacity to block a measure have been characterized as veto players (Tsebelis 2002). Legislatures have a veto. However, they also have a persuasive capacity. If the government is contemplating a particular action or policy, members of the legislature may – by speeches, motions or meetings with ministers – make clear their opposition. The government may decide not to proceed because of pressure from parliamentarians: ministers may feel they need to maintain the goodwill of the parliamentarians (especially if they are members of the same party) or they may find the arguments they advance compelling. There may even be the hint of coercion, Members intimating they may later vote down the proposal. Whatever the reason, ministers have been persuaded to act in a way contrary to that they had intended. They have exercised choice. It is thus possible for outcomes to be affected without the legislature having formally said 'no' to government.

The *elitist* approach sees power in terms of agenda-setting, rather than in terms of what happens once an issue is on the agenda. It defines power in terms of controlling access to the political agenda. A particular group – an elite – can serve as a gatekeeper, determining what can and, most important of all, cannot be allowed on to the political agenda. Shared attitudes on the part of the elite may determine that certain matters are too important to be allowed to get on the agenda. This has been characterized as 'non-decision making' (Bachrach and Baratz 1962). However, this view of power generates methodological problems: trying to identify what has been kept off the agenda is clearly fraught with difficulty. How issues are resolved once they are on the political agenda can frequently be observed: conflict is often public, or reports of conflict (of internal cabinet or party fights) find their way into the public arena. It is difficult to identify the issues that are kept off the agenda through the actions of a particular body, especially when that body may itself not be clearly discernible or act in an organized manner. This view is thus problematic, but may none the less have some utility for the study of legislatures. This is not so much because legislatures form part of the elite, but because the actions – actual or anticipated – of the legislature may have some impact on an elite. Carl Friedrich (1963) identified the 'law of anticipated reactions'. If a governing body – a president, prime minister or cabinet – anticipates a negative reaction from the legislature, it may decide not to bring an issue on to the political agenda. As Cox and Morgenstern (2002, p. 446) have observed, 'the venerable "rule of anticipated reactions" makes even primarily reactive institutions, such as Latin American legislatures, relevant'. In the UK, a bill may not be brought forward because of an expected hostile reaction from government backbenchers or the House of Lords. A policy or action may not be pursued in case it is the subject of critical review by a select committee or is raised on the floor of the House. A governing elite may control access to the agenda and operate in its own interest, but self-interest may dictate anticipating the reaction to an issue once it is allowed on to the agenda.

The *institutional* approach is concerned with the impact of institutions on shaping outcomes. The focus is not so much the conflict over a particular issue but rather the structures and processes through which the conflict takes place. The result of a football match may be determined by a penalty shoot-out. From a pluralist view, the team with the player who scores the winning penalty has exercised power over the other team. However, the institutional view stresses that the goal is scored within the context of a clearly defined game with specific rules governing the use of the penalty shoot-out. Had some other rule been in place, then the outcome might have been very different. The institutional view covers both the fact that the rules and processes can affect outcomes, and the acceptance of the rules by players and observers. Acceptance of the process underpins stability.

In the context of legislatures, structures and procedures can affect outcomes (Norton 2001b). The need for measures to go through several stages, or to be passed by a particular time, affects what is brought forward by the executive. The rules may create bottlenecks, limiting how many measures can be brought forward at any one time. Acceptance of the process, at both the elite and the mass level, also renders the legislature powerful, as it is accepted that a measure is not legitimate if it has not received the assent of the legislature. The courts enforce the law as passed by the legislature. It is especially powerful in systems where there is no recognition of any alternative to the legislature as the body for legitimizing measures of public policy.

It is thus apparent that the perception of the decline of legislatures derives from a particular view of power. Indeed, it can be claimed to be a narrow view, even within a pluralist framework, derived primarily from an emphasis on coercion. Because legislatures do not regularly say 'no' to the executive, and substitute policy of their own, they are deemed to be in decline. However, once we go beyond the pluralist view, then we can see legislatures in a new perspective. The very fact that there are so many of them suggests that there is more to them than law 'making'. Looking at the different definitions of power is suggestive of a wider relevance. That relevance becomes more defined if we look at the functions, or tasks, that legislatures perform.

The functions of legislatures

The generic name of legislatures masks rather than illuminates what they in fact do. Their core defining role, as suggested by our opening sentence, is not to *make* law but rather to *give assent* to it. For some that has not only been their core but their only function. The parliament of the former German Democratic Republic (East Germany), for example, sometimes met on only three days a year to approve measures put before it, an example of what Michael Mezey (1979) has defined as a 'minimal legislature'.

With the collapse of the Soviet-dominated regimes of central and eastern Europe, the number of such legislatures declined significantly. Furthermore, such legislatures have been exceptional. Most legislatures engage in other activities and have wider consequences for their political systems. Their significance lies not so much in law-making but rather in a range of other functions they fulfil. Those functions will vary in extent and significance over time, and from legislature to legislature. Indeed, even in central and eastern Europe during the era of Soviet domination, there was some variation in activity and consequences. The Polish parliament (the Sejm), for example, exhibited a capacity for some independent action that set it apart from its German neighbour. A limited variation continues to be found in some legislatures in non-democratic nations (Allmark 2012).

There is, then, more to legislatures – much more – than formulating (making) law. This is apparent from a cursory observation of the demands made in Britain of the House of Commons and its members. The House of Commons spends as much time dealing with other items of business as it does with legislation. Question time and debates on declaratory motions are not part of the law-making process. Some of the most significant occasions in the House that have had a major political impact have had nothing to do directly with legislation: for example, when both Houses of Parliament were recalled in August 2011 to discuss the riots which had occurred in London and some other cities a few days before. The most extensive media coverage, to which we have already referred, is of the partisan clash between the Prime Minister and the Leader of the Opposition during the Prime Minister's weekly appearance at the dispatch box to answer questions. Constituents will write to Members of Parliament (MPs) seeking their intervention in cases where benefits have not been paid or where some government department has apparently mishandled a request or complaint. No change in the law is being sought, yet members of the legislature – in their capacity as members – are expected to act, and *do* act, in pursuit of particular demands. In surveys of what constituents expect of their MP, the constituency service role ranks significantly higher than the collective task of law-making or exercising an oversight of the executive (Norton 2002a, pp. 29–30). Expectations of MPs as constituency workers have increased markedly since the 1960s (Norton 2002a, pp. 20–9; 2012b).

Britain may enjoy a legislature that is distinctive for its longevity, but observation of other legislatures suggests that it is not unusual in the range of its activities and the demands made of it. Most parliamentary assemblies have a facility for asking oral questions on the floor of the

House (Bruyneel 1978; see also Martin 2011). A fixed period for asking such questions – question time – is a feature of many European parliaments. In some countries, such as Austria and Finland, the procedure for asking questions is enshrined in the constitution. Constituency work occupies the time of parliamentarians in many – though by no means all – countries (see Cain *et al.* 1987, Norton 2002a).

Formally, then, as well as in practice, expectations of legislatures extend beyond involvement in the formal process of law-making. Hence the apparent paradox falls. Legislatures cannot be assessed solely in terms of their capacity to make law. Given this, a prerequisite is to identify the functions that they variously fulfil.

In a seminal study, Robert Packenham (1970) identified a total of 11 functions of legislatures. He defined functions in terms of consequences for the political system. In other words, they were not necessarily planned or formally delineated tasks undertaken by the legislature. The functions are listed in Table 1.1. Packenham drew on a study of the Brazilian congress in order to identify them. His study of that legislature allowed him to determine a rank ordering – those at the top of the list had the greatest consequences for the political system, and those at the bottom the least. The decisional functions such as lawmaking, on which pluralists concentrate, came towards the end of the ranking. Those functions would clearly rank higher in any analysis of the United States Congress but, as Packenham observed, 'what knowledge we have suggests that the Brazilian case is much closer to the mode than the U.S. Congress'. For Packenham, it is the other functions that merit particular scrutiny. 'In fact, even if it [the Brazilian congress] had no decision-making power whatsoever, the other functions which it performs would be significant.'

Packenham's delineation is neither original nor exhaustive. Walter Bagehot, in *The English Constitution* (1867), provided a list of functions of the House of Commons more than a century before Packenham's work appeared. They were five in number: the elective (choosing the government); expressive ('to express the mind of the ... people on all matters which come before it'); teaching ('to teach the nation what it does not know' and so alter society); informing (to raise grievances and make people hear 'what otherwise we should not'); and, finally, the legislative function, of which of course it would be preposterous to deny the great importance'. Parliament's responsibility in the sphere of finance he subsumed under the last heading listed here. A year short of a century after Bagehot's work appeared, Samuel Beer identified another function – that of support mobilization; that is, helping to raise popular support

Table 1.1   Packenham's legislative functions

Legitimation
Latent (through meeting regularly and uninterruptedly)
Manifest (the formal stamp of approval)
'Safety valve' or 'tension release' (outlet for tensions)

Recruitment, socialization and training
Recruitment
Socialization
Training

Decisional or influence functions
Law-making
'Exit' function (resolving an impasse in the system)
Interest articulation
Conflict resolution
Administrative oversight and patronage (including 'errand running' for
   constituents)

Source: Derived from Packenham (1970).

for a particular measure of public policy. It was, he contended, a function
that was significant in the USA but not in the United Kingdom (Beer
1966). It is a function that, to some extent, marries Bagehot's informing
and teaching functions.

Nor are the functions Packenham identified free of criticism. His
inclusion of latent legitimation is open to criticism on the grounds that it
should not rank alongside the other functions listed, but rather be
regarded as a consequence of the fulfilment of the other functions. If a
parliament carries out the tasks expected of it by citizens, then it may
generate a latent body of support for the political system. Meeting regularly and without interruption – part of the process of institutionalization
– may develop some familiarity on the part of citizens, but such consistency may not itself generate a significant body of support. Such characteristics did little to prevent the collapse of regimes in central and eastern
Europe in the late 1980s. Some regularity in meeting may be necessary,
but not sufficient to build up latent support.

Packenham's work none the less marked a major advance. It is significant for its breadth, sophistication and empirical support. It still provides
the most extensive delineation of functions available in the field of
comparative legislative studies. In an adapted form, it will provide the

basic structure for this study. It will be adapted in two ways. First, it will be reworked to provide slightly greater breadth and sophistication. The category of seeking a redress of grievance will be employed, thus separating out – and going beyond – the errand-running activity identified by Packenham; the law-making category will be broken up into the various stages of the legislative process; and the study will be complemented by a consideration of parliament's capacity to educate and to mobilize support for particular policies. Second, it will not be utilized in the rank order provided by Packenham. Instead, the functions will be grouped under two basic heads: government and the citizen.

Parliament, like other legislatures, serves as a buckle between the citizen and the government, and the buckle may not always be a strong one. However, what is important for our immediate purposes is that parliament has two sets of relationships, one with those who govern and one with the citizen. The relationships are not mutually exclusive but they are analytically separable. The focus of scholarly attention has been on the link with the executive and, in particular, on the capacity of parliament to affect government in the initiation and formulation – the making – of public policy. In short, the focus has been a pluralist one, concerned with observable decision-making.

The relationship with the citizen has rarely been explored to the same extent as parliament's relationship with the executive. The literature is growing but is still relatively sparse. Yet the link is a vital one, underpinning the health of a political system. How parliamentarians act on behalf of citizens can generate a latent body of support. That action may involve persuasion. That persuasion may be two-way, with parliamentarians influencing the action of ministers on the one hand and citizens on the other. That persuasion may be at the collective level – parliamentarians influencing the policy or actions of government or of organized groups (attentive publics) or the wider citizenry (general public) – or at the level of the individual, where an MP's actions influence the behaviour of a minister or a citizen.

Political authority, according to Richard Rose, rests on the twin pillars of effectiveness and consent. 'An organization that cannot effectively influence the society around it is not a government. A government that acts without the consent of the governed is not a government as we like to think of it in the western world' (Rose 1979, p. 353). A government needs to be able to govern, and it needs to be powerful in pluralist terms. However, its legitimacy as a governing body derives, in a parliamentary system, from its relationship to the legislature. Any government normally requires the assent of the legislature to get its measures enacted. It may –

in most cases, usually does – receive this assent, but the process by which it does so has to be accepted as legitimate by the population. The legislature thus needs to be powerful in institutional terms. Institutional structures and processes can serve as an important constraint on government. The latent body of support that Packenham identifies as an important element of legitimation may, as we have suggested, derive from the fulfilment of the other functions he identifies. By fulfilling a range of functions, legislatures may thus underpin popular support for the political system.

Explaining Parliament in Britain

The role of legislatures is thus more complex than that suggested by pluralist writers. This work seeks to give shape to that complexity. It does so by following the structure already identified: first, the relationship of Parliament and government; and, second, the relationship of Parliament and the citizen. The foregoing analysis helps shape the structure of the book. It also provides the basis of the analytic framework. Legislatures have proved to be adaptable bodies. Some have a history dating back several centuries: the English Parliament (which later combined with the Scottish one to form the British Parliament), the Icelandic parliament (the *Althingi*) and the Manx parliament (the *Tynwald*) compete for the claim to be the oldest extant legislature. As we shall see, Parliament in Britain has had a chequered history, weathering a number of conflicts, but it has adapted and endured. It has been characterized by continuity and change, with the balance between the two frequently proving problematic. The basic premise of this study is that Parliament has adapted in recent times in a particular way. Recognition of Parliament's power to determine the outcome of public policy has moved, to a large degree, from the coercive to the persuasive. Its capacity to persuade has become more significant in giving voice to the needs and demands of citizens. Political stability rests on its capacity to make its voice heard, and in a way that meets the expectations and concerns of citizens.

Parliament and government

Parliament exists because of government. Parliament was formed out of body summoned by the monarch and its relationship to the government is the only one that has been dominant and direct throughout its existence. In responding to the demands and actions of government, it has become more structured, both in its institutional form and in the tasks it fulfils. It has a range of consequences.

In Part I, we draw on Packenham's taxonomy in looking at the consequences of Parliament for recruitment and training, legislation (the law 'making' function), and scrutiny of government (oversight). We look first at Parliament as the recruiting agency for executive office. It is one of the functions that makes Parliament powerful – in institutional terms – in that it has a virtual monopoly as a recruiting agency for executive office. We then devote most of the section to legislation, analysing the pre-legislative stage (initiation and formulation) and the legislative process within Parliament. Again, the importance of the study is to be found in the institutional as well as the pluralist view of power. Measures requiring parliamentary approval are laid before Parliament and go through a specified process. Both Houses have highly developed rules and procedures. Every bill has to go through several stages in each House. It is at the stage of debate and approval that Parliament becomes most visible in the legislative process. The government is normally assured of getting the measures it wants, but the content of those measures may be influenced by the actions of MPs and peers. The need to go through the highly institutionalized legislative process limits government.

Beyond Whitehall

Our study, however, is not confined to the relationship to British government. Until relatively recently, works on Parliament were so confined. The generation – the making – of public policy rested with *the* government. Parliament's principal and direct relationship was necessarily with Her Majesty's government. However, in recent decades, it has had to come to terms with the existence of several levels of government. The capacity to determine public policy in a number of fields has moved from the British government to different tiers of government – to the European Community, now the European Union, and to elected administrations in Scotland, Wales and Northern Ireland. As R. A. W. Rhodes (1994, p. 151) observed, 'To talk of the hollowing out of the state is to signal there are potentially dramatic changes underway in British government. Government is smaller. Both central and local government are losing functions to other agencies and to the EU'. Such dramatic changes have had significant consequences for Parliament: policy-making competence has passed to bodies over which it exerts no coercive capacity. Nor has the transfer of competence been confined to governmental bodies. Parliament has enacted measures that have resulted in a new juridical dimension to the British constitution. The courts have acquired new roles, both as a consequence of membership of the EC, devolution, and the enactment of the Human Rights Act.

Parliament has authorized the transfer of policy-making competences to these other bodies and has sought to adapt to their existence. Its relationship and how it has adapted constitutes the focus of Part II. Lacking a coercive capacity in relation to each of these bodies, both Houses have sought to generate a structured means of persuasion. Their attempts to do so constitute, to some degree, work in progress. Parliament has worked on generating institutional means of persuasion while those bodies which it seeks to persuade have themselves continued to evolve.

Parliament and citizen

In Part III, we look at the relationship of Parliament to citizen. Parliament stands as the authoritative buckle between government and citizen. It is the body through which the people choose government and the body through which they seek to make themselves heard by government. That relationship in recent decades has become more demanding and extensive and, as a result of the changing nature of government, more complex.

We open by examining the importance of Parliament as a representative body. We then focus on MPs as the principal link between the individual and government, serving as 'grievance chasers' (in traditional terminology, seeking a redress of grievance) and as a safety valve for constituents wanting to give vent to particular problems and concerns. In Chapter 12 we look at Parliament's role as a means of expressing particular interests and demands channelled through parties and, at a more particular level, through organized (and not so organized) groups. Having looked at the relationship of citizen to Parliament, we address in Chapter 13 the relationship of Parliament to citizen and consider how the institution informs and educates the public.

The issue of reform

We conclude by looking at the issue of parliamentary reform. The extent to which Parliament is able to fulfil the functions ascribed to it has long been the subject of dispute, not least by those who analyse it from a pluralist perspective. Even from an institutional perspective, some see the institution as constrained by the political capacity of government to change the rules to suits its purposes. Parliament may not only be unwilling or unable to say no to government, but may also lack the political will or resources to fulfil effectively other functions ascribed to it. Such perceptions are longstanding, gaining greater traction at some periods than others, with some politicians and commentators pressing for reform. Those demands are at times fuelled by controversies surrounding Parliament, either in terms of what the institution does or does not do, or because of the behaviour of individual members. In 2009, as we shall see, the House of Commons faced a barrage of public criticism following a scandal over MPs' expenses. That scandal gave an impetus to reform of the House.

Some press the case for change within the existing parliamentary structures, seeing the answer as to be found within Parliament itself. Others regard such changes as essentially marginal, believing that Parliament will only be able to fulfil the roles expected of it by the people if there is basic constitutional change. If Parliament is to act as the representative body of the nation, is it in need of fundamental reform?

2

The Development of Parliament

In legal terms, Parliament is not just the House of Commons and House of Lords: it is the Queen-in-Parliament. The assent of the monarch is necessary for a measure to be recognized by the courts as constituting an Act of Parliament. However, the queen, as sovereign, occupies a position distinct from the two Houses, forming what Bagehot referred to as a 'dignified' element of the constitution. Her actions as sovereign are determined almost exclusively by convention (Norton 2010a). As such, her actions are predictable, involving little, if any, real scope for independent, and hence partisan, judgement. The role of the monarch will not form part of our enquiry. That will accord with popular perceptions of what constitutes Parliament: few electors would include the monarch if asked to define the term.

Many electors, though, would tend to define Parliament in terms of the House of Commons. It is not uncommon for writers on British politics to use 'Parliament' as a synonym for the House of Commons. In this study, though, the focus is on both Houses occupying the Palace of Westminster. The House of Lords may be a poor relation, but it is still part of the family.

However, though both Houses may be part of the same family, they are certainly not twins. Compared to other legislative bodies, both are extremely active chambers, each typically sitting for more than 150 days each year. Few other legislatures can match this figure (Select Committee on Sittings of the House 1992). They are also large bodies. The Commons has 650 members and the House of Lords in mid-2012 had almost 790. (There is no fixed membership number for the House of Lords: the figure fluctuates as new members are created and members die.) No other bicameral legislature comes close in terms of the combined membership. However, compared to one another, the two chambers differ markedly. They have different origins, different practices and procedures, different roles and – formally since 1911 – different powers. The House of Commons is not dissimilar in character to many other elected first chambers; indeed, some legislative chambers in Commonwealth countries are modelled on the House. The House of Lords, as an unelected chamber, is not unique, but the nature of membership (appointment for life in most cases) and its practices and procedures render it distinctive. The unelected chamber is subordinate to the first. In the event of conflict, the House of Commons can, if it insists, eventually get its way. The United Kingdom thus has what is termed asymmetrical bicameralism. Historically, it has not always been thus.

The House of Commons

The House of Commons is the younger, but now the more politically significant, chamber. However, it is only in the years since 1832 that it has established itself as the politically superior chamber.

Origins

The House has its origins in the thirteenth century. There was a practice of the king holding a royal court on special occasions, to which leading figures were called, supplemented in between by summoning the principal prelates and tenants-in-chief (usually earls and barons) to offer their counsel in the kings' court, the *Curia Regis*. In 1254, when the King needed money, two knights from each shire were also summoned to Court 'to consider ... what aid they will be willing to grant us in our great need' (McKenzie 1968, p. 15). Ten years later, at a time of considerable conflict, Simon de Montfort – then the most powerful baron and effectively ruling the country – issued writs in the king's name for the return of four knights from each shire to discuss the state of the realm. The following year – 1265 – he issued writs for the return not only of two knights from each shire but also of two leading figures (burgesses) from each borough. This, as McKenzie noted, is often seen as the beginning of the House of Commons: 'the Commons had arrived' (McKenzie 1968, p. 15).

In 1275, Edward I held his 'first general Parliament', to which knights, burgesses and citizens were summoned in addition to the barons and leading churchmen (McKenzie 1968, p. 17). He held some 30 Parliaments during the first 25 years of his reign. However, those summoned from the local communities, or *communes* (Commons), played no part in the deliberations on high policy. Nor were they always summoned. There is no evidence, for example, of their having been summoned to more than four of Edward's Parliaments. However, their attendance became more regular under Edward II, and they were summoned regularly after the accession of

Edward III in 1327. 'Having for a long time been accorded *some* signifi-cance, the presence of the Commons in Parliament had at last come to be regarded as essential' (Roskell 1993, p. 7).

The Commons grew in importance in the fourteenth and fifteenth centuries. There were various clashes between the king and Parliament, not least over taxation. There was pressure for Parliament to be summoned on an annual basis. The king tended to summon it only when he felt he needed it, usually to vote for more money. Relations between Henry IV and his Parliaments were 'constantly uneasy and fraught' (Roskell 1993, p. 2). The king not only decided when Parliament would meet but also where it would sit. A number of cities were the sites for parliamentary sittings, though the most frequent venue was Westminster. Some sittings were very short, but a number lasted for weeks at a time. There were reigns when the number of Parliaments summoned was considerable.

There was also one other significant development in the fourteenth century. At various times, the knights and burgesses met separately from the churchmen and nobles, and so there developed the separation of the two chambers. It was also during this time that the Commons acquired functions that are still associated with it today.

Early functions

The knights and burgesses had initially been summoned to confirm the assent of local communities to the raising of additional taxation. There was no suggestion that they had the power to refuse that assent. Nor was such assent sought for all forms of taxation. However, in 1341, the king agreed that the people should not be 'charged nor grieved to make common aid or to sustain charge' without the assent of Parliament (White 1908, p. 364). Granting money – known as supply – thus became an important parliamentary function.

Even before the measure of 1341, Parliament had begun to use its power of the purse to ensure that public petitions were accepted by the king. Citizens had the right to petition the monarch for a redress of griev-ances. Parliament presented such petitions and began to make the voting of supply conditional on a redress being granted. The first known instance of this was as early as 1309 (White 1908, p. 369). From such petitions developed what came to be called statutes, which required the assent of the Commons, the Lords and the king, and were thus distin-guishable from ordinances, which were the product solely of the king. Statute law soon displaced ordinances as the most extensive form of written law, and in the fifteenth century the task of writing statutes was taken from the King's scribes and undertaken instead by the Commons.

Those returned to Parliament also began to take an interest in how money was being collected as well as how it was spent. As early as 1340, commissioners were appointed to audit the accounts of the collectors of subsidies. Where public officials were found wanting, Parliament used its power to remove them through impeachment, with the Commons voting impeachment, and the Lords trying the case. Though impeachment has since fallen into disuse, it provided the basis for the development of Parliament's scrutiny of administrative actions.

Sixteenth to eighteenth centuries

Parliament's position was strengthened under the Tudors, when monarchs needed supply and the support of Parliament in their various political and religious battles. Henry VIII had little difficulty gaining the support he wanted in his battles with Rome, but in so doing he accorded Parliament a significant status in helping to determine the high policy of the realm. During the Tudor era, a seat in the House of Commons became something to be sought after, rather than service in the House being treated simply as an expensive chore. It was also during this era that there were the first signs of embryonic specialization by the Commons. In 1571 there is the first official reference to a bill being sent to a committee of the House. Committees to undertake particular enquiries – select committees – were often employed in both Tudor and Stuart Parliaments.

The seventeenth century witnessed the clash between an assertive Parliament and a monarch believing in the divine right of kings. James I and, more especially his son, Charles I, variously denied the privileges of Parliament, and the clash between Charles and Parliament resulted in civil war. The defeat of the royalist forces brought in its wake not only the abolition of the monarchy but also of the House of Lords. The country was ruled by a council of state, elected by what came to be known – for fairly self-evident reasons – as the Rump Parliament, followed by military dictatorship. With the Restoration in 1660 came a revival of traditional institutions: there was a deliberate attempt to revert, unconditionally, to the position as it had been at the beginning of 1642.

Charles II, who became king upon the restoration of the monarchy, was a popular monarch, but tension resurfaced under his successor, James II, resulting in a clash between the king and a Parliament resistant both to his claims to the divine right of kings and to his Roman Catholic faith. In 1685, the Commons refused to grant the king money to maintain a standing army. It also refused to repeal the Test Acts, which restricted public office to Anglicans. James decided to dispense with the services of Parliament and began to rule by prerogative powers, 'suspending' various laws, including the Test Acts. His actions incited leading politicians to invite the Protestant Dutchman, William of Orange, James' son-in-law, to bring a military force to England. He did so and James fled the country.

On the invitation of peers and former members of the Commons, William summoned a convention that proceeded to offer him and his wife, Mary, the throne, which it declared James to have abdicated. However, the offer was conditional. The convention promulgated a declaration of right, embodying 13 articles affecting the rights of Parliament. The suspending of laws without the approval of Parliament was declared to be illegal; the dispensing power – to exempt individuals or groups from the provisions of particular acts – was forbidden; and the levying of taxation without the assent of Parliament was prohibited.

On 13 February 1689, William and Mary accepted both the throne and the declaration of right. The declaration was subsequently embodied in statute as the Bill of Rights and the convention turned, retrospectively, into a Parliament. According to G. M. Trevelyan (1938), James II had forced the country to choose between royal absolutism and parliamentary government. It chose parliamentary government.

The dependence of the monarch on Parliament was thus established. Increasingly, the monarch withdrew from the tasks of parliamentary management. Those tasks were assumed by the King's ministers, and the eighteenth century witnessed the emergence of a cabinet and a Prime Minister, and a powerful but not overly assertive House of Commons. Many MPs sat for rotten boroughs controlled by members of the aristocracy. The combination of aristocratic control and royal patronage was usually sufficient to ensure a majority for the king's ministry.

The nineteenth century

During this period, parliamentary politics was confined to a political elite. The aristocracy and the landed interests had a political voice, but few others had. Industrialization, as we noted in Chapter 1, created powerful pressures. There were demands for reform, and at the beginning of the 1830s, the Whigs – who had been the 'outs' in politics for a quarter of a century – found themselves in power and in a position to introduce a reform bill. The 1832 Reform Act enlarged the electorate by 49 per cent.

In so doing, it helped to loosen the grip of the aristocracy on the Commons, but did not enlarge the electorate to such an extent that large-scale party organization was necessary to contact and mobilize electors. Many sources of royal patronage were also eliminated and an Act of 1809 made the selling of seats illegal. 'The cumulative effects of the restrictions on royal revenues and adjustments to election laws were increasingly evident in the policy bargains reached between the sovereign and parliament' (Congleton 2011, p. 349). The consequence was a greater scope for independent action by MPs. The Act thus heralded what has been described as a 'golden age' of Parliament. MPs turned governments out and put new ones in (Bagehot's elective function), and variously overruled government policy: 'There was always a possibility that a speech might turn votes; the result of a division was not a foregone conclusion' (Campion, 1952, p. 15).

Too much should not be made of this golden age. The domain of public policy was very limited – most bills passed were private, rather than public – and defeats were not excessive in number. Furthermore, the period was a short-lived one. Pressure from a burgeoning urban middle class and from artisans contributed to a further major Reform Act in 1867. This was followed by measures to restrict corrupt practices and to introduce secret ballots. With the passage of the Representation of the People Act in 1884, the majority of working men were allowed to vote. The measures transformed the political landscape, as mass parties developed in response to the new situation. In the words of Richard Crossman (1963, p. 39), 'organized corruption was gradually replaced by party organization'.

The consequences for the House of Commons were profound. On the one hand, its superiority over the unelected Upper House was established, but on the other, it effectively lost two of the functions ascribed to it by Bagehot. The elective function passed to the electorate, and the legislative function passed, in effect, to the cabinet. Party came to dominate parliamentary activity. Government achieved control of the timetable. Whips – MPs appointed to keep fellow supporters informed of business and to ensure that they turned out and voted – became prominent figures in the life of members (Norton 1979, pp. 10–14). By the start of the twentieth century, party cohesion was a well-established feature of parliamentary life: MPs voted loyally with their parties (Lowell 1924, pp. 76–8). The outcome of votes was predictable: 'The task of the House of Commons became one of supporting the Cabinet chosen at the polls and passing its legislation ... By the 1900s, the Cabinet dominated British government' (Mackintosh 1977, p. 174).

The twentieth century

The party leadership in government was able to utilize its parliamentary majority to ensure that those features of the nineteenth-century House that were to the benefit of government were retained, while those that were seen as a hindrance were diminished or removed. Hence the emphasis on an amateur House, with issues being debated on the floor, was maintained. A majority was easier to deploy on the floor. A few critical voices could be lost among the cries of loyal supporters. The use of investigative select committees facilitated critical scrutiny. What use there had been of select committees was reduced drastically.

However, the use of standing committees for taking the committee stage of legislation was extended. Standing committees were to the benefit of the government's legislative programme: more bills could be considered at the same time, avoiding a queue for detailed consideration on the floor of the House. From 1907, all bills were referred to a standing committee unless the House voted otherwise. Government was able to deploy its majority in a standing committee. Before the 1940s, a minister's parliamentary private secretary (an MP who was a minister's unpaid helper) used to act as an unofficial whip, but after 1945 it became standard policy to appoint whips to standing committees.

Government also became less willing to divulge information to the House. Increasingly, MPs were expected to defer to the superior knowledge of government. As government bills came to dominate the legislative agenda, and as those bills became more complex, the House failed to generate the resources to keep pace with those developments. Hence, in its relationship with government, the House exhibited the limitations mentioned in the introduction. It lacked both the political will and the institutional resources to challenge the measures formulated by government.

In terms of the relationship with citizens, the twentieth century witnessed some significant developments. One was the enlargement of the electorate. Under the provisions of the Representation of the People Act 1918, the franchise was extended to women aged 30 years and over. It was extended to encompass women aged 21 and over – thus bringing the female franchise in line with the male – in 1928. The voting age was lowered to 18 years by the Representation of the People Act of 1969.

However, for much of the century, an increased electorate did not entail a significant increase in the demands made of local MPs. MPs frequently were amateurs for whom parliamentary service was not a career occupation (see King 1981; Riddell 1993). For many Conservatives, it was a public duty and something often to be combined with other activities, such as practising at the Bar or serving as a company director or landowner. For some Labour MPs, it was essentially an end-of-career activity, a reward for long service in the cause of the party or a trade union. Where there were demands made of MPs by constituents, they were not always welcome. Even if many had wanted to be more active in dealing with their constituencies, there was the problem of limited resources. Payment for MPs was introduced only in 1912 (the princely sum of £400 a year) and saw few increases thereafter. Indeed, it was in fact reduced for three years in the 1930s because of the Depression.

For many MPs in post-war Parliaments, service was not always particularly rewarding, and for some without independent means it was difficult to survive. For those achieving ministerial office, and those amateurs who took some delight in watching – as one put it in the title of her autobiography – 'from the wings' (Cazalet-Keir 1967), parliamentary life had some purpose. For others, Westminster offered little more than 'corridors of frustration' (Teeling 1970). Members had little opportunity to influence public policy. Constituency activity absorbed some of an MP's time, but being recognized as a 'good constituency Member' was seen as an admission that one was not destined for government office. Serving as the link between citizens and government was not seen as the most rewarding, or productive, of activities. The link was essential, but not necessarily strong.

Recent changes

Since the 1950s there have been a number of changes that have relevance for our later analysis. There have been significant developments both inside and outside Parliament which have changed both the nature of the institution and the political environment in which it operates. We shall return later to those external to Parliament. The changes within the House can be grouped under six headings. The first three – background, resources, and behaviour – cover members and what they do. The next two – structures and procedures, and visibility – relate to the institution. The last one covers relations with the citizen: constituency activity.

Background

There has been a notable change in the background of MPs. This has been seen to some extent in terms of socioeconomic background, but even more so in terms of career aspirations.

Members of Parliament have become more middle class in background, a continuation of a trend. There was a substantial change in the background of Conservative MPs in the nineteenth century (Rush 2001, pp. 97–100). The landed interest gave way to business and the professions. Those with private means have largely disappeared. In recent decades, the Conservative Party has, if anything, become more middle class than before (see Nott 2002, p. 129). 'Traditionally, the Conservative may be regarded as the party of business, but it is even more the party of the middle class' (Rush 2001, pp. 98–9). Conservative MPs are more likely to be university-educated than before, those drawn from non-Oxbridge universities becoming more prominent in the party's ranks. (The non-Oxbridge MPs have replaced MPs who had not had a university education rather than those who were Oxbridge educated.) The number educated at the leading public schools and Oxford or Cambridge universities has declined, most notably so in recent years. Though most Conservative MPs are public-school and university educated, only a small number are now drawn from the leading public schools; in 2010, only 19 (including Prime Minister David Cameron) out of 306 Conservatives elected had been to Eton and only three to Harrow (Criddle 2010, p. 326). The move, it has been suggested, 'marks ... a retreat of the upper middle class from political careers now more arduous because full-time, lower in status and less well paid than in much of the private sector' (Criddle, Childs and Norton 2005, p. 27).

The proportion of manual workers in the ranks of the parliamentary Labour Party (the PLP) declined from 1945 to 1979 – from approximately one in four to one in ten – with only slight variations thereafter. Of the 258 Labour MPs elected in 2010, 9 per cent were drawn from manual backgrounds (Criddle 2010, p. 327). The number of university-educated MPs on the Labour benches increased – from just over a third in 1945 to over half by 1970, and to two-thirds by 2001. By 2010, the figure was almost three-quarters (73 per cent). The typical Labour MP in 2010 was educated at secondary school and university; 36 (14 per cent) had been educated at public school and university.

Members of both parties are now typically drawn from middle-class professions (Criddle 2010, p. 327). Lawyers are to be found on both sides of the House, as are political organizers and journalists (see Rush 2005, pp. 39–40). Labour MPs are also drawn from the ranks of public-sector professionals, lecturers and teachers. The Conservative benches are supplemented by company executives and directors. Not only are there very few industrialists, landowners or miners, there are also relatively few scientists, engineers, architects and accountants.

The explanation for the dearth of MPs drawn from highly special-ized professional backgrounds can be found in the fact that not only has there been something of a convergence in social background, but there has also been a convergence in terms of career goals. There has been a marked growth in the number of career politicians. These are politicians who, in Max Weber's words, 'live for politics'. For them, parliamentary life is long-term and more important than any other pursuit (Buck 1963; King 1981). Britain has always had career politicians, but what has been notable has been the growth in their number in recent decades, squeezing out the MP for whom parliamentary service came at the end of another career or, indeed, preceded going off to do something else with one's life (Riddell 1993, 1995). Career politicians devote them-selves to Parliament, or rather to their parliamentary careers. They serve as political researchers, advisers or consultants before being elected (Judge 1999a, pp. 107–8). For them, re-election is a necessary but not sufficient condition for political advancement. They therefore apply themselves to raising their constituency profile. For promotion to the front bench, they need to impress their party leaders, so they busy themselves raising their profile in the House. This often entails asking questions, speaking in debates, and tabling motions (see Rush 2001, Ch. 6). For the career politician, being an MP is a full-time, and often demanding, job.

MPs have thus become more middle-class and career-oriented over time. Though there has been a convergence in class terms, there has been a more recent divergence in terms of gender, race and sexual orientation. As we shall see in Chapter 10, the number of women, openly gay members, and members drawn from ethnic minority backgrounds has grown in the period since 1997. The change was marked on the Labour benches in 1997 and on the Conservative benches in 2010.

Resources

Before the 1960s, MPs had few resources other than their salaries and travel allowances and, for most, a school-type locker in which to keep their papers. When not in the chamber, they found seats in the library and, given the lack of offices and a limited number of meeting rooms, held meetings with visitors (including secretaries, if they had them) on seats in the corridors. Salaries were not generous (prior to an increase in 1964, an MP's salary was £1,750 per annum) and some Members, especially on the Labour benches, found it difficult to cope. Conditions improved from 1964 onwards. MPs since have been better resourced, both individually and collectively. The increase in individual resources, though, has not always been free of controversy.

The salary was variously increased (in 1964, for example, from £1,750 to £3,250 a year) and in 1969, a secretarial allowance of £500 a year was introduced. A subsistence allowance was introduced in 1972. The secretarial allowance evolved into an office cost allowance but by 2004 this had been disaggregated into a range of allowances. In addition to their parliamentary salary (£57,485 in April 2004), MPs could claim more than £100,000 in allowances, including staffing, constituency offices, and an additional cost allowance for non-London MPs for overnight accommodation when away from home. This last allowance, enabling MPs to claim expenses to maintain a second home, proved controversial when, in 2009, data on expense claims were obtained by *The Daily Telegraph* and published, showing some MPs had made claims that were unethical and, in some cases, illegal. The resulting scandal resulted in a reform of the expenses regime, with responsibility for policing and paying expenses being transferred from the House authorities to an independent body (the Independent Parliamentary Standards Authority – IPSA), and, as we shall see, in a decline in public trust in the House of Commons. IPSA in 2011 was also given responsibility for determining MPs' pay and setting the level of any increase in pay.

In 2012, an MP's salary was £65,738 a year, and each Member could claim allowances to cover the cost of running an office and employing staff, having somewhere to live in London or their constituency, as well as travelling between their constituency and Westminster. Members holding particular responsibilities in the House, such as Speaker, Deputy Speaker or chair of a select committee, receive a higher salary.

Though the expenses claimed by MPs have not been free of controversy, they have been necessary to enable them to create the facilities necessary to cope not only with their Westminster responsibilities, but also with their expanding constituency duties. Given the technology now available, many MPs concentrate their office resources in the constituency. In the 1950s and 1960s, concentrating resources in the constituency usually meant having the spouse do the administrative work while the MP replied in longhand to letters from constituents.

Physical resources have expanded. Extra office space has been created in the Palace of Westminster. The old Scotland Yard buildings – on the Victoria embankment a hundred yards (about 91 metres) from the Palace of Westminster – were taken over to provide more office space. They have been complemented by two major office buildings: No. 1 Parliament Street, a complex of modern offices built behind the original

Georgian façade of several buildings; and Portcullis House, a large, purpose-made building dominating Bridge Street, opposite the Elizabeth Tower of the Palace of Westminster. The buildings are all connected, enabling MPs to reach the chamber without leaving the parliamentary estate. The completion of Portcullis House meant that no MP was without a dedicated office.

The resources available collectively to MPs have also expanded, especially in post-war years. In 1972, the House of Commons Library – housed principally in six large rooms overlooking the River Thames on the principal floor in the Palace – had a staff of 55; by the year 2000, it had a staff of 200. The Library offers not only a traditional library service, but also a research service, staffed by highly-qualified researchers – there are eight subject teams – who are able to provide extensive independent briefing packs for MPs at short notice. The Library has a Parliament and Constitution Centre, created in 1999, to provide a focus for its work in the field of Parliament and the constitution. It also publishes a wide range of research papers and standard notes for use by parliamentarians, but which are now also made publicly available. MPs are great consumers of Library services. In 1973, the Library dealt with 3,291 enquiries; in 2009–10, it dealt with more than 23,000 requests for oral or written briefings and reference information. MPs also have the facility of a searchable database, providing access to most information produced by Parliament.

MPs are now able to work in dedicated offices, supported by secretarial and research staff, and use television screens to follow proceedings in the chamber and their computers (or hand-held electronic devices) to access library research material and other data available on the parliamentary intranet.

Behavioural changes

The behaviour of MPs has changed markedly over the past half-century, especially in the chamber and the voting lobbies. Given the rise of the professional politician, there is far more competition in catching the Speaker's eye. There is far greater demand to take part in debates and question time (Rush 2001, pp. 154–7; Franklin and Norton 1993). Most significant of all, though, has been the change in behaviour in the voting (division) lobbies. Members have proved to be relatively more independent in their voting behaviour. As we have seen, cohesion was a marked feature of parliamentary life by the end of the nineteenth century. This cohesion was maintained throughout the first seven decades of the twentieth century, reaching a peak in the 1950s. In two sessions (parliamentary years) in the 1950s, not a single Conservative MP voted against the party line. In the 1960s, one distinguished American commentator was able to declare that cohesion had increased so much 'until in recent decades it was so close to 100 per cent that there was no longer any point in measuring it' (Beer 1969, pp. 350–1). Shortly afterwards, it did become relevant to measure it.

The early years of the 1970s saw a significant increase in cross-voting by Conservative MPs (Norton 1975; 1978a). They voted against their own leaders more often than before, in greater numbers and with more effect. On six occasions, despite the government enjoying an overall majority of seats in the Commons, cross-voting resulted in the government being defeated. Cross-voting also became a feature of Labour MPs after a Labour government was returned to office in 1974, contributing to most of the 42 defeats suffered by the government in the 1974–9 parliament (Norton 1980; 2004c). The number of defeats on the floor of the House, combined with defeats in standing committee, ran into three figures (see Norton 1980; Schwarz 1980). The defeats took place on a number of important issues, including economic policy and the government's key constitutional policy of devolving powers to elected assemblies in Scotland and Wales (Norton 2004c).

Some degree of independent voting has been maintained in succeeding Parliaments (Norton 1985; Cowley and Norton 1999; Rush 2001, pp. 170–6). In 1986, the government lost the second reading of the Shops Bill (Regan 1987; Bown 1990), when 72 Conservative MPs voted with the Opposition to defeat it, the first time in the twentieth century a government with a clear overall majority had lost a second reading vote. The Conservative government of John Major (1990–7) suffered four defeats as a result of cross-voting by Conservative MPs. Following a major defeat on the Maastricht Bill in 1993 – on the social chapter of the Maastricht Treaty – it had to seek a vote of confidence.

Though large majorities achieved by the Labour government in 1997 and 2001 served to absorb dissent by Labour backbenchers, dissension by Labour MPs increased significantly (Cowley 2002a; 2005; Cowley and Stuart 2004a; 2004b). In March 2003, 139 Labour MPs voted against the government on the issue of war with Iraq, the largest rebellion by government backbenchers in modern British history (Cowley and Stuart 2004a). Dissent continued into the Parliament of 2005–10. Indeed, the two Parliaments of 2001–5 and 2005–10 proved to be the most rebellious of post-war Parliaments (Cowley 2007, www.revolts.co.uk). In the first session of the 2005–10 Parliament, the government suffered no less than four defeats, on anti-terrorism legislation and racial and religious hatred

(Kelly, Gay and Cowley 2006). The defeats were the tip of an iceberg. The Government 'scraped past other votes with miniscule majorities; won other votes thanks to a series of retreats and deals; and won yet others only thanks to the support of the Conservatives. Three key policies of the Blair era only passed the Commons thanks to Conservative support: encompassing foreign policy (Iraq), domestic policy (schools reform) and defence (Trident)' (Cowley 2007, p. 27).

Though the first session of a Parliament under a new government usually produces fairly cohesive behaviour by government supporters, there was no such cohesion under the unusual conditions of coalition government in 2010. The government produced measures that attracted opposition from Conservative MPs, from Liberal Democrat MPs and in some cases from both (see Norton 2012a). By the end of 2011, there had been no less than 179 votes in which one or more coalition MPs had voted against the government, representing a rebellion rate of 43 per cent of votes (Cowley and Stuart 2012, pp. 8–11). Contrast this with the two sessions in the 1950s when there was no dissent by *any* government supporter. Independence in voting behaviour has become a more significant feature of the House of Commons than is popularly recognized.

The cause of this behavioural change has been the subject of considerable debate (Norton 1978a; 1987; Schwarz, 1980; Franklin, Baxter and Jordan 1986; Rush 2001, pp. 176–83, Kelso 2009, pp. 24–6). Clearly, issues are crucial. European integration has been the subject of considerable dissent, especially on the Conservative benches (Cowley and Norton 1999). Issues, however, are necessary but not sufficient conditions to explain the change in behaviour. Some of the issues were not new but the willingness to vote against the government on such a scale, and to rob it of its majority, was. The behavioural change has been ascribed to the changing background of MPs – a generational explanation – as well as to the relaxation of the convention that a defeat necessarily involves the government's resignation. However, the changing background of MPs does not explain the sudden change in behaviour in the 1970s; there was little correlation between a new generation of MPs and dissenting behaviour. There was no change in the convention covering government defeats in the division lobbies. A government defeat *per se* was not sufficient to trigger a resignation or a general election; the defeat had to be on a vote of confidence for that to happen (Norton 1978b). There was nothing new in this; it had been established in the nineteenth century. The remaining explanation is the 'poor leadership' thesis, advanced by this writer, ascribing the trigger-

ing effect for the dissension to Edward Heath's style of prime ministerial leadership in the 1970–4 Parliament (Norton 1978a). Heath ignored
his backbenchers on important issues, generating such a degree of
resentment and frustration that some of his supporters found themselves impelled to express their disagreement, publicly and forcefully,
by voting against the government, and on occasion denying it a majority. Once triggered, such behaviour developed a momentum, ensuring
that it outlived the prime minister responsible for unleashing it. As one
dissenter stated, when you had voted against the government once, it
was much easier to do it a second time.

These behavioural changes should not be exaggerated, as cohesion
remains a very marked feature of parliamentary behaviour (Cowley
2002a, p. 6). Even in the 2005–10 Parliament and in the Parliament
returned in 2010, complete party cohesion constitutes a feature of most
votes, with the results in virtually all cases being predictable. Despite one
or more of its MPs dissenting in more than four out of every ten votes in
the period from May 2010 to September 2011, the coalition government
lost none of them. The change in behaviour is relative. Prior to 1970, a
government with an overall majority was guaranteed a majority if it
pressed ahead with a measure. Since then, it has usually been assured a
majority but cannot quite take it for granted.

Structures and procedures

The late 1970s and since has seen some MPs flexing their new-found
political muscle in order to extend their resources and to create a more
specialized infrastructure, though the flexing has been somewhat
sporadic. There have been three notable changes: the introduction of
departmental select committees, meetings in Westminster Hall, and the
Backbench Business Committee.

Departmental select committees.   There are two principal phases in the
development of the committees: their creation in 1979 and enhancement
in 2010. Departmental select committees were created in 1979 and
marked a major departure from the chamber-orientated House that had
been dominant since the advent of party government. Their introduction
constituted the most important reform of the latter half of the twentieth
century; possibly of the whole century. They exist to 'examine the expenditure, administration and policy' of the relevant department and associated public bodies. Fourteen were established in the 1979–83 Parliament,
covering most government departments, and they have increased in

number since; for every department, there is now a departmental select committee. At the beginning of the 2010 Parliament, 19 were appointed; four can also meet concurrently as the Committees on Arms Exports Controls.

The committees have become a permanent, and indeed a pervasive, feature of the parliamentary landscape. They are now central to the task of pre-legislative scrutiny (see Chapter 4) and administrative oversight (Chapter 6). They absorb the energies of almost a third of all MPs: just over 200 MPs serve on them. They are complemented by a number of other investigative committees, including Public Administration, Political and Constitutional Reform, European Scrutiny, Environmental Audit and the long-standing Public Accounts Committee. They are active bodies, choosing their own topics for inquiry, meeting usually weekly, engaging in extensive evidence-taking, and publishing a raft of reports, formally to the House but in practice directed at government (Drewry 1989; Hawes 1993; Jogerst 1993; see also George and Morgan 1999; Natzler and Hutton 2005; Hindmoor, Larkin and Kennon 2009).

Their activity is reflected not only in the number of reports they publish – usually more than 50 a session – but also in the physical expansion of the parliamentary estate. Such has been the demand for them in the Palace of Westminster that two floors of committee rooms in the Palace of Westminster have been complemented by a floor of state-of-the-art committee rooms in Portcullis House.

Despite being active and often independent bodies, the involvement of the whips in organizing names for appointment to the committees was seen by many to undermine their independence. Appointment as chairs of committees was on occasion seen as rewards to former ministers. Pressure for change resulted in a committee recommending in 2009 that the chairs of committees should be elected by the House as a whole and the members of each committee elected by their respective parliamentary parties (House of Commons Reform Committee 2009). This was agreed and implemented at the start of the 2010 Parliament. Some chairs, as for the Treasury committee, were hotly contested. The elections were seen to enhance both the status and the independence of the committees. Those who chaired them were put there by the House and not the party whips and could speak with some independent authority.

Meetings in Westminster Hall.   Committee meetings are not the only parliamentary activity that draws MPs from the chamber. The House in 1999 introduced a parallel chamber, an idea borrowed from the Australian Parliament. Though the proposal was initially contentious, some members fearing it would draw attention away from the chamber, the innovation was soon widely accepted and made a permanent feature. Back-bench MPs came to see it as a means of supplementing and not supplanting proceedings in the chamber, providing a valuable opportunity to raise issues.

Meetings are held each week in the grand committee room off Westminster Hall – the sittings are styled as meetings in Westminster Hall – in order to hold short debates on topics raised by private members as well as on select committee reports. The meetings are open to all MPs who wish to attend. Unlike the chamber, no votes are permitted and the room has fixed desks arranged in a semi-circle around a raised dais. Though meetings attract few MPs, they provide the opportunity for those with a particular interest to attend and speak.

Backbench Business Committee. Another recommendation of the Reform of the House of Commons Committee, which reported in 2009, was that backbench business in the House should be allocated by a Backbench Business Committee, comprising back-bench MPs elected by the House, and not by the Government. This recommendation was accepted and in 2010 the House elected members to the newly-formed committee. The committee has responsibility for determining back-bench business on 35 days, 27 of them on the floor of the House (the remainder in Westminster Hall). It invites MPs to put forward proposals for debate and has variously selected topics that the government may prefer not to be considered. Among topics chosen in the first year of its existence was the war in Afghanistan (enabling MPs for the first time to vote on the issue), whether or not prisoners should be allowed the right to vote, and whether there should be a referendum on withdrawing from membership of the European Union.

These changes constitute the principal structural changes, though they are not the only changes to have been made (see Norton 1986; Brazier, Flinders and McHugh 2005; Cowley 2007, pp. 18–22). There have also been some substantial changes in procedure and processes, not least the legislative process. These have encompassed pre- and post-legislative scrutiny in addition to the actual legislative process. Since 1997, a number of bills each session have been published in draft with each being sent to a parliamentary committee (usually a departmental select committee but occasionally a joint committee of the two Houses) for scrutiny, enabling members to make recommendations for change before the measure is formally introduced and ministers become relatively unwilling to see changes.

In 2006, standing committees were succeeded by public bill committees for the consideration of bills (see Chapter 5). Whereas the former could only consider the contents of the bills before them, and discuss changes on the basis of motions (to agree clauses or make amendments), the latter can receive evidence, both oral and written. Public bill committees can and do hear from witnesses before reverting to the procedure previously utilized by standing committees, discussing a bill clause by clause.

Since 2008, following a recommendation of the House of Lords Constitution Committee and the Law Commission, Acts of Parliament have also been subject to post-legislative review. Most Acts three to five years after enactment are subject to review by the relevant government department to determine if they have met their objectives. The reviews are then sent to the relevant departmental select committee, though by 2012 only one committee (the Justice Committee, see Chapter 5) had undertaken an enquiry based on a review.

Though the changes in structures and processes have generally favoured the House, there have also been developments that have strengthened government. In particular, the use since 1997 of programme motions – that is, timetable motions for bills – has been much criticized, not least for the extremely tight timetables imposed on some bills. The pressure of the timetable undermines, for example, the effectiveness of public bill committees, with little time for committee members to consider the evidence placed before them before they revert to considering each clause of the bill before them (Levy 2010). This continuing hold on the business of the House by government has underpinned continuing criticism, especially from a pluralist perspective, of the extent to which the House is still the creature of government. MPs may be more able to debate what government is doing but government normally gets its way.

Visibility

The other major change is in the visibility, both of Members individually and of the House and its proceedings. Members are now not only able to be seen locally at surgeries and public meetings, but, as we shall see (Chapter 13), have been able to invest in the new technology to host websites, blogs and twitter feeds, and variously to keep constituents informed through e-mail lists. The activity of Members is also variously monitored, through websites such as *TheyWorkforYou. com*, and people can email MPs through the similar sites as well as directly.

The House has also become a more open institution. Until the 1970s, one could read about debates but not listen to them, other than by sitting in the public gallery. In the mid-1970s, there was an experiment where debates were broadcast, and sound broadcasting of the debates in both Houses began on a permanent basis in 1978. People could now listen to what went on in Parliament, though the effect was not necessarily positive: the sound of MPs bellowing support or dissent proved to be unattractive. But pressure built up to admit television cameras, and the House of Lords admitted them in 1985. The House of Commons lagged behind, voting to admit them in 1988, and with the cameras beginning to transmit proceedings the following year. The cameras record proceedings on the floor of the House and, selectively, in committee. The television coverage initially proved both more extensive than had been anticipated, and also more popular, both with MPs and the viewing public. What had started out as an experiment was soon made permanent.

More recently, a dedicated BBC Parliament Channel has been complemented by a web site, BBC Democracy Live, which enables viewers to watch proceedings not only from the Commons and the Lords, but also the chambers of the Scottish parliament, National Assembly for Wales, the Northern Ireland assembly and the European Parliament. Transcripts of committee hearings are also placed on the Internet shortly after they become available. Committee reports are available on the Internet. Some committees have also undertaken online consultations on particular proposals.

Constituency activity

MPs have always had a clear territorial base, being sent to Westminster from a particular county or borough. (Constituencies continue to be divided into county and borough constituencies.) As we have seen, the size of the electorate increased in the nineteenth century; single-member constituencies became the norm in the 1880s and MPs – not least with further expansions in the franchise – came to represent a growing number of electors. Whereas an average English county constituency at the beginning of the twentieth century had fewer than 15,000 electors, by the beginning of the twenty-first it had in excess of 70,000. Despite the increase in the numbers, there was not a substantial increase in constituency demands made of a typical MP in the first half of the century. However, that changed in the 1960s and in succeeding decades (see Norton and Wood 1993; Norton 1994b; 2002a; Rush 2001, pp. 207–11), with MPs moving from being local dignitaries and benefactors to information providers and powerful friends (Norton 1994b), being expected to pursue grievances on behalf of constituents and protect the interests of the constituencies.

These demands helped transform the role of the MP, providing an extensive constituency face to the existing Westminster face of the Member, and ensuring that the position became much more of a full-time one. Members devoted an increasing amount of time to their role (see Norton 2012b), with constituents according priority to the role over and above the Westminster duties of the MP. A survey of MPs newly-elected in 2010 found that they estimated that they spent 59 per cent of their time on constituency business (Hansard Society 2011, p. 6). The reasons for the change we will explore in greater detail in Chapter 11. One apparent consequence of MPs' willingness to engage in constituency casework has been that constituents see the local MP in a more positive light than the House of Commons. Whereas levels of trust in the House of Commons have fluctuated, trust in the local MP prior to 2009 tended to remain constant and positive. As we shall see, following the expenses scandal of 2009, the local MP remains more trusted than the House of Commons.

MPs are elected on a party basis but expected nonetheless to serve the constituency on an individual, in essence non-partisan, basis. They are expected to serve the interests of constituents. The expenses' scandal of 2009 suggested that some were a little too keen to serve their own interests. The disappearance in the first half of the twentieth century of MPs of independent means had left Members reliant on a salary and resources that some deemed inadequate to the increasing demands of the job. The tensions this created resulted in some seeking to supplement their salary through using expenses in a way that was found to breach the spirit and sometimes the letter of the rules (and the law). Changes introduced in 2010 and 2011 were designed to introduce greater rigour and transparency to the system, while also providing MPs with the resources necessary to fulfil their Westminster and constituency duties. The scandal and resulting changes nonetheless failed to reduce the tension inherent in the relationship. On the one hand, constituents expect MPs to serve effectively as grievance chasers on their behalf, but look warily at any attempts to increase the allowances available to MPs, even though they may be necessary to fulfil the tasks that electors expect of their elected representatives.

The nature of the House of Commons and its members has thus undergone significant and disparate change in the last half-century. These changes, as we shall see, have also to be seen within a wider constitutional context.

The House of Lords

The House of Lords can claim to have its origins in the earliest medieval courts, the Anglo-Saxon *Witenagemot* and its successor, the Norman *Curia Regis* of the twelfth and thirteenth centuries, summoned by the king to help discern and declare the law and to proffer advice before the levying of new taxes. As we have noted, the *Curia* comprised the leading barons and churchmen of the kingdom. If a baron attended regularly, it became common for his heir to be summoned following the baron's death. The court thus acquired a body of attenders there by virtue of being their fathers' sons rather than in their own right as tenants of the king.

In the thirteenth century, as we have seen, the king summoned knights and later burgesses to court. In the fourteenth century, the barons and churchmen started to deliberate separately from the knights and burgesses, thus creating the two bodies we now recognize as the House of Lords and the House of Commons.

Formally, the two Houses were co-equal, though the principle of the Commons being responsible for initiating taxation was soon conceded. Henry IV affirmed the position in 1407 and the Commons defended it after the Restoration when the Lords attempted to initiate bills to raise taxes. Indeed, the Commons extended its privilege, denying the right of the Lords to amend money bills (McKenzie 1968, p. 70). In other matters, the House of Lords was equal to the Commons.

Indeed, in political terms, their lordships came to exert considerable influence over members of the Commons, not formally but through their control of parliamentary seats. Most, though not all, of the MPs returned for 'pocket' boroughs owed their positions to the patronage of peers. A table compiled about 1815 showed that 471 parliamentary seats were controlled by 144 peers and 123 commoners (Ostrogorski 1902, p. 20). Some members of the Lords preferred to make their political presence felt through their surrogates in the Commons rather than through their own House. In the Lords, each had one voice. In the Lower House, they might control several.

Franchise and boundary reforms undermined this control. The House of Lords, though, remained a powerful body. It used its powers to initiate and, perhaps more importantly, to vote down bills. It continued to use this power despite the fact that its legitimacy as a co-equal body was undermined by the widening of the franchise. An unelected chamber had difficulty withstanding the claims of an elected chamber. As Lord Shaftesbury noted during the passage of the 1867 Reform Bill, the House might get away with voting down a particularly unjust or coercive bill, but to do so more than once would not be permitted. 'It would be said, "The people must govern, and not a set of hereditary peers never chosen by the people"' (quoted in Norton 1981, p. 21). The House – Conservative-dominated, as it had been since William Pitt the Younger created a record number of Tory peers in the late eighteenth century (Baldwin 1985, p. 96) – did vote down more than one contentious Liberal bill, and the outcry that Shaftesbury had anticipated was heard. The latter half of the nineteenth century saw calls for the reform, or even the abolition, of the Upper House. The policy of 'mend or end' became popular in Liberal circles. In 1893, the Lords threw out the Home Rule Bill. The following year, the Liberal Party conference voted in favour of abolishing the Lords' power to veto bills.

The nineteenth century thus ended in a situation where the House of Commons could claim political but not legal supremacy over the unelected House of Lords. The situation was likely to prove untenable in the event of the return of another Liberal government, and so it proved. The twentieth century saw major reform to the second chamber. In the first half of the century, under a Liberal and then a Labour government, the reform was of its powers. In the second half of the century, under a Conservative and then a Labour government, it was of composition. What started out at the beginning of the century as a coequal chamber comprising predominantly members sitting by virtue of inheritance ended as a subordinate chamber composed predominantly of members chosen in their own right.

Reform: powers

The Liberal Government of 1906 introduced a number of measures that proved too radical for the tastes of the Conservative majority in the Upper House. The Lords threw out or emasculated several major bills, including an Education Bill, before finally rejecting the Budget in 1909 'until it had been submitted to the judgement of the country'. This precipitated a general election in 1910 followed, after the failure of a constitutional conference to discuss the future of the Lords, by another at the end of the year. The first election was held to get support for the passage of the budget and the second on reforming the second chamber. The result was the passage of the Parliament Act of 1911 (see Ballinger 2011, Norton 2012d). The king had agreed to create a sufficient number of new Liberal peers should that be necessary in order to ensure a majority for the bill. In the event, it was not necessary: the number of Conservative 'hedgers' outnumbered the 'ditchers' – those who wanted to make a last-ditch stance against reform.

The 1911 Act provided that a non-money bill could be delayed by the Lords for a maximum of two successive sessions, the bill being enacted if passed by the Commons in the next session. Money bills – those dealing exclusively with money and certified as such by the Speaker – were to become law one month after leaving the Commons, whether approved by the Lords or not. The subordinate position of the House was thus enshrined in statute. In succeeding decades, the House essentially acknowledged its position as a politically inferior chamber and rarely challenged the principle of measures sent to it by the Commons.

The subordinate position of the House found further confirmation during the period of Labour government from 1945 to 1951. Shortly after the return of the Labour government, the Conservative leader in the Lords, Lord Cranborne, later Lord Salisbury, expressed the view that the House should not reject the second reading of a bill promised by the government in its manifesto. What became known as the Salisbury convention has remained in force ever since, and indeed, been extended, the House not usually voting on the second reading of a bill embodied in the government's programme for the session. The formal powers of the House have also been further limited. Under the Parliament Act of 1949, the two-session veto on non-money bills was reduced to one session.

Reform: composition

Reform of composition in the latter half of the twentieth century took place in two stages. The first entailed the introduction of life peerages and the second the removal of most hereditary peers.

The inferior position of the House after 1911 appeared to limit peers' interest in taking part in its activities. In the 1940s, the House had a membership of over 800, but of those 'only about 100 attend regularly and of these perhaps sixty of them take an active part in its business' (Gordon 1948, p. 139). The House rarely met for more than three days a week, and on those days would often not sit for more than three hours. Votes were rare and when they were taken peers voted on party lines (Bromhead 1958). Limited powers and limited activity led to little outside interest in the House. Even MPs gave it little attention, some looking upon it as providing, through its gallery, no more than a convenient place for depositing unwanted guests. When it did attract attention it was from critics who wanted to reform it or – the preference of some Labour MPs – do away with it altogether.

Rather than allow the chamber to atrophy, the Conservative government of Harold Macmillan decided to invigorate it, and in 1958 achieved the passage of the Life Peerages Act, which introduced the provision for peerages to be held solely for the lifetime of the holder. This allowed for the elevation to the peerage of many, such as trade unionists and other Labour supporters, who objected to the hereditary principle. The addition of life peers – the number of new creations increasing over the years – added to the size of the House (by 1998, the number exceeded 1,200) as well as the activity; life peers were disproportionately active in the work of the chamber. Having introduced an Act to enable new peerages to be created, the same Conservative government was also responsible for an Act – the 1963 Peerages Act – that allowed hereditary members of the Upper House to renounce their peerages. The measure had been championed for some years by the second Viscount Stansgate – Tony Benn – who wanted to give up his peerage in order to return to the House of Commons. However, the act also worked to the advantage of two Conservative peers (Lords Home and Hailsham) who, given the facility to renounce, could then seek the Conservative leadership following Harold Macmillan's resignation in 1963. Lord Home was the successful candidate for the succession and renounced his peerage in order to contest a seat for the elected House.

The second major change came in 1999. The Labour government in 1968 had attempted to reform the composition of the House by phasing out the membership of hereditary peers, who continued to dominate the House. The bill to reform the House ran into opposition: some opponents on the left thought it did not go far enough (they preferred an elected chamber or no chamber at all), while some on the right thought it went too far, preferring to leave things as they were. The opponents combined to delay the bill and – while it was never defeated in a vote (the opponents simply wore the government down) – the government decided not to proceed. There was no further major reform attempt for another 30 years. Then, in January 1999, another Labour government – secure in a large majority in the House of Commons – introduced a bill, the House of Lords Bill, to remove hereditary peers from membership of the House. In order to ensure the passage of the bill through the House of Lords, the government agreed to an amendment to retain 92 hereditary peers in the House (90 to be chosen by peers and two to sit ex officio). The bill was passed successfully and was enacted at the end of the 1998–9 session.

The House of Lords Act removed more than 550 hereditary peers from membership. From November 1999, the House has comprised predominantly life peers. The change also affected the party composition of the House, transforming it from one with a preponderance of Tory members

Table 2.1   The changing membership of the House of Lords, 1999–2012

Grouping	Jan 1999	Dec 2004	Mar 2012
Conservative	473	203	217
Labour	168	201	238
Liberal Democrat	67	68	90
Cross-bench	310	173	186
Law Lords*	12	12	0
Lords Spiritual**	26	26	25
Other***	0	10	30

Notes: Excludes peers on leave of absence, suspended, or excluded as, e.g., law lords or MEPs.

* Judges appointed under the Appellate Jurisdiction Act 1876 to fulfil the judicial functions of the House. They were excluded under the provisions of the Constitutional Reform Act 2005 when they became members of the Supreme Court. The Act also excludes other members who hold judicial office.

** The two Archbishops and the Bishops of London, Durham and Winchester, and the twenty-one most senior Bishops in the Church of England. There was one vacancy waiting to be filled in March 2012.

*** Includes members of other parties, such as the Democratic Unionists, Ulster Unionists and members of the United Kingdom Independence Party (UKIP) and non-affiliated peers, such as those who serve as Chairman and Deputy Chairman of Committees and members who hold various public offices outside the House.

Source: Data derived from House of Lords website.

to one in which no single party dominated. Further creations of life peers in 2004 helped to bring the number of Labour peers close to parity with Tory peers and in succeeding years Labour became the largest party in the House. The scale of the change, in terms both of numbers and party strength, can be seen from the data in Table 2.1. The House is clearly different from that existing before 1999 and has been transformed compared with the Tory-dominated house of hereditary peers that existed prior to 1958.

The changing nature of the House

The changes in the powers and composition of the House are not the only changes to have occurred in the Upper House. There are other changes which have taken place, some related to, the others independent of, the change in the composition of the House.

Behaviour

The House of Lords has seen something of a revival in terms of attendance and activity. The introduction of life peers represented a major spur to greater activity, as they proved to be relatively more active than hereditary peers; as a result of the influx of life peers, attendance has increased. By the end of the 1980s, the average daily attendance exceeded 300. More than 700 peers attended one or more sittings each year, and of those, more than 500 contributed to debates (Shell 1988). In other words, well over half of all peers made the effort to turn up one or more times during each session. The relative position improved after 1999, with the disappearance of most hereditary peers, and the hereditary peers selected to remain being among the most active. In the period from 2001 to 2005, the average daily attendance in each session exceeded 360 and from 2005 to 2009 it was 400 or higher (House of Commons Library 2011a, p. 5); by 2010–11, it was closer to 500. Not only was this more in absolute terms than the figure in the 1980s, expressed as a proportion of the membership it marked a significant shift, from a quarter to more than half. There is a substantial body of regular attendees. The House is usually packed for Question Time and for major debates on contentious issues. The increase in attendance has also made possible the creation of more committees.

The greater activity of the House is reflected not only in attendance but also in sittings. The House now sits on more days, and for longer hours, than it did in earlier decades. It sometimes sits for slightly more days a session than the House of Commons. (In October 2011, for example, it resumed sitting a week earlier than the Commons.) The number of days it sits and the length of sittings make it, as we have noted, one of the busiest legislative chambers in the world (see above and House of Lords 2003, p. 11).

There has also been a change in voting behaviour, though the change is not that obvious on the surface. The removal of most hereditary peers in 1999 changed the political composition of the House and consequently the vulnerability of the government to defeat. Before then, a Labour government was vulnerable to defeat at the hands of the Conservative opposition. (Cross-benchers did not usually turn up in sufficient numbers to make a difference.) The Labour government of 1974–9 suffered frequent defeats (a total of 362; see Baldwin 1995, p. 241). A Conservative government was liable to defeat at the hands of its own back-benchers (either by vote or staying away or in conjunction with cross-benchers). The Conservative government of 1979–97 suffered 241 defeats, a substantial number but many fewer per session than suffered by

Labour. After 1999, the Labour government was vulnerable to defeat if the Liberal Democrats voted with the Conservatives (Russell and Sciara 2007). Though there were more cross-benchers than Liberal Democrat peers, Liberal Democrats were much more assiduous in their attendance and voting. The government suffered an average of 40 defeats a session, a total of 528 by the time it left office in 2010 (House of Commons Library 2011a, p. 5). The creation in 2010 of a coalition resulted in the Government having a combined strength notably greater than the Labour opposition (see Table 2.1), meaning that it was vulnerable to defeat only if the cross-bench peers turned out in large numbers and voted disproportionately with the opposition, or coalition peers voted against their own side. In the event, there were occasions when cross-benchers acted in this way (and some when coalition peers voted against their own side or abstained), with the result that in the long session of 2010–12, the government was defeated 48 times in the House of Lords. Governments have thus been vulnerable to defeat in the House of Lords, but as a consequence of different political configurations.

The defeats, though more numerous than in the Commons, nonetheless remain exceptional. The House proceeds largely by way of agreement, with most amendments to bills being accepted without a vote taking place. Fewer than 2 per cent of amendments made to bills in the House of Lords are achieved through defeating the government.

Structures and procedures

The House has become a more specialized body. Until the 1970s the House was very much a chamber-orientated body. This changed with the creation of a European Communities Committee to consider documents emanating from the European Community. This has developed into an extremely active committee (now titled the European Union Committee). It can consider the merits of documents and it works through a number of sub-committees (seven in the period from 2004 to 2012 and six since 2012). About 70 peers are engaged in the regular scrutiny of EU documents, and as we shall see (Chapter 7) it has established a formidable reputation for its work.

The EU Committee is now complemented by other investigative select committees: the Science and Technology Committee, the Economic Affairs Committee, the Constitution Committee and the Communications Committee, the last of these examining the media and the creative industries. The House has also established two select committees to assist with the examination of secondary legislation: the

Delegated Powers and Regulatory Reform Committee and the Secondary Legislation Scrutiny Committee (known until 2012 as the Merits of Statutory Instruments Committee). The House also makes use of *ad hoc* committees, each typically appointed for a session in order to examine a particular issue. They have included in recent years committees to examine the Barnett Formula, HIV/AIDS, the law on adoption, public service and demographic change, and small and medium sized enterprises (SMEs). The House also joined with the Commons in 2001 to set up a Joint Committee on Human Rights.

The House also now regularly utilizes Grand Committees for the committee stage of bills. The normal practice previously was for the committee stage of Bills to be taken on the floor of the House. The Grand Committees are held in committee rooms, and can sit while the House is sitting, thus saving some of the time of the House. Any member of the House can attend, though only those particularly interested in the measures tend to do so, providing for fairly informed scrutiny, and no votes can take place. Any contested amendment on which members wish to vote has to be considered again when the bill returns to the chamber for the report stage. The procedure is used primarily for measures that are not contentious between the parties, though in 2011 a large and contentious Bill – the Welfare Reform Bill – was sent to a Grand Committee despite the Opposition voting against it being taken in this way.

Resources

The House now has an active body of committees complementing what takes place in the chamber and absorbing the commitment of a wide range of members. This activity places a strain on the relatively limited resources of the House. So too does the increasing size of the House. Whereas there were 666 members in the immediate wake of the 1999 House of Lords Act, the number increased significantly under the premierships of Tony Blair and David Cameron. By March 2012, as we have seen, there were almost 790 members. There have been problems in generating resources to keep pace with the growth in the active membership and the work of the House. Though ostensibly occupying half of the Palace of Westminster, the House of Lords has far less space at its disposal than is the case with the House of Commons. Both the House and its members have to maximize the use of the limited space.

Recent years have seen some improvements in the resources available to the House, but these have been limited. Peers receive no salaries, only allowances, and these are paid on the basis of attendance, though some allowance can be claimed to cover parliamentary work during recesses. The allowances have been increased in recent years, but remain modest. Until 2010, members could claim for overnight accommodation, subsistence, and secretarial and research support, up to specified maxima, in addition to travel costs. However, following an expenses scandal not dissimilar to that of the Commons, where some peers were found to be claiming travel and overnight accommodation allowances while living in London – with two subsequently being convicted and imprisoned – the House approved a new scheme, where peers, regardless of where they lived, could claim only a single daily allowance of either £300 or, if not attending the whole day, £150, in addition to travel costs. There is no separate provision for accommodation or secretarial or research support: any such support has to be funded out of the daily allowance. For their principal income, peers tend to rely on the jobs they hold outside the House. While the House of Commons is increasingly a House of career politicians, the Lords sees itself as being a House of experience and expertise, utilizing the experience and skills of members drawn from a range of backgrounds. (Members are usually appointed to committees because of their expertise in the areas covered by the committees.) Opposition parties – as in the Commons – also receive money now to support them in fulfilling their parliamentary duties, though there is no payment to individual members of the Opposition front bench, other than the leader and chief whip.

Office space has increased in recent years, with the House acquiring buildings across the road from the Lords. The House acquired 2 Millbank and more recently 1 Millbank, the two adjoining buildings occupying a significant free-standing block: the former was closed while both were refurbished, the new 'island site' being opened in September 2011 to accommodate committee staff and more than 150 members. The pressure on space means that peers do not have individual offices, but instead have to share accommodation. Most who want a desk have one, though some peers, by choice or necessity, work instead in the Library or other working areas, such as the Royal Gallery or the Peers' Writing Room. For any members who have secretaries or researchers, there is little space to accommodate them.

The facilities may not appear generous, though the pressure on space is compensated to some extent by the attractiveness of the surroundings. The House, like the Commons, has its own Library, with research staff (though not as numerous as in the Commons), and members are entitled to computers and other technical support.

Visibility

The other major change is, as in the Commons, that of the televising of proceedings. As we have already noted, the Lords admitted the cameras in 1985, four years ahead of their entry to the Commons. In the first four years, Lords debates received late-night coverage and, despite the timing, relatively good viewing figures, but the coverage was largely squeezed out once the cameras started recording proceedings in the Commons. Lords debates, and some committee meetings, are carried on the Parliament Channel and proceedings in the chamber can be seen in real time on BBC Democracy Live. All committee meetings are webcast and, as with committees in the Commons, transcripts of evidence are placed on the Parliament website, along with committee reports and other material. The House has also been proactive in promoting awareness of its work (see House of Lords Information Committee 2009), not least through the use of new media – Facebook, Twitter, Flickr and YouTube – and in an outreach programme, peers visiting schools and other organizations to speak about the work of the House.

The House of Lords has thus seen major changes since the start of the twentieth century, not only in terms of its powers and composition, but also in terms of its operation. It has been characterized as a full-time House of part-time members – an active chamber drawing on members whose expertise derives from work normally pursued outside the House. It has changed in its relationship to the first chamber from being a co-equal to being a complementary chamber. As an unelected chamber, it remains, as we shall see (Chapter 14), the subject of debate, with proposals for reform or even abolition.

The changing constitutional environment

Both Houses have thus experienced notable changes in recent years. These changes, as we have noted, have taken place in the context of significant developments in the wider polity. Parliament is no longer the only legislature engaged in debating measures that will be applicable in part or the whole of the United Kingdom. The European Parliament is now a major law-effecting body, and a substantial body of law in the UK derives from European legislation. Parliament has approved legislation creating a Scottish Parliament, a National Assembly for Wales, and a Northern Ireland Assembly. The functions normally ascribed to Parliament on which it previously had a virtual monopoly (almost but not quite, because for 50 years from 1922 to 1972 Northern Ireland had its own parliament at Stormont), are now being exercised by a range of bodies.

These developments have injected a new juridical element to the UK constitution. The courts can determine that provisions of UK law conflict with EU law. They also serve in effect as constitutional courts for Scotland, Wales and Northern Ireland, ensuring that the devolved administrations and legislatures act within the powers given them. The courts have also acquired a further role as a consequence of Parliament enacting the Human Rights Act 1998, bringing into UK law most of the provisions of the European Convention on Human Rights. As a result, the courts, as we shall see (Chapter 9), have acquired the power to determine whether legislation enacted by Parliament complies with the provision of the Convention.

At the same time, there has been a perceived centralization of decision-making power within British government. The Prime Minister has become, according to some commentators, more presidential, meaning that he has become more detached from his own party and his own cabinet (Foley 1993; Norton 2003b), operating as if elected directly by the people and hence deriving his authority from them rather than from Parliament. The result has been a declining engagement with Parliament by the Prime Minister (Dunleavy and Jones 1995). This presidential tendency was compounded under the Blair government by a limited knowledge of government itself and by a tendency for ministers to follow the Prime Minister in focusing on executive rather than parliamentary duties (Norton 2003b). The presidential tendency, combined with devolution, has contributed to a fragmentation of power, leaving a range of power sources located at some distance, constitutionally as well as geographically, from Parliament.

These developments challenge Parliament's hegemony as the body for giving approval to measures of public policy. There are now other elected bodies that confer assent and which can claim to speak for the people in deliberations on measures of public policy. Parliament has to compete with other bodies to be heard by the institutions of the European Union. With the concentration of executive authority in Downing Street, Parliament faces a challenge also to make itself heard by the British government. The challenge has been to adapt to a changing constitutional environment.

Conclusion

Both Houses of Parliament have a history spanning several centuries, and they have had significant consequences for the political system. At times, they have been important allies – and on occasion adversaries – of the monarch. In the seventeenth century, Parliament was a major actor in shaping the nation's constitution.

Though the institution, like other Western legislatures, has not been able to withstand the forces identified in the introduction, it remains a central part of the body politic. It is not, and never has been for any continuous period in its history, a policy-making body. It continues, though, to have important consequences for the political system. Neither House is a static body. Recent years have seen remarkable changes both inside and outside Parliament. Both Houses are more active, more specialized, better resourced, and more visible than before. The specialization of Parliament – with both Houses operating through committees – has been especially important in transforming the institution. On the face of it, Parliament should be in a better position than before to be heard and to influence government. The need to do so is greater as it faces challenges from changes in executive authority and a more crowded political landscape. The remaining parts of this work examine whether or not Parliament has met the challenge.

Part I
Parliament and Government

3

Recruiting Ministers

Government ministers are drawn from, and remain in, Parliament. The significance of this well-known fact is often overlooked, but it has fundamental implications for the ways in which government and Parliament function.

Ministers in Parliament

It is a convention of the constitution that ministers must normally be drawn from the ranks of MPs and peers. There is no legal requirement. It is something that has derived from political circumstance. Monarchs needed the support of Parliament (see Chapter 2) and it was therefore prudent to have their ministers in a position to marshal and contribute to that support. In modern British politics, MPs expect ministers to be answerable to them for their actions; that means coming to the dispatch box to answer questions and respond to debates. Exceptionally, a Prime Minister may appoint someone who is not in Parliament. However, once appointed, the minister is usually brought into Parliament. Traditionally, this has been achieved by elevating the minister to the peerage or engineering election to the Commons through a by-election; nowadays, prime ministers tend to stick to the former route, since victory in a by-election cannot be guaranteed.

An attempt was made through the Act of Settlement of 1701 to sever the link between ministers and Parliament by making 'placemen' – holders of office of profit under the Crown, a category that includes ministers – ineligible for membership of the Commons. This provision, though, was not to come into effect until the death of Queen Anne and was modified, while she was still on the throne, by an Act of 1706. This allowed ministers to retain their seats provided they sought re-election.

Though this put them to trouble and expense and was not repealed until as late as 1926, only very occasionally did it result in the office-holder's defeat, since the convention was soon established that it was ungentlemanly to oppose a member seeking re-election. (Cannon and Griffiths 1988, p. 441)

The succession to the throne of the Hanoverian George I, who spoke no English, added enormously to the king's dependence on ministers to manage Parliament. The most stable administrations proved to be those led by ministers who enjoyed the confidence of both the monarch and the House of Commons.

The practice of ministers being drawn from, and remaining in, Parliament is thus long-standing. What has been noteworthy about the twentieth century and later has been, first, a decisive shift to the Commons as the pool from which ministers are drawn; and, second, the increase in ministerial numbers. Ministers have become less aristocratic and more numerous.

The shift to the Commons

As the franchise was extended and the Commons became the dominant of the two chambers, so the greater was the emphasis on having ministers in the Lower House, answerable to elected representatives. In the nineteenth century, it was not uncommon to have a preponderance of peers in the cabinet and, indeed, for the Prime Minister to be a peer. The twentieth century opened with the third Marquess of Salisbury still occupying the premiership. Since then, there has been a decisive, but not necessarily rapid, shift of emphasis to the Commons.

In 1923, George V had to choose between Viscount Curzon and MP Stanley Baldwin for the premiership. He chose the latter, principally because the Labour Party had become the official Opposition and had no members in the Lords. However, the King's action has been taken as establishing the convention that the Prime Minister must be drawn from the Commons. This was, in effect, confirmed in 1940 when Lord Halifax, favoured by some Labour members for the premiership, recognized that his membership of the Upper House precluded him from the post.

We have already alluded to the events of 1963 (see Chapter 2), when the Queen sent for the fourteenth Earl of Home to ask him to form a government: he relinquished his title and, as Sir Alec Douglas-Home, was returned to the Commons at a by-election (see Shepherd, 1991, pp.

149–59). The occasion was exceptional and only made possible by the passage of the Peerages Act 1963. Lord Home was eligible to renounce his peerage within the time limit stipulated. He was also the beneficiary of the fact that the Conservative Party had no formal means of electing a leader, with the choice being left to the monarch in the event of no obvious leader emerging. Today, election of the leader is by party members – from 1965 to 1997 it was by Conservative MPs – and members of the House of Lords, no longer joining the House by reason of inheriting their titles, cannot renounce their peerages. (The 1963 Act applied only to hereditary peers and, furthermore, stipulated a time period; all the hereditary peers remaining in the Lords are now out of time.) The choice of leader, in other words, must fall on a member of the Lower House.

The emphasis on being answerable to an elected House has also resulted in fewer peers serving in the cabinet. Churchill included six peers in his first peacetime cabinet in 1951. Harold Macmillan included five in his cabinet in 1957. He was the last premier to have a duke (his own nephew-in-law, the Duke of Devonshire) in his government as a junior minister. In both cases, the numbers were quite generous and included a qualitative dimension: a number of peers were given senior positions. Since then, no prime minister has drawn as heavily on the Upper House for members of the cabinet.

Two members of the cabinet were, up to 2005, necessarily drawn from the Lords – the Lord Chancellor and the Leader of the House of Lords – with the minimum number also usually, though not always, constituting the maximum. The separation of the office of Lord Chancellor from the speakership of the House of Lords – with the result that the Lord Chancellor need not necessarily sit in the Lords – reduced the number from two to one. However, Prime Ministers have on occasion appointed peers as departmental ministers. The cabinets of Margaret Thatcher occasionally contained a departmental minister who was in the Lords; the most senior was Lord Carrington as Foreign Secretary (1979–82). Tony Blair briefly had one departmental minister in the House – Lady Amos as International Development Secretary (2003) – and Gordon Brown appointed two (Lord Mandelson as Business Secretary and Lord Adonis as Transport Secretary). Under David Cameron, two peers were appointed to his cabinet in 2010 – the Leader of the House, Lord Strathclyde, and party co-chair (holding the office of minister without portfolio) Baroness Warsi.

Below cabinet level, peers are more numerous in ministerial ranks. It is useful for Prime Ministers to appoint a peer as one of the ministers in a department, as it means that there is then a minister free from constituency duties and therefore someone who can carry most of the routine ministerial tasks during an election campaign, when the other ministers are busy campaigning. None the less, as we shall see, peers still constitute a minority – usually about a fifth – of government ministers.

Growth in numbers

Over the twentieth century and into the twenty-first, the size of the cabinet has not changed significantly, usually comprising 20 or so senior ministers. In 1901, the cabinet had 19 members; in 2011, it had 23. There have been some variations, partly reflecting a variation in the number of government departments, and conditions of war have seen the formation of an inner, or war, cabinet, but the basic membership has shown no significant increase. Where there has been an increase has been in the number of ministers outside the cabinet.

At the beginning of the twentieth century, the number of ministers of cabinet rank (senior ministers not in the cabinet, such as the Paymaster General) and junior ministers (such as the parliamentary secretary to the local government board) was not much larger than the number of ministers in the cabinet. Indeed, the number was only larger because of the inclusion of the whips. Since then, the growth in government responsibilities has resulted in a significant increase in the number of ministers. At the beginning of the twentieth century, there were 30 ministers outside the cabinet; by 1997 there were 80 (Theakston 1987, pp. 42–3; Brazier, 1997, pp. 12–13). The growth has been especially pronounced in the years since 1945, and the change has been qualitative as well as quantitative. A new post of minister of state – just below cabinet rank – was created in 1950, and most departments now have one or more of them, in addition to the more traditional parliamentary secretaries.

The number of ministers, in total and by rank, in the coalition government as at 1 August 2012 is shown in Table 3.1.The largest department – Business, Innovation and Skills (BIS) – had seven ministers in addition to the cabinet minister (though two ministers served jointly in other departments). In 1901, no department had more than one junior minister attached to it. There is a statutory limit on the number of paid ministerial posts. The number of ministers appointed in recent years has exceeded the limit, with the result that several serve as unpaid ministers. In 2012, there were 13 ministers in this category, 10 of them in the House of Lords.

Table 3.1   Number of government ministers in Parliament, 1 August 2012

Rank	House of Commons	House of Lords	Total
Cabinet ministers (including PM)	21	2	23
Ministers of state*	26	4	30
Law officers	2	1	3
Under-secretaries of state**	29	9	38
Whips***	17	10	27
Total	**95**	**26**	**121**

Notes: * Includes the Leader of the House of Commons and the Financial Secretary to the Treasury
** Includes the Economic Secretary, the Exchequer Secretary and the Commercial Secretary to the Treasury,
*** Including the Chief Whip in both Houses.
Source: Data derived from published lists of ministerial positions.

Consequences for ministers

The fact that ministers are drawn from, and remain within, Parliament – and are drawn predominantly from the House of Commons – has a number of consequences in terms of the recruitment and training of those who are to form the government of the United Kingdom.

Ministerial recruitment

Politicians seek membership of a legislature because they believe that such membership will be of value to them: 'Membership may have immediate political value, long-range career value, and financial value, as well as value calculated in less tangible ideological and psychological terms' (Mezey 1979, p. 224).

Of these, the long-range political career is the most important for our purposes. It is also distinctive. For anyone seeking to undertake public service, there are alternatives to serving in Parliament. For anyone seeking financial gain, there are far more remunerative positions to pursue than that of being an MP or, for that matter, a minister. (Indeed, there are various instances of people turning down offers of ministerial jobs or being highly selective because they were being paid more for doing other jobs; see, for example, Nott 2002, p. 124; Renton 2004, p. 3.) For anyone seeking to have some influence on public policy, there are again alternatives to being an MP: for example, a senior civil servant, policy adviser (in, for example, Downing Street) or head of an influential pressure group. For anyone seeking to find a platform for a particular ideological viewpoint, there are again alternatives: journalism, or serving in a policy research body or think tank. However, for anyone wishing to become, and make a career of being, a government minister or, ultimately, to occupy the premiership – the top of what Disraeli called the greasy pole – there is only one route. Parliament, in effect, enjoys a virtual monopoly in terms of recruitment.

As we have noted, someone – usually not a politician – may be elevated to ministerial office without being in either House at the time of appointment. However, such instances are exceptional and – equally important in this context – unpredictable. In other words, anyone *seeking* a career as a minister cannot plan to do so through a route other than membership of the House of Commons.

The House of Commons thus serves as a magnet for those wanting to exercise political power as ministers. As one American observer noted. 'the British House of Commons may play an insignificant role in policymaking ... [but] as the only channel to top executive office it has the special attractiveness of "the only game in town" for the politically ambitious' (Matthews 1985, p. 22). In institutional terms, the House is a powerful body.

This thus distinguishes Parliament from political systems where the executive and legislature are elected independently of one another. In the USA, for example, there are multiple career lines. For anyone seeking the presidency or a cabinet post there is no single and predictable career course to follow, but rather a range of options: state politics (primarily the governorship), the federal legislature (House or Senate), public service, education or business. Congress therefore does not constitute the exclusive pool from which cabinet officers or presidential candidates are drawn. Of recent presidents, for example, Ronald Reagan, Bill Clinton and George W. Bush did not serve in Congress. None the less, members of the House or Senate may be chosen for cabinet posts. In the European Parliament, there is no such likelihood: '[T]he European Parliament's situation has remained unchanged since 1979; it offers no links to "external" governmental opportunities for upward mobility. The only way up is out' (Westlake 1994, p. 6).

The first act of a politician in Britain wanting ministerial office is therefore to obtain a parliamentary candidature. In order to stand any chance of election, this means getting selected as a candidate for one of the main parties. That is the first, but not the only step to take, for election by itself is rarely sufficient. Exceptionally, a new MP – whose reputation for particular qualities has preceded him (never, as yet, her) – may be offered a ministerial post straight away, but in practice, most members have to serve an apprenticeship in the House before being offered a government post. Once elected, they are socialized into the parliamentary process through various rituals and procedures, such as the maiden speech, using certain modes of address in the chamber, and conventions on where to sit. For the purpose of advancement, they need to learn how to use the practices and procedures to their benefit. Some have difficulty in doing so, some may not want to, but for those seeking office it is usually a necessity.

There are more MPs on the government side of the House than there are posts to be filled: the ratio is usually in excess of three to one. Consequently, there is competition for places on the treasury bench (the traditional name for the government front bench). This was particularly the case on the Conservative benches following the creation of a coalition government in 2010, with 20 per cent of ministerial posts going to Liberal Democrats. The chamber and the committee rooms serve as arenas in which ambitious members seek to get themselves noticed by those with the capacity to influence their promotion to office. This means the Prime Minister, senior ministers and – most important of all for getting a foot on the first rung of the ministerial ladder – the whips. There is always a whip present in the chamber, and the whips play a central role in advising the Prime Minister on the performance of members. In the words of one former whip, they are 'vital in determining whether Members climb the parliamentary ladder to senior positions, slip from high office, or remain forever on the back benches waiting in hope' (Major 1999, p. 78; see also Brandreth 1999, p. 369; Renton 2004, pp. 62–9, 79–83).

To establish a reputation in the House, members may focus on the chamber – making speeches, tabling oral questions and generally making themselves visible, as well as being obliging to the whips (Shephard 2000, pp. 85–6) – or on making a mark as an effective committee member. Serving as a member, or chair, of a select committee – or as an officer of a back bench party group – can also help to establish a member's reputation. Exceptionally, a member may get noticed and promoted on the basis of a particular speech. Francis Maude was given office in 1985, two years after being elected to Parliament, reputedly because he made a speech that was noticed by Margaret Thatcher, who happened to be in the chamber at the time. More usually, reputations – and contacts – are made over a period of time.

A member may be promoted to ministerial office straight from the back benches, or go via the position of parliamentary private secretary (PPS). A PPS is an unpaid assistant to a minister, helping with the minister's political arrangements, providing a link with back bench opinion, and ferrying messages between the civil servants' box in the chamber and the minister on the front bench. (PPSs by convention sit on the bench behind the treasury bench.) A PPS can acquire some knowledge of how a department is run and at the same time acquire a ministerial champion who can mention his or her particular qualities to the whips and the prime minister. Becoming a PPS is often seen as the first rung to achieving ministerial office, and MPs are variously chosen as PPSs because they are perceived to have ministerial potential (Norris 1996, p. 147; see also Norton 1994a). That potential is not always realized – perhaps they fail to shine, or their patron does not carry clout with the PM – and for some the height of their political career is serving as the parliamentary private secretary to a minister of a state, the length of the title being in an inverse relationship to its political importance.

A training ground

The fact that ministers are drawn from the ranks of parliamentarians ensures that Parliament serves as the recruiting agency for ministerial aspirants. However, equally significant is the fact that ministers remain within Parliament. A consequence of this is that Parliament is important not only for nurturing future ministers but also serving as a training, or testing, ground for ministers.

The fact that ministers will remain within Parliament may itself be a significant factor in influencing the choice of backbenchers for ministerial office. Skills that are appropriate to handling oneself in the House may take precedence over other qualities. A good speaker or someone who in committee has demonstrated a good grasp of detail may hold an advantage over a colleague who may be a good administrator but who cannot hold the House during debate or has a poor grasp of what is being discussed in committee.

Once in office, a minister is expected to be able to perform competently at the dispatch box during debates and at Question Time. A good performance can contribute to a minister's standing and future career prospects, while a poor speech can mar advancement. 'Several ... ministers would find it hard to win a prize for parliamentary oratory ... As a result, they often had a far more difficult time than they deserved' (Norris 1996, p. 82). On occasion, it can contribute to a minister's downfall.

Nicholas Fairbairn, for example, ceased to be Solicitor General for Scotland in 1982 after his disastrous handling of a debate on a controversial legal case.

Given the emphasis on performance in the chamber, ministers tend to take seriously their appearances at the dispatch box. Some prepare rigorously; and some get very tense. One junior minister recalled that her secretary of state 'was not only meticulous in preparation but was also nerve-racked before questions and debates, refusing to eat, and smoking enormous numbers of cigarettes. He infected the rest of us with pre-appearance nerves, especially me, as a brand-new minister not over-endowed with parliamentary confidence' (Shephard 2000. p. 137). A poor speech at the dispatch box can undermine the morale of the parliamentary party and, in the process, the minister's reputation and that of the government. One MP recalled a debate in which a cabinet minister had no effective answer to a question consistently posed to her in debate. 'So unconvincing was she that several people who came along with the intention of abstaining ended up voting against the government' (Mullin 2011, p. 292); the minister lost her job the following year. A good speech can lift it and enhance a reputation. Following particularly important debates, senior ministers sometimes hold post mortems to discuss how a speech at the dispatch box has been received (see, for example, Lang 2002, p. 289; Nott 2002, p. 267).

Performance outside the chamber is also important. A minister needs to be able to master the detail of legislation when it is going through committee, and to handle questions from critical MPs – usually, but not always, opposition MPs – when appearing before a select committee. It is important for ministers to maintain good relations with their own supporters. An ability to mix easily – to be clubbable – is not a prerequisite for achieving and retaining office, but it is an advantage. A minister can generate goodwill by spending time chatting to MPs in the Commons tea room or when they are going through the division lobbies. A minister may invite worried backbenchers to come and discuss their concerns. If a policy or measure looks likely to upset members, the minister may write what is known as a 'Dear Colleague' letter (a letter sent to all MPs in the parliamentary party explaining the reasons for bringing the proposal forward). Goodwill can prove to be a protective shield. A poor standing with backbenchers can make a minister vulnerable in the event of a policy or administrative mistake.

Ministers may attract criticism because of a particular speech or, more likely, a particular pattern of poor performances at the dispatch box. A minister who lacks confidence at the dispatch box, who fails to gauge the mood of the House, or who is obviously not in command of the facts will attract mutterings from the back benches and these will be noted by the whips. In his first government reshuffle, for example, Tony Blair removed one cabinet minister who had a reputation for indecisiveness as well as for being a poor performer at the dispatch box.

On occasion, ministers may lose office not simply because there are private mutterings on the back benches but because there are public demands for them to go. Various ministers during the period of Conservative government from 1979 to 1997 resigned after losing the confidence of Conservative MPs. These included the Foreign Secretary, Lord Carrington, in 1982, Trade and Industry Secretary, Leon Brittan, in 1986, and National Heritage Secretary, David Mellor, in 1992. Some ministers in Tony Blair's government left office after criticism not only from Opposition MPs but also from government backbenchers. One example was Geoffrey Robinson, the Paymaster General, in 1998 (Robinson 2000, p. 233). Under the coalition government of David Cameron, the Government Chief Whip, Andrew Mitchell, resigned in 2012 after criticism from Tory MPs following an altercation the minister had with a police officer in Downing Street.

Remaining as members of a body which may not choose them but can influence their future has, then, a significant influence on ministers. Resignations as a result of upsetting backbenchers may be few in number but serve as a salutary reminder to other ministers. It is an exceptionally thick-skinned minister who is unconcerned about his or her parliamentary reputation, and it is a rare, and usually imprudent, minister who neglects government backbenchers.

Parliament is thus a vital training ground or, to put it perhaps more accurately, an environment in which ministers have to learn to survive. Most do so without undue difficulty, but knowing they have to survive in that fairly closeted environment influences both their perceptions and their behaviour.

Wider consequences

The fact that ministers are drawn from and stay within Parliament also has other consequences for Parliament and for government. One of the benefits that flow to government, in the form of control, represents a problem for Parliament. However, there are beneficial consequences for both. For Parliament, there are what may be seen as essentially beneficial consequences in terms of career attractiveness, stability in membership, proximity to ministers, and socialization. For government, there are important consequences – mainly, but not wholly, beneficial – in terms of control, ministerial selection and legitimation.

Parliament

Career attractiveness

As we have seen, for anyone seeking to influence public policy through holding national ministerial office, there is little or no alternative to seeking a seat in the House of Commons. Gaining a parliamentary majority is essential for a political party to carry out its programme. Being in Parliament is essential to forming part of the government.

The hold of the Commons over ambitious politicians is remarkable. The main parties have a large pool from which to select their parliamentary candidates; the number of applications to succeed a retiring MP often runs to three figures. Recent years, as we have noted (Chapter 2), have seen a rise in the number of career politicians. The result, as we shall see, has been a more active House.

The attraction of sitting in the House is reflected not only in quantitative but also in qualitative terms. Those holding influential positions in government or other bodies continue to give up their posts to become MPs. Despite the growing power of the European Parliament to determine EU legislation, British politicians are more likely to view membership of the European Parliament as a stepping stone to a seat in the House of Commons, rather than the other way round. Liberal Democrat leader, Nick Clegg, who became Deputy Prime Minister in 2010, had been an MEP from 1999 to 2004 before entering the House of Commons in 2005. Leading government advisers and journalists seek parliamentary candidatures. In 2004, the Chancellor of the Exchequer's economic adviser, Ed Balls – regarded as a powerful influence on the Chancellor's thinking – gave up his post to be selected as Labour candidate for a safe Labour seat. At the same time, an assistant editor of *The Times*, Michael Gove, was selected as a Conservative candidate to fight a safe Tory seat.

For some politicians, being an MP is an end in itself (see Searing 1994). For others, it is a means to an end, usually deciding public policy as a minister or, failing that, influencing those who are ministers. So long as government is drawn from, and remains within, Parliament, then a seat in Parliament remains highly prized by ambitious politicians.

Stability in membership

A stable membership allows for some degree of continuity. Experience can be drawn on, and there is the potential for a corporate spirit to develop. There would thus appear to be an advantage to the House in having some measure of continuity in its membership.

Given that those intent on a political career have no alternative path to pursue, the Commons loses relatively few members as a result of competing job opportunities. Some younger members have left the House because they felt there was little prospect of promotion from the back benches, or because they found the environment less than congenial, but these are few in number. The injection of new blood into the House is achieved predominantly through a change in electoral fortunes and in the retirement of members at the end of their political careers. Very few MPs under the age of 65 voluntarily give up their seats. The greater career orientation of members appears to have contributed to longer parliamentary careers, especially in the years since 1945 (Rush 2001, p. 131).

Stability is obviously affected by a massive swing in political fortunes at a general election. The general elections of 1906, 1945, 1997 and 2010 resulted in a large body of new MPs, but other elections have not had such a dramatic effect. Whereas the 1997 election produced an extensive turnover of members – 39 per cent of the membership was new – the 2001 general election was remarkable for its low turnover. Very few seats changed hands and a relatively small number of MPs retired; the consequence was that only 15 per cent of the MPs in the 2001 Parliament were new. This was closer to the norm than was 1997. The result is a House of Commons with stability in membership that is relatively high by international comparison. Most MPs will continue in post from one Parliament to the next.

Ministerial ambition is not the sole explanation for such stability. Many ex-ministers remain in the House, as do some backbenchers who know their chances of promotion to office are slight. The fact that ministers remain in Parliament may be a partial explanation for the presence of those not destined for future office. They remain close to those who are in office.

Proximity to ministers

The fact that ministers remain in Parliament is valuable to other members in that it ensures a closeness that can be utilized by each House collectively, and by members individually. Ministers have offices in the Palace of Westminster as well as in their departments. MPs can arrange to see them in the House. Some ministers will also spend time meeting members in the tea and dining rooms, not least for reasons of raising their profile among potential back bench supporters. In the 1997–2001 Parliament, Home Secretary Jack Straw was described as 'the senior minister most often in the tea rooms' (Cowley 2002a, p. 160). Ministers will be present in the House to take part in debates and answer questions; the minister replying to a debate normally remains throughout to listen to the speeches. Some will attend to listen to other ministers in debate.

Given that they are members, ministers are also entitled to vote. They are thus present during divisions. As the process of voting takes several minutes – usually at least twelve minutes for each division – ministers spend some time rubbing shoulders with back bench supporters in the division lobbies. This presents an opportunity – and a much-used one – for backbenchers to talk to ministers and put over particular points. Conversely, ministers often utilize the opportunity to track down members they want to see. Such opportunities for face-to-face contact are recognized by members as invaluable for increasing the likelihood of a positive response to a request: a minister finds it more difficult to say no when facing the member making the request.

Socialization

The fact that ministers start life as MPs and remain as members ensures – or is likely to ensure – that they are familiar with parliamentary norms and expectations. Aspirant ministers have to know their way round the institution. A survey by the Study of Parliament Group of new MPs first returned in the 1992 general election found that approximately half of them regarded themselves as 'very familiar' or 'somewhat familiar' with parliamentary procedure. Once elected, they face the same demands and pressures as their other colleagues. And once elevated to ministerial office, those demands do not necessarily cease. Ministers in the House of Commons retain constituency responsibilities (see Chapter 10). They have to carry out tasks as MPs and not solely as ministers. They have to contact fellow ministers in their capacities as constituency MPs, and fellow ministers may approach them in a similar capacity.

There is thus socialization into the parliamentary process of those who are to form the political elite (Rush and Giddings 2011). Though ministers are answerable to Parliament, they are also members of the very institution to which they are answerable. They mix with backbenchers, rubbing shoulders with them – sometimes literally, in a crowded lobby – when they vote. They are themselves likely to return to the back benches at some stage, be it by choice or by prime ministerial diktat. This reduces the likelihood of ministers ignoring and not understanding Parliament's needs and expectations. Indeed, not understanding those needs and expectations may facilitate a speedy return to the back benches. Some ministers may be poor at handling the House, but they generally grasp and are integrated into its practices and procedures. They are an integral part of the institution. This contrasts with those political systems where there is a separation of executive and legislature, increasing the potential for misunderstandings between the two.

Government

Control

Party dominates Parliament and political behaviour. We have seen in preceding chapters the conditions that made this possible. For its continuance in office, government is dependent on a parliamentary majority. Formally, this should ensure parliamentary control of the executive, but in practice, the flow of control is the other way. In the eighteenth century, control could be achieved through royal patronage and placemen in the Commons, but since the last third of the nineteenth century, it has been achieved through party.

The presence of ministers in Parliament is not the cause of party control (see Crowe 1986) but serves to facilitate it. Being in Parliament means ministers have a platform to lead and to persuade their supporters. Ministers can serve as an important reference group for loyal and ambitious backbenchers. 'Some MPs model themselves after the front-bench group, especially those backbenchers who seek higher office themselves' (Crowe 1986, p. 164). In debate, frontbenchers are the focus of attention. And ministers collectively constitute a significant voting force.

Ministers are bound by the convention of collective responsibility, a convention requiring that ministers do not oppose a policy once it has been agreed. Some uncertainty existed in the nineteenth century as to whether the convention applied to junior ministers. In the twentieth century and since, there has been no such ambiguity (Norton 1989b, pp. 34–5). It encompasses all ministers, and in recent years has been employed to constrain the activities of parliamentary private secretaries (Norton 1989a, pp. 234–6; 1989b, pp. 35–6); PPSs voting against the government can usually expect to lose their posts. The result is a block vote at the disposal of government. Given the increase over the twentieth century in the number of ministers, and the increase since 1997 in the number of PPSs, it is now a sizeable block (see House of Commons Library 2011b, p. 5). In 1900, there were 33 MPs in government posts and 9 PPSs. In 2011, there were 95 MPs in government posts and 46 PPSs, constituting 21 per cent of the House. In the event of an expected difficult vote, as over Iraq in 2003 and student fees in 2010, this block vote – normally referred to as the payroll vote, even though it includes unpaid PPSs – is much in evidence.

The government can also exercise control through patronage. Research shows that, in the 1997–2001 Parliament, there was a correlation between those with ambitions for ministerial office and voting loyally for the government (Cowley 2002a, pp. 109–10). Those disclaiming ambition for office were more likely to rebel.

Ministerial selection

The fact that ministers must be drawn from the ranks of MPs and peers – predominantly the former – has important consequences for British politics. It limits the pool from which the Prime Minister can select ministers. In the USA, the president has a very wide pool: cabinet members may be drawn from a wide range, extending not only beyond Congress but also beyond politics. The president may appoint academics, lawyers and leading bankers. A Prime Minister has no such luxury; ministers are chosen from the Prime Minister's own party and, within this party, from those who are usually within a certain profile in terms of age, experience and political acceptability. The only latitude there is to go beyond the pool is by appointing someone to the Lords, a route utilized on occasion by Prime Ministers Tony Blair, Gordon Brown and David Cameron.

Though the limited pool facing the Prime Minister may be seen as extremely constraining, it does mean that the Prime Minister will usually know well those selected to serve in the cabinet. There will already have been an opportunity to work with them and observe them in action.

Thus, as we have noted already, the fact that ministers have to survive within a parliamentary environment has some effect on ministerial selection. An ability to handle oneself in the House is an advantage for anyone keen to become a minister. A Prime Minister is also influenced by the support a potential or existing minister has on the back benches. Some ministers are deemed to be immune from dismissal because of their support on the back benches. Others may be vulnerable if they have little support and depend for their patronage solely on the prime minister or another senior minister.

For a potential or serving minister, then, parliamentary skills are highly prized. Arguably, they may be too highly prized. There is the danger that parliamentary skills may be elevated over skills that may be just as necessary to control and lead a government department. A minister capable of strategic thinking, with a good grasp of future policy requirements, and a capacity for hard work and administration, may make little progress – indeed, may lose office – if these are not matched by a capacity to handle oneself in debate and in one's relations with backbenchers. Indeed, as one former minister noted, the emphasis on parliamentary skills may have a negative effect on running a department:

> Performance at the dispatch box, or in debate, gave no indication of the ability of a minister to get things done in his department. Indeed, I came to believe that the ability to carry the House of Commons led individuals to think that they needed to put less effort into running their departments. (Golding 2003, p. 19)

On this analysis, therefore, it is possible to argue that, far from lacking power, Parliament is too powerful. Ministerial membership in Parliament imposes constraints in ministerial selection, with a prime minister unable to exploit alternative avenues – because none exist – in ministerial recruitment. It also dictates attention to parliamentary performance to the potential detriment of effective departmental management and innovative thinking. Some highly intelligent ministers have been poor performers at the dispatch box.

Legitimation

The fact that ministers are drawn from the ranks of parliamentarians and remain within Parliament contributes to the legitimation of government. Membership of the legislature confers some status on ministers, over and above that accruing from being ministers. That ministers in the Commons have fought elections to be returned to Parliament as MPs gives them a particular status; and the knowledge that they are subject individually to re-election as members adds to their presumed sensitivity to electors' opinions. Membership in Parliament, with procedures geared to ministerial leadership, also provides an authoritative platform for ministers. Press conferences may give them greater media coverage, but making a statement in the House confers greater legitimacy.

Remaining within Parliament also adds a particular burden to the workload of ministers (see James 1992, pp. 19–29). They have variously to be present, not just to take part in Question Time and debates, but also to vote and to support fellow ministers in important debates. As MPs, they have to pursue constituency casework. Douglas Hurd recalled that when he was Foreign Secretary: 'Foreign colleagues were amazed in an interval of some international conference to watch me signing replies to individual constituents on their personal problems, and to learn that I had earlier dictated these replies myself' (Hurd 2003, p. 312). The burden on individuals is heavy and they may therefore have mixed feelings about having to shoulder the twin burden of ministerial office and parliamentary membership. It can also create problems for government in that ministers cannot devote their energies exclusively to running their departments, though the existence of several ministers in a department now helps to spread the burden. However, from the perspective of government, the balance of advantage clearly favours the present integration of ministers in Parliament.

Conclusion

The Act of Settlement of 1701 almost resulted in a formal separation of ministers from Parliament. However, that was avoided and ministers continue to be selected from and remain within the ranks of MPs and peers.

From a pluralist view of power, that has rendered Parliament a weak body in policy-making. The governing party has its leaders in Parliament. Procedures are structured in order to facilitate ministerial leadership. Ministers open and close debates. Only ministers can move certain motions, especially those relating to money and to sittings of the House. The presence of ministers and PPSs ensures that the government has a substantial 'payroll' vote at its disposal. Because ministers are drawn from the ranks of parliamentarians, the Prime Minister enjoys extensive patronage powers: those seeking advancement are likely to follow his or her wishes. If government supporters show signs of wavering, the whips – and ministers – are able to move quickly to respond and to persuade them to stick with the government. Mass parties and the existence of parliamentary government – government being drawn from and remaining within Parliament – has ensured the hegemony of government over Parliament.

However, viewed from an institutional perspective, the position makes Parliament powerful. Those wishing to change British society through control of public policy have to acquire office through the House of Commons. This applies collectively – that is, to parties – and individually – that is, to those seeking ministerial office. Parliament enjoys a monopoly as a recruiting agency for government. Within Parliament, ministerial aspirants are socialized into parliamentary life and have to demonstrate their skills as debaters. As we have noted, this not only renders Parliament powerful, but possibly too powerful; it limits the pool from which ministers can be drawn. Able people outside the House are excluded from consideration. Some able people in the House may also be excluded, or have short ministerial careers, because they are poor performers at the dispatch box. Some commentators, and indeed politicians have described parliamentary life as theatre. However, in this case, the players have the opportunity to influence who have the leading parts.

4

The Making of Public Policy

The capacity of legislatures to affect the content of public policy is, as we noted in Chapter 1, a central concern of legislative scholars (see Olson and Mezey 1991). From empirical observation, it is clear that the capacity to affect policy varies from one legislature to another.

In terms of their impact on public policy, three types of legislature can be identified: policy-making, policy-influencing, and those with little or no policy affect. The essential characteristics of each are identified in Table 4.1. Policy-making legislatures can involve themselves in the drawing up – the making – of policy. Policy-influencing legislatures have the formal capacity to amend, even to reject, measures of public policy placed before them, but they are essentially dependent on government to put forward those measures. Even if they reject a measure, they look to government to formulate and bring forward a replacement. The legislature itself does not seek to generate – to make – policy. It lacks the political will, the institutional resources or even, in some cases, the

Table 4.1   Types of legislatures

Policy-making legislatures
Have the capacity to amend or reject policy brought forward by the executive, and the capacity to formulate and substitute policy of their own.

Policy-influencing legislatures
Have the capacity to amend or reject policy brought forward by the executive, but lack the capacity to formulate and substitute policy of their own.

Legislatures with little or no policy affect
Lack the capacity both to amend or reject policy brought forward by the executive and to formulate and substitute policy of their own. They confine themselves to assenting to whatever is placed before them.

Source: Norton (1990a, p. 178).

constitutional power to do so. Legislatures with little or no policy effect exist primarily to give assent to measures laid before them.

For most of its history, Parliament has not been a policy-making body. The monarch came to depend on Parliament to assent to both supply and legislation (see Chapter 2). Demanding a redress of grievance before granting supply could be construed as initiating some change in the monarch's policies. But for most of the centuries of its existence, Parliament has looked to the executive – first the monarch, then the king's government – to bring forward measures for it to consider. Even in the wake of the Glorious Revolution of 1688, those responsible for the Bill of Rights wanted 'a real, working, governing King, a King with a policy' (F. W. Maitland, in Wiseman 1966, p. 5).

The position has been exacerbated by the growth of party. The rise of party in the nineteenth century heralded the consolidation of policy-initiating power in the hands of the executive. Increasing demands on government by organized interests resulted in more public legislation and an increasing domination by government of the parliamentary timetable.

This development has not been peculiar to Britain. In the typology of Table 4.1, Parliament is a policy-influencing legislature. So too are most legislatures of Western Europe (Norton 1990c, 1998a) and of the Commonwealth. The category, in fact, is the most crowded of the three. The number has been swelled by the democratic legislatures of southern (Leston-Bandeira 2005) and central and eastern Europe (Olson and Norton 1996; 2008), but even prior to their emergence it was the most populous category. What is noteworthy, but not altogether surprising given the effects detailed in Chapter 1, is that the first category – that of policy-making legislatures – is sparsely populated. The only major national legislature to have occupied the category on any consistent basis is the US Congress. It is joined by the state legislatures of the USA (see Mezey 1979, ch. 2). The separation of powers in the USA, combined with an ideological consensus that has militated against the emergence of strong parties (Norton 1993a; Lipset 1997), has resulted in a legislative system that stands apart from others.

The policy-making process

The process by which a proposal is translated into public policy is often a complex and lengthy one. Four principal stages in the process can be identified: initiation; formulation; deliberation and approval; and implementation.

Initiation is the first stage of a formal process. Within the policy process in the UK, it embraces two elements. The first is generating a particular policy proposal, and the second is agreeing that it should be brought before Parliament for approval. The decision to bring something before Parliament rests principally with the government, a role it shares with private members – any MP or peer can put forward a bill – but for constitutional and political reasons, the government is the principal generator of bills. Only ministers can propose bills making a charge on the public revenue and, as we have seen, Parliament looks to the executive to bring measures forward. The government's position is enhanced by its political hegemony.

In terms of *formulation,* we mean putting the flesh on the bones of a particular proposal. There are two elements to this stage as well. Those responsible for introducing the measure have to agree the detail. In the case of a government bill, for example, that would be the ministers in the relevant department and, subsequently, the appropriate cabinet committee. Second, there is the formal construction of the document. In the case of legislation, that means drawing up a bill. For government (and some private members') bills, this task is undertaken by trained lawyers known as parliamentary counsel. Where the proposal does not involve primary legislation, such as a document to be placed before an international body, the formal construction will usually be undertaken by departmental civil servants.

The stages of initiation and formulation may thus be taken to form the essential stages of policy-making. They involve the putting together – the crafting – of a coherent proposal that is intended to be applied in a particular community. Once a measure has been agreed, it is then laid before Parliament. Parliament is rarely involved prior to the formal introduction of the measure. However, there are exceptions, and these are growing in number. Parliament is involved increasingly at the stage between formulation and the formal introduction of the bill before Parliament. This stage is essentially discretionary – not all bills go through it – and it involves the publication of bills in draft, offering Parliament the opportunity for pre-legislative scrutiny.

The remaining stages complete the process from making to application. *Deliberation and approval* entail consideration of the full and published measure by Parliament and the formal giving of assent to it by the Queen-in-Parliament. Without that assent, it cannot constitute an Act of Parliament and be enforced as the law of the land.

Implementation constitutes the carrying into effect of the policy. The nature of the implementation will vary depending on the nature of the

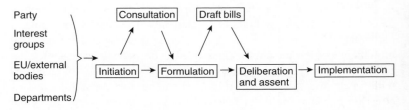

Figure 4.1   The policy-making process

policy. Some measures can be implemented through administrative action by officials, such as the payment of a new kind of benefit, while some are implemented through police action, as with the enforcing of a ban on a particular activity.

The stages of the policy-making process are shown in simple diagrammatic form in Figure 4.1. The purpose of this chapter is to focus on the first two stages of the process. What role does Parliament play in policy-making? Our initial assumption, based on history and comparative observation, is that it is a minor one; however, recent empirical evidence points to it being somewhat less minor than before.

Initiation

Bills do not suddenly emerge from the ether. They are the product of a perceived need for a change in the law. Most bills that achieve passage, as we shall see, are introduced by government, in responding to demands that it deems are legitimate and sufficient to justify legislative action. The demands to which it responds derive from a variety of sources.

A major source is the party. The political parties contest elections on the basis of increasingly bulky and detailed election manifestos. These provide the basis for the government's flagship legislation during a Parliament, though in 2010 there was no one party manifesto that determined government policy: negotiations between the Conservative and Liberal Democrats led to a coalition agreement being drawn up (Laws 2010; Wilson 2010; Norton 2010b) and this provided the framework for government policy. Winning parties have a very good record of implementing manifesto promises (Hofferbert and Budge 1992, pp. 151–82). However, a party manifesto is no guarantee of success. Ministers may decide not to pursue particular proposals: there may not be time, the proposals may have been overtaken by events, or they may not be translatable into legislative form. They may encounter opposition within government itself.

Furthermore, bills derived from manifesto commitments constitute only a minority – about a tenth – of the legislation introduced by government (Rose 1984, p. 70). Government will also introduce legislation as a response to particular crises; for example, to deal with international terrorism, or in order to give effect to international agreements it has negotiated. Some will emanate from EU commitments. Certain bills, such as the Finance Bill, are brought forward as a matter of course. Most, though, derive from government departments as a result of pressure from and discussion with interest groups and other bodies (Rose 1984, pp. 70–2). Road safety groups and families that have lost loved ones in road accidents may press for a tightening of the laws on reckless and careless driving. Employees whose pensions are under threat because of depleting pensions funds or because their companies have become insolvent may demand legislation to protect their pension rights. Divorced fathers who have limited access to their children may press for a change in the law to allow them equal access with the mothers. If ministers find their cases persuasive, they may agree to bring forward appropriate legislation.

Bodies seeking to change public policy may lobby parties to try to influence the party manifestos, but the main – indeed, usually, the first, and often only – port of call is a government department. A survey of business associations and unions found that meeting civil servants was rated the most effective of seven types of pressure group activity (Mitchell 1997, reported in Grant 2000, p. 64). As Wyn Grant noted, when figures were aggregated, 'over 90 per cent of respondents selected a channel of influence involving the executive branch as the most effective' (Grant 2000, p. 64). Another study found that in order to influence ministers, groups place as much emphasis on the mass media as they do on Parliament (Rush 1990). MPs may play a limited role as facilitators, helping to introduce representatives of a group or company to a minister, but their intervention is neither essential nor, consequentially, always sought. As one group in a 1986 survey of interest groups commented: 'We usually go to the minister direct without MPs' assistance ... Our comments do bear fruit, there are lots of examples where they have' (Rush 1990, p. 272).

The essential link for organized interests is thus government departments. The links, as we have noted (see Chapter 1), have become extensive and institutionalized. The policy style involved in negotiations between civil servants and representatives of outside groups has been characterized by Jordan and Richardson (1982) as one of 'bureaucratic accommodation'. It is in the interests of both sides to produce a mutually agreeable proposal, which is then passed upwards for ministerial assent.

Such negotiations are geared essentially to achieving incremental change: an adjustment, for example, to some existing regulation. For more substantial change, especially that involving major legislation, the principal figure is the minister.

A minister is the key figure in the legislative process. Once ministers are appointed to head departments, they normally like to generate some flagship bill that will help to make their name. However, most of the bills that emanate from their departments are the product of negotiation between their officials and outside groups. These bills are likely to have been brought forward regardless of which party is in power, and indeed are likely to be resurrected if they fall because of a general election and a new party takes office. The important role of the minister here is as gate-keeper. Even though most measures percolate up to a minister, rather than originating in the minister's office, it is up to the minister to agree to the proposal going forward.

If a minister agrees that change is necessary, this is no guarantee that a bill will be brought forward. It is not unusual for proposals to be put out for consultation, governed by a clear set of guidelines; interested bodies usually have 12 weeks to respond. Consultation tends to be extensive – all interested bodies are normally sent copies of the consultation paper – and invited to comment. It may take the form of a Green Paper, where different legislative proposals are canvassed. The government may issue a White Paper, which embodies a statement of what it intends to do. Though now more extensive than before, not all proposals will be subject to consultation; there may not be time, or the proposal may be a manifesto commitment to which the government is strongly committed. In the five-session 2005–10 Parliament, the government issued (excluding Departmental annual reports and expenditure plans) a total of 76 White Papers.

The next stage is for the minister to persuade colleagues of the need for legislation. The proposal goes to the relevant cabinet committee. Much of the deliberation takes the form of the circulation of papers, the minister setting out the proposal and members of the committee responding. Getting clearance from the committee is a necessary but not sufficient condition for introducing a bill. Legislative proposals then have to go to the Parliamentary Business and Legislation Committee, chaired by the Leader of the House of Commons, which decides which bills will be included in the government's programme for the next parliamentary session. Bids from departments always exceed the slots available: 'There is no shortage of candidates. There never is' (Cook 2003, p. 76). There is limited time available and so the committee has to be selective in its choice of bills to be brought forward. Departments may find that their bills, especially if of a minor, technical nature, may have to wait to a later session.

Bills approved by the Committee are then prepared for introduction. Ministers may be responsible for bringing bills forward, but they are not responsible for writing them.

Formulation

Once a bill has been approved for introduction, the relevant department draws up instructions as to what should go in the bill. The officials in the department who engage in this task are lawyers. This constitutes the first leg of this stage of the process. However, it is the second leg that is the most important. Though departments draw up instructions as to what they want to include, they are not responsible for drawing up properly formulated bills.

Drafting bills is a highly specialized art, undertaken, as we have noted, by lawyers known as parliamentary counsel. They form the Office of Parliamentary Counsel; housed in an office in Whitehall, they are formally part of the Cabinet Office but operate as a distinct entity. They are highly trained, principally through on-the-job training; it takes about seven years to become qualified to draft a bill, even longer to take on a major complex measure (Bowman 2004, p. 96). They work under considerable pressure – Robin Cook as Leader of the House of Commons referred to their 'Stakhanovite commitment to their job' (Cook 2003: p. 210) – and, to cope with the demands made on them, their number has been significantly expanded in recent years. In 1997 there were 36 parliamentary counsel; in 2012 there were approximately 50. (The figure excludes ten who are normally seconded to assist the Law Commission and HM Revenue and Customs.) They usually work in teams, a team of two or three usually dealing with each bill, though a slightly larger number will work on measures such as the annual Finance Bill. Indeed, the complexity of a measure, such as a Finance Bill, may require ten or more.

Counsel are important figures in that they have the power to tell departments that a particular principle cannot be embodied in legal form. A principle, however acceptable, cannot always be translated into the detail of legislation, amenable to interpretation and application by the courts. They will also advise on the best way to achieve a particular intention (Engle 1983; Bowman 2004). They also try increasingly to ensure that the language of bills is clear and accessible, without sacrificing the need to render them in sufficiently precise form for legal application. In drafting bills, they will bear in mind the parliamentary rules governing such matters as scope and hybridity (a hybrid bill is a public bill affecting private interests). If in doubt, discussions take place with the clerks in both Houses, with whom they have a close working relationship.

Parliamentary counsel have traditionally prepared bills ready for their introduction to Parliament. However, in recent years, there has been a growing practice of publishing bills in draft. The terminology is misleading; 'drafting a bill' refers to drawing up a bill in properly constituted form ready for formal parliamentary consideration (see Chapter 5), whereas a 'draft bill' refers to a bill drawn up, sometimes but not always in properly constituted form, in advance of its introduction to Parliament. (A better way to think of a draft bill is as a preliminary, or rough, bill.) The Conservative government of John Major (1992–7) published several bills in draft, the Labour government returned in 1997 extended the practice, and the coalition government has maintained it. The rationale for this is to enable consultation to take place on the particular provisions of a bill. Through such consultation it is possible to see if the provisions meet the purpose of the bill, if the provisions are too broadly drawn or may have unintended effects, or if they suffer from other defects.

Publication of bills in draft is especially important for Parliament. A draft bill provides the opportunity for parliamentary involvement at the formulation stage. Parliamentarians get to comment on it *prior to* it being laid officially before Parliament for approval. Involvement at this formative stage has the potential to be more productive than at later stages, when the government has determined precisely the provisions it wishes to be embodied and to which it is publicly committed.

There is thus a much greater opportunity than before for Parliament to engage in pre-legislative scrutiny. Draft bills may be considered by a departmental select committee in the House of Commons or by a joint committee of both Houses. Though government has conceded that bills should normally be published in draft (see Kennon 2004, p. 477), not all can be – and most still are not. Between 1997 and 2010, out of 471 bills introduced by government, 76 – or 16 per cent – were published in draft (Constitution Committee 2010, p. 7). In the first session of a new government, there will not be time for the principal bills to be considered in draft: the government will need to introduce several bills at the start of the session, and measures introduced as a response to crises may need to be enacted swiftly. Certain bills, such as the Finance Bill, do not permit of such scrutiny.

None the less, the publication of bills in draft has, as we shall see, provided scope for parliamentary involvement at the second stage of the legislative process – in effect, Parliament operating at the interface between the stages of formulation and formal deliberation – and given it a capacity to influence the content of legislation to a greater extent, arguably, than has been witnessed since the advent of party government.

The impact of Parliament: decision-making

The different definitions of power enable us to view Parliament from three distinct perspectives. Viewed from a pluralist perspective, Parliament is essentially a marginal body. As we have seen, MPs and peers are not involved centrally in the initiation and formulation of legislation. It is overwhelmingly a government-centred activity. However, though Parliament may be a marginal actor in the process, it is not a nonexistent one. And its involvement in recent years has grown rather than diminished. That involvement can be considered under three headings, each corresponding to a particular part of the policy-making process: agenda setting; initiating legislation; and pre-legislative scrutiny.

Agenda setting

Parliament may play a role as one of the bodies putting pressure on government to introduce measures. In marketing terms, government departments are targets for bodies seeking a change in the law. However, Parliament can serve as a channel for reaching the target. MPs enjoy proximity to ministers. They can raise issues and ensure a ministerial response in a way that the ordinary citizen cannot.

There are various mechanisms available to MPs and peers to bring issues on to the political agenda. We shall explore these in more detail in later chapters. They may write to ministers, they may (individually or in groups) arrange meetings with a minister (or arrange for representatives of affected bodies to meet ministers), or they may utilize structures or procedures within Parliament itself. On the floor of each House, members may employ questions and motions. Away from the floor, there are two unofficial routes, those of party groups and all-party groups, and one official route, that of select committees. There is also the opportunity to table early day motions. These means are not mutually exclusive, and several or all may be utilized to achieve consideration of a particular policy.

We shall be exploring these means of ensuring that the voices of different bodies in society are heard by government in later chapters. They serve an important role – some of them an increasingly important one – in ensuring that government is aware of particular problems and concerns. By bringing an issue on to the agenda, it is possible that it may prompt action – including legislative action – by government. These range, for example, from reform of the law on homosexual relations – prompted by a debate initiated in the House of Lords by Lord Arran (Richards 1970, p. 76; McManus 2011, pp. 52–7) to the more recent ban on fox hunting.

However, what MPs and peers are doing more frequently through using these devices is not setting the agenda but rather reinforcing demands already voiced by different bodies – in effect, emphasizing the case for, and often against, issues already on the agenda, and trying to ensure that they achieve sympathetic treatment by ministers.

Initiating legislation

The principal focus under this heading is private members' legislation. Any MP or peer can introduce a bill. In the Lords, the convention is that the government does not oppose such a bill, so most pass through all their stages in the House. They rarely get any further, though, because there is no time for them in the Commons. In the Commons, MPs can introduce bills through one of three routes: the ballot; the ten-minute rule procedure; and the presentation bill – or unballoted – procedure.

Each session, a ballot is held for MPs wishing to introduce private members' bills; most MPs put their names in. The top 20 names drawn have an opportunity to nominate when their bills should be considered on one of the Fridays set aside each session for such bills; the top six or seven are normally assured of their bills having a full debate on second reading. This constitutes the main route for the introduction of bills likely to have some chance of enactment.

A ballot is also held for bills introduced under the ten-minute rule. Taken after Question Time on Tuesdays and Wednesdays, a member has ten minutes to make the case for the bill. Another member may then speak against it, also for ten minutes, and the motion is then put for the member to have leave to introduce the bill. If it is opposed, a vote takes place. If leave is given, the bill still stands little chance of becoming law as there is no time allotted to debate it.

The final method is simply to introduce a presentation bill. No ballot is involved. The member simply gives notice of the intention to introduce the bill; it is put on the order paper and then given a formal first reading – there is no debate – and it is printed (though some members do not even bother to go this far, bills remaining in name but not in substance). There is no time in the parliamentary timetable to debate these bills. Their titles are read out at the end of business on Friday. A single objection is sufficient to block a bill from progressing any further. A government whip will usually be present to ensure that a bill's passage is blocked. A short, widely supported and non-contentious bill may get through, but most fail to escape a cry of 'object'.

There are two views of private members' legislation that appear to be widely held. One is that they represent the exception to the rule in respect of the reactive role of Parliament. They represent the means, albeit a limited one, by which legislation can be initiated within Parliament. The second, related to the limited capacity, is that very few private members' bills are passed. MPs can initiate legislation, but they rarely do so successfully.

Both views are, or were, open to challenge. Although MPs and peers can introduce private members' bills, only a small number originate effectively from the sponsor. A great many, if not most, originate from interest groups, official reports or government departments. Indeed, private members' legislation provides a useful means through which some of the bills favoured by departments, but which were not included in the government's legislative programme for the session, may make it to the statute book. They are known as 'hand-out bills', ready to hand out to any MPs who are successful in the ballot and who would be interested in taking them through. The attraction of such bills to backbenchers is that they come properly drafted – by parliamentary counsel – and have government support; they are therefore likely to make it to the statute book. The government achieves its legislation and the private members in whose names the bills are introduced are able to claim the measures as 'theirs'.

If not originating from a department, a private member's bill stands a good chance of having originated from an interest group. Not only will groups lobby MPs to introduce particular measures, they may even draft them as well. Many organizations, such as the Consumers' Association, have become adept at drafting bills. If the bill finds favour with the government, it will be reviewed by parliamentary counsel. Failing that, it will be up to the members to make their own arrangements. Those members who rely on their own skills or those of sympathetic bodies run a high risk of finding that the bill is technically flawed. Where drafting is deficient, sponsors will often agree to accepting amendments to remedy the problem.

Table 4.2   Private Members' Bills, 2005–10

	Introduced	Successful
2005–6	116	3
2006–7	96	4
2007–8	100	2
2008–9	112	5
2009–10	67	7
Total	491	21

Source: Compiled from House of Commons Information Office, *Sessional Information Digests* (2005–10).

There are thus incentives to bring forward bills prepared and proffered by outside bodies. The fact that a number are hand-out bills may also explain the other caveat to the generally held view of private members' bills. Far more have tended to be passed than is popularly realized, though the numbers have dropped in recent years. In the quarter-century up to 2005, about nine private members' bills became law each session (Rogers and Walters 2006, p. 230). However, the number dropped towards the end of the period and in the 2005–10 Parliament it averaged four a session (Table 4.2). Of the 21 successful bills in the Parliament, 15 were ballot bills, 4 were private members' bills introduced in the Lords, and 2 were presentation bills. The seven bills that were successful in the final session are listed in Table 4.3.

In the sessions prior to 2005, for every private member's bill that passed, there were usually about eight or nine others that do not make it. In the 2005–10 Parliament, there were more than 20 unsuccessful bills for

Table 4.3   Private members' bills passed, 2009–10 session

Title of bill	Bill's sponsor
Anti-Slavery Day	Anthony Steen (Con)
Co-operative and Community Benefit Societies and Credits	Lord Tomlinson (Lab)
Debt Relief (Developing Countries)	Andrew Gwynne (Lab)
Marriage (Wales)	Lord Rowe-Beddoe (Ind)
Mortgage Repossessions (Protection of Tenants Etc)	Dr Brian Iddon (Lab)
Sunbeds (Regulation)	Julie Morgan (Lab)
Sustainable Communities Act 2007 (Amendment)	Alistair Burt (Con)

every successful bill. On the face of it, MPs and peers appear to devote time to introducing bills which stand little or no chance of success.

The bills that are successful usually introduce modest changes in the law, though some do involve important changes in the law – the 1997 Knives Act, for example, made it an offence to carry knives as offensive weapons. Unless government agrees, bills cannot make a charge on the public revenue (other than incidentally). There is limited time available and government rarely makes extra time available in its own parliamentary schedule. Most, therefore, focus on adjustments to existing laws or introduce small changes that enjoy broad support. One may conclude therefore that private members' legislation makes relatively minor changes to the law and that MPs and peers are generally devoting their energies unnecessarily to bills that will never make it to the statute book.

Such a conclusion, though, would be misleading. Private members' bills, as we have seen, can result in some changes to the law. Only MPs and peers can introduce such bills and these individuals thus serve as gatekeepers; they can decide what is brought forward. There is thus a very limited initiating role, even if the measures are prepared by others. (Bills introduced by ministers are, after all, also prepared by other people.) However, the most important role fulfilled by private members' legislation is not that of initiating legislation but rather agenda setting and reinforcing the case for change. Private members' legislation takes up little time in the Commons – usually less than 5 per cent – but it is valuable time for raising issues. Ten-minute rule bills hardly ever make it to the statute book, so why do MPs bother introducing them? Principally, because ten-minute rule bills are discussed in prime parliamentary time. It is a way of raising an issue, not only verbally but also by vote; if the motion is contested, a high vote in favour can demonstrate parliamentary support for action. Speaking after Question Time is early enough to attract media attention; there will be ministers on the treasury bench, usually waiting for the next business.

Private members' bills may rarely become law, but a number serve to prompt pressure for a later change in the law. Private members' bills to ban hunting with hounds helped to put pressure on the Blair government to introduce a bill of its own in 2002. The previous Tory government blocked a disability discrimination bill introduced by a Labour backbencher but later, after attracting widespread criticism, introduced its own Disability Discrimination Bill (Berry 1996). The fact that a bill is not passed does not mean that it has not had an effect. The fact of debate is valuable for making views known and getting them on the record, a point of relevance to discussion in later chapters. There may be a result in future years when government decides that it should act on the issue. Private members' legislation may be put under the heading of initiation, but more often than not debate of such legislation forms a sub-set of our previous category. As the sponsor of the Disability Discrimination Bill, Roger Berry, put it, reflecting on his experience: 'the final lesson must surely be that even failed private members' bills can have an impact. Or, more correctly, campaigns can be mounted around such bills that can ultimately bring about change' (Berry 1996, p. 144).

Pre-legislative scrutiny

The opportunity for Parliament to scrutinize bills before they have been formally introduced – while they are still, in effect, at their formative stage – has become a significant one since 1997 as a result of bills being published in draft. Indeed, some of the bills are brought forward as very rough drafts: sometimes the clauses are not even formally drafted and the government instead makes available statements of what it intends to include. When the Parliamentary Business and Legislation Committee of the cabinet considers the legislative programme for the session, this will now encompass not only the bills to be laid before Parliament but also those that will be published in draft. They are then announced in the Queen's Speech.

Draft bills provide Parliament with an opportunity to influence government before it decides for certain what will be in the measure. As we have seen, between 1997 and 2010, 76 bills were published in draft. Not all were given parliamentary scrutiny, either because they were published too late or the relevant departmental select committee was too busy. However, most are considered, usually by the relevant departmental select committees in the Commons. These committees specialize in the relevant area and are already in place. On occasion, though, bills may be considered by a joint committee of the two Houses. Establishing a joint committee takes time; potential members have to be approached and then both Houses have to agree motions establishing the committee. (There is also the problem of establishing party strength; the government has an overall majority in the Commons but not in the Lords.) Joint committees, though, are especially appropriate for bills that cut across sectors, involve particularly large and complex subjects, or where there is particular expertise on the subject in the House of Lords. They can also serve to relieve the pressure on departmental select committees, some of which are under particular pressure because of the number of bills in their

Table 4.4   Draft bills subject to parliamentary scrutiny, 2010–12 session

Draft bill	*Committee considering the bill*
Draft Civil Aviation Bill	Transport
Draft Defamation Bill	Joint Committee
Draft Detention of Terrorist Suspects (Temporary Extension) Bills (two bills)	Joint Committee
Draft Defamation Bill	Joint Committee
Draft Electoral Administration Provisions	Political and Constitutional Reform
Further Draft Electoral Administration Provisions	Political and Constitutional Reform
Draft Enhanced Terrorism Prevention and Investigation Measures Bill	Home Affairs
Draft Financial Services Bill	Joint Committee
Draft Groceries Code Adjudicator Bill	Business, Innovation and Skills
Draft House of Lords Reform Bill	Joint Committee
Draft Recall of MPs Bill	Political and Constitutional Reform

Source: Compiled from Parliament website.

sector. Of the 12 draft bills published by the coalition government in the long 2010–12 session (Table 4.4), no less than six were referred to joint committees.

The committees have to move quickly to scrutinize the draft bills. In doing so, though, they can, and do, summon evidence and by so doing put a lot of useful information in the public domain. They can draw on outside expertise in a way that – as we shall see (Chapter 5) – is often not possible once the bill is introduced. Evidence from those who have chaired or served on the joint committees has been that they have fulfilled a valuable role, resulting in effective scrutiny at a formative stage, enabling the government to accept many of the recommendations made by the committees (see Greenway 2004; Moonie 2004). Indeed, as Kennon (2004, p. 490) has noted, 'there is considerable evidence from recent replies that the government does accept many of the recommendations'.

The experience of the joint committee on the Communications Bill in 2002 illustrates the capacity of Parliament to influence outcomes. Of the 148 recommendations made in its report, no less than 120 were accepted. The report was also influential in the subsequent debates on the bill, especially in the House of Lords. (The committee had been chaired by a peer: the film director, Lord Puttnam.) Another joint committee having a significant impact was that established in the 2002–3 session to consider the draft Civil Contingencies Bill, a major measure designed to provide for extraordinary executive powers in times of emergency. The committee took written evidence, including from other parliamentary committees, before publishing its extensive report; in its response, the government accepted in full or in part most of the committee's 50 recommendations, including that of narrowing the scope of what constituted an emergency. As the government conceded, pre-legislative scrutiny had 'assisted the development of the bill significantly' (Cabinet Office 2004, p. 3). The bill was ultimately in a very different form from the one the government had originally intended.

Pre-legislative scrutiny is a relatively new area of parliamentary activity, one that gives Parliament a valuable opportunity to scrutinize, in a structured manner, government proposals for law. By being able to have some input at the formulation stage, parliamentary influence is maximized. It also provides the House with valuable information for when the bill is introduced, including from external bodies who submitted evidence to the committee. It also ensures that there are members – those who served on the committee – who are already knowledgeable about the bill. There remain major limitations, however, Parliament remains a reactive body. The government decides which bills are published in draft and whether committees will have time to scrutinize them (see Hansard Society 2004, p. 5). Pre-legislative scrutiny also imposes burdens, in terms of time, resources and members' commitments. However, the benefit to Parliament through engaging in such scrutiny is considerable.

The impact of Parliament: anticipated reaction

When we look at the capacity of Parliament to keep things off the agenda – as opposed to trying to get them on – we see its impact from another perspective. The impact is limited and difficult to observe and quantify, but what evidence we have suggests that Parliament is at least considered before measures are introduced.

There are two points at which anticipated reaction is salient. The first is when a minister is working up a proposal. Ministers do not want to alienate their own supporters and would prefer to take through Parliament a bill that earns them plaudits rather than condemnation from these allies. An ambitious minister may thus be influenced, some-times certainly consciously, by anticipation of parliamentary reaction, and sometimes possibly subconsciously. The minister will discuss the proposal within the department. MPs and peers, as such, have no formal involvement, though ministers' parliamentary private secre-taries (see Chapter 3) may participate in the preliminary discussions and, along with the relevant whip, give some advice on what back bench reaction is likely to be. Anticipated reaction may thus prove to be important. Given the privacy of discussions, and the fact that antic-ipated reaction may lead to a provision being deleted rather than inserted, it is difficult to quantify or even to generalize about the extent of such anticipation. There is little empirical evidence of it having a significant impact, though there is anecdotal evidence of ministers being especially concerned about reactions in the House of Lords. The support of back bench MPs can usually be assumed, but the support of peers cannot.

The second point is after a minister has decided to put forward a proposal and it has gone through the relevant cabinet committee. The cabinet considers likely parliamentary reaction. In evidence to the House of Lords Constitution Committee in 2004, the Leader of the House of Commons, Peter Hain, revealed that, as chairman of the Legislative Programme Committee, he asked what consultation had taken place on each proposed bill, especially in respect of whether it was controversial or not: 'is it likely to create difficulties for the Government in the House?' (Hain 2004, p. 2). Ministers had to say to what extent difficulties or areas of controversy had been addressed.

When the government's proposed legislative programme is being considered in cabinet, the chief whips are especially important in indicat-ing likely parliamentary reaction. One newly-appointed Commons chief whip recalled that, on appointment, 'the decisions regarding the treat-ment of parliamentary business, the cajoling of ministers to think not only of their departments but also of the reaction of other MPs to what they had planned, and the persuading of colleagues to attend or not to rebel lay with me' (Renton 2004, p. 22). If a hostile reception is anticipated, then the bill may not be proceeded with, or time will be given either to persuading members of the value of the measure or addressing their particular concerns. In practice, it is more likely to be the last two courses rather than not proceeding with the measure, but anticipated reaction none the less is a factor of cabinet deliberations.

The impact of Parliament: institutional constraints

The final perspective is institutional: concerned not so much with the constraints deriving from behaviour but rather from procedures. This in many respects is the most powerful constraint. There is only so much time available in a parliamentary session. Every bill, as we shall see (Chapter 5), has to go through several stages in each House. The government can impose timetable motions to expedite the passage of bills in the Commons, but even so there is a finite number of MPs available to serve on public bill committees, and bills are normally sent to committee around the same time in the session. This is a consequence of another feature of the parliamentary process: the fact that bills (though now with some exceptions) fall unless passed by the end of the session. This creates what Robin Cook (2003, p. 11) has termed the 'tidal wave principle', with the bulk of the government's bills having to be introduced at the start of the session, in order to complete their passage in time.

The government is also constrained by the procedures of the Upper House. The government cannot impose timetable motions in the Lords; the Upper House is a self-regulating chamber and the government lacks a majority. The House guards its procedures jealously, and the government has, therefore, to work within established procedures and, indeed, resources.

Working within these procedures restricts the number of bills the government can introduce. In an ideal world, it may want to get its whole programme through within the session. But it cannot. This is not because its own supporters won't vote for it, but because of the procedural hurdles. Hence the government limits the number of bills it brings forward each session. The committee deciding the programme for the session serves as a gatekeeper, deciding which bills deserve priority for introduction (see Cook 2003, p. 76). More bills will be turned down because they cannot be accommodated during the session than because a negative reaction is anticipated from backbenchers.

The government's business managers play an especially important role in determining how many measures can be accommodated within the session. As one chief whip recalled, 'if I were asked in Cabinet or committee whether I thought a bill we were discussing would get through Parliament by Easter, in the way the Secretary of State presenting the legislation wanted, I only had to say that I thought it would be very difficult to achieve such a target date, and that would be the last word' (Renton 2004, p. 23). This reflects not only the power of the whips in dealing with business, but also the constraints of parliamentary time and procedures.

There are also constraints imposed by limited resources available to government. This is notably the case with parliamentary counsel. Their number, as we have noted, has been expanded to cope with demand, but they remain fully stretched (Cook 2003, pp. 210–11, 261; Bowman 2004). However, this particular limitation may itself be the product of limited parliamentary time and the tidal wave principle. Hence the size of the Parliamentary Counsel Office is linked to the number of bills that can be accommodated by the parliamentary process. If there was a great deal more time, more parliamentary counsel would doubtless be recruited.

There is also a significant constraint deriving not only from parliamentary procedures as such, but also the form in which measures have to be laid before Parliament. Bills have to be drawn up in a very precise form – they are not simply broad statements of principle. The rules governing the form are detailed and precise (see Gifford and Salter 1996). Bills have not increased significantly in number since the nineteenth century (Drewry 1985), but their length has. They have become more complex. This places demands on parliamentary counsel and on the parliamentary timetable. There is little scope for more time – bills have increasingly to be levered into the process – and the government thus finds itself constrained by what is manageable in terms of the parliamentary process. It may seek to change some of the rules governing that process, but the changes are not likely to affect the overall body of rules and procedures that constrain it (Norton 2001b).

The constraints imposed by the parliamentary process limit the flow of bills. They may also have served to trigger the downfall of a prime minister. At a cabinet meeting in 1990, Prime Minister Margaret Thatcher berated the Leader of the House of Commons, Sir Geoffrey Howe, for his failure to have certain bills ready for the new session. A few hours later, Howe decided to resign, the incident in cabinet being the final straw that broke the camel's back. In so doing, he triggered a series of events culminating in Margaret Thatcher being challenged for leadership of the Conservative Party, and her resignation as party leader and subsequently Prime Minister.

Conclusion

Parliament does not figure largely as a significant influence in the introduction and content of bills, but it may contribute to the pressure that induces government to introduce a bill. Increasingly, it plays a role in the formulation stage of legislation through engaging in pre-legislative scrutiny, an activity that continues to expand. The initiative continues to rest – almost wholly, and compellingly – with government, which remains the generator of public policy. In so far as Parliament has an impact on government, it is principally as a constraint rather than a prompt. Its practices and procedures limit what government can bring forward. Anticipated reaction may be a constraint, but the most important question for ministers is not 'Will our side cause trouble?' but rather 'Do we have the time?'

5

Legislation

The third stage of the policy-making process – that of deliberation and assent – is undertaken, at least for UK legislation, by the Queen-in-Parliament. The two Houses of Parliament are responsible for the deliberation, and the two Houses plus the Crown are responsible for giving assent. The assent of the monarch is governed by convention (see Chapter 2). A bill has to go through several parliamentary stages before it can be submitted to the Queen for formal approval and hence become an Act of Parliament. The essential stages are listed in Table 5.1.

Legislative process

All bills dealing with finance begin their passage in the Commons, but given the pre-eminence of the Commons, so do most other bills. However, a number each session are introduced first in the House of Lords. This avoids an excessive imbalance in the legislative workload during the parliamentary session. If the Lords only considered bills after they had first been through the Commons, it would have a light workload in the first half of a session and an impossible one in the second half.

As can be seen from Table 5.1, the stages in both houses are analogous. However, the way in which the two houses deal with bills is not identical.

The House of Commons

Most legislation considered by the House is government legislation. Government bills enjoy priority, other than on the Fridays set aside for private members' bills. About a third of the time the chamber is occupied by the consideration of government bills, but considerably more time is taken up in the public bill committees established to consider the bills.

Table 5.1   Legislative stages in Parliament

House of Commons	
First reading	Formal introduction. Title is read out. The bill is then published. At least two weekends are meant to elapse before moving to the next stage.
Second reading	Debate on the principle of the bill.
Committee	Consideration of clauses and amendments proposed. This normally takes place in a public bill committee, though some bills are taken in committee of the whole house (or sent to a second reading committee).
Report	Bill considered again in the House, when further amendments are possible.
Third reading	Final approval of the bill, usually taken immediately after the report stage.
Lords' amendments	After the bill has been approved, it is sent to the House of Lords. If the House of Lords makes amendments, these have to be considered by the Commons.
House of Lords	
First reading	Formal introduction of the bill. At least two weekends elapse before the next stage is taken.
Second reading	Debate on principle. The House by convention does not vote on a bill that has appeared in the government's programme. Fourteen days elapse before the next stage is taken.
Committee	Committee stage is normally taken either in committee of the whole house or in grand committee (which any peer can attend but in which votes do not take place). On bills of considerable length and complexity, there is a fourteen day gap before the next stage.
Report	Further consideration of amendments, especially covering issues not resolved in committee. Three days then elapse before the third reading can be taken.
Third Reading	Unlike the Commons, the Lords can and does consider amendments after the formal motion for third reading and before considering the motion 'That the bill do now pass'.
Commons' amendments	If the bill originates in the Lords and the Commons makes amendments, the Lords considers the amendments.

Note: If the two Houses cannot agree an amendment, it may go back and forth – 'ping pong' – between the two Houses until one gives way; otherwise the bill falls. Only when both Houses have agreed the text of the bill can it be sent for Royal Assent. Exceptionally, a bill may be sent for Royal Assent under the provisions of the Parliament Act 1949, under which a bill may be enacted without the consent of the Lords if the Lords has rejected the bill in one session and the Commons has passed the same bill in the second session.

First and second readings

When a bill is introduced, it is given a first reading. This is a purely formal stage: the title of the bill is read out and a date for the second reading given; the bill – at this stage in dummy form, merely a long and short title on a piece of paper, with the names of the bill's sponsors – is also ordered to be printed. If the bill is not starting in the Commons, but coming from the Lords, these formal proceedings are dispensed with; the bill is scheduled for second reading with no prior proceedings on the floor of the House.

The bill is normally printed within days of its first reading and, indeed, in the case of most government bills, within a day. Second reading normally takes place about two weeks later. It is considered desirable for at least two weekends to elapse between first and second readings, though this is not an established rule and is not always adhered to. Second reading constitutes the first occasion the House has to discuss the measure. If it is a non-contentious bill, it may exceptionally be referred for its second reading debate to a committee, but otherwise – the usual practice – it is taken on the floor of the House.

Second reading constitutes the debate on principle. Some uncontroversial bills are given a second reading without debate. Others will be subject usually to a half-day or full-day debate – in effect, roughly a three-hour or a six-hour debate. Bills of constitutional importance may be given two or more days. In the 1997–8 session, the three bills dealing with devolution – the Government of Wales Bill, the Scotland Bill and the Referendums (Scotland and Wales) Bill – each had two days for second reading. (Just over 20 years earlier, the ill-fated predecessor to these measures – the 1976 Scotland and Wales Bill – was given four days.) The Greater London Authority Bill in 1998, the House of Lords Bill in 1999, and the House of Lords Reform Bill in 2012 were also each accorded two days.

Second reading debates are wide ranging. Taken on the floor, the minister moves second reading and explains the contents and case for the bill, the minister's shadow on the opposition front bench outlines the opposition's stance, and then backbench members have the opportunity to catch the Speaker's eye and contribute. At the end of the debate, an opposition frontbencher and a minister reply to what has been said. Opponents may divide the House – that is, force a vote. If it is a government bill, approval – as we shall see – is usually assured.

Committee stage

Once the House has approved the principle, the bill is sent to committee for detailed consideration. Unless the House votes otherwise, this will be a public bill committee. Until 2006, bills were referred to standing committees which were standing in name (Standing Committee A, B etc) but not in composition. Members were appointed for each particular bill and, crucially, could only consider the Bill as put before them, examining it clause by clause, debating any amendments to a clause before agreeing that the clause stand part of the bill. The committees were not empowered to take evidence. The House voted in 2006 to replace standing committees with public bill committees – that is, committees that were empowered to take evidence. Now, when a government bill is sent to such a committee, and the bill has not been subject to pre-legislative scrutiny, the committee will hear oral evidence from witnesses as well as receive written evidence from those with an interest in the measure.

A committee can comprise between 16 and 50 members, though the usual practice is to appoint at the lower end of the range, usually between 16 and 25. For major bills such as the annual Finance Bill, the committees are larger.

The composition of each committee will reflect the party strength on the floor of the House and, indeed, will take the form of the House in miniature, with ministers, a whip and back bench supporters on one side, and opposition frontbenchers, a whip and backbenchers – plus usually a member or members from one of the smaller parties – on the other. As in the chamber, the two sides sit opposite one another, presided over impartially by an MP drawn from the panel of chairs – a body of senior MPs chosen for their ability to undertake such a task.

The committee is constrained by the decision taken by the House on second reading. It cannot reject the principle of the bill nor consider an amendment that goes against the principle. It is also precluded from considering any amendment that does not fall within the scope of the bill's long title.

Uncontentious bills that are likely to pass without discussion, bills for which immediate passage is sought, and bills of major constitutional significance will usually be taken for committee stage on the floor of the House – that is, in committee of the whole house (CWH). The first type is taken on the floor for convenience: there is little point in assembling a committee. The second is taken to expedite proceedings – there is usually some urgency attaching to the measure and taking it on the floor avoids a committee having to be appointed and assembled, and then reporting back to the House. The third is taken in order that all members may have an opportunity to deliberate on a matter of great import. The principal measures in this category are those entailing significant constitutional change.

In the 2009–10 session, the Digital Economy Bill fell in the first category: it had started life in the Lords, where it had seven days in committee (and three on report); it needed only one day in committee and so was taken on the floor. (There was no report stage: if a Bill is taken in committee of the whole House and is not amended, it moves straight to third reading.) An example of a bill that fell in the second category in the same session was the Terrorist Asset-Freezing (Temporary Provisions) Bill, which was taken for second reading, committee stage and third reading on the same day in the Commons and completed its passage in the Lords the following day. A bill in the third category in that session was the Constitutional Reform and Governance Bill which, among other provisions, put the civil service on a statutory basis. Whereas bills in the first two categories take up little time in the chamber, those in the third can each occupy several days.

Report and third reading

When a bill has completed its committee stage, the committee having gone through it, considered (and approved or rejected) amendments. and approved each clause and any new clauses proposed by members, the bill is then reported to the House.

This stage provides an opportunity for all members to consider the bill, and further amendments can be, and usually are, made. There is no consideration of each clause, and amendments that essentially repeat amendments that failed in committee are not usually selected for consideration. Though the report stage usually occupies only one or two sittings, they can prove to be long ones because of the number of amendments tabled. About 10 per cent of the time of the House is taken up with the report stage of government bills. In the 2005–6 session, when the House sat for 1,572 hours, 200 hours were taken up with report stage, though in subsequent sessions the time taken was well under 10 per cent. In the 2008–9 session, for example, when the House sat for a total of 1,049 hours, 78 hours were taken up with the consideration of bills on report; in the 2009–10 session, when the House sat for 540 hours, it was 42 hours.

After the report stage, a bill is given a third reading. This is the final debate on the measure, limited to its contents, and more often than not is taken immediately following report. Debate is usually short and does not figure prominently as a drain on the time of the House. Opponents may force a division. Once past this hurdle, the bill then goes to the other chamber.

House of Lords

Whereas the Commons devotes about a third of its time to considering legislation, the Lords usually devotes most of its time to discussing the bills placed before it (see Walters 2004, p. 216). Usually, it occupies more than half the time of the House, typically between 50 and 60 per cent of the time each session. In the Lords, a bill has to pass through the same stages as in the Commons. However, Lords procedure differs from that of the Commons. The House is more rigorous in its rules governing the intervals between stages. Practice in those stages also differs from those of the Commons.

It is possible for a debate to take place on first reading, and on very rare occasions that has happened. Second reading is the debate on principle. This may take a whole day; sometimes, as in the Commons, two days may be devoted to it, as happened with the House of Lords Bill in 1999. Committee stage is taken on the floor of the House or in grand committee. Utilizing grand committee enables a bill to be considered without occupying the time of the chamber, but consideration of the bill is not much different to taking it in the chamber in that any peer can attend. As in the chamber, this enables those peers with an interest in particular parts of the bill to participate. (The only difference is that votes cannot be taken in grand committee, though in practice it is rare for votes to take place in committee of the whole House.) Proceedings are also less formal than at other stages, so members may intervene more than once during discussion of an amendment. Committee stage may take several days.

The grand committee is used for bills that are not particularly contentious between the parties, and several are now sent to grand committee each session. In the 2009–10 session, for example, bills committed to grand committee included the Bribery Bill, Child Poverty Bill, Cluster Munitions (Prohibition) Bill, Flood and Water Management Bill, Northern Ireland (Assembly Members) Bill, and the Third Parties (Rights against Insurers) Bill.

The House also has provision for other types of committee to consider bills, though they are rarely employed. They include the special public bill procedure, similar to the public bill committee in the Commons. The

House may also refer a bill to a select committee, which can not only take evidence but also produce a considered report. This is rarely employed, though in 2004 the House sent the Constitutional Reform Bill (to abolish the office of Lord Chancellor and create a supreme court) to a select committee.

Following committee, there is then the report stage, when issues unresolved in committee can be considered again.

There is a major difference with procedures in the Commons in that all amendments tabled by peers are considered. In the Commons, there is not time to debate all the amendments that are submitted, so only some are selected for consideration: the chair makes the selection in committee and the Speaker makes the selection at report stage. The Lords are not so restricted. Again in sharp contrast with the Commons, there are no means of curtailing proceedings. In the Commons, proceedings can be timetabled through the use of programme motions which stipulate how much time is provided to consider particular parts of a bill, but no such facility to restrict proceedings exists in the Lords. The principal limitation at report stage is that no amendment can be considered if it has been voted on at committee stage.

Following the report stage, the bill moves to its third reading. Again, in contrast with the Commons, there is a stipulated interval between the two stages. Furthermore, amendments can be, and frequently are, tabled at third reading, though significantly fewer in number than at the report stage. The motion for third reading is usually agreed formally and the House then moves to amendments. Once those are dealt with, the House approves the bill on the motion 'That the bill do now pass.' The provision for amendments at this stage allows an issue to be considered thoroughly. The government may agree to bring forward an amendment at report stage in response to debate in committee; if there is a problem with the government's amendment, there is the opportunity to return to the issue at its third reading.

Once a bill has been considered and passed by the Lords, it then goes back to the Commons (if it originated there) so that it can consider any amendments made by the second chamber. (If a bill originates in the Lords, the reverse applies, and any Commons amendments are sent to the Lords.) In the event of an amendment proving unacceptable to the Commons, it goes back to the Lords. The process has the potential to be a lengthy one if the second chamber insists on its amendment. If this happens, the process is known as 'ping pong'. In practice, most amendments prove acceptable to the Commons and, in the event of a clash, the House of Lords usually defers – though not always immediately – to the elected chamber. Ultimately, if the bill originates in the Commons, the Commons can get its way under the provisions of the Parliament Act 1949 (see Chapter 2). The Act has only been invoked four times since its passage, the most recent occasion being in November 2004 on the Hunting Bill to ban foxhunting in England and Wales.

Private members' bills

Private members' bills have to go through the same stages as government bills listed in Table 5.1. Both categories of bill constitute public legislation. However, the time for consideration of private members' bills in the Commons is limited, confined principally to ten (or sometimes more) Fridays and taking up less than 5 per cent of the time of the House in each session. Most bills introduced are not debated (see Chapter 4), and those that are face considerable hurdles.

Opposition to the bill by government is usually fatal. No bill that has been the subject of a division on second reading has subsequently made it to the statute book without government time being provided (Marsh and Read 1988, p. 49). Even government support does not guarantee its passage. Opponents may try to talk the bill out. On a Friday, the House sits at 9.30 am, and if debate is still continuing at 2.30 pm the bill under consideration falls to the back of the queue on subsequent Fridays, where it can easily be blocked (see Chapter 4). To prevent that happening, a bill's sponsor may move a closure motion: a motion that requires the question to be put immediately. However, for a closure motion to be carried, there must not only be a majority but also at least a hundred members voting in favour. Achieving that figure on a Friday is notoriously difficult. And if the bill has not been debated for very long, the Speaker will not even allow a closure motion to be moved. Hence, as we recorded in Chapter 4, there is a preference on the part of members successful in the ballot to opt for measures that enjoy government or widespread support, thus maximizing the chances of getting them on to the statute book.

In the Lords, the practice again is different. There is only one procedure. A peer can introduce a bill and the bill then awaits a slot in the timetable for the session: bills introduced early in the session are more or less guaranteed time for debate. Though private members' bills are taken on some Fridays when the House sits, they are also taken on other days. Those likely to attract considerable attention tend to be scheduled for Fridays. By convention, the government does not oppose their passage.

Individual members, though, may oppose them and may table numerous amendments: as these have to be debated, they can result in a bill not completing committee stage. (Usually only one slot is provided for committee stage, so if the amendments are not cleared by the end of the day, the bill does not proceed further.) Even if a bill clears the Lords, there is usually no time for it to be considered in the Commons: it joins the back of the queue of private members' bills on a Friday and, as with the other bills (see Chapter 3), a single cry of 'object' prevents it going further. Nonetheless, though few such bills make it to the statute book, four did so, as we have noted (Chapter 3), in the 2005–10 Parliament, at a time when the number of private members' bills making it on to the statute book was declining.

Private legislation

There are essentially two types of legislation. The first, and most important, is public legislation, which enacts measures that apply to the whole community. This category includes both government bills and private members' bills. The second category is that of private legislation, which gives specified powers to particular individuals or bodies – for example, to give legal authority to Network Rail to acquire and build a railway track on a particular piece of land, or to a local authority to undertake a particular activity. There is also a category of bill that falls between the two, known as a hybrid bill: this embodies a public policy that affects the particular interests of some individuals or bodies in a way that does not apply to all individuals and groups within the category.

A private bill has to go through analogous stages to public bills, but the purposes of the stages differ and the bill itself is not initiated by government or by private members, but by petition from the body sponsoring it. At second reading, the House affirms the principle conditionally. At committee stage, proceedings are quasi-judicial, with counsel representing petitioners. Witnesses are heard under oath. Government sometimes takes an interest in such measures, but normally leaves it for the House to decide. The majority of private bills have no political or, for most MPs, constituency implications. It is therefore a form of legislation that does not impinge much upon the consciousness of MPs and peers. (There are occasional exceptions, such as the Mersey Tunnels Bill in 2004, which provided, among other things for an increase in the bridge tolls.) Where members do take an interest, they can have a powerful influence: a single cry of 'object' is sufficient to force a debate. Nowadays relatively few such bills are introduced – in recent years the number in each session has been in single figures – and most are not debated, with the result that they occupy little time: over the three sessions of 2007–10, the Commons sat for over 2,905 hours, with fewer than 12 – under 0.5 per cent of the time – being devoted to private business.

Secondary legislation

There is one other category of legislation, and that is secondary legislation. Acts of Parliament frequently confer powers on ministers (and sometimes other bodies) to make orders; for example, to change the level of fees set for a particular service or to say how many governors may serve on the governing bodies of state schools. These powers comprise what is known as secondary, or delegated, legislation. They are now extensive in number, both in the total that now exist and in terms of the number brought in each year. They are extensive in number because they are attractive to government: they provide flexibility and enable changes to be made without having to bring in a new bill.

Orders are usually promulgated as statutory instruments (SIs). The act incorporating the power to make orders will stipulate what parliamentary approval, if any, is required. Important orders are normally subject to what is known as the affirmative resolution procedure; that is, they require parliamentary approval in order to take effect. Others are subject to the negative resolution procedure; that is, they take effect unless Parliament votes them down. Other, less significant, orders are not subject to any parliamentary consent at all; some simply have to be laid before Parliament and others are not even subject to that requirement. Before the 1970s, the number of statutory instruments laid before Parliament in each session was usually several hundred. Since 1970, the number has usually been well over a thousand, and in some sessions more than 1,500.

Given the number, there is not sufficient parliamentary time available to consider every statutory instrument. Once brought forward, they are considered by the Joint Committee on Statutory Instruments. (If they require only the approval of the Commons, the MPs on the committee sit as a Commons committee.) The committee checks the SIs to ensure that they are properly drawn; that is, within the powers granted and are not deficient in terms of drafting. The committee reports and it is up to government to decide whether to take any action. The committee has no formal powers and it is possible that an instrument may be approved by the House before the committee has reported. However, it is possible for adverse reports to influence the withdrawal of an instrument, though that rarely happens. The work of the committee is seen as worthwhile but largely unexciting.

Statutory instruments that require parliamentary approval under the affirmative resolution procedure are considered by the Commons, but usually in a committee on delegated legislation. Only a small number are debated in the chamber. In 2008–09, the House devoted just over 19 hours – just under 2 per cent of the time in the session – to debating such orders. Those subject to the negative resolution procedure are considered only if members table a motion (known as a prayer) to annul them, and even then time is usually found to debate them only if the motion is tabled by the Opposition front bench. Very few are debated on the floor. In two of the five sessions of the 2005–10 Parliament, none was debated.

The House of Lords has a somewhat more extensive method of scrutiny. In 1993 it created a Delegated Powers Committee – now titled the Delegated Powers and Regulatory Reform Committee – to consider whether the delegated powers embodied in a bill, and the provisions for their parliamentary scrutiny, are appropriate. It variously recommends, for example, that an order-making power should be subject to the affirmative resolution, rather than the negative resolution, procedure. Its recommendations are normally accepted by government. The committee, however, only deals with what may be termed the input end of delegated legislation; that is, the inclusion of the powers in bills. In 2003, the House appointed a committee – the Select Committee on the Merits of Statutory Instruments – to consider the output end, that is, the orders laid before Parliament. This committee examines all SIs subject to either the affirmative or negative resolution procedure and is empowered to draw to the attention of the House any instruments that have important political or legal implications; are inappropriate because of changes since the parent Act was passed; implement EU legislation inappropriately; or achieve their policy objectives imperfectly. The committee was re-named the Secondary Legislation Scrutiny Committee in 2012 when its remit was extended to cover orders made under the Public Bodies Act 2011 to abolish or transfer functions of public bodies.

For SIs requiring approval, the Lords usually takes them on the floor of the House rather than in committee (though some, primarily Northern Ireland orders, are now taken in grand committee). They are variously taken at the end of business or in what is known as the 'dinner hour'; that is, when the House adjourns the business for at least an hour, usually around 7.30 pm, to enable those taking part in debate to have dinner. The hour is occupied by other business, either a question for short debate (QSD) (see Chapter 6) or orders. Most debates are on SIs subject to the affirmative resolution procedure, but on occasion the opposition moves a motion to annul an instrument subject to the negative resolution procedure, or to regret the introduction of an order, for the purpose of forcing a debate. Before 1999, the practice had developed of the House not voting against SIs, but there are now occasions when peers will force a vote.

Post-legislative scrutiny

For ministers and indeed parliamentarians generally, the end of the legislative process is seen as royal assent. Success is measured in terms of getting a bill on to the statute book. Relatively little attention has been given to the effect of Acts of Parliament. Exceptionally, provision has been made for post-legislative review. The 2001 Anti-terrorism, Crime and Security Act provided that, within two years of its enactment, the secretary of state was to appoint a committee to conduct a review of the Act. Otherwise, it tended to be a case of review when a measure had clearly gone badly awry. The Child Support Act 1991, for example, established a Child Support Agency, but the agency did not work out as intended as was subject to investigation by select committee. Most Acts, though, have gone unconsidered by Parliament.

Following a recommendation in 2004 by the House of Lords Constitution Committee – which favoured systematic post-legislative scrutiny and the appointment of a parliamentary committee to oversee such scrutiny – the government referred the matter to the Law Commission. It too favoured systematic post-legislative review and in 2008 the government announced that in future most Acts, three to five years after their enactment, would be subject to review by the sponsoring government department to determine if they had achieved what they were designed to achieve. A number of reviews were undertaken before the end of the Parliament and the practice of reviewing Acts was continued under the coalition government formed in 2010. These reviews are published and sent to the relevant departmental select committee in the Commons. It is then a matter for the committees to determine if they wish to undertake an inquiry. However, no dedicated committee on post-legislative scrutiny has been established and departmental select committees are usually too busy with other business to pursue the departmental reviews. There is only the occasional sporadic inquiry. In 2012, for example, the Justice Committee undertook post-legislative scrutiny of the Freedom of

Information Act 2000, but other committees have not engaged in similar inquiries.

The effect of Parliament?

Viewed from a pluralist perspective, what impact does Parliament have on legislation? Jean Blondel *et al.* (1970) referred to the concept of Parliament's 'viscosity' – that is, the capacity to impede the flow of a stream: in effect, Parliament's capacity to constrain or to change the bills placed before it. Does Parliament exercise an independent capacity to alter a bill, resulting in it leaving Parliament substantially different in content from when it was introduced?

The answer is that it does so, but usually only at the margins. The impact of Parliament on government bills, similar to its impact on the initiation of measures, is sporadic. In the Commons, the investment of considerable time and effort does not result in a significant viscosity. Government is normally assured of having its measures passed. Moreover, it is normally assured not only of the principle of the bills being accepted but also the detail. In the Lords, the outcome is somewhat less certain.

Saying no to government

Parliament rarely exercises its coercive capacity (see Chapter 1). As can be seen from Table 5.2, the government will almost always succeed in having its bills passed by Parliament. Government, for the reasons discussed in preceding chapters, normally enjoys an overall majority in the House of Commons, with that majority ready to ensure its measures are passed. As explained in Chapter 2, the House of Lords abides by the Salisbury convention and does not vote on the second reading of bills that are in the government's programme. Whatever it may do to the detail, the House does not vote against the principle.

The years in which governments have been most likely to fail with bills have usually been election years. The government did not wish to signal that it planned to hold a general election during the session, so usually introduced a full legislative programme. When it called the election, not all of its bills would have completed their passage through Parliament, so some were sacrificed. The largest number of bills lost by the Labour government of Tony Blair was in the short session of 2000–1, cut short because of the calling of the general election: on that occasion,

Table 5.2   Government bills, 2005–10

Session	Government bills			
	Introduced	*Passed*	*Failed*	*Carried over*
2005–6	58	54	2	2
2006–7	33	29	1	3
2007–8	32	30	0	2
2008–9	26	22	1	3
2009–10	23	23	0	0

Source: Derived from House of Commons, *Sessional Information Digests,* 2005–10.

five bills were lost. In 2009–10, however, the Brown government was prepared to do deals with the Opposition, resulting in bills being severely amended rather than lost. Such a loss to government is unlikely to be repeated in later parliaments, given the introduction of fixed-term Parliaments through the Fixed-term Parliaments Act 2011. The date of future elections is now fixed (other than in exceptional circumstances), thus removing the uncertainty and existence of short sessions deriving from the prime minister's capacity to ask for a dissolution of Parliament.

In other sessions, the government may lose a bill because it finds it does not have the time available to get it through, or decides not to proceed with it. However, a bill listed as having failed in one session may still make it to the statute book by being reintroduced in a subsequent session.

Government, then, is in greater danger of losing bills because of timetable and managerial problems than because of the behaviour of MPs or peers. The chances of a government being defeated on second reading are rare. It occurred only three times in the Commons in the twentieth century (in 1924, 1977 and 1986) and only one of these was when the government had an overall working majority (on the Shops Bill 1986; see Chapter 2). The chances of losing a vote at third reading are similarly slim. It happened, exceptionally, in 1977 on the Local Authority Works (Scotland) Bill, when the government did not anticipate a vote taking place.

In the Commons, the party majority that ensures the passing of bills on second and third reading is also deployed to ensure that government gets its way on the detail of bills. Even if government backbenchers were tempted to go against their own leaders, various constraints operate other than merely political ones. One is structural. The *ad hoc* formation of public bill committees militates against the development of a body of expertise and a corporate, possibly bipartisan, feeling. Another factor is time. Given the size of bills, there is often little time to consider the detail adequately. Members of public bill committees do not have much time to absorb evidence given to them before they have to consider amendments to the bill (Levy 2010). This is compounded by partisanship. If a bill is strongly opposed, the government is likely to introduce a programme motion to ensure its expeditious passage. This then results in some clauses not in fact being the subject of debate. Partisanship also affects the choice and questioning of witnesses appearing before committees.

As a result, public bill committees are in a weak position and are characterized by the partisanship that exists in the chamber. For MPs, serving on a committee is often frustrating. Government backbenchers have traditionally been encouraged to remain silent in order not to delay proceedings; so some have used the opportunity to read and reply to correspondence, only half-listening to committee proceedings. There is often little expectation by other members that their activities will have any tangible effect.

Once a committee reverts to considering amendments to the bill, most time is spent agreeing government amendments and rejecting opposition ones. Usually about 90 per cent of amendments accepted in committee are moved by the government. Very few amendments are carried against the wishes of the government. Even were government to be defeated in committee, it would still have the option of seeking to reverse the defeat, in practice, at report stage.

The chances of MPs saying no to government are thus relatively slim. The position differs in the House of Lords, however. The House may not divide on second reading of a bill, but it is willing to say no to government when it comes to the detail. As we noted in Chapter 2, the government suffers defeats in the Lords; of these, virtually all are on amendments to bills. Prior to the passage of the 1999 House of Lords Act, a chamber with a preponderance of Conservative peers was more liable to defeat Labour governments than Conservative governments (though both suffered at the hands of the House). The position changed in 1999 (see Chapter 2). Since then, the government has faced a House in which no single party has a majority and is therefore vulnerable to other parties – or the main opposition party and cross-bench peers – combining against it. Opposition parties or, especially in the Parliament returned in 2010, cross-bench peers, have proved willing to vote against the government in support of particular amendments. The numbers of government defeats

Table 5.3   Government defeats in the House of Lords, 1999–2012

Session	Number of defeats
1999–2000	36
2000–1	2
2001–2	56
2002–3	88
2003–4	64
2004–5	37
2005–6	61
2006–7	45
2007–8	29
2008–9	30
2009–10	14
2010–12*	48

* Exceptional two-year session.
Source: House of Lords and Constitution Unit, University College London.

per session are given in Table 5.3. The House appears more willing to defeat the government than was the case preceding the removal of the hereditary peers.

The government is thus more vulnerable to defeat in the Lords than in the Commons. However, the defeats in the Lords are not necessarily definitive. The House is not able, except in particular circumstances, to be a veto player (see Chapter 1). When the House amends a bill against the wishes of the government, those amendments require the approval of the Commons. If the Commons disagrees with the Lords, the Upper House usually does not insist on its amendments. If it does persist, the amendments shuttle between the two Houses until one side gives way.

It is rare for the Lords to persist with an amendment. The government may accept defeats imposed by the Lords, either on their merits or because the Lords amendment finds some support among the government's own supporters, but acceptance is at the discretion of government. Only if proceedings on a bill are close to the end of the session, or if the government is keen to ensure the quick passage of a measure, is the Lords able to act as a veto player and, as such, ensure that the government accepts its amendments. Nonetheless, research has shown that government has accepted over 40 per cent of defeats imposed by the Lords and, somewhat counter-intuitively, has tended to accept the more significant amendments (Russell and Sciara 2008).

Persuading the government

Parliament, then, rarely says no to government. The Lords may require it to think again, but the government can use its Commons majority if necessary to overturn a defeat in the Lords. Where Parliament has somewhat more effect (though, again, the impact is limited) is in persuading government (see Chapter 1) to change its mind.

In the Commons, MPs can lobby ministers to accept a particular amendment and may threaten to vote against a proposal of which they disapprove. The threat may be sufficient to induce ministers to act. (Voting against the government is usually a sign that earlier attempts at persuasion have failed.) The government survived the vote in January 2004 on the second reading of the Higher Education Bill by a majority of five votes. This was seen as a narrow government victory, but it was achieved by making concessions to MPs who were threatening to vote against the government. A similar approach had been adopted on a number of bills where there has been significant opposition from government backbenchers. In 1998, Home Secretary Jack Straw made a number of concessions to backbenchers in order to smooth the passage of the Criminal Justice (Terrorism and Conspiracy) Bill; a plan to include incitement to commit offences abroad, for example, was withdrawn (Cowley 2002a, p. 32). Straw also made concessions during the passage of the Immigration and Asylum Bill in 1999 (Cowley 2002a, pp. 52–4). Other ministers sought to pacify dissenters. When one back bench opponent of the government's proposals regarding incapacity benefit, part of the Welfare Reform and Pensions Bill in 1999, went to see the Social Security Secretary, Alistair Darling, he was asked: 'What's your price?' (Cowley 2002a, p. 47). The government ran into opposition from Labour MPs to its provision to establish foundation hospital trusts in the 2003 Health and Social Care (Community Health and Standards) Bill. Fearing not just back bench dissent, but possible defeat, the government made various concessions:

> It introduced a cap on the income that the new foundation hospitals could earn from private patients; it ensured that NHS pay arrangements applied to foundation hospitals ... it promised to make all hospitals foundation trusts within five years: and it improved the arrangements for local consultations. When John Reid, the Secretary of State for Health, faced the Commons before the crucial vote in November, he was quite open (indeed, almost boastful) about the extent to which the bill had been amended as a result of back bench

pressure. He then added another major concession, agreeing to a review of the operation of the first wave of trusts after twelve months. (Cowley and Stuart 2004b, p. 309)

MPs are thus able to put pressure on ministers to persuade them to amend bills as they go through Parliament. On rare occasions, the government has decided not to proceed with a bill. In the 1984–5 session a Civil Aviation Bill also ran into opposition from Conservative MPs and was dropped; an Education (Corporal Punishment) Bill ran into trouble in both Houses, especially the Lords, and suffered a similar fate (Silk 1987, pp. 113–14). In 2004, the government decided not to proceed with a bill to remove the remaining hereditary peers from the House of Lords. Ministers were not only worried by the possible reaction in the Lords but also by how their own backbenchers might behave in the Commons; there was the possibility that Labour MPs, supported by MPs from other parties, might seek to amend it to introduce more radical changes. As the government were unable to find ways of making the bill 'amendment proof', they dropped it. A later, more radical bill on the Lords was also dropped: the coalition government decided in 2012 not to proceed with the House of Lords Reform Bill, providing for a largely elected House of Lords, after most Conservative MPs, other than ministers and PPSs, failed to support the bill on second reading.

By a variety of means, backbenchers may thus persuade ministers to amend bills. As a result, some measures are enacted in a form very different from that in which they entered the House; very occasionally, a bill might not even be proceeded with. MPs can thus make a difference. However, the occasions when MPs do achieve changes to bills are relatively rare. Though rebellions are more frequent than in the past, more often than not government backbenchers are united (see Chapter 2). Some changes may be achieved by force of argument, but again this appears to be relatively rare. Most government bills will leave the Commons in the form that ministers want them. Even when government makes concessions, they are often marginal or cosmetic. In the 1997–2001 Parliament, it was noted that 'concessions were often small. The accusation about certain ministers was that although they may give ground, in policy terms, it was always "the minimum they can get away with"... Negotiations with ministers rarely yielded anything that discontented backbenchers wanted' (Cowley 2002a, p. 180). When concessions were offered, even though they did not meet the full demands of the rebels, a sufficient number of rebel MPs were prepared to go along with the government to ensure that it had a majority.

The government may thus be persuaded by MPs to make changes, but such occasions are the exception rather than the rule. Again, there is a contrast with the House of Lords. Government does not enjoy a majority in the Lords. The House sees itself as a House of experience and expertise (see Chapter 2). Although there is a high level of party cohesion in the Lords (Norton 2003a), ministers cannot necessarily rely on their own supporters to back them. They remain vulnerable to opposition parties and the cross-bench peers combining against them. These conditions induce ministers to listen to what is said in debate and, on occasion, concede to the force of argument and/or the potential of losing a vote. Ministers have to assume that well-informed members will be taking part in a debate. They will normally therefore be well briefed and engage in a discourse with members, often in an environment that lacks the partisanship of the Commons. Also, debate tends to attract little media coverage, so ministers feel less of a need to become defensive. It is also usually on the detail of the bill, so no great principles are at stake. Ministers may thus find the environment more conducive to accepting amendments from opposition parties and individual members than is the case with their counterparts in the Commons.

The number of amendments made to bills in the Lords each year is substantial. It is not unusual for anything between a few hundred to two or three-thousand amendments to be made in a session. In 2007–8, for example, 2,625 amendments were agreed and in the 2008–9 session the figure was 1,824. The 1999–2000 session was remarkable in that no less than 4,761 amendments were made. On the surface this seems an impressive number. Most, though, emanate from the government itself. One study of the 1988–9 session found that non-government amendments accounted for well under 10 per cent of the amendments accepted by the House (Miers and Brock 1993, p. 103). However, the figure underestimates the persuasive impact of the House and predates the reform of 1999. The fact that a minister introduces an amendment is not evidence that the proposal originated with government. Ministers variously bring forward amendments at report stage to give effect to commitments made to peers at committee stage. A peer may introduce an amendment, the minister may indicate some sympathy or support and offer to bring forward a government amendment at report stage if the peer withdraws the amendment. (The advantage of a government amendment is that its drafting is likely to be more technically competent.) Ministers may thus introduce amendments as a consequence of dialogue with peers and sometimes in order to avoid a defeat. Anticipating trouble on a bill, the government may move to avert it. Thus, for example, the coalition government created in 2010 has been active in seeking to accommodate the case for change made by members. If the government is defeated and the amendments go to the Commons, negotiation remains a feature of proceedings; ministers may be willing to accept some defeats, but not others. The Lords is more likely to pursue an issue if it is one on which government supporters in the Commons are not united.

The Lords can thus make some difference to legislation, more so than the Commons, since the government cannot rely on a majority in the Lords. By argument, threat of defeat or actual defeat – forcing the Commons to think again – the Lords may persuade the government to accept changes to its bills. There have been some notable cases in recent years, including that of the Anti-terrorism, Crime and Security Bill, introduced in November 2001 following the terrorist attacks in the USA on 11 September. The government was keen for the expeditious passage of the bill. The Lords made amendments and then insisted on some of them; some found support among Labour MPs in the Commons. As a result of Lords pressure, changes were made covering the proportionality in disclosure of information, appeals, the confinement of new police powers to anti-terrorism and national security, and the removal of an offence of inciting religious hatred. Such high-profile cases are rare but they demonstrate the capacity of the Upper House to pursue an issue and, without a capacity to say a definitive 'no' to government, to persuade government to accept changes.

Institutional constraints

How useful are the other views of power in analysing Parliament in the legislative process? That of agenda-setting as such does not apply, since we are concerned here with measures once they are on the agenda. However, once there, anticipation may be relevant, since a bill may run into opposition from government backbenchers and, anticipating defeat or bad publicity, the government may amend the measure or not pursue it. However, this involves events once an issue has been brought forward, and the opposition is usually observable.

The institutional view has a continuing utility; this is apparent from Table 5.1. A bill has to go through several stages in each House. Not only that; the bill also has to be considered by the two Houses on a consecutive basis, not a concurrent one – that is, one House has to finish with it before the other considers it. As we have seen, there are also intervals between the stages. These stages are not always followed in the Commons, but they are adhered to in the Lords, unless the House is persuaded not to impose them;

for example, because the measure is accepted as urgent. Government therefore has to ensure that bills are passed within the time available.

The session itself provides a constraint on government. Bills not passed by the end of the session fail. Both Houses have introduced provisions enabling some bills to carry over from one session to the next. In the Lords, for example, a bill may be considered for carry-over if it has been subject to pre-legislative scrutiny. (In the 2003–4 session, the House also agreed to carry over the Constitutional Reform Bill after it had been subjected to scrutiny by a select committee.) However, as is apparent from Table 5.2, few bills are carried over. The government's legislative programme is thus based on limited time and what Robin Cook referred to, as we have seen (see Chapter 4), as the 'tidal wave' principle, most bills being introduced at the beginning of the session and then cascading down to committees later in the session. Government has to get its planning right. If it miscalculates, it may not get its bills through; mostly it does, but not always. Though it can employ programme motions in the Commons, it has no means of curtailing discussion in the Lords. The existence of established rules and procedures may also be exploited by MPs and peers to put pressure on government to accept amendments. The Lords tends to be in a position to persuade government to accept changes at the very end of a session if one or more bills have not yet got through all their stages. In order to get them through and on to the statute book, ministers will do various deals with the opposition parties in the Lords to ensure that they get through. Even if the government has a united Commons majority in support of the measure, they cannot put that majority to good effect if they have miscalculated the time needed to get the measure through.

Conclusion

We have drawn attention to Blondel's concept of viscosity: that is, the capacity to constrain a stream. The terminology has a particular utility. If we see legislation as the stream, then the institutional arrangements constitute the river bed. The government may be able to change the rules – in effect, widen the river bed – but doing that on an extensive basis is difficult. It therefore has to ensure that it gets its flow of bills largely within the existing institutional framework.

In seeking to constrain the legislative stream, Parliament is limited. The limitation is essentially political in the House of Commons: the government enjoys a majority and so will normally get passed the measures it wishes to be passed and normally in the form that it wishes. Furthermore, through the use of its majority to pass programme motions, it can ensure that they are passed fairly expeditiously. The result of programme motions is that some bills reach the House of Lords with substantial parts never having been considered by MPs. In the Lords, the constraint is constitutional. Though the House achieves considerable change to the detail of bills, it accepts that the Commons is entitled to get its way, especially in terms of legislative goals. The Commons determines the ends; the Lords focus on the means.

Once bills have been introduced by government, they are almost certain to be passed. The weakest part of the process has historically been at the committee stage in the Commons. The introduction of public bill committees marked a considerable advance of the use on standing committees, but they remain limited by reasons of time and partisanship.

Clearly, as we have seen, Parliament has *some* impact, and sufficient to make it a relevant target for pressure-group attention – more so in the twenty-first century than ever before – but it remains, at best, a proximate actor and, at worst, a marginal one in determining the content of measures of public policy.

6

The Administration of Government

The policy-making process is not confined to generating, discussing and approving law. Parliament also fulfils the function identified by Packenham (1970) (see Chapter 1) as 'administrative oversight'. This encompasses scrutinizing decisions taken by government that do not require legislative sanction, as well as the conduct – the actual administration – of departments. Much administration carried out is routine, but ministers have to act within their powers. They may act under the royal prerogative – that is, carrying out powers that still reside in the Crown, but are exercised by ministers in the name of the monarch – or under powers granted by statute. The royal prerogative remains important, since it encompasses powers such as that of declaring war. As we have seen, powers granted by statute usually take the form of delegated legislation.

By what means, then, does Parliament engage in administrative oversight, and what impact does it have? The means available can be grouped under two general headings: those available in the chamber, and those available outside the chamber. The latter category, as we shall see, can be sub-divided into formal and informal means.

Inside the chamber

The principal means of scrutiny inside the chamber are debates and question time. Both suffer from a range of limitations.

Debates in the Commons

Debates are the oldest method by which the two Houses subject the actions of the executive to critical scrutiny. There are several types of debate, other than those – covered in Chapter 5 – on the second and third readings of bills. In the Commons, there is the annual debate on the

address – usually five days devoted to debates on the Queen's Speech
outlining the government's programme for the year. There are also
debates in which the topics are selected by the Opposition, by committees
of the House, by ballot, as well as by government itself.

Opposition

There are 20 *opposition days* each session. These are days on which the
subject for debate is chosen by opposition parties. The Leader of the
Opposition chooses the topic on 17 and the leader of the second largest
opposition in the House selects the subject on the other three. (The government now also provides some time for debate on topics selected by the
other parties.) Each day may be utilized for one full-day or two half-day
debates. Subjects chosen during the 2008–9 session are listed in Table 6.1.
Some extra time may also be found (unallocated days) and in the lengthy
2010–12 session several additional days were given to the opposition
parties. If the Opposition is dissatisfied with the conduct of government, it
may also table a motion of no confidence in the government. Such motions
are tabled very sparingly, but when tabled, time is found to debate them as
a matter of urgency. The last speech of Margaret Thatcher as Prime
Minister in 1990 was in a debate on a motion of no confidence.

Committees of the House

There are now debates in which the topics are determined by committees
of the House. The Liaison Committee (comprising the chairs of select
committees) selects the topics on three estimates days each session and
the Backbench Business Committee nominates the subjects on days
given over to backbench business. Both constitute a major departure from
the business being determined by government or opposition.

The provision for three *estimates days* in each session was introduced in the 1982–3 session – the first debate was in March 1983 –
providing for debates on estimates selected by the Liaison Committee.
Estimates of government expenditure used to be approved without
debate; the introduction of estimates days allowed for some discussion,
though in practice the committee tends to select for discussion those
that have been the subject of select committee inquiries. It is possible
for two topics to be debated on an estimates day. Table 6.2 lists the esti-
mate day topics in the last two sessions of the 2005–10 Parliament. As
is apparent from the table, the Liaison Committee tends to opt for
subjects of topical interest.

Table 6.1   Opposition days, 2008–9

Date	Subject(s) of debate
21 January 2009 (1)	Emergency Care
21 January 2009 (2)	Savers
28 January 2009	Heathrow (Third Runway)
2 February 2009 (1)	Government Capital Expenditure*
2 February 2009 (2)	Parliament Standards (Constitutional Reform)*
3 February 2009 (1)	Skills and Further Education
3 February 2009 (2)	Child Protection
11 February 2009 (1)	Housing Waiting Lists
11 February 2009 (2)	Royal Mail
24 February 2009 (1)	Law and Order
24 February 2009 (2)	British Agriculture and Food Labelling
10 March 2009 (1)	Unemployment
10 March 2009 (2)	European Working Time Directive
18 March 2009	The Economy
25 March 2009 (1)	Iraq War Inquiry
25 March 2009 (2)	Business Rates and the Recession
29 April 2009	Gurkha Settlement Rights*
18 May 2009 (1)	Skills in the recession
18 May 2009 (2)	Mid-Staffordshire NHS Foundation Trust
9 June 2009 (1)	Knife crime
9 June 2009 (2)	Government housing policy
10 June 2009	Dissolution of Parliament [unallocated half-day]**
15 June 2009 (1)	Rural Communities (Recession)
15 June 2009 (2)	Business Rates
24 June 2009	Iraq Inquiry
6 July 2009 (1)	Young people in the recession
6 July 2009 (2)	Identity Cards
15 July 2009 (1)	US/UK Extradition Treaty
15 July 2009 (2)	Caring for the Elderly
19 October 2009	Economic Recovery and Welfare
21 October 2009 (1)	Equitable Life*
21 October 2009 (2)	Political response in the UK to climate change*
27 October 2009	Parading in Northern Ireland [unallocated half-day]***
28 October 2009 (1)	Local spending
28 October 2009 (2)	Future of the Territorial Army

* Liberal Democrat days.
** SNP/PC day.
* DUP day.

Source: House of Commons Library, Opposition Day Debates Since 1997, Parliamentary Information List (PIL), SN/PC/03190, 30 March 2012.

Table 6.2   Estimates days, 2008–10

Date	Principal subject
2008–9	
16 Dec. 2008	Energy prices, fuel poverty, OFGEM
16 Dec. 2008	Dental services
9 March 2009	Economic situation
9 March 2009	Railways
2 July 2009	Looked-after children
2 July 2009	Road safety
2009–10	
10 Dec. 2009	Students and universities
10 Dec 2009	Central and local government
10 March 2010	Alcohol
10 March 2010	Road users (taxes and charges)
[no third day because of dissolution of Parliament]	

Source: House of Commons *Sessional Information Digests*.

The introduction of the estimates days constituted an important inno-vation in that it represented business being determined by a committee of the House. That has been complemented significantly by the creation of the *Backbench Business Committee*. As we have seen (Chapter 2), this came into being in 2010 and has made a notable impact on parliamentary life. The committee, comprised of eight backbench MPs, selects the topics for debate on 35 sitting days (of which not least 27 are in the cham-ber). The business is deemed to be backbench business, excluding private members' bills and the half-hour adjournment debates at the end of each day (see below). Previously, backbench business was allocated by government.

The committee, following its appointment, decided to operate in a transparent manner and invites members to appear in public before it to make a case for debating their nominated subjects. In considering the subjects, the committee takes into account topicality and timing, why holding a debate is important, the number of MPs who are likely to take part, and whether a debate has already been held or is likely to be arranged through other routes. The coalition government also introduced a procedure for e-petitions and announced that any petition gaining 100,000 signatures would be eligible for debate in the House: what this meant, in practice, was that any such petition was passed on to the Backbench Business Committee for consideration. Though the committee has selected topics that have been the subject of e-petitioning in this way, it has only done so where an MP has supported it and there have been others indicating that they would take part in a debate on the subject.

We have already seen (Chapter 2) the sort of topics selected by the committee. They have tended to be topical and frequently issues that have proved embarrassing for government or, in one case, the House authorities. Some have been notable for attracting a good attendance. Among the subjects chosen for debate in the long 2010–12 session were the war in Afghanistan, the strategic defence and security review, contaminated blood products, privacy and the Internet, immigration, banking reform, fisheries, the future of pubs, drugs policy, anti-Semitism, prisoners' voting rights, onshore wind energy, the Big Society, education performance, student visas, responses to the riots, a national referendum on the EU, NHS care of older people, metal theft, and charging for access to Parliament.

The debate on Afghanistan enabled MPs to vote on the issue for the first time. The debate on prisoners' voting rights embarrassed government in that it demonstrated overwhelming opposition to giving prisoners the right to vote, even though the government was required to review the provision as a consequence of a decision by the European Court on Human Rights (which found against the UK blanket ban). The debate on a referendum on the EU created a major split in Conservative ranks when 81 Conservative MPs voted in favour of such a referendum. The debate on charging access to Parliament focused on a proposal by the parliamentary authorities to charge for tours of the Elizabeth Tower in the Palace of Westminster. Opposition to the proposal was so strong that it was withdrawn.

The committee chooses the topics, though the actual dates allocated for backbench business are determined by government. Nonetheless, the creation of the committee added a major new dimension to the capacity of the House, through a committee, to determine what is to be discussed, rather than leaving the decision to government.

By ballot

There are also debates which are determined by ballot. These cover primarily debates held in Westminster Hall and, somewhat more long-standing, the adjournment debate held at the end of each day's sitting.

Debates in Westminster Hall (see Chapter 2) allow backbenchers to raise issues of concern. Though not held in the Commons chamber, proceedings are the equivalent of proceedings in the chamber: they are televised and are published in *Hansard*, the official report of Commons debates. Sittings are held on Tuesdays and Wednesdays from 9.30 am to 11.30 am, and from 2.30 pm to 5.00 pm, and on Thursdays from 1.30 pm to 4.30 pm, presided over by a Deputy Speaker or senior member of the panel of chairs.

The Tuesday and Wednesday sittings provide the opportunity for a series of short debates. Backbenchers wanting to initiate debates send their names to the Speaker and a ballot is held. The first debate lasts for 90 minutes and is followed by a 30-minute debate. In the afternoon sessions, a 90-minute debate is followed by two half-hour debates. (Thursday sittings are dedicated to discussing select committee reports and general debates.) Examples of debates on a single sitting day are shown in Table 6.3. Each debate not only gives the initiating backbencher the opportunity to make a short speech, but it also provides an opportunity for a number of other MPs to speak – especially in the 90-minute debates – before a minister replies. (This is normally a junior minister, but exceptionally a senior minister has replied.) Members are thus able to have their views recorded, and to ensure that there is a response by the government. As can be gleaned from Table 6.3, the debates provide an opportunity to raise issues of constituency or regional concern, and issues of social concern outside the normal context of party debate.

Although debates in Westminster Hall were treated warily by some members when first introduced, they are now generally accepted as a useful complement to the chamber itself. Attendance is usually small – sometimes fewer than a dozen members – but numbers are not particularly pertinent in the context of what MPs wish to achieve. The debates allow backbenchers to raise issues they would otherwise not generally have the opportunity to raise in the chamber, and certainly not for the

Table 6.3   Sittings in Westminster Hall, 18 April 2012

Time	MP initiating debate	Subject of debate
9.30–11.00 a.m.	Dr Julian Lewis (Con)	Proposed closure of acute mental health beds in Hampshire
11.00–11.30 a.m.	Justin Tomlinson (Con)	Encouraging young entrepreneurships
2.30–4.00 p.m.	Elfyn Llwyd (PC)	MOD Logistics Bicester
4.00–4.30 p.m.	Lindsay Roy (Lab)	High Speed 2 in Scotland
4.30–5.00 p.m.	Neil Carmichael (Con)	Review of flood defences

length of time afforded by Westminster Hall. The opportunity afforded can be shown in terms of the number of hours that sittings occupy.

Back bench members also have the opportunity to raise a topic in the *half-hour adjournment debate* at the end of each day's sitting in the chamber. The topics, or rather the Members proposing the topics, are selected by ballot for each debate, other than on a Thursday, when the selection is made by the Speaker. Each 'debate' is confined to half an hour (unless preceding business finishes early), with the member initiating the debate speaking for ten to fifteen minutes, perhaps allowing another member to intervene for a few minutes, and the remaining time being occupied by the minister responding. No vote is taken. As with debates in Westminster Hall, the attendance is small (sometimes no more than the member initiating the debate, the junior minister who is replying, and the duty whip) but again is considered a useful opportunity to raise an issue. The occasion is used most frequently to raise specific constituency matters, but may also be utilized to discuss more general issues of policy and administration such as, for example, problems of solvent abuse and water fluoridation.

Government

The other main type of debate is that on *government motions*. These may take the form of substantive motions, inviting the House to approve or take note of some action or proposal, or they may take the form of adjournment motions, allowing the House to discuss a particular topic but without having to reach a particular decision on it. These adjournment debates are distinct from the half-hour adjournment debates just discussed, and are usually employed when the government itself has no fixed position and/or when it wishes to invite a wide-ranging discussion.

Some substantive motions tabled by the government will tend to be of a procedural or 'domestic' nature – proposing, for example, the creation of a new select committee, an amendment to existing pensions arrangements for members, or a vote of thanks to a retiring Speaker or Clerk of the House. Others, however, will be on items of public policy. In the period since 2001, for example, there have been several debates relating to the international situation. Table 6.4 lists the 18 substantive motions discussed in the 2008–9 session and the five held in the shorter 2009–10 session, and shows the mix of procedural and substantive motions that characterize the list each session.

In combination, then, these different types of debate provide the House with opportunities to discuss myriad aspects of policy and executive

Table 6.4   Government substantive motions, 2008–10

Date	Subject
2008–9	
8 Dec. 2008	Speaker's Committee on the search of Offices on the Parliamentary Estate
9 Dec. 2008	European Affairs
15 Jan. 2009	Gaza
29 Jan. 2009	Armed forces personnel
5 Feb. 2009	Afghanistan and Pakistan
26 Feb. 2009	Welsh affairs
5 Mar. 2009	Support for women during the economic downturn for the future
31 Mar. 2009	The economy
20 Apr. 2009	Defence procurement
14 May 2009	Swine flu
3 June 2009	Stroke services
16 June 2009	European affairs
18 June 2009	Food, farming and the environment
16 July 2009	Afghanistan and Pakistan
20 July 2009	Select Committee on Reform of the House of Commons
15 Oct. 2009	Defence policy
2 Nov. 2009	Tackling anti-social behaviour
5 Nov. 2009	Climate change: Preparation for the Copenhagen Climate Change Conference
2009–10	
1 Dec. 2009	Fisheries
3 Dec. 2009	European Affairs
22 Feb. 2010	Reform of the House of Commons Committee Report, HC 111, Rebuilding the House
15 Mar. 2010	Defence in the world
18 Mar. 2010	The Intelligence and Security Committee Annual Report

Source: *Sessional Information Digests 2008–09, 2009–10* (some errors in dates in the *Digest* corrected).

actions. Tables 6.1 to 6.4 are noteworthy for the diversity of issues covered. They are also notable for the amount of time they occupy.

About one-third of the time spent on the floor of the House, sometimes more, is occupied by these various types of debate, including the annual debate on the address. In the 2008–9 session, the House sat for 1,049 hours, and just over 400 of them were taken up by these various debates.

More than 400 hours also tend to be taken up by debates in Westminster Hall. The aggregated number of hours is thus substantial and could not be matched in the period prior to the introduction of debates in Westminster Hall.

Debates in the Lords

In the House of Lords, the variety is not quite so great. In Chapter 5 it was mentioned that most of the time of the House is now occupied by legislation. Debates occupy over 20 per cent of the time of the House. The principal debates are held on dedicated debate days (previously Wednesdays, but Thursdays since the 2005–6 session), accounting for about 15 per cent of the time of the House. The topics for debate are selected by each of the parties, plus the cross-bench peers, and there are a number of days where the topics, nominated by backbench peers, are selected by ballot. There are usually two debates on each debate day. The total time allotted for both debates is five hours. These debates provide an opportunity for all peers who are interested in speaking; unlike in the Commons, there is no need to catch the Speaker's eye for permission to speak, as there is no authority figure to make such a choice. Instead, peers sign up on a speakers' list in advance of the debate and their names are published shortly before the debate. Peers speak in the order they appear on the list, which is agreed by the whips earlier in the day. (The names are usually listed to ensure that there is some alternation between the different groupings.) The time is then divided between the number of speakers, and peers are advised of how long they each have available to speak. If many peers sign up, each may only have a few minutes to speak.

The process of debate in the Lords may seem artificial, but it has proved to be effective. Peers who wish to speak do so; and knowing that they have a limited time to speak, they choose their words carefully. Because speeches are short, no member is able to go on for too long or to dominate proceedings. (If they attempt to, they are reminded of the time limit.) Given that in most (though not all) debates, the majority of speakers will have some experience or expertise relevant to the subject, the result often is a well-informed, and informative, debate. The topics themselves, especially those chosen by ballot or selected by the crossbenchers, often tend to fall outside the framework of partisan conflict. Peers are thus able to raise issues of concern to groups outside Parliament and to ensure that there is a government response; each debate is replied to by a minister.

About 5 per cent of the time in the House is taken up with questions for short debate (QSDs, previously known as 'unstarred questions'). They are the equivalent of the half-hour adjournment debates in the Commons, but take up more time. If they are held in the dinner hour, they last for 60 minutes. If they are taken as the last business of the day, they last for up to 90 minutes. In this time, it is possible for several peers to contribute. (As with other debates, they sign up in advance.) On occasion, more than half-a-dozen peers may speak before a minister replies to the question. On occasion, as with debate days, so many peers decide to speak that they have only a few minutes each.

Towards the end of the session, the demands of legislative scrutiny are such that debate days are devoted to dealing with bills and there are few questions for short debate. However, for most of the session, these debates provide valuable opportunities for backbenchers, often specialists in the field, to raise issues of current concern. They are not the only debates, however. Some time is given to debating, similar to that occupied in the Commons on government motions. There is the same mix of procedural motions and debate of substantive issues, such as the situation in the Middle East and European affairs. Time is also found to debate reports from select committees. In the Commons, some committee reports are debated, especially now in Westminster Hall, but there is a problem with finding time to debate all those that may merit discussion. In the Lords, if a select committee recommends that a report it has issued be debated, then time is found to discuss it. The House has resolved that time should normally be found in prime time but this is often not possible and some are debated during Friday sittings (the House sits on some Fridays to deal with such debates as well as to approve SIs) and some in grand committee. The number of select committees (see below) is now such that there is sometimes a list of half-a-dozen and a dozen or more reports awaiting debate. The advantage of debating the reports is that there is a ministerial reply. The government cannot get by solely by responding in writing.

Some select committee reports are also debated on a Thursday, following general debates. Thus, for example, on 1 December 2011, two debates initiated by cross-bench peers – one on nursing by Baroness Emerton and one on international development policy by the Earl of Sandwich – were followed by a debate on the report of the ad hoc select committee on HIV/AIDS, introduced by the committee chair, former Conservative cabinet minister, Lord Fowler.

Both Houses thus have a range of means available to raise and debate issues that are of concern to citizens, and where the topic of debate is not necessarily in the gift of the government.

Question Time

The House of Commons sits at 2.30 pm on Mondays, 11.30 am on Tuesdays and Wednesdays and 9.30 am on Thursdays. (Prior to October 2012, it sat at 2.30 pm on a Tuesday and 10.30 am on Thursdays.) If it sits on a Friday, it meets at 9.30 am, but there is no Question Time and it is therefore excluded from this discussion.

After prayers, any formal announcements by the Speaker (such as of the death of a member) and any private business (taken formally), Question Time commences. It lasts until one hour from the commencement of the sitting (that is, until 3.30 pm on Mondays, 12.30 pm on Tuesday and Wednesday and 10.30 am on Thursday). Departments answer questions on a rota basis, each one coming up every four weeks. All questions are tabled to the appropriate secretary of state, but all ministers in a department will be involved, dealing with those questions that fall within their particular remit. During questions to the Secretary of State for Business, Skills and Innovation, for example, questions dealing specifically with universities will normally be answered by the minister with responsibility for higher education.

Small departments, and ministers without departmental portfolios, such as the Deputy Prime Minister (if there is one) or Chancellor of the Duchy of Lancaster, are given slots towards the end of Question Time. The prime minister makes an appearance each Wednesday, from noon until 12.30 pm. Prior to 1997, Prime Minister's Question Time occupied two fifteen-minute slots, one on a Tuesday and one on a Thursday. When Tony Blair became Prime Minister, he aggregated the time and moved the session to Wednesday.

MPs can table questions up to three sitting days in advance (five days for questions to the Secretaries of State for Northern Ireland, Scotland, and Wales) – until 2003 it was ten sitting days – and are limited to one question per department on any day and no more than two in total on the day (it is thus possible to ask a question of the minister preceding Prime Minister's Question Time as well as of the Prime Minister). Because of the large number of questions tabled – which may run into three figures for the larger and more popular departments, such as the Treasury – there is a random computer shuffle to determine the order in which they are taken. Only the top 25 are published (fewer if a department is not taking up the whole of question time) and the rest are treated as lost. Not all of the 25 will necessarily be dealt with in the time available; those that are not reached receive a written answer.

Question Time begins with the Speaker calling the member in whose name the first question stands. The member stands and simply announces the number of the question. (Given that the question is on the order paper, time is saved by not reading it out.) The relevant minister then rises and reads out a prepared answer. The member is then called again in order to ask a supplementary question and, at the discretion of the Speaker, one or two other members may also be called to ask supplementaries. If a member of the opposition front bench rises after the first supplementary, he or she takes precedence. The process is then repeated for subsequent questions on the order paper.

Since 2007, the questions to a minister who has a period of 30 minutes or more conclude with what are termed topical questions. If the minister is answering for the whole of question time, the last 15 minutes are given over to topical questions; the time is reduced for those who have less than the full hour. These take the form of asking the minister to make a statement on departmental responsibilities and are utilized in order to enable members to then raise issues they regard as of immediate interest.

Questions must be confined to matters for which the answering minister has responsibility. This creates a problem at Prime Minister's Question Time, as there is no Prime Minister's Department. To avoid a question being transferred to the departmental minister responsible for the subject covered by the question, members developed the practice of asking the Prime Minister if he would pay an official visit to a particular place or – what is now the standard question – to list his official engagements for that day. The MPs lucky enough to have come high in the ballot then have an opportunity to put the questions they really wanted to ask in the form of supplementaries.

Though questions are required to be precisely that – questioners may not make statements or advance arguments – they are not necessarily information-seeking but rather means of raising issues and criticizing (or praising) ministers. Ministers may well know the content of supplementary questions from their own supporters – who brief the minister so that a response demonstrating the government's strengths can be given – whereas supplementaries from opposition members have to be guessed at; the opposition members will often try to catch the minister out with an unexpected (but in order) supplementary.

Prime Minister's Question Time is seen as the cut-and-thrust of political conflict between the two sides of the House, and in particular between the Prime Minister and the Leader of the Opposition. It is a focus of media and indeed Members' attention, the House usually being crowded. However, it presents an exaggerated picture of Question Time.

Questions to departmental ministers will not necessarily be as sharply partisan and are characterized at times by informed questioning by a small number of members pursuing issues of concern to constituents and others in society.

In addition to oral questions, which are published on the order paper, members may also seek to put an urgent question: these must, as the name implies, be of an urgent character and relate to a matter of public importance or the arrangement of business. An application has to be made to the Speaker before a set time in the morning and, if he agrees that it fulfils the criteria, the question is taken at the end of Question Time (or at 11.00 a.m. on a Friday). It used to be rare for a Speaker to allow an urgent question. In the 12 months before John Bercow became Speaker, only two were allowed. Speaker Bercow, since his election in 2009, has proved far more willing to accept such questions: by February 2012, he had allowed 89.

Members also have the option of tabling questions for a written answer. These are printed, along with the minister's reply, in *Hansard*. Written questions allow members to obtain information in a form that may not be possible on the floor (in tabular form, for example), or to receive answers to questions that may not be reached in Question Time. Members may stipulate a particular date on which they wish to receive the answer (as long as three days' notice has been given) – known as priority written questions – but a member may not table more than five such questions on any one day. Otherwise, they are free to table questions without stipulating a date; ministers are expected to try to answer such questions within a week of their being tabled.

Given the freedom to table written questions, it is perhaps not surprising that the use of these is popular among MPs. The number tabled each session is usually in excess of 50,000 (Table 6.5). As can be seen from Table 6.5, in the long 2005–06 session it reached 94,000. Written questions are an important part of MPs' activity. They are especially useful to members of the opposition front bench as well as opposition backbenchers for raising and pursuing issues (Young *et al.* 2003, p. 17).

Questions are seen, not least by MPs themselves, as an important means of subjecting ministers and departments to critical scrutiny. One survey of MPs on both sides of the House in the early 1990s found there was general agreement that questions were important for holding ministers to account (Franklin and Norton 1993, ch. 4). Oral questions were seen as being marginally more important than written questions in this context. Written questions were deemed to be more important than oral questions for obtaining information that would otherwise be difficult to acquire.

Table 6.5　Number of questions tabled, House of Commons, 2005–10

Type of question	Session				
	*2005–6**	*2006–7*	*2007–8*	*2008–9*	*2009–10***
For oral answer***	5,353	3,736	5,151	4,113	1,924
Priority written	15,374	10,590	12,351	8,907	4,307
Non-priority written	79,667	47,235	61,006	47,285	21,160
Total	100,394	61,5461	78,508	60,305	27,391

* Long session.
** Short session.
*** Figures for oral answer refer to the number tabled and not the number answered. Only about a half will be reached in time to receive an oral answer.
Source: *Sessional Information Digests, 2005–10.*

In the Lords, Question Time is also taken at the start of a sitting from Mondays to Thursdays, but differs notably from that in the Commons in four respects. The first is in terms of time: Question Time occupies a maximum of 30 minutes. The second is in terms of scope: whereas the Commons goes for breadth, trying to get through as many questions as possible, the Lords go for depth. No more than four questions are permitted to appear on the order paper. This allows for about eight minutes per question, thus giving time for several supplementaries, enabling a particular subject to be pursued in some detail. Consequently, ministers have to be well briefed, not least given the expertise of those who may be asking the questions. The third is in terms of ministers who reply: there is no rota system for departments. Questions are not tabled to particular departments but instead are addressed to Her Majesty's government. Questions can be tabled up to a month in advance (though the final question on Tuesdays, Wednesdays and Thursdays is a 'topical question' chosen by ballot two sitting days in advance), and on any particular day one may deal with the economy, another with foreign affairs and so on. In this case, the relevant treasury minister will be in attendance to answer, as will the relevant foreign office minister. A minister may thus make a several appearances at the despatch box in the course of a week. The fourth difference is that there is less partisanship than in the Commons: questions can be tabled to seek information and in order to pursue an issue outside the context of party politics. Some are very specific to the interest of the questioner, which may cover a matter of general public concern, such as the international situation, and others may be more parochial, such as responsibility for digging up roads in London.

Table 6.6   Number of questions tabled, House of Lords, 2005–10

Type of question	Session				
	*2005–6**	*2006–7*	*2007–8*	*2008–9*	*2009–10***
Oral	743	519	595	484	248
Written	7,374	5,118	5,814	5,655	2,906

* Long session.
** Short session.
Source: Derived from *The House of Lords at Work*, sessions 2005–6 to 2009–10.

There is also another notable difference between the two Houses. Peers are less likely to table questions than are MPs. Even so, there are limits in order to prevent any peer dominating Question Time. No peer should have more than two questions on the order paper at any one time, or have more than one question on any one day. In an average session, about 500 questions will be asked (Table 6.6). There are other procedural differences. The peer with the question rises and says 'I beg leave to put the question standing in my name on the order paper', and, after the supplementary to the minister, other peers intervene to put supplementaries. As there is no Speaker with powers to call people to put questions, the House must decide who should ask a supplementary if two peers persist and neither gives way; in practice, the Leader of the House normally comes to the dispatch box to suggest that peer X should perhaps be heard, and then peer Y. The normal convention is to give way to another peer, and a question coming from one side of the House should be followed by a question from the other side.

Peers may also table questions for a written answer, though the number tabled each session – usually between 5,000 and 6,000 (Table 6.6) – is, again, small relative to the number in the Commons, though it is growing. Some peers are regular questioners, but most will tend to ask questions when they in fact want information. Some will pursue issues central to their area of expertise; the leading lawyer, Lord Lester of Herne Hill, for example, frequently tables questions on issues of human rights. The questions should be answered within a fortnight. Departments which fail to answer questions within that time are listed on the order paper, a form of naming and shaming.

Outside the chamber

There are various means available to MPs to raise issues other than through debates and questions. Indeed, these means have expanded noticeably in recent decades. The most prominent of these comprise select committees and represent the formal means of engaging in administrative oversight. At the informal level – informal in that they are not officially-designated agencies of the House – there are back bench groups and all-party groups. Members also have the option of pursuing matters individually, for example, through a meeting with, or writing to, a minister.

Select committees

Select committees are appointed to consider a particular issue. They were used frequently in earlier times, such as during the Tudor era, but were largely, though not wholly, squeezed out by the advent of party government in the nineteenth century. They can be divided into two types: domestic committees and investigative committees. Domestic committees cover such matters as catering and management functions. Each House has several such committees. They are intrinsic to the smooth running of each House, but they need not concern us here as they are not tools of administrative oversight.

Investigative select committees in the Commons fall into one of two categories. There are the departmental select committees and there are other investigative committees, of which the oldest and most important is the Public Accounts Committee.

Departmental select committees

The creation of departmental select committees in 1979 added a major new dimension to the work of the Commons (see Chapter 2). As we have noted, their creation constituted the most important reform of the latter half of the twentieth century. At the start of the 2010 Parliament, there were 19 of them (Table 6.7). The committees are multifunctional. Formally, as we have seen, they exist to consider the administration as well as the policy and expenditure of departments. Finding out what departments have done, why and with what effect, constitutes a central part of their activities.

The committees are responsible for determining their own agenda and they have significant advantages over the use of the floor of the House to

Table 6.7   Departmental select committees, 2010–12

Committee	Chair
Business, Innovation and Skills	Adrian Bailey (Lab)
Communities and Local Government	Clive Betts (Lab)
Culture, Media and Sport	John Whittingdale (Con)
Defence	The Rt Hon. James Arbuthnot (Con)
Education	Graham Stuart (Con)
Energy and Climate Change	Tim Yeo (Con)
Environment, Food and Rural Affairs	Anne McIntosh (Con)
Foreign Affairs	Richard Ottaway (Con)
Health	The Rt Hon Stephen Dorrell (Con)
Home Affairs	Keith Vaz (Lab)
International Development	The Rt Hon. Malcolm Bruce (Lib Dem)
Justice	The Rt Hon. Sir Alan Beith (Lib Dem)
Northern Ireland Affairs	Laurence Robertson (Con)
Science and Technology	Andrew Miller (Lab)
Scottish Affairs	Ian Davidson (Lab)
Transport	Louise Ellman (Lab)
Treasury	Andrew Tyrie (Con)
Welsh Affairs	David C. T. Davies (Con)
Work and Pensions	Dame Anne Begg (Lab)

subject departments to sustained scrutiny. Debates and questions can be deployed only for sporadic scrutiny of particular programmes and activities. Committees can pursue a particular issue at some length. They can do so by questioning not only the appropriate minister but also the relevant civil servants. They can also call witnesses from other bodies to offer their knowledge and advice, and they do so frequently; the majority of witnesses are not drawn from government departments. Oral evidence is supplemented by the submission of written evidence, both solicited and unsolicited. The committees are also empowered to appoint, and most do appoint, one or more specialist advisers – outside experts paid on a daily basis – to assist them throughout a Parliament or for particular enquiries, as well as appointing specialist assistants – usually highly-qualified graduates in the field, employed on a fixed-term contract for two or three years.

The chairs of the committees are divided between the parties. As we have noted (Chapter 2), since the start of the 2010 Parliament the chairs are elected by the House and members by their respective parties.

Table 6.8   Subjects covered by selected select committees, 2010–12

Select Committee on Business, Innovation and Skills
- The New Local Enterprise Partnerships: An initial assessment
- Sheffield Forgemasters
- Government Assistance to Industry
- Is Kraft Working for Cadbury?
- Rebalancing the Economy: Trade and Investment
- Trade and Investment: China
- Time to Bring on the Referee? The Government's proposed Adjudicator for the Groceries Code
- Pub Companies
- Government Reform of Higher Education
- Pre-appointment Hearing: Appointment of Director of the Office for Fair Access
- Stamp Prices
- Debt Management

Select Committee on Foreign Affairs
- Future Inter-Parliamentary Scrutiny of EU Foreign, Defence and Security Policy
- FCO Public Diplomacy: The Olympic and Paralympic Games 2012
- FCO Performance and Finances
- The UK's Foreign Policy Approach to Afghanistan and Pakistan
- The Implications of Cuts to the BBC World Service
- The Role of the FCO in UK Government
- The FCO's Human Rights Work 2010–11
- UK–Brazil Relations
- Piracy off the Coast of Somalia
- UK–Turkey Relations and Turkey's Regional Role
- Departmental Annual Report 2010–11

Select Committee on Culture, Media and Sport
- Channel 4 Annual Report
- Pre-Appointment Hearing with the Government's Preferred Candidate for Chairman of the BBC Trust
- Funding of the Arts and Heritage
- BBC Licence Fee Settlement and Annual Report
- Pre-Appointment Hearing with the Government's Preferred Candidate for Chairman of the SC4 Authority [joint report]
- 2018 World Cup Bid
- Football Governance
- Spectrum
- 1175 Channel 4 Annual Report

Source: Derived from House of Common website: committee section.

Fourteen of the committees each have 11 members; defence, justice, and Welsh affairs each have 12, the Treasury committee has 13, and the Northern Ireland committee 14.

Each committee normally meets every week while the House is sitting, with meetings lasting between one to two hours. They may undertake extensive, long-term inquiries or short, rapid ones. Some will have single sessions on a particular subject or an annual meeting with the minister; for example, the Treasury Committee has a session with the Chancellor of the Exchequer each year. The topics chosen may reflect a committee in a proactive or a reactive mode. That is, a committee may seek to influence an issue just as it is coming on to the political agenda, or it may decide an issue already clearly on the agenda and one generating concern. As we have seen (Chapter 4), select committees may also play a role in pre-legislative scrutiny, enabling them to influence legislation at an early stage. The range of subjects on which the committees undertake enquiries, and subsequently issue reports, is diverse. Examples of that diversity are shown in Table 6.8, which lists subjects covered by three committees – Business, Innovation and Skills (BIS), Foreign Affairs, and Culture, Media and Sport (CMS) – in the first, long session of the 2010 Parliament.

The committees take evidence, both oral and written, before drawing up and agreeing a report. The reports are published in paper form and are also available on the Internet. The committees are prolific in output and have become more so over time. In a typical Parliament in the first quarter-century of the committees' existence, over 400 reports would be published. In the 2005–10 Parliament, the number exceeded 600 (Table 6.9). As Table 6.9 shows, more than 150 reports were published in each of two succeeding sessions.

The committees have thus invested considerable time and energy in reviewing government action in the different sectors of public policy. By their questioning of ministers and civil servants, they have required the occupants of government departments to explain and justify particular policies and particular actions. They have been able to do so by virtue of their special status. Though the committees cannot force the attendance of ministers and civil servants, there has usually been no problem in achieving the attendance of the witnesses sought. Ministers do not wish to attract the parliamentary opprobrium that would result from a refusal to attend. Civil servants cannot make comments to the media. Appearing before committees, they can speak only in the name of their ministers, but none the less, by appearing they are in a position to provide information and explanations that would probably not otherwise be put in the public domain.

Table 6.9   Number of departmental select committee
reports,* 2005–10

Session	Number of reports published
2005–6	86
2006–7	134
2007–8	152
2008–9	154
2009–10	84
Total:	*610*

* Excludes reports from the Environmental Audit Committee
which are listed in the *Sessional Information Digests* with
departmental select committee reports.
Source: Data calculated from *Sessional Information Digests,*
2005–10.

Committees are thus able to ensure that ministers and civil servants are
subjected to scrutiny in a public authoritative forum, eking out explanations and data that otherwise might not be forthcoming. In so doing, they
have ensured what, in Judge's terminology (1990, p. 167), is a greater
transparency of departments, ensuring that their actions are more visible
to Parliament as well as to the public and outside groups. Through issuing
reports and recommendations they also have some impact on departmental thinking. This impact does not usually extend to initiating significant
new policies, but it can affect the implementation of existing policies and
administrative practices. By taking evidence from interested bodies, the
committees have the potential also to look at policies from different
perspectives and by so doing may influence government to re-examine
and re-appraise existing policy positions (Judge 1990, p. 198).

Other committees

In addition to the Backbench Business Committee, domestic committees,
and the departmental select committees, the Commons has five investigative committees that cut across departmental boundaries – the longstanding Public Accounts Committee (PAC), and the Environmental Audit
Committee, the European Scrutiny Committee, the Political and
Constitutional Reform Committee and the Public Administration
Committee – and two that straddle the categories of domestic and investigative: the Liaison Committee and the Procedure Committee (Table
6.10).

Table 6.10   Non-departmental investigative select committees, 2010–12

Committee	Chair
Environmental Audit	Joan Walley (Lab)
European Scrutiny	William Cash (Con)
Liaison	The Rt Hon. Sir Alan Beith (Lib Dem)
Political and Constitutional Reform	Graham Allen (Lab)
Procedure	The Rt Hon. Greg Knight (Con)
Public Accounts	The Rt Hon. Margaret Hodge (Lab)
Public Administration	The Hon. Bernard Jenkin (Lab)

First appointed in 1861, the PAC primarily undertakes value-for-money audits of government programmes. The audits themselves are undertaken by, and on the initiative of, the Comptroller and Auditor General, who heads the National Audit Office, a body with a staff of approximately 800. The Comptroller and Auditor General presents reports to the committee, reports that are often short but generally numerous: about 30 or 40 per session, focusing on how money is spent and whether it is used most efficiently to achieve its intended purpose. Given the number of reports, the PAC cannot spend too much time on any particular one, and tends to hold one hearing, rather than several, on any given report. The Permanent Secretary of the relevant department will normally appear as the witness in the capacity of accounting officer.

If not satisfied with the responses, the committee can issue a critical report. By virtue of the nature of the enquiry by the National Audit Office and the status of the PAC, such reports are treated seriously in Whitehall. Committee recommendations are considered by the Treasury in consultation with the relevant department and, if accepted, put into effect according to Treasury instructions. If not accepted, a reasoned reply has to be given to the committee. The committee, traditionally chaired by a senior opposition MP, may then choose to return to the matter at a later stage. PAC reports and enquiries contribute substantially to the scrutiny of the administration undertaken by the house, forcing departments to justify their actions in spending monies in the way that they do.

The Environmental Audit Committee is of more recent origin. It was formed in 1997 to consider to what extent the policies and programmes of departments and non-departmental public bodies 'contribute to environmental protection and sustainable development', and to audit their performance against such targets as may be set for them by ministers. Whereas the PAC conducts a financial audit, this committee – as its name implies – undertakes a 'green' audit. (Both committees are unusual in that each also has a minister serving on it – a Treasury minister in the case of the PAC and the Minister for the Environment on this committee – but each sits ex officio and does not attend.) The Committee has been extremely active and in the first, long session of the 2010 Parliament had examined and reported on sustainable food, carbon budgets, air quality, green economy, sustainable development in the national planning policy, the 10 per cent emission reduction programme for central government, solar power feed-in tariffs, protecting the Arctic, and wildlife crimes.

The European Scrutiny Committee was previously the Select Committee on European Legislation and had a fairly narrow remit in terms of considering proposals and other documents presented by the European Commission to the Council of Ministers. It was responsible for reporting to the House documents that were of legal and political significance and whether such documents merited debate. It fulfilled a worthwhile role but it was essentially reactive. Its terms of reference were later expanded, providing it with an opportunity to address wider issues of concern (see Chapter 7). It has utilized the opportunity to report on such issues as the role of national parliaments in the EU and successive European treaties.

The Political and Constitutional Reform Committee is the newest of the committees, having been established at the start of the 2010 Parliament. Between 1997 and 2010, the House had a Select Committee on the Modernisation of the House of Commons, which made recommendations on reforming the House. It addressed such issues as the legislative process, select committees, sittings of the House, and how the House could reconnect with members of the public. It was succeeded in 2010 by the Political and Constitutional Reform Committee with a somewhat wider remit, looking at constitutional reform. Within the first two years of its existence, it had investigated, among other topics, Parliament's role in conflict decisions, electoral administration, political party finance, the rules of royal succession, codifying the UK constitution, prisoner voting, a statutory register of lobbyists, and proposals for the recall of MPs.

The Public Administration Committee was created in 1997, bringing together two existing committees: the Select Committee on the Parliamentary Commissioner for Administration (the Ombudsman) and the Public Service Committee, which was concerned especially with the civil service. The Committee thus has responsibility for receiving reports from the Ombudsman, who investigates complaints of maladministration (see Giddings, 1998), and 'to consider matters relating to the quality and standards of administration provided by civil service departments, and other matters relating to the civil service'. The committee has tended to range more widely than its terms of reference suggest, and has looked more at the whole sphere of public administration. (It has even been known to go beyond that – in looking, for example, at House of Lords reform.) It has proved to be a prolific committee, frequently examining issues that are of topical concern. In the first session of the 2010 Parliament, for example, it examined, among other topics (and one-off evidence sessions), good governance and civil service reform, the use of IT, the work of the ombudsman, smaller government, public appointments, strategic thinking in government, oversight of administrative justice, and the honours system.

The Liaison Committee is the body that draws together all the chairmen of the select committees of the House. (This includes domestic committees, so it is a large body.) It has various administrative functions, not least in relation to the budget and activities of select committees. As we have seen, it chooses the subjects for estimates day debates. However, it also has an investigative role, and has pursued the issue of the role of select committees. In 2000, for the first time, it took evidence in public, when it called the then Leader of the House, Margaret Beckett, to give evidence. It has also acquired a new role as a result of the prime minister agreeing in 2002 to appear twice a year to answer questions from members. The first such session took place in July of that year. The appearances have since moved from two a year, each of two-and-a-half hours, to three, each lasting approximately 90 minutes. Given the limited time and the size of the committee, specific themes are now selected for the sessions. In the Prime Minister's appearance before the committee in September 2011, for example, they were developments in Europe: impact on the UK, and government, politics and the media; in March 2012, they were Iran and Syria, and the accountability of public services.

The Procedure Committee is a more long-standing committee and, as it name shows, is concerned with examining the procedures of the House. It has reported on such matters as the committee structure – its 1978 report led to the creation of the departmental select committees – as well as private members' legislation and Question Time. More recently it has examined such issues as e-petitioning.

These committees are complemented by a Regulatory Reform Committee to examine draft Legislative Reform Orders under the Legislative and Regulatory Reform Act 2006 and a Joint Committee on Human Rights (see Chapter 9). In total, the House has 34 select committees, only five of which are primarily domestic.

The House of Commons, which for much of the twentieth century had very few permanent investigative select committees, is now a much more committee-orientated House, in essence changing the very nature of the institution. There is extensive activity taking place in committee rooms in the different parts of the parliamentary estate, especially on Tuesdays and Wednesdays. The committees themselves do not necessarily confine themselves to Westminster and have power to meet elsewhere to take evidence. This power is sometimes employed to take evidence abroad as well as in different parts of the United Kingdom.

House of Lords

The House of Lords is not dissimilar to the Commons in that it has seen a notable expansion of committee activity in recent years. Until the 1970s, it was very much a chamber-orientated institution. That changed with the creation of the European Communities Committee in 1974. The committee worked through sub-committees, and the House developed a reputation for its thorough and informed inquiries in the field of European legislation. It was facilitated by terms of reference that enabled it to look at the merits of documents. The committee – now the European Union Committee – works through six sub-committees and we shall be examining its work in more detail in Chapter 7.

The European Communities Committee was joined in 1979 by another permanent committee – the Science and Technology Committee. These two comprised the main investigative committees of the House, supplemented on occasion by *ad hoc* investigative committees. A further committee was added in 1993, when the Delegated Powers Committee came into being. The committee – now the Delegated Powers and Regulatory Reform Committee – has responsibility, as we have seen (see Chapter 5) – for examining order-making powers that are included in bills. The largest addition to the committees of the House came in 2001, when two new committees – the Constitution Committee and the Economic Affairs Committee – were created, along with a joint committee of both Houses – the Joint Committee on Human Rights. Another committee – the Select Committee on the Merits of Statutory Instruments – was appointed in December 2003. As we have seen (in Chapter 5), its role is to report to the House on statutory instruments that are of political or legal significance, or are inappropriate or imperfectly drawn to achieve their objectives. In 2012, it became the Secondary Legislation Scrutiny Committee. The House also appointed a Communications Committee to examine the media and the creative industries. First appointed in 2007, it has proved an energetic committee in examining the ownership and role of the media in the United Kingdom.

Table 6.11   Investigative select committees in the House of Lords, 2012–13

Committee	Chairman
Communications	Lord Inglewood (Con)
Constitution	The Rt Hon. Baroness Jay of Paddington (Lab)
Delegated Powers and Regulatory Reform	Baroness Thomas of Winchester (Lib Dem)
Economic Affairs	The Rt Hon. Lord MacGregor of Pulham Market (Con)
European Union	Lord Boswell of Aynho (non-affiliated)
Sub-Committee A	Lord Harrison (Lab)
Sub-Committee B	Baroness O'Cathain (Con)
Sub-Committee C	Lord Teverson (Lib Dem)
Sub-Committee D	Lord Carter of Coles (Lab)
Sub-Committee E	Lord Bowness (Con)
Sub-Committee F	Lord Hannay of Chiswick (Cross-bench)
Secondary Legislation	The Rt Hon. Lord Goodlad (Con)
Science and Technology	Lord Krebs (Cross-bench)

The number of committees has thus grown and they are listed in Table 6.11. They are designed to complement those in the Commons by covering topics that transcend particular policy sectors and are not confined to particular departments. There is some overlap. The Political and Constitutional Reform Committee in the Commons (and to some extent the Justice Committee) overlap with the Lords Constitution Committee, though liaison between committee clerks ensures that there is no unnecessary duplication.

The committees are also designed to play to the strengths of the House, with members appointed because of their expertise in the field. The chairman of the Science and Technology Committee is usually a distinguished scientist. At the start of the 2010 Parliament, it was Lord Krebs, an expert on ecology and animal behaviour, and former chief executive of the Natural Environment Research Council. When the economic affairs and constitution committees were first established, the House appointed Lord Peston, who had been professor of economics at the University of London to chair the former and a professor of government – the writer of this volume – to chair the latter.

The Committees, like their Commons counterparts, tend to be prolific. The European Union Committee, working through its subcommittees, has been especially productive, notably so in examining the impact of proposed treaty changes, including the Lisbon treaty. Those that report on legislation, as well as undertaking policy inquiries, such as the Constitution Committee, have tended to influence legislation as it passes through the House.

Back-bench and all-party groups

MPs and peers can also examine what government is doing through informal processes; that is, processes that are not formally established by either House and do not form part of parliamentary proceedings, but are created by parliamentarians and operate within the Palace of Westminster.

Back-bench groups

The twentieth century saw a notable institutionalization of the parties in Parliament (see Norton, 1979). The main parties developed an infrastructure that provided the means for backbenchers to discuss issues of common concern and to convey their views to party leaders. Parliamentary parties retain their own organization, independent of the party whips. Each parliamentary party – the Conservative is known as the 1922 Committee (see Norton 1994a) and Labour as the Parliamentary Labour Party (PLP) – usually meet once a week when the House is sitting. Meetings tend to be used to announce future business and often to listen to speakers, who may be leading frontbenchers or outside speakers. The two largest parties have had a sufficient number of members to sustain various committees, or groups, to cover particular areas of policy. These used to be especially numerous and influential on the Conservative benches (Norton 1979; 1994a) but other pressures on MPs' time, and the reduction in the size of the parliamentary party, led to a reduction in numbers. Instead of committees covering virtually every government department, the parliamentary party has policy groups covering broad areas of policy, such as the constitution. All Conservative MPs and peers are eligible to attend each meeting.

The Parliamentary Labour Party has a series of subject groups, usually one for each government department. The groups meet regularly to discuss issues of concern within the policy area. (There are also regional groups to discuss issues of concern to each region.) The groups usually meet fortnightly to discuss forthcoming business relevant to the sector, and on occasion to hear from outside speakers as well as ministers. Each

Labour MP can be a voting member of no more than three groups but is able to attend any group he or she wishes. Attendance fluctuates depending on the topic under discussion. In the Parliament returned in 2010, the Liberal Democrats also created backbench groups to act as a forum for debate and expressing a party view independent of the coalition government.

The party infrastructure is important to enable MPs to make their views heard by party leaders (Norton 1979) and to do so within the closed confines of the parliamentary party; they are not engaging in a public dialogue (though reports of meetings may be leaked). It is less easy for a minister to shrug off criticism in a crowded party meeting – confined to party supporters – than is possible in the chamber where the criticism is coming from one's political opponents. Critical comments in a party meeting may serve to alert the whips, and ministers, to the fact that there is a problem with a policy.

All-party groups

MPs (and peers) increasingly have the opportunity to join with members of other parties on issues that cut across party lines. All-party groups have grown in number in recent years, covering not only policy areas but also cultural and sporting interests. The first all-party group was the Parliamentary Science Committee in 1933, which was reformed as the Parliamentary and Scientific Committee (PASC) in 1939 (Powell 1980), providing 'a unique forum for the exchange of ideas between the parliamentary and scientific worlds' (Wakefield of Kendal 1980, p. 5), and the number has grown since then, not least in the twenty-first century. By 1988, there were 103 all-party subject groups and 113 country groups (Jones 1990, p. 125); by 2004, the number had grown to 303 subject groups and 116 country groups; and by 2012, there were no less than 432 subject groups and 136 country groups.

The country groups exist to foster links with the country concerned. The subject groups vary in their purpose. Some exist to enable members to meet and enjoy common interests, such as bridge or chess. Most, however, serve primarily to raise awareness of the topic they cover. This is especially so with those concerned with social issues – encompassing, for example, breast cancer, epilepsy, hospices, learning disabilities, mental health, motor neurone disease, pensioner incomes, and poverty. Some of the groups exist in name only. Others are active, holding meetings regularly with outside speakers, and lobbying ministers and civil servants. Some also arrange photo opportunities for publicity to raise public awareness.

The all-party groups provide a means of contact between outside organizations and MPs, and serve also as a means of reaching ministers through parliamentarians. All-party groups are especially attractive to interest groups as they operate outside the context of party – the groups cannot be accused of siding with any particular party – and are a means of identifying and keeping in touch with sympathetic MPs and peers. As a result, many all-party groups receive support from outside organizations, especially in the form of administrative support. One study in 2012 found over 300 all-party groups received support from outside group, with 80 providing parliamentary passes to staff with outside interests (Ball and Beleaga 2012).

For MPs and peers, membership of all-party groups enables them to keep informed of subjects of particular interest to them. In the words of one MP, 'all-party groups allow MPs to band together over a common interest' (Barbara Follett, quoted in Moyes 2004, p. 21). Ministers are also likely to be sympathetic to such groups, given that the members cannot usually be seen to be acting in a partisan way or out of self-interest.

All-party groups constitute an important and increasingly pervasive part of the parliamentary landscape. Each party MP (and peer) receives with the weekly party whip an all-party whip, listing the forthcoming meetings of all-party groups. There is usually a long list for each week. Some, as we have said, are more active than others. Some have proved to be influential. Their attraction to outside groups is a particular feature, which is both a strength – in terms of the information it produces – and a weakness. As one lobbyist noted in identifying the strengths and weaknesses of different parliamentary bodies, all-party groups 'can mobilize support on occasions (e.g. VAT on books)' but, as a weakness, are seen as 'too influenced by pressure groups' (Miller 1990, p. 55). A survey of MPs and peers in 2012 found that 48 per cent agreed strongly or tended to agree that all-party groups 'are prone to be manipulated by public affairs and lobby groups for their own purposes' (Speakers' Working Group on All-Party Groups 2012, p. 7). The links with outside groups has variously come in for critical scrutiny and in 2011 the Speakers of the two Houses established a working group to examine the role of all-party groups. The group reported in 2012 and recommended, among other things, greater transparency, especially in relation to income and expenditure.

Meetings and correspondence

MPs and peers can also operate at an individual level in scrutinizing what government is doing. They meet ministers and correspond with them.

Writing to ministers is usually in pursuit of constituency casework (see Chapter 9) but it is also a device for obtaining information from ministers and ensuring that they are aware of particular issues that concern members. As such, it can be seen as supplementary to parliamentary questions, requiring ministers to respond to particular points, but to do so less publicly and usually at greater length. A parliamentary question may elicit a short response, but a letter to a minister can result in a reply two or three A4 pages in length, explaining in some detail why a particular policy has been pursued or what plans government has made to deal with an issue. A letter also enables the member to develop a query, or make a point, in a way that is not possible in a parliamentary question.

Correspondence may be supplemented by personal contact. A member may arrange a private meeting with ministers to pursue particular points about the conduct of their departments. Such contact may be through a scheduled meeting, at the department or in the minister's room in the Palace of Westminster, or through a chance – or, indeed, planned – meeting in the division lobby, corridor or tea room. Such contact is a regular feature of activity in the division lobbies, being popular with members for the reason already noted in Chapter 3: it is difficult for a minister to give a negative response when face to face with a member making a particular request.

The important point about these informal means is that they supplement the formal means available. In combination – and it is the combination that is important – these various devices result in both Houses of Parliament, and the Commons in particular, devoting considerable time and attention – both on and off the floor – to the actions and administration of government.

Impact?

But what impact does all the time and energy devoted to the conduct of government in fact have? Looked at from a pluralist perspective, Parliament's capacity to affect decisions through administrative oversight is extremely limited. However, by drawing on the other perspectives of power, we are able to develop a more subtle understanding of Parliament's impact on the administration of government.

Limitations

Parliament exercises very little coercion in undertaking administrative oversight. The activities we have outlined are very rarely subject to a vote. There is virtually no opportunity for Parliament to say no definitively to government. Even when votes take place, as may happen on opposition days, they are declaratory; they have no legal force. The one occasion when the House of Commons can be powerful is in passing a vote of no confidence in government. Until 2011, it was a convention that, when defeated on a vote of confidence, the government resigned or requested a general election (Norton 1978b). The convention has since been superseded by statute. Under the Fixed-term Parliaments Act 2011, the passing of a vote of no confidence triggers a general election if a new government, enjoying the confidence of the House, is not formed within 14 days. (The last time that a government actually lost a confidence vote was in 1979; the last occasion before that was 1924.) Generally, in engaging in administrative oversight, Parliament is operating in persuasive rather than coercive mode.

To what extent, then, is Parliament able to influence government? From a pluralist perspective, there are obvious problems in attempting such an evaluation. For one thing, there is the problem of disentangling the scrutiny of administration from the other tasks fulfilled by Parliament. The scrutiny itself, as we have seen, takes different forms and embodies a range of consequences. For another, there is the problem of generating criteria for measuring Parliament's impact (Nixon 1986; Judge 1990). Even if the contours were clear, generating measurable objectives offers a virtually insurmountable obstacle.

Taken purely in terms of observable decision making, there is little evidence of Parliament affecting policy outcomes regularly and significantly. There are, for example, occasions when select committees have recommended a certain action and the government has then taken the action recommended. It is plausible to assume cause and effect, though that cannot be proved: the government may have intended to take the action anyway. Conversely, the government may reject a report, only for its recommendations to find their way on to a ministerial agenda a few years later (what is known as the 'delayed drop' effect), though again one cannot prove cause and effect. As Peter Riddell has noted, committees have influenced various policy changes on the part of government, but these are the exception and not the rule (Riddell 2000, p. 213). Furthermore, 'ministers can, and frequently do, disregard or ignore findings with which they disagree without much of a political stir' (Riddell 2000, p. 213). One attempt at assessing the work of a particular committee was that of Hindmoor, Larkin and Kennon. They concluded:

There are examples where the Education Committee appeared to have an impact on policy. Successive secretaries of state all identified areas where a committee inquiry changed existing policy or caused new policy to be made, and there are more recent cases outside the timeframe of this study, such as the Education and Inspections Bill 2007, where the committee's role in the development of the legislation was highly visible. But demonstrating broader patterns of influence on policy is difficult. In comparing committee reports with government legislation there are certainly instances of correlation, but causation is much harder to establish. Where there was influence, this was more often a result of the committee's role as a mediating forum between the backbenches and government. As a former special adviser said to us, a Select Committee is 'useful to have on your side'. (Hindmoor *et al.* 2009, p. 86)

The committees are limited in terms of what they can cover. They have limited resources – of which time is one – to scrutinize the whole gamut of government activity. They necessarily have to be selective, and policy tends to be more attractive than administration or estimates. Furthermore, 'witnesses do not always make it easy for committees to do their work' (Negrine 1992, p. 406). Though committees normally get the witnesses they want, they do not always get the answers they want, civil servants being prohibited from giving information on internal discussions, inter-departmental negotiations, or anything that is commercially sensitive. Ministers and their officials can prove to be tight-lipped, offering nothing of substance.

There is little evidence that opposition day debates affect government actions, other than exceptionally: they are simply part of the partisan conflict in the chamber and are rarely reported by the media. The debate on Ghurkha settlement rights in 2009 (see Table 6.1) was exceptional in that it produced a government defeat and a change of policy, but it stands out simply because of its rarity. Debates themselves are a misnomer, in that there is rarely a 'debate', and members deliver set-piece orations, often – after the front bench speeches – to an almost empty chamber; and the outcomes of debates are usually predictable. Prime Minister's Question Time is regularly deemed to be newsworthy by the broadcast media, again because of its partisan content, but not the questioning of departmental ministers. At Question Time, there is limited opportunity to question the whole range of departmental activities. There is a substantial list of topics on which ministers will not answer questions, including arms sales and budgetary forecasts. The randomness of question selection militates against pursuing an issue in a sustained manner.

The result is that Parliament cannot claim to subject the conduct of government to continuous and comprehensive scrutiny. Much, if not most, of what government does avoids parliamentary attention. When it *is* the subject of such attention, the attention is frequently sporadic and fleeting, affected by partisan considerations, time pressure and lack of knowledge. Ministers have various ways of deflecting probing by members, and to ignore recommendations for a change in practice or policy.

Strengths

Parliament's capacity to review government actions and administration is, then, clearly limited. However, it is not so limited as to be of no consequence. Indeed, it can be argued that Parliament, limitations notwithstanding, has the capacity to influence government. To tease out the capacity to persuade we can bring in the other perspectives of power.

The elitist, or agenda-setting, perspective is useful for drawing attention to what Parliament *can* do as much as to what it does do. Parliament may serve to keep certain matters off the agenda through the government anticipating reaction to parliamentary questioning or inquiry. In other words, it may have a deterrent effect. Knowing that an issue *may* be raised in the House, ministers and civil servants might be wary of pursuing a particular policy if they believe that it would attract adverse public reaction. Debates and questions may draw out something that government may not wish to be drawn out. The creation of the departmental select committees is especially important in this context. A committee may choose to investigate a particular policy. Committees choose their own agendas, usually after consultation with the department, but they may opt to pursue a subject government would prefer them not to. Ministers and civil servants may be more inclined than before to anticipate that their work might be subject to inquiry by a committee able to take evidence and to publish a report. As Peter Riddell (2000, p. 213) observed, 'ministers have to provide detailed replies to reports and that concentrates minds in Whitehall – as does the need to present evidence'.

The deterrent is likely to be greatest where there is consistency in scrutiny. This is notably the case with committees that examine every bill to ensure compliance with particular standards. The Joint Committee on Human Rights, for example, has chosen to consider every government bill (a practice now extended to *all* bills) to ensure that it is compliant with the provisions of the Human Rights Act. It has also started examining them to ensure that they also meet obligations embodied in other international human rights obligations (see Chapter 7). In the opinion of its founder chairman, Labour MP Jean (now Baroness) Corston, the committee has affected outcomes, both directly and indirectly: 'Here it is the *threat* of parliamentary scrutiny, and an adverse opinion from us, that is the key factor. This threat, I believe, is much enhanced by the comprehensiveness of our coverage' [emphasis in original] (Corston 2004, p. 165).

The deterrent capacity of committees has arguably also been enhanced by two independent developments. One has been the introduction of television cameras to the Palace of Westminster. A minister's appearance before a committee will attract the cameras if it looks as though the minister is in for a rough time. The other development is the growing link between the committees and the floor of the House. When first established, they operated largely in isolation, with few reports being debated by the House; over time, however, opportunities to debate reports has increased, first through estimates days and now debates in Westminster Hall. In the Lords, the opportunity to debate reports is better established; the change in the Lords has been the increase in the number of investigative committees.

Ministers and officials may thus decide, consciously or even subconsciously, not to pursue a particular policy for fear of parliamentary investigation. The extent to which this happens is impossible to determine, certainly not in any quantitative sense. Even if ministers claim they have been deterred from pursuing a particular line, one cannot prove that anticipated parliamentary reaction was the cause. One illustration of this, though focused on decision-making, was the claim by Margaret Thatcher when Prime Minister that 'I would like to be tougher on public spending. But I have to do what I think we can get through Parliament' (quoted in *The Times*, 11 January 1982). She may have been deterred by the prospect of being given a hard time in debate by Tory as well as Labour MPs. Then again, she may not have intended being tougher anyway, but none the less wished to assuage the criticism of those pressing for more radical action. All we can say is that Parliament has the potential to induce non-decision making on the part of government. Ministers remain within Parliament (see Chapter 3) and depend on the goodwill of their own supporters, not only for getting measures through but also to aid their own advancement. Given that, it would seem plausible to argue that ministers do not put parliamentary reaction totally out of their minds in the course of determining their policy and future actions.

There is also the positive side of agenda setting. That is, members may induce certain issues to be brought on to the agenda. This may be achieved through the obvious route of seeking to initiate a debate or it may be the result of tabling questions. Ministers devote considerable time to preparing for Question Time. This applies to the prime minister as well as to senior ministers. The Prime Minister will go over possible questions with a team of advisers, assisted by a small unit in 10 Downing Street, which draws together material from departments. Senior ministers will draw together junior ministers and senior officials in order to prepare. A parliamentary question ensures that the issue is brought before a minister; it may alert ministers to something of which they were not aware and which may merit further attention or action. Indeed, it can be argued that parliamentary questions assist administrative oversight through ensuring that ministers are briefed about a range of issues within their departments and which, without the prompt of members' questions, may otherwise not be put before them by civil servants. Again, the extent to which this contributes to agenda-setting in any significant sense is questionable, but there is a persuasive case that it helps to keep ministers abreast of developments for which their departments have a responsibility.

The extent to which an agenda setting capacity has been expanded in recent years is also significant. The introduction of Debates in Westminster Hall and the creation of the Backbench Business Committee have increased significantly the capacity of MPs to raise issues, some of which may not have been considered in the House in recent years if at all, complementing the agenda-setting capacity of select committees.

The institutional approach may be of even greater utility in assessing Parliament's capacity to engage in administrative oversight, and induce ministers and civil servants to act in a way that they would not otherwise. The relevance of the institutional approach is perhaps best illustrated by Peter Riddell's observation about select committees: 'Select committees are now part of ministers' lives and therefore part of the policy-making debate' (Riddell 2000, p. 213). The same applies to debates and Question Time, as well as the other, not least the new, institutional means of administrative oversight. In other words, the behaviour of ministers is shaped by the institutional framework of Parliament.

The extent to which it shapes behaviour is illustrated by comparison with other legislatures. In some legislatures, ministers have the option of choosing which questions they wish to answer; and some may not even bother to turn up for Question Time. In Westminster, there is no question of departmental ministers not being on the Treasury bench for Question Time. They may sometimes be adept at side-stepping questions, but they offer some response and then have to contend with sometimes hostile supplementaries put to them. When major debates are held, either on opposition days or in government time, senior ministers will be present to argue and defend the government's case. Some of the debates may be hostile to government actions, criticism of government coming from their own backbenchers as well as from opposition parties. The creation of a coalition government in 2010 added a new dimension in that the government comprised not one but two parliamentary parties and was pursuing policies at times that attracted opposition from backbench members of one, and sometimes both, of them (Cowley and Stuart 2012).

The ministerial guidelines issued by the prime minister emphasize that ministers should make important policy announcements to the House of Commons. Ministers may be adept at handling the House, especially given a supportive majority, but the important point is that they present themselves to the House; it is part of the culture to which they have been socialized. They know the environment in which they will be operating. It is usually a supportive one, but on occasion may not be; a poor performance at the dispatch box may render the government's position vulnerable (see Chapter 3); on occasion, a minister may be fighting for his or her political life. In 2003, Prime Minister Tony Blair was arguing for the government's life in seeking parliamentary support for the war with Iraq. Just as avoiding paying income tax is legal but evading it is not, so being economical with the truth at the dispatch box is permissible, but misleading or lying to the House is not. Ministers therefore have to be careful what they say. This has nothing to do with the size of the government's majority. It is one of the accepted rules of the game, and ministers play by the rules (Norton 2001b).

This institutional framework is important because it shapes ministers' behaviour and induces them to act in a way that otherwise they would not. That may sometime be in terms of decision-making, but more pervasively it is in terms of putting material in the public domain that otherwise would not be there. If MPs and peers did not ask questions or debate issues, then much of the material embodied in ministers' answers and speeches might not be revealed at all. Much of the material generated through the devices we have outlined may not be of great import, but some of it is. Select committees have contributed significantly to the process, extracting from ministers and civil servants information that is important, both quantitatively and qualitatively. Indeed, it can be argued that, prior to the passage of the Freedom of Information Act, the select committees were the most important contributors to open government in the United Kingdom.

The structures and procedures we have detailed thus facilitate the release of information by government, and hence the means by which government can be judged; or at least judged more objectively than would be the case if these devices did not exist. They help to open up government, not only to Parliament itself but also to the media, interested organizations – who are the most frequent consumers of select committee reports – and the public. The public acquire information principally through television and the print media, though the Internet provides expanding scope for direct access.

As Nevil Johnson (1988, p. 165) observed, the select committees were created under a government that adhered to a traditional view of parliamentary government: 'It is a view of the constitution which can accommodate strengthened select committees as critical organs of the House, but it has no place for committees with pretensions to the status of parallel governments.' The committees have therefore not served as decision-making bodies – they have no coercive capacity – but what they are able to engage in is a discourse with departments. They serve not simply as conduits for raw data, but rather engage in informed dialogue to enhance the understanding of government actions and intentions. They have expert advisers to assist in the process and thus engage in informed dialogue. Treasury officials know, for example, that the advisers to the Treasury Committee will run their economic forecasts through different economic models (Laugharne 1994). In the Lords, it is the members of the committees who are usually experts or have experience in the field.

As Johnson argues, the committees:

> are accepted by the departments as regular interlocutors, and can to some extent build on their accumulated experience of the sector of government entrusted to them. All this helps ensure that the House of Commons, ministers, and the departments all see the committees as regular elements in the processes of discussion, debate, and exchange of information through which public decisions are implemented. As a result organs of the House are latched on to the work of the executive in a more secure fashion than previously. (Johnson 1988, p. 167)

The select committees thus add to the existing parliamentary means for prising out of government information and explanations. They contribute to a parliamentary framework for questioning and opening up of government, and are an established part of the parliamentary landscape. Regardless of the size of its parliamentary majority, government has to work within this framework of administrative oversight. Ministers accept that the framework and how it operates is legitimate. They are socialized to the process and accept it, on the grounds of both principle and self-interest (Norton 2001b). Ministers one day will cease to be ministers and the mechanisms now used to scrutinize them may prove to be useful tools in their own hands.

Conclusion

Parliament devotes a substantial amount of time to questioning the actions of government, including the implementation of policy goals (a decision to commit troops abroad, for example) and more mundane administration of public programmes (payment of benefits, for example). It has a range of devices at its disposal. However, even as devices for eking out information, each suffers from certain limitations. MPs are limited in what they may ask questions about. Partisanship in Question Time is tending to squeeze out genuine information-seeking (Norton 1993b, pp. 201–3). The select committees will never be able to scrutinize more than a fraction of the policies and actions of government, and they are liable to focus on policy to the detriment of administration and expenditure. Their utility as scrutinizing bodies will vary considerably, depending in large part on the quality and commitment of the members, and in particular the chair. Partisanship in the House of Commons will ensure that debates are characterized by high levels of generality rather than informed and forensic scrutiny.

Those devices, none the less, have considerable consequences for government. They provoke responses in the form of information, explanation and justification. They absorb the time and intellectual energy of ministers and senior civil servants. They shape behaviour. They create a critical environment for the discussion of particular programmes and actions. They ensure greater openness on the part of government. Use of these parliamentary tools may occasionally influence a change of policy or minister or, more frequently, some change in administrative techniques and departmental practices. Furthermore, they have expanded in number in recent years. The opportunities to raise issues and force a response from government have become more extensive and institutionalised. Their very existence, and the occasional observable impact they sometimes have on policies and careers, may have a pervasive deterrent effect throughout the corridors of power.

Part II
Beyond Whitehall

7

Parliament and the European Union

The history of Parliament, as we have seen (see Chapter 2), has been the history of its relationship to the executive, and its capacity to affect public policy has been determined largely by changes in that relationship. It acquired the capacity to determine supply (the raising of money) and legislation; it other words, a coercive capacity. However, political pressures have largely curtailed the use of that capacity. Parliament has had to adapt to these pressures and, as we have seen, has done so through developing its persuasive capacity to affect outcomes.

Parliament has also had to adapt to other, significant developments. The period since 1970 has seen major constitutional change, on a scale largely unparalleled in modern British political history (Stevens 2002, p. xiii; Norton 2003b; King 2007; Bogdanor 2009; 2011). The 'hollowing out' of the state has had profound consequences for the nation's constitutional arrangements, given that the United Kingdom, unlike many other west European nations, has not been used to government being conducted at different levels. The modern history of the United Kingdom has been one of policy being made by the executive – the Prime Minister and cabinet – and assented to by Parliament. Parliament has been structured and has operated on the basis of policy-making competence resting with Her Majesty's government.

As a result of policy decisions by government, assented to by Parliament, designated powers – coercive and persuasive – have been transferred to other bodies, both within the UK and beyond its shores. These changes derive from no intellectually coherent view of constitutional change (see Norton 2007a; 2007b) but rather are measures deemed politically expedient or a response to perceived particular problems and needs. They have not primarily been directed *at* Parliament but have had major consequences *for* Parliament. They have served to transform the constitutional landscape, fragmenting power – hollowing out the British state – and creating particular challenges for Parliament.

The three principal changes are membership of the European Community (now the European Union); the devolution of powers to elected bodies in different parts of the United Kingdom; and the passage of the Human Rights Act 1998, incorporating most of the provisions of the European Convention on Human Rights into British law. They have had major consequences for Parliament, both individually and collectively. In this chapter, we address membership of the European Union.

Membership

The UK became a member of the European Community (EC) on 1 January 1973. The reasons for applying for membership were essentially economic and political. The issue of membership has been politically fraught, European integration constituting a major political fault line in British politics, both major parties being divided on the issue and both changing their stance on integration since the issue came on to the political agenda (Norton 2012c). Membership and moves towards further integration, through successive treaties, have not only created major problems for the political parties – having difficulty in carrying all their supporters with them – but also problems for Parliament in adapting to the new situation.

Membership of the Community resulted in the transfer of several policy-making competences to the institutions of the EC. These competences – the capacity to promulgate law in certain sectors – have been expanded with successive treaties. The Single European Act, which took effect in 1987, not only transferred more sectors to the EC domain, but it also strengthened the powers of the Community institutions at the expense of the national institutions of the member states. This was achieved principally through the extension of qualified majority voting in the Council of Ministers, the principal decision-making body of the Community, composed of ministers from each of the member states. Previously, unanimity had been the norm: each country had thus been a veto player. Later treaties – those of Maastricht, Amsterdam, Nice and Lisbon – further extended the fields of competence as well as instituting various institutional changes. Under the Maastricht Treaty, the EC became the European Union, comprising three pillars (the European Community (EC), common foreign and security policy (CFSP), and justice and home affairs); it also strengthened the position of the European Parliament. The Lisbon Treaty did away with the three pillars and combined them in a single entity. Other treaties provided for enlargement of the EU: with the accession of Bulgaria and Romania in 2007 the number of Member States reached 27, with Croatia scheduled to join in 2013. There has thus been a significant dynamic to EC/EU development.

The challenge for Parliament has been to keep pace with this development and to do so within a unique constitutional framework. Parliament provided the legal basis for membership through enacting the European Communities Act 1972 (Norton 2011a). This not only gave the force of law to existing EC law, it also gave it to future EC law promulgated under the treaties. In other words, the assent of Parliament would not be required to those measures: it would already have been given, in effect, under the terms of the 1972 Act. Parliament could determine how best to give effect to European directives, but it had no power to say no to them. Another consequence was that in the event of any conflict between EC and UK law, the matter was to be resolved by the courts.

After the UK became a member, Parliament decided to establish some means of scrutinizing EC activity. This was intended to give it a greater capacity to influence ministers prior to meetings of the Council of Ministers. As such, Parliament was developing the means to engage in a form of pre-legislative scrutiny. The difference between this and the pre-legislative scrutiny discussed in Chapter 4 is that, in the case of the EC, Parliament was operating at one remove from the decision-makers. Furthermore, there was nothing at that stage beyond pre-legislative scrutiny. It had no formal role in the process; its power was purely persuasive.

How, then, has this pre-legislative scrutiny developed? Both Houses have created a distinct process for dealing with proposals for European law.

The House of Commons

The principal work in the House of Commons is carried out in committee, both for the initial consideration of EU documents and also primarily for debate of documents that are deemed to merit further consideration. What time is devoted in the chamber to EU affairs is as likely to be for occasional debates on the UK's continued membership of the EU as it is for the detailed consideration of legislative proposals emanating from Brussels.

European Scrutiny Committee

In the Commons, EU documents are deposited with the European Scrutiny Committee. The Committee began life in 1974 as the Select

Committee on European Secondary Legislation. It considered legislative proposals emanating from the Commission but its terms of reference have been expanded to encompass 'EU documents', which includes Green and White papers of the Commission, draft recommendations, resolutions and conclusions, and the draft of the annual budget. The committee also keeps under review developments within the EU which have implications for the UK as well as monitoring business in the Council of Ministers, the negotiating position of UK ministers, and the outcome of Council meetings. It has also acquired, under the Lisbon Treaty, an enhanced scrutiny role. As we shall see, under the 'yellow' and 'orange' card procedure stipulated in the Treaty, national parliaments can report to the Council of Ministers and European Parliament proposals that they believe do not comply with the principle of subsidiarity.

Anything up to a 1,000 documents each year are classed as EU documents and as such are deposited with the Committee. Each has to be sent within two days of their receipt by the Foreign Office. (Some minor documents are now listed rather than being deposited with the Committee.) Within ten days, the relevant government department submits a detailed explanatory memorandum, explaining – among other matters – the legal base under the treaty provisions, the government's position, the effect on existing UK law, and the financial implications. The memoranda tend to be detailed and informative, often helping to make sense of what otherwise may appear to be impenetrable documents.

The documents are considered by the European Scrutiny Committee and sifted into one of four categories:

(i)   those of sufficient legal or political importance to justify debate;
(ii) those of legal or political importance but not warranting debate;
(iii) those of no legal or political importance; and
(iv) those of legal or political importance in respect of which the committee is not yet in a position to decide whether debate would be justified.

The committee, which has 16 members, is aided by a professional staff of 14, and normally publishes a report on the documents considered following each weekly meeting. Usually between a third and a half – sometimes more – of the documents are deemed to be of such significance as to require further consideration. In 2008–9, for example, 902 documents were considered and 456 were deemed of legal and/or political significance (European Scrutiny Committee 2010, p. 3).

For those that the committee considers merit further consideration, it may decide to 'tag' a document: that is, not recommend the document as such for debate, but list it on the order paper when it is relevant to a debate that is taking place. For the more politically or legally important documents, it recommends them for debate in a European Committee or, occasionally, on the floor of the House. In 2008–9, 72 were recommended for debate.

While this consideration takes place, the documents are subject to what is known as the 'scrutiny reserve'. Under this, ministers are expected to withhold agreement in the Council of Ministers to any proposal 'which has not completed scrutiny or which awaits a resolution of the House'. The only exceptions are where the committee has indicated that agreement need not be withheld, or the minister concerned considers that 'for special reasons' agreement should not be withheld. Such special reasons have been taken by government to include the need to avoid a legal vacuum and the desirability of getting a measure of benefit to the UK into force as soon as possible. In practice, a small number of proposals are accepted each year by the Council prior to debate in the Commons, even though recommended by the committee for further consideration. Despite this, the scrutiny reserve is seen as a useful means available to Parliament – it applies to scrutiny in both Houses – to give it some leverage in discussing EU proposals with ministers.

In addition to considering the documents deposited with it, the committee also fulfils its wider role to monitor developments within the EU and undertakes various inquiries, examining the impact of proposed changes as well as the process by which they are considered. In 2011, for example, it reported on the procedure for opting into international agreements and enhanced Parliamentary scrutiny of opt-in decisions (European Scrutiny Committee 2011) and in 2012 it reported on the Treaty on Stability, Co-ordination and Governance and its impact on the eurozone and the rule of law (European Scrutiny Committee 2012). We shall examine later its work in respect of the yellow and orange card procedure under the Lisbon Treaty.

European committees

Most documents recommended for further consideration are taken in one of three European Committees. They were previously known as European Standing Committees. Each one deals with a number of specified policy sectors (see Table 7.1). Whenever a document is referred to a particular committee, 13 MPs are nominated to serve on the committee

Table 7.1   European Committees, House of Commons

Committee	Covering matters within the responsibility of the Departments
A	Energy and climate change; environment, food and rural affairs; transport, communities and local government; forestry commission; and analogous responsibilities of the Scotland, Wales and Northern Ireland offices.
B	HM treasury (including HM Revenue & Customs); work and pensions; foreign and commonwealth office; international development; home office; ministry of justice (excluding those responsibilities of the Scotland and Wales offices which fall to Committee A); together with matters not otherwise allocated.
C	Business, innovation and skills; education; culture, media and sports; health.

for that particular document. Usually, two members of the European Scrutiny Committee and two members of the relevant departmental select committee are included among the membership. A member of the panel of chairs is appointed to chair the meeting. Any MP who is not a committee member can attend and seek to speak, though not to vote or move a motion.

The meeting can spend up to an hour questioning the relevant minister. (This can be extended for up to a further 30 minutes at the discretion of the chair.) The questioning can be useful and influence the minister's thinking. A motion is then put – usually a 'take note' motion – and debated for up to 90 minutes; amendments can be proposed. After the committee has completed its deliberations, and agreed a motion, the government moves a motion in the House; this is usually the same motion – though it need not be – as that agreed by the committee. (On one occasion, a committee agreed a motion different from that preferred by government; but the government moved its preferred motion in the House.) The motion is not debatable, though it can be voted on.

Floor of the House

The Scrutiny Committee can recommend that a document be debated in the chamber rather than in a European Committee. However, it is at the government's discretion as to whether such a debate takes place. It rarely agrees to such debates, so the time taken by EU documents on the floor of the House is very small. In the 2008–9 session, for example, only four documents were debated on the floor of the House, occupying a total of five-and-a-half hours (0.5 per cent of the time during that session). In the 2009–10 session, only 14 minutes were taken up discussing EU documents. Apart from the discussion of EU documents, there are two debates each year prior to the six-monthly meetings of the European Council, the body comprising the heads of government of the member states. The time taken by the general debates usually exceeds that taken by scrutiny of particular documents.

Select committees

Departmental select committees can examine European issues that impinge on departmental responsibilities, and the Scrutiny Committee may request comments from them. A weekly report on EU developments is circulated to them. In 1989, the Procedure Committee advised against the creation of a single committee to consider EC policy issues, preferring to leave the task with the existing departmental committees. However, the demands made on the time of select committees are such that very little time is devoted to EU matters. Some committees, such as that for environment, food and rural affairs, have given time to EU issues, including the common agricultural policy and the common fisheries policy, but no committee undertakes systematic scrutiny of EC legislation. Conflicting priorities are likely to ensure that this remains the case.

The House of Lords

Like the Commons, the House of Lords has a committee for the scrutiny of draft EU legislation. However, its work is more extensive than its equivalent in the Commons. It encompasses, in effect, the work done in the Commons by the Scrutiny Committee *and* the European Committees. Its scrutiny is of a different nature. The two Houses seek to avoid duplicating the work of each other, and engage in complementary activities. Whereas the Commons goes for breadth, examining all documents, the Lords goes for depth, examining some documents in great detail (Norton 1996a).

The European Union Committee

In 1974, the House of Lords created a European Communities Committee (see Grantham and Moore Hodgson 1985, pp. 118–32), renamed in 1999 as the European Union Committee. It is appointed to consider documents

Table 7.2   Sub-committees of the House of Lords European Union Committee
2012–13

Sub-committee	Sectors covered
A	Economic and financial affairs
B	Internal market, infrastructure and employment
C	External affairs
D	Agriculture, fisheries, environment and energy
E	Justice, institutions and consumer protection
F	Home affairs, health and education

and report to the House on those that it considers raise matters of principle and policy, and questions to which the Committee believes the attention of the House should be drawn. As such, it can comment on the merits
of proposals.

The committee has a chairman (a salaried post) and 18 members. It
meets fortnightly, operating principally through six sub-committees.
(The number has varied over the years between five and seven.) The
sub-committees are known by letters of the alphabet (Sub-Committee A
and so on) and each has responsibility for considering documents in a
number of sectors (see Table 7.2). Each usually has 12 members (one
currently has 13); at least two are members of the main committee and
the rest are co-opted. As a result, almost 70 peers are actively involved
in committee work. Other peers may attend sub-committee meetings,
thus allowing the sub-committees to benefit from members' expertise in
particular areas.

Committee deliberations are notable for their lack of partisanship. The
main committee is chosen to reflect the broad political balance within the
House, but interests and experience largely determine which peers are
appointed to the committee or co-opted to the sub-committees, and which
become chairmen. Of the members of the committee at the beginning of
2012, five had served as members of the European Parliament (one of
them as President of the Parliament), two were former UK Ambassadors
to the United Nations (one of them having also served as a European
Commissioner and the other as an EC Assistant Under-Secretary), and
four had been government ministers, one of them as Minister of
Agriculture. Another was a Nobel Prize winner. In terms of political affil-
iation, 5 were Conservative, 5 Labour, 5 cross-bench, 3 Liberal
Democrat, and one (the chairman) classed as non-affiliated.

Whereas sub-committees cover particular sectors, the main committee
looks instead at cross-cutting topics as well as taking evidence from

every incoming EU presidency and from the UK minister for Europe after major meetings of the European Council.

EU documents are submitted to the Lords as well as the Commons. The chairman of the EU Committee undertakes a weekly 'sift', sorting out the more important documents that require further consideration, from the less important documents. In this, he is assisted by an expert legal adviser as well as by the clerk of the committee. Documents deemed to be important – generally anything between a quarter and a half of the total – are then sent to the relevant sub-committees. It is then open to the sub-committees either to clear the proposals without subjecting them to further scrutiny, or to undertake inquiries. In 2008–9, of 845 documents sent to the committee, 403 were referred to sub-committees; in 2009–10, of 766 documents, 325 were referred (EU Committee 2010).

If a sub-committee decides to undertake an inquiry, it can be a short one, with some evidence taken, and followed by a letter to the appropriate minister, or it can be a substantial inquiry, with oral and written evidence taken and a report made to the House. The inquiry need not be confined to a particular document. It may look at particular aspects of EU activity or even anticipate events. Typically, a sub-committee begins a meeting by considering documents referred to it – some of which may be revised versions of earlier proposals – before moving on to take evidence, in public, as part of a specific inquiry. When undertaking full-scale inquiries, a specialist adviser will normally be appointed, and bodies such as the EU Commission, professional and trade organizations, and other organized interests – including pressure groups – will be invited to submit evidence. Evidence from the government will be invited as a matter of course. Sub-committees have also variously invited Members of the European Parliament to give evidence. Some will also undertake occasional visits in order to obtain evidence.

When a sub-committee has completed an inquiry, a draft report is submitted to the main committee for approval, and the committee decides whether the report should be sent to the House for information or for debate. The reports themselves are often substantial documents and, though addressed to the House, copies are sent not only to the UK government but also to the EU Commission, Parliament and the UK representative in Brussels.

The remit of the committee is such that its inquiries will often range widely. It will scrutinize EU documents to get some idea of the direction in which the Union appears to be moving in particular sectors and may then undertake, through the appropriate sub-committee, what amounts to a forward-looking enquiry. It undertook an extensive inquiry into the consequences of the Lisbon Treaty. Among subjects on which it reported in 2011–12 were the euro area crisis, the EU financial framework from 2014, the EU strategy for economic growth and the UK national reform programme, and future inter-parliamentary scrutiny of EU foreign, defence and security policy. Whether a report is recommended for debate or not, the government publishes a reply within two months of publication.

The floor of the House

The committee will usually make 30 or more reports a year to the House, with about half of these recommended for debate. When a report is recommended for debate, then it will be debated. However, pressure on time means that some reports are squeezed into inconvenient times, with some debates being held on Fridays or in grand committee. Debates on EU Committee reports occupy a relatively small part of the House's time – usually less than 3 per cent per session – but the debates serve a valuable purpose. When a report is debated, the issue gains a more public airing and a minister replies on behalf of the government. Some are not short debates; they can be substantial, lasting for several hours.

Given the need to move quickly to influence some EU decisions, the practice of undertaking short inquiries followed by letters to relevant ministers is frequently employed. The correspondence is regularly drawn together and published.

External links

Parliament has developed links with EU institutions. There is a British Parliament Office in Brussels, with two clerks from the Commons and one from the Lords seconded to monitor developments in the EU. Although Parliament has not accorded significant rights to UK Members of the European Parliament (MEPs), there are regular meetings of members of the Commons Scrutiny Committee and the Lords EU Committee with UK MEPs. In 2008–9, for example, they discussed Europe's response to the financial crisis, the Lisbon Treaty, and the Czech Council Presidency/Commission 2009 work programme (European Scrutiny Committee 2010, p. 13). Some members of the Scrutiny and EU Committees attend, and are active participants in, the twice-yearly meeting of the Conference of European Affairs Committees – known by the French acronym COSAC – which draws together representatives from such committees to discuss matters affecting national parliaments and to share best practice (Tordoff 2000, European Scrutiny Committee 2010, pp. 11–12). The chairman and officials of the Scrutiny and EU Committees will visit Brussels, for meetings with EU officials, as well as the country holding the EU presidency.

Both Committees are also developing bilateral links with counterpart committees in other legislatures. Co-operation between national parliaments has developed over the years, with sharing of information now much more developed than before and with a scrutiny website (IPEX), created in 2006, to provide a platform for the electronic exchange of EU-related information between national parliaments (Norton 2007c, p. 215). Each national parliament thus has a greater awareness than before of what other parliaments are doing, without waiting for a meeting of COSAC.

There are also links now with the devolved legislatures in the UK, with twice-yearly meetings of the EC-UK Forum, comprising the two Westminster committees and the Scottish Parliament, National Assembly for Wales and the Northern Ireland Assembly.

Lisbon Treaty and the yellow card procedure

Prior to the Lisbon Treaty, which took effect in 2009, national parliaments had no formal role in the European law-making process. As we have seen, all they could do was scrutinize and seek to influence national government. The Lisbon Treaty, however, accorded them a role, albeit a modest one.

Under a protocol to the treaty, national parliaments are accorded a role in scrutinizing legislative proposals to see if they conflict with the principle of subsidiarity (that decisions are taken at the most appropriate level). If a parliament (or a chamber in the case of a bicameral legislature) considers that a proposal does breach the principle, it may within an eight-week period submit a reasoned opinion to the institution proposing the law. If a third or more of national parliaments (or one-quarter in the field of co-operation in criminal matters) submit opinions, then the institution has to review the proposal with a view to maintaining, amending or withdrawing it (the yellow card procedure) If more than half the Member States submit opinions, and the institution decides to maintain the proposal, it must then submit a reasoned opinion in support of its decision to the Council and the European Parliament, each of which can strike down the proposal (the orange card procedure).

Under this process, a unicameral legislature has two votes and each chamber of a bicameral legislature has one vote. The Commons and

Lords can thus operate independently in reaching an opinion on a proposal. Both Houses have judged some legislative proposals to fall foul of the principle of subsidiarity. When the respective committee judges a proposal not to comply with the principle, a motion is put to the House and, if agreed, a reasoned opinion is then submitted. In 2010, the Commons submitted reasoned opinions in respect of three proposals and the Lords in respect of two. Of these, one was common to both Houses (the seasonal workers directive). Only the Polish Senate submitted a higher number of reasoned opinions (four) than the Commons. Though opinions were submitted in respect of 12 legislative proposals, in no case was the number of opinions sufficient to force a reconsideration. The closest was in respect of the seasonal workers directive, which in the view of nine chambers fell foul of the principle of subsidiarity.

Though no legislative proposal has been referred back, national parliaments are active in considering proposals under this provision. In 2010, 20 chambers submitted reasoned opinions. Under the Lisbon Treaty protocol, it is also open to national parliaments, through their national governments, to apply to the Court of Justice for judicial review of EU legislation on the grounds that it infringes the principle of subsidiarity. To date, though, the court has not struck down any measure on those grounds.

Parliamentary adaptation

How successful has Parliament been in adapting to the changed constitutional landscape created by EU membership? In terms of the pluralist view of power, we can see that there has been a significant change. Parliament has transferred significant power – coercive and persuasive – to other bodies, in this case the institutions of the EU.

Formally, the transfer of coercive powers has not been complete. Parliament cannot strike down or amend EU law made under the provisions of the treaties. However, it retains a coercive capacity in relation to new, or amendments to existing, European treaties. Under the Constitutional Reform and Governance Act 2010, the prerogative power to ratify treaties was transferred to Parliament. However, even before that, Parliament enjoyed some leverage in relation to implementing new treaties. It had to enact any measures necessary to give effect in UK law to the treaties. Given that the treaties normally require a change in UK law, Parliament was thus in a position to refuse to make such changes.

Parliament has never utilized such power, but the passage of the European Communities (Amendment) Act 1993, giving effect to the provisions of the Maastricht Treaty, was politically fraught. It was only achieved – as with the passage of the original European Communities Act in 1972 (Norton 2011a) – through the government resorting to a vote of confidence. Parliament also formally retains ultimate control in that UK membership of the EU rests on the European Communities Act 1972. There is now provision under the Lisbon Treaty for a Member State to withdraw, but that provision notwithstanding Parliament could bring membership to an end by repealing the 1972 Act. Were it to repeal the 1972 Act, the general view of constitutional experts is that the courts would enforce it under the doctrine of parliamentary sovereignty.

In reality, however, the chances of Parliament exercising its coercive capacity are very limited. The fact that it exists is important, but the political reality is that it is not going to be exercised other than in the most exceptional circumstances. What is important, therefore, is how Parliament has developed a persuasive capacity. As we have seen, it has done so principally through the creation of committees which exist to scrutinize EU documents and seek to exert influence prior to proposals being discussed in the Council of Ministers.

The committees are limited by the extent to which they operate independently of the chamber. As we have seen, few EU documents are debated in the Commons. Furthermore, the committees have a persuasive capacity only. Unlike some other parliaments of Member States of the EU (such as Austria, Denmark, Finland, Hungary, Slovakia and Sweden), there is no capacity to mandate a minister in the Council of Ministers; that is, to stipulate what the minister may or may not agree to. Instead, Parliament is what is known as a documents-based system (as with the Irish, Italian and Czech parliaments). The two Houses can seek to influence national government, but the capacity to do is limited when the government enjoys a majority in the House of Commons.

There are further limitations, especially in the case of the House of Commons. Though debates on Britain's continued membership of the EU attract the attention of a good many MPs, very few are interested in detailed examination of EU documents. Membership of the European Scrutiny Committee is not highly prized and there can be problems with persuading members to serve on a European Committee. Membership of the European Committees did move from being *ad hoc* for each document to being permanent for each Parliament, but this created problems in ensuring enough members attended to maintain a quorum. The practice reverted to the appointment of members on an *ad hoc* basis.

The introduction of the yellow and orange card procedure under the Lisbon Treaty was designed to provide a more significant role for national parliaments, part of the overall intention of the treaty to address the 'democratic deficit' in the EU. It has been seen as crafting a means for national parliaments collectively to influence policy, to act as a new channel for linking citizens with the EU, and to serve as a forum for debating the merits of proposed legislation (Cooper 2012, pp. 441–65). There are, though, notable limitations. It entails national parliaments being involved in a relatively late stage of the law-making process – when proposals have already been drawn up – rather than at the initial stages. The stance is essentially reactive and the powers conferred are limited, essentially to inviting the institution generating the proposal to think again. The scope of the provision is also narrow, being confined to the principle of subsidiarity. Very few legislative proposals fall foul of that principle. A more significant principle in this context is that of proportionality (the measure being proportionate to achieving the stipulated goal), but that does not fall within the remit of the yellow and orange card procedure. As a result, the inclusion in the Lisbon Treaty of a role for national parliaments has some symbolic significance, but its practical effect is, at best, modest. As the European Scrutiny Committee observed, the provision added little to existing practice, given that such scrutiny was long-established practice, and the legislative decisions on subsidiarity continued to rest with the EU institutions (European Scrutiny Committee 2010, p. 7).

However, as persuasive bodies, both Houses are arguably as effective as they can be within the context of executive–legislative relations in the UK – that is, if a government does not wish to be persuaded, there is little a committee can do. In the context of the EU, the work of the European committees at least serves to focus the minds of ministers and officials; and it can at times influence the nature of the debate within the EU. The work of the European Union Committee in the Lords is seen as being particularly good at contributing to debate, both within government and in the institutions of the EU.

Given the constraints within which Parliament operates, it could be argued that it has adapted as well as it can in relation to EU membership. The combination of the scrutiny reserve and the explanatory memoranda that accompany European documents is valuable. It is the combination that is important. The way in which the two Houses complement one another in exercising systematic scrutiny – the House of Commons, as we have mentioned, going for breadth, and the House of Lords for depth – is also a distinctive feature of the UK Parliament.

The persuasive capacity of Parliament is not, however, easily demonstrated in observable outcomes, as there are few changed decisions that can be attributed to the work of the scrutiny committees. However, the work of the committees is seen in a somewhat different light when viewed from the other perspectives of power. In terms of agenda-setting, or non-decision-making, then the deterrent effect becomes important. Ministers and officials know that EU documents will be considered.

Viewed from the institutional perspective, we can see what has happened in two different lights. New institutional structures, or processes, have been created within and beyond the UK, and they have acquired legitimacy through an Act of Parliament. They exist independently of Parliament. On the other hand, Parliament has created its own institutional arrangements and the committee process in respect of EU document is well established and accepted by government. Hence, as we have seen, all EU documents are deposited with Parliament and it is up to the scrutiny committees, advised by legal experts, as to what action to recommend. The explanatory memoranda, as we have noted, help to focus the minds of ministers and civil servants. The scrutiny reserve serves as something of a constraint on government. It is a means of forcing a minister to think more deeply about a proposal and to justify it or the government's stance on it. The committees recognize that the scrutiny reserve should not be utilized unreasonably and so, in effect, a balance exists; the government complies with the scrutiny reserve knowing it is not being overly used.

The committees are not in a position to say no to government, but government accepts the institutional process: all documents flow through the European committees. The *process* is important and limiting, inducing in effect a dialogue between ministers and the committees.

Conclusion

Parliament has had to adapt to a changing constitutional landscape. The changes have seen it transfer some of its law-effecting powers elsewhere. However, given the dominance of the executive in its relationship to Parliament, the coercive capacity of Parliament is arguably not as great as, on the surface, it appears to be. Rather, Parliament has sought to adapt to the changed conditions by creating new mechanisms to scrutinize and influence government. The formality of coercion has, in effect, been replaced by a more politically realistic capacity to persuade. That capacity is arguably not as well developed as it might be. There are dangers in

scrutiny being hived off to committees if those committees do not enjoy
a clear link with the chamber – a particular problem in the Commons with
EU documents. There is also the problem that the effectiveness of the
procedures depends on members being willing to make them work. As we
have seen, attendance at European Committees in the Commons is problematic. The involvement of the Lords, characterized by a greater
commitment by members, has offset this to some extent, but it remains a
problem. The challenge for Parliament is trying to cope with the growing
demands made of it.

8

Parliament and Devolution

The end of the twentieth century witnessed a major change in the structure of the governmental framework of the United Kingdom. During the latter half of the twentieth century, pressure had built up in Scotland, and to a lesser extent in Wales, for policy making to be made by bodies closer to the people, rather than being centralized in London (see, e.g., Birch 1977; O'Neill 2004; Jefferson 2011). A scheme of devolution was recommended by a Royal Commission (the Kilbrandon Commission) in 1973. There was an ultimately unsuccessful attempt by the Labour government of 1974–9 to create a Scottish parliament and a somewhat less powerful Welsh assembly. The Labour government returned in 1997, with a large parliamentary majority and a manifesto commitment to implement the policy, was successful in its attempts to achieve devolution. It extended beyond Scotland and Wales to Northern Ireland, which had experience of its own legislature, having had a parliament from 1922 to 1972. Following referendums in Scotland, Wales (Norton 2010d, pp. 275–6) and, in a somewhat different context, Northern Ireland (Norton 2010d, pp. 287–9; Walker 2012, pp. 146–9), powers were devolved from the centre to these three parts of the United Kingdom.

Devolution is not dissimilar to EU membership in that Parliament has transferred specified powers to other bodies. In the case of Scotland and Northern Ireland, legislative and executive powers were devolved. In the case of Scotland, the 129-member Scottish Parliament is able to legislate in all areas, other than those reserved to Westminster (such as foreign and defence policy, fiscal matters and social security policy). Further powers, notably an extension of tax-raising powers, were devolved under the Scotland Act 2012. Northern Ireland has a system of government that is *sui generis*, with a power-sharing executive and portfolios allocated according to party strength and with no collective ministerial responsibility. The 108-member Northern Ireland Assembly can legislate in 'transferred matters', in effect areas not reserved to Westminster. Powers that remain with Westminster comprise those which can never be transferred ('excepted matters') and those which may at some stage be transferred ('reserved matters'). In the case of Wales, executive powers only were devolved initially, with Westminster legislating for Wales as well as England, but under the Government of Wales Act 2006 a process of transferring legislative powers also began. Following a referendum in March 2011, the 60-member National Assembly for Wales was empowered to legislate in devolved matters without the need for Westminster approval.

Members of the Scottish Parliament (MSPs) and members of the National Assembly for Wales (AMs) are elected by the additional-member system (AMS) and members of the Northern Ireland Legislative Assembly (MLAs) by the single-transferable vote (STV). In Scotland and Wales, members occupy new purpose-built buildings – in Holyrood in Edinburgh for the Scottish Parliament and in Cardiff Bay for the National Assembly for Wales. In Northern Ireland, members occupy the building at Stormont, on the outskirts of Belfast, which was the seat of the old Northern Ireland Parliament.

The Scottish Parliament has been an active body since its inception (Arter 2004a, p. 72). It has developed an extensive committee system, with each committee combining both a legislative and an investigative role. The committees have even been empowered to initiate bills. It has sought to distinguish itself from the Westminster Parliament and to develop a more consensual style of policy-making. It has also sought to achieve input from the public, not least through the use of public petitions. The Northern Ireland Assembly also works through committees: it has 12 committees to scrutinize the departments of the Northern Ireland executive – the equivalent of departmental select committees – and six permanent standing committees, such as a Public Accounts Committee. The smaller National Assembly for Wales has established five committees to cover particular policy sectors, such as enterprise and business, as well as five to cover more procedural and governmental issues, such as petitions and public accounts.

Though the Scottish Parliament operates in a way that is certainly different from Westminster (see Winetrobe 2004), it has been heavily influenced by Westminster. Many of the Scottish politicians who were initially responsible for developing the Parliament were also Westminster MPs (see Constitution Committee 2003). Party became a central feature of the institution, with party cohesion and party conflict characterizing proceedings (Arter 2004a; 2004b). The committees became heavily involved in considering bills brought forward by the executive. The situation is not dissimilar in Wales, where the Welsh Assembly government was led from 2000 to 2009 by a former Welsh Labour MP, Rhodri

Morgan. In Northern Ireland, the political parties are distinctive to the province, but the leaders have also been Westminster MPs (though in the case of Sinn Fein MPs not taking their seats).

However, the politics of the area covered by the elected body have shaped the development of each body, not least the presence of a significant nationalist party. Each has also had to cope with the politics of coalition. In the case of Northern Ireland, power-sharing between the parties has been a constitutional requirement. In Scotland and Wales it has been at times a political necessity, Scotland witnessing a Labour-Liberal Democrat coalition (1999–2007) and Wales a Labour-Plaid Cymru administration (2007–11). In the case of Scotland, the position has since changed to witness the Scottish National Party (SNP) forming a minority administration (2007–11) and then being elected in 2011 with an absolute majority (69 seats out 129). In short, not only has the constitutional structure of each elected body been distinctive, but so too has its politics.

Whitehall and Westminster

The challenge for Parliament, and indeed for government (see Constitution Committee 2003; Trench 2004a), has been to adapt to the changed conditions.

If anything, government has been able to adapt more quickly and effectively than has Parliament. When the elections were first held to the Scottish Parliament and National Assembly for Wales, the dominant party was the Labour party. As Labour was also in power in Westminster, the relationship between the executives was smooth. This was enhanced by the fact that the Labour politicians leading the new administrations in Holyrood and Cardiff Bay were drawn from Westminster – not just former (or still) Labour MPs but former ministers. They were thus able to have contact as colleagues, indeed party colleagues. The smooth transition was also facilitated by the fact that the British civil service remained a unified service. There was a separate Northern Ireland Civil Services (NICS), but otherwise there was just one home civil service (Constitution Committee 2003). This again made for good relations between officials: they often knew one another and shared the same ethos. The devolution legislation created the framework for resolving disputes between the UK government and the elected Scottish and Welsh administrations, but this formal framework was rarely used; most contact was informal.

The challenge was somewhat greater for Westminster. There was no established framework for dealing with the new situation. The experience of the Northern Ireland parliament from 1922 to 1972 hardly set a useful precedent. During the period of rule by a Unionist majority at Stormont, the Westminster parliament had largely ignored the province. The MPs elected to Westminster from Northern Ireland constituencies were predominantly Unionists. They were few in number (for most of the period the province sent 12 MPs to Westminster), the Ulster Unionist MPs were incorporated in the ranks of the Conservative parliamentary party, and had a less than sparkling attendance record. They were viewed essentially as second-rank Northern Ireland politicians – the first rank stayed at home to run the Stormont parliament – and their votes were rarely crucial to the outcome of votes in the Commons (Norton 1996b, pp. 129–42).

Westminster was thus not well prepared to deal with the new situation. At one level, it did mirror the earlier situation in relation to Northern Ireland in that the effect was to move Scottish matters largely off the parliamentary agenda at Westminster. Matters that fell within the remit of the Scottish administration and parliament were for resolution in Holyrood. By convention, the Secretary of State for Scotland cannot be asked about matters that are the responsibility of the devolved body. Indeed, this has raised questions about the need to retain the post of a Secretary of State for Scotland; given that there was little for the post-holder to do, the Constitution Committee of the House of Lords in 2003 recommended that the post be abolished. Though the government retained it, so that Scotland had a voice in cabinet when reserved matters were considered, it was effectively regarded as a part-time post, variously being combined with another one. Thus, for example, Alistair Darling combined being Transport Secretary with the post of Scottish Secretary (2003–6) and Des Browne was both Secretary of Defence and Scottish Secretary (2007–8). A similar situation pertained in Wales, with Peter Hain serving as Secretary of State for Wales from 2002 to 2009 while also serving for most of that time in other Cabinet offices: Leader of the House of Commons (2003–5), Northern Ireland Secretary (2005–7) and Work and Pensions Secretary (2007–8).

Though Parliament has the capacity to legislate for Scotland in devolved matters, it chooses not to do so, other than by invitation. If Westminster is considering a bill that the Scottish Parliament believes is also appropriate for Scotland, then – rather than passing a separate bill itself – the Scottish Parliament invites Westminster to extend the scope of the measure to Scotland. It does so through agreeing to what were initially known as 'Sewel motions' (named after the Scottish Office minister, Lord Sewel, when the Scotland Bill was going through

Parliament) but are now styled Legislative Consent Motions. In practice, such motions have been far more extensive than was initially envisaged (see Page and Batey 2002). By June 2012, a total of 107 had been passed. However, although the motions are passed by the Scottish Parliament, they are in effect brought forward by the Scottish executive and discussions about the legislation essentially take place on a government-to-government basis rather than a parliament-to-parliament basis. The same applies also to the other devolved bodies, which may also pass Legislative Consent Motions. The motions normally relate to specific provisions of a Bill rather than to the whole measure.

The challenge for the House of Commons has thus been to develop a means for scrutinizing government policy in reserved areas as it applies to the devolved parts of the United Kingdom as well as develop its own working relationship with the Scottish Parliament, National Assembly for Wales and Northern Ireland Assembly.

Scrutiny

The principal means of scrutinizing government policy in respect of the devolved parts of the United Kingdom has fallen to the relevant departmental select committees. This has created particular challenges. This affects both composition and remit. In terms of composition, committees are required to reflect proportionately party strength in the House. The limited political strength of the Conservatives in Scotland means that the party is not able to appoint members to the committees who sit for Scottish constituencies. In the 2010 general election, only one Conservative MP was returned in a Scottish seat (as was the case in 2001 and 2005). As the MP returned in 2010 (David Mundell) was appointed a minister, this meant that all four Conservative members appointed to the committee represented English constituencies. Conservative strength is somewhat greater in Wales than in Scotland. Even so, in the case of the Welsh Affairs Committee, three of its five Conservative members in 2010 were drawn from English constituencies.

Party strength, though, poses a more serious challenge for the Northern Ireland Committee, given that there are no MPs elected in Northern Ireland representing any of the principal UK political parties. This has meant some special provisions have been made for the committee. Unlike other committees, which usually each have 11 members, the Northern Ireland Committee has 14, enabling some MPs from the province to serve on it. In the new Parliament returned in 2010, 5 of the members were drawn from the province (two Democratic Unionists, one SDLP, one Alliance, and one Independent). The remaining members comprised 5 Conservatives (including the chair) and 4 Labour MPs.

In terms of responsibilities, as the Scottish Affairs Committee noted in its annual report in 2009, 'as a result of the Scotland Act 1998 and the Scottish Parliament receiving full legislative powers on 1 July 1999, much of what other committees can and do scrutinise lies outside of our remit' (Scottish Affairs Committee 2009, p. 3). It does little, for example, in respect of draft legislation (indeed, few bills relating exclusively to Scotland are brought forward – the Scotland Bill in 2011–12 was unusual), there are few major public appointments made by the Scotland Office, and there are rarely any treaties that fall within the remit of the Scotland Office. Against that, though, has to be set the fact that the House has vested the committee with a distinct responsibility and that is to establish and maintain relations with the Scottish Parliament on behalf of the House.

In pursuit of its scrutiny role, the committee has variously examined the devolution settlement and the various changes undertaken or proposed to that settlement: these have included the proposals of the Commission on Scottish Devolution (the Calman Commission, 2007–9) for greater powers to be transferred – implemented in large measure through the Scotland Act 2012 – and the demand of the SNP government in Scotland for a referendum on Scottish independence. Its more regular reports – it produces approximately four or five a year, though the long session of 2010–12 enabled it to be especially productive (see Table 8.1) – have covered policy matters that fall within the remit of the UK government. These have included, for example, credit unions, the press industry, health and safety, the student immigration system, postal services, the Crown Estate, blacklisting in employment, and poverty, all as they affect Scotland.

In pursuit of its responsibility to maintain relations with the Scottish Parliament, the committee makes various visits to Scotland. Some of these are to meet different organizations or to launch a committee report. However, some are to engage in dialogue with the parliament or its committees. In 2009, for example, it held a meeting in Glasgow with the parliament's EU and External Relations Committee. It also on occasion takes evidence from MSPs or Scottish parliamentary bodies. In its inquiry into credit unions in Scotland, for example, it heard from representatives of the Scottish Parliament cross-parliamentary group on tackling debt. This, though, is exceptional. Most evidence is presented by affected bodies and the committee hears more frequently from members of the UK government, most notably the Scottish Secretary.

Table 8.1   Reports by the Scottish, Welsh and Northern Ireland Affairs Select Committees 2010–12

Scottish Affairs Committee
The Referendum on Separation for Scotland: Do you agree this is a biased question?
The Crown Estate in Scotland
The Referendum on Separation for Scotland: Unanswered Questions
Student Immigration System in Scotland
The Scotland Bill
UK Border Agency and Glasgow City Council
Video Games Industry in Scotland
Postal Services in Scotland

Welsh Affairs Committee
Inward Investment in Wales
Representation of Consumer Interests in Wales
Pre-Appointment Hearing with the Government's Preferred Candidate for the Chairman of S4C Authority
S4C
Proposed Legislative Competence Orders Relating to Organ Donation and Cycle Paths
The Future of Newport Passport Office
The Implications for Wales of the Government's Proposals on Constitutional Reform
The Severn Crossings Toll

Northern Ireland Affairs Committee
Fuel Laundering and Smuggling in Northern Ireland
Corporation Tax in Northern Ireland
Air Passenger Duty: Implications for Northern Ireland

The Welsh Affairs Committee fulfils a similar but not identical role to that of its Scottish counterpart. As the Secretary of State for Wales told the Committee in 2007 'we are not a spending department' (Welsh Affairs Committee 2010, p. 5). Rather, the committee focuses on government policy in respect of Wales and also – again a particular task vested in it by the House – providing a link with the National Assembly for Wales. This particular role resulted in it acquiring a task of pre-legislative scrutiny (something not shared by the Scottish Affairs Committee) of Legislative Competence Orders in Council. These were the means by which legislative competence was variously transferred in particular areas from Westminster to the National Assembly for Wales. The committee devoted resources to considering each order, in so doing effectively doubling its workload. Between 2007 and 2011, 15 such orders were made. The responsibility, though, was relatively short-lived. The coalition government formed in 2010 triggered a provision under the Government of Wales Act 2006 for a referendum in Wales to enable the assembly to pass legislative measures in all devolved areas. Following a yes vote in the referendum in March 2011 (just over 63 per cent voted yes), the need for Legislative Competence Orders ceased, so the committee reverted to a role not dissimilar to that of the Scottish Affairs Committee.

The Northern Ireland Committee had a particularly onerous task at various points prior to 2007 given that for some of the period responsibility for the government of Northern Ireland rested with the UK government, law being made by Orders in Council subject to assent by both Houses of Parliament. Even after a Northern Ireland Assembly was created, the assembly was suspended briefly in 2000 and then again from October 2002, and was dissolved in April 2003. However, in 2007 agreement was reached on the formation of an executive and assembly in the province and so responsibility passed from London to Stormont. As the Committee recorded in 2010, 'The establishment of the Northern Ireland executive saw our remit significantly reduced and most of our work since has been concerned with policing and justice and with cross-border issues' (Northern Ireland Affairs Committee 2010, p. 3). Some of the issues it considered in the new Parliament returned in 2010 are shown in Table 8.1. In addition to particular inquiries, it also follows the practice of the other committees in holding one-off evidence sessions with the Secretary of State.

The House also has Grand Committees for Scotland, Wales and Northern Ireland. These committees comprise all the MPs holding seats in that part of the UK, though MPs drawn from other parts of the UK may be added. The committees may hear statements from ministers, question ministers, and discuss issues affecting that part of the UK; also some bills and delegated legislation may be sent to them for discussion. In practice, the effect of devolution has resulted in them meeting infrequently and then usually only for general debates. The Welsh Grand Committee, for example, met to discuss four matters in 2008–09, but only met once in both the 2009–10 and the long 2010–12 sessions, on each occasion to discuss the government's programme as it affected Wales.

Inter-parliamentary contact

When the Constitution Committee of the House of Lords investigated inter-institutional relations in the UK in 2002, it found that there was no effective mechanism for contact between the legislative bodies. There were particular problems with respect to Wales (Constitution Committee 2003). The challenge has been to develop relations between the devolved assemblies and Westminster. Part of the problem was keeping track of developments in the different legislatures and of ensuring there was an opportunity for input to be fed in to Westminster from the devolved bodies when relevant legislation was being considered. This was especially the case with Wales, given its dependence on Westminster for legislation, especially in the period prior to the transfer of legislative competence in 2011.

Various attempts have been made to increase co-operation. These have included ensuring Parliament is better informed when legislative consent motions have been passed or sought as well as practical adjustments, such as enhancing facilities for members of devolved bodies to visit Westminster and for MPs and peers to visit devolved bodies. Among proposals advanced, but not acted upon, was one for a joint liaison committee of the Scottish and Westminster parliaments and another for a 'super' Scottish Grand Committee, bringing together MPs, MEPs and MSPs from Scotland.

The principal structural link, though, is through the departmental select committees. As we have seen, the Scottish, Welsh and Northern Ireland Affairs Committees have been vested with responsibility for maintaining contact with the devolved bodies. There are also now regular meetings between clerks in the different bodies. Initially, contact was facilitated by the fact that the presiding officers of the three devolved legislatures were also members of the House of Lords (Lord Steel in Scotland, Lord Alderdice in Northern Ireland and Lord Elis-Thomas in Wales), and so had contact when in the Lords, but that ceased to be the case when they retired (Lord Steel in 2003 and Lord Alderdice in 2004) and no such institutional link remains.

Parliamentary adaptation

Devolution has created two problems for Parliament. One is internal to it, deriving from the fact of devolution, and the other affects the relationship between the different parts of the United Kingdom, deriving from the asymmetrical nature of devolution.

Internal challenges

The transfer of law-effecting powers to Scotland, Northern Ireland and more recently Wales has left the Westminster Parliament with little to do with respect to the different parts of the United Kingdom, other than England. As such, it undertakes no role comparable to that for EU legislation. The distinction between the two is significant. EU law applies throughout the European Union, and hence is applicable throughout the United Kingdom, but the Scottish Parliament has no remit beyond the borders of Scotland.

Parliament has therefore had to struggle to define and develop a relationship with the elected legislative bodies in the different parts of the United Kingdom. This it has done through the departmental select committees. They provide a systematic means of scrutinizing government policy as it affects Scotland, Wales and Northern Ireland, and – as we have seen – the committees seek to maintain contact with the respective devolved legislatures. However, two problems remain. One is establishing a link with the chamber. This has been a problem especially in the House of Commons. As we have seen, matters that fall within the remit of a devolved body cannot be raised in the House. There is a tendency, therefore, to leave it to the select committees to address issues relating to devolution. In the House of Lords, there is no committee dealing specifically with the devolved parts of the UK – the issue of devolution, as a constitutional issue, falls within the remit of the Constitution Committee, but is but one of many such issues considered by the committee – and matters affecting Scotland, Wales or Northern Ireland have, therefore, to be considered, where appropriate, in the chamber. Discussion is facilitated by the fact that several peers are or have been members of the devolved bodies. As we have seen, the first presiding officer of each was a peer. A number of ministers in the devolved bodies have been elevated to the peerage following their ministerial service. (For example, the Democratic Unionist Lord Bannside – Ian Paisley – was First Minister of Northern Ireland when the new power-sharing administration was formed in 2007, Liberal Democrat Lord Wallace of Tankerness was Deputy First Minister in Scotland 1999–2005 and Labour peer Lord McConnell was First Minister in Scotland 2001–7). Some, like the original presiding officers, have served simultaneously as members of a devolved body and the House of Lords, such as, in the case of the Scottish Parliament, the Earl of Selkirk (Conservative) and Lord Foulkes (Labour).

The other problem has been keeping pace with developments in respect of devolution. It has been difficult to establish a steady-state relationship when the powers of the devolved bodies keep changing. As we have seen, the situation in respect of Wales has changed significantly as a consequence of the Government of Wales Act 2006 and the 'yes' vote in the March 2011 referendum on the transfer of legislative powers. In 2011, the government appointed a commission (the Silk Commission) to examine the financial accountability of the Welsh government and National Assembly for Wales and issues of fiscal devolution and accountability in Wales. Further powers were ceded to Scotland by the Scotland Act 2012, but the SNP government in Scotland pressed for a referendum on Scottish independence. Agreement was reached with the UK government on holding such a referendum in 2014. Though parliamentary committees in Westminster have been able to contribute to debate on these developments – the Constitution Committee of the Lords and Scottish Affairs Committee in the Commons both producing important reports on the proposed referendum (Constitution Committee 2012a; Scottish Affairs Committee 2012) – the problem has been to establish a means of monitoring devolution holistically. Each House, especially the House of Commons, has had to adapt to the various changes in the different parts of the United Kingdom, but without the equivalent of an over-arching committee, such as the EU Scrutiny Committee. It is rather analogous to the Lords having the EU Committee sub-committees, but without having the EU Committee itself.

The West Lothian Question

The UK-wide problem derives from the asymmetrical nature of devolution, in that devolution has only occurred in parts of the United Kingdom, with no devolution in England. Parliament at Westminster thus combines being both a UK Parliament for certain issues and an English Parliament for others. This creates a problem in terms of voting by MPs. MPs sitting for Scottish seats are entitled to vote on issues affecting the English health service, but MPs representing English seats are not entitled to vote on matters affecting Scottish health services, given that this is a matter for the Scottish Parliament.

This problem has been styled the 'West Lothian Question', after the then Labour MP for West Lothian, Tam Dalyell, who raised it in debate on devolution in the 1970s. The issue, though, was by no means a new one and had been raised during debate on Irish home rule in the nineteenth century (Norton 2011b, pp. 177–9). The problem in the nineteenth century proved as intractable as it did in the twentieth century. Various proposals were put forward during debates on Irish home rule, including excluding members from Ireland from sitting in the Westminster parliament, excluding MPs from Irish seats voting on issues other than 'Imperial' issues, and reducing the number of seats in Ireland. The last of these was applied in the case of Northern Ireland during the existence of the Stormont parliament (1922–72). The number of seats was less than the population of the province would otherwise justify. After the Stormont parliament was suspended and then abolished, legislation was introduced to increase the number of Northern Irish seats. During the existence of the Stormont parliament, MPs returned to Westminster from Northern Ireland retained the same rights as all other MPs. This was only challenged in the 1964–6 Parliament, when the government had a miniscule overall majority and the votes of Northern Ireland MPs may have made the difference to the outcome of a particular vote (Norton 2011b, p. 179).

The proposals for what in the nineteenth century was known as the 'in and out' option (MPs from the devolved part of the UK only voting on UK wide issues) and for reducing the number of MPs were advanced following devolution in 1999. Various committees, commissions and individual parliamentarians advanced the proposals or variants thereof (see House of Commons Library 2012). The Conservative Party in particular favoured 'English votes for English laws', that is, only MPs sitting for English seats being able to vote on legislation that affects only England. Following the formation of a coalition government in 2010, it persuaded its partner party, the Liberal Democrats, to agree to setting up a Commission on the West Lothian question.

Critics of the proposal for allowing only MPs from English seats to vote on English-only legislation argued that it would create two tiers of MPs and make it difficult especially for a Labour government, reliant on its seats in Scotland, to pass legislation affecting only England if, as is more often the case, the Conservatives hold a majority of seats in England. There is also the problem of identifying legislation that applies exclusively to England (or to England and Wales); even if dealing ostensibly with English law, it may have significant consequences for other parts of the United Kingdom.

In practice, the only proposal that has been implemented has been that of reducing the number of MPs returned from Scotland. (There has been no equivalent change in Wales or Northern Ireland.) The number of Scottish seats was reduced in the 2005 general election from 72 to 59, but this took account only of the fact that Scotland was already over-represented in relation to the size of its population. The reduction brought the electoral quota in Scotland into line with that in England, which did not have its own parliament. Critics argued that, to take account of Scotland having its own parliament (equivalent to what happened in Northern Ireland with the original Stormont Parliament), then a further reduction in the number of seats was necessary.

When he was Lord Chancellor, Lord Irvine of Lairg famously said that the best way to deal with the West Lothian Question was not to ask it. His comment acknowledged that it was a largely unanswerable question. The only clear solutions were either repealing the devolution settlement, so that there was no devolution, or creating an English parliament, thus ensuring symmetry. One compromise would be English regionalism, with regional parliaments, but this largely faded from view following a large 'no' vote in a referendum held in the North-East of England in 2004.

The problem was exacerbated by concerns in England over the method of funding the different parts of the United Kingdom (the Barnett formula), with Scotland, Wales and Northern Ireland being perceived as enjoying disproportionately higher funding than England. Added to the perceive unfairness of Scottish MPs being able to vote on English issues, this created what became known as the 'English question', essentially the question of how England copes with the post-devolution settlement. Some bodies, not least but not only English nationalist bodies, made the case for an English Parliament. The Campaign for an English Parliament (www.thecep.org.uk) has argued that whereas Scotland, Wales and Northern Ireland each has a legislative body as a distinct nation, 'England has nothing. The British government refuses to give any such political and constitutional recognition to England.' As England developed a distinct identity, so, it argued, it needed its own parliament.

The constitutional position was also muddied by the demands in Scotland for independence. If the SNP achieved a 'yes' vote in an independence referendum, what would be the effects for the rest of the United Kingdom? One argument was that independence would not have a major structural implication for Parliament. The Act of Union supposedly represented a joining of two parliaments, but in practice meant Scottish MPs joining English MPs at Westminster (Bradley and Ewing 2007, pp. 75–6), so independence for Scotland would simply result in the removal of Scottish MPs from Westminster. Others, however, envisaged more profound changes. The Welsh First Minister, Carwyn Jones, argued that in the event of Scottish independence the House of Lords should be recast as a federal chamber.

Parliament has thus had to adapt to changes to the relationship between the different parts of the United Kingdom as well as address, or rather seek to keep abreast of, demands for further change. In large measure,

Parliament has been in response mode, dealing with demands emanating from the different parts of the United Kingdom. The UK government has occasionally taken the initiative, as with the appointment of the Silk Commission in 2011, but much of the impetus for change has come from outside London.

Conclusion

Devolution, like membership of the European Communities, has created notable problems for Parliament. It has had to adapt to a new situation. Though there has been some experience of a devolved legislature, in the form of the Stormont Parliament in Northern Ireland from 1922 to 1972, it constituted a limited, and not exactly helpful, precedent on which to draw.

The principal challenge has been institutional. In terms of its formal powers, Parliament retains the capacity to legislate for the whole of the United Kingdom, even against the wishes of the devolved bodies. In practice, it chooses not to do so, but there is no legal prohibition to it doing so. The political reality means that, in any event, its coercive capacity has not been exercised, given executive dominance of Westminster. It had devolved powers that previously were utilized by the executive enjoying majority control in Westminster.

Having devolved powers to other bodies, it then had the challenge to adapt to the new situation. This is analogous to the situation in respect of the EU. Having transferred some legislative competences to the institutions of the then European Communities, the two Houses then established committees to engage in a form of pre-legislative scrutiny. With devolution, the House of Commons has handed over responsibility for scrutiny to extant departmental select committees. The situation differs, though, in that there is not a single 'devolution' committee and there is no regular pre-legislative scrutiny to be undertaken. The House may thus be argued to have adapted less well to devolution than it has to membership of the European Communities.

A number of proposals have been advanced to enable Parliament to achieve a better overview of devolution and to develop closer links with the devolved bodies. Achieving change, though, remains a challenge. Westminster has still not fully come to terms with the implications of devolution. The sheer number of MPs from Scotland, Wales and Northern Ireland in Westminster means that MPs generally are aware of the issue of devolution, even if they rarely have the opportunity to discuss it. For

MPs sitting for Scottish seats, there is the frustration of knowing that many issues that concern their constituents cannot be raised in the House. For MPs representing English seats, there is the knowledge that their colleagues from Scotland can vote on matters that affect only England and almost certainly have a lighter workload than they do.

The need for greater co-operation has been recognized by the different bodies that have addressed the relationships between the different legislative bodies in the UK. As we have seen, various proposals have been advanced. However, as the Scottish Affairs Committee in the Commons observed, 'it is political will that will drive forward real change' (Scottish Affairs Committee 2010, p. 3). Much of the debate, rather like membership of the EU, has been at the level of constitutional change – an English parliament, English votes for English laws, Scottish independence – rather than focused on the more systematic scrutiny of the devolution settlement and relations between Westminster and elected bodies in Scotland, Wales and Northern Ireland.

Though England dominates the UK in terms both of population and wealth – with over 85 per cent of both – the issue of devolution remains a highly salient political issue. For Parliament, it is a case of both addressing demands for constitutional change and adapting its practices and procedures. Though there is still a lot that could be done, not least in achieving a more holistic view of devolution, both Houses have adapted to the changed situation since 1999. The use of committees has enabled the Commons to achieve some scrutiny of government policy as it affects different parts of the United Kingdom and to develop some links with the elected bodies in Scotland, Wales and Northern Ireland. The situation denies neatness and symmetry, but Parliament has at least coped with the political realities of a complex and shifting constitutional framework.

9

Parliament and the Courts

Constitutional change in recent decades has had a further consequence for the constitution: that has been to create a new juridical dimension. The courts, previously subordinate to Parliament – a position confirmed in 1688–9 under the judicially self-imposed doctrine of parliamentary sovereignty – have acquired a new role (Norton 2005).

This dimension derives principally from three major constitutional changes. Two comprise the changes that we have discussed in the preceding two chapters: membership of the EU and devolution. The other is the incorporation of most of the provisions of the European Convention on Human Rights into UK law through the Human Rights Act 1998.

One consequence of membership of the EC was that, as we have noted (Chapter 7) any case involving a conflict between European and UK law was to the resolved by the courts. Under the European Communities Act 1972, questions of law are to be determined by the European Court of Justice or in accordance with decisions of that court. Cases in the UK that reach the Supreme Court are, unless the justices consider that the law has already been settled by the ECJ, referred to the ECJ for a definitive ruling.

The UK courts are enjoined to interpret UK law in so far as possible to render it compatible with EC law, but in the event of conflict European law is to take precedence. The full implications of this were not fully recognized at the time of UK membership and only became apparent as a result of some high-profile cases in the 1990s. In the *Factortame* case in 1990–1, the European Court of Justice held that UK law may be suspended while a final determination was made in cases where there appeared to be a *prima facie* clash with EC law. In the *Ex Parte EOC* case in 1994, the law lords struck down a provision of an Act of Parliament, the 1978 Employment Protection (Consolidation) Act, because it conflicted with EU law (Maxwell 1999; Double 2004). Following the case, *The Times* declared that 'Britain may now have, for the first time in its history, a constitutional court' (cited in Maxwell 1999, p. 197).

Though there have been few cases of such prominence since, the Supreme Court variously refers cases to the ECJ. Thus, for example, in 2012 it considered a case which it had referred to the ECJ to determine the meaning of 'worker' under a European directive. A barrister who had sat as a fee-paid Recorder was not eligible for a pension under UK Regulations but claimed that he should be so entitled under the EU Part-Time Workers Framework Directive. Cases such as this may not attract much attention, but they reflect a significant role now undertaken by the courts. They have the power to override a provision of UK law, albeit a power given them by an Act of Parliament.

Devolution has also had an impact. The courts are, in effect, constitutional courts for Scotland, Wales and Northern Ireland. The devolved bodies can only act within the terms of the legislation that created them. The interpretation of that legislation falls ultimately to the courts. What are formally termed 'devolution issues' were dealt with initially by the Judicial Committee of the Privy Council (see, for example, O'Neill 2001; Winetrobe 2002) before responsibility was transferred to the UK Supreme Court following its creation in 2009. The role of the courts is thus significant in constitutional terms, though the number of devolution issues reaching the Supreme Court is relatively small. In the period from October 2009, when responsibility transferred to the Supreme Court, up to the beginning of 2012, there were, for example, 31 applications to appeal in Scottish criminal cases, but in only 11 cases was leave to appeal granted (Supreme Court 2012, p. 3).

In addition, the courts have acquired a significant role as a result of the enactment of the Human Rights Act 1998, which brought most of the provisions of the European Convention on Human Rights (ECHR) into UK law. The convention lays down basic human rights. It forbids torture, slavery and compulsory labour, and decrees the right to liberty and security of person, and to respect for a private and family life. It also decrees the right to freedom of thought conscience, religion, expression, freedom of assembly and freedom of expression. All of these rights are to be secured without discrimination on grounds such as race, sex, colour of religion.

The convention was produced under the aegis of the Council of Europe, an intergovernmental consultative organization formed in 1949. British lawyers were involved in drafting the convention. It was agreed in 1950 and the United Kingdom ratified it in 1951. The United Kingdom was thus committed to it under international law, but successive governments made no attempt to incorporate it into domestic law. After UK citizens were permitted to appeal to the European Court on Human Rights in

Strasbourg, a number of high profile cases were won against the UK government. As a result, the government introduced legislation to bring UK law into line with the decisions of the Strasbourg court. A number of lawyers and politicians argued the case for the provisions of the convention to be incorporated into UK law. They contended that cases taken directly to the Strasbourg court took years to be decided and those lost by the UK government were an embarrassment to the nation. They also argued that incorporating the provisions of the convention in UK law would provide citizens with a clearer statement of their rights and help create a rights culture. Opponents argued that it would result in power being transferred from elected politicians to unelected judges.

The Labour government elected in 1997 was committed to incorporating the provisions of the ECHR into UK law. It published a White Paper entitled *Rights Brought Home* and then introducing the Human Rights Bill to give effect to its commitment. It was enacted in 1998.

As a consequence of the Act, the courts have to interpret rights enshrined in the convention. The Act maintained the doctrine of parliamentary sovereignty. As a result, the courts are not empowered to strike down measures that fall foul of the ECHR. If a higher court deems a particular provision of UK law to conflict with a convention right, it can issue a declaration of incompatibility. It is then up to Parliament to bring the law into line with the convention, and it has established a fast-track procedure for doing so.

The scale of the change wrought by the Act was such that judges had to be trained in interpretation of the convention. As a result, the main provisions of the Act were not put in place until 2000. The influence of the convention on judges has extended beyond a simple interpretation of the Act, extending to development of the common law (Klug and O'Brien 2002). Parliament, too, has also had to adapt to a new role. It could be argued by some that it is a diminished role. In part, it has transferred a coercive capacity – in practice if not formally – and has had to adapt by developing its capacity to persuade. In this respect, it mirrors its changing relationship with British government

Human Rights Act

The Human Rights Act makes it unlawful for public authorities to act in a way that is incompatible with convention rights. A public authority acting under statutory powers may be challenged because those powers contravene convention rights. It is under section 4 of the Act that the higher courts can issue declarations of incompatibility. When such a declaration is made, Parliament can then act to rectify the position by bringing the law into line with the courts' interpretation of the convention, either by enacting a new law or through a remedial order (a statutory instrument subject to affirmative resolution in both Houses). The first use of the remedial order – the fast-track route for bringing the law into line with the convention – came in 2001 to make amendments to sections of the Mental Health Act found to be incompatible with the convention. A further remedial order was introduced in 2004 to rectify an incompatibility between the Naval Discipline Act 1957 governing the composition of naval courts martial and convention rights to a fair hearing before an independent and impartial tribunal.

The courts have thus acquired a further and important role. By 2011, a total of 27 declarations of incompatibility had been made, though not all were upheld when appealed to the House of Lords or its successor, the Supreme Court. Of the 27, 19 had become final by the end of 2011 (Ministry of Justice 2011, p. 5). The consequence of judicial interpretation of the ECHR has been that various decisions taken by Parliament and enshrined in law have been overturned or modified by the courts.

In 2002, for example, the courts held that the Home Secretary's power under the Crime (Sentences) Act 1997 to set the minimum period that must be served by a prisoner subject to a mandatory life sentence was incompatible with Article 6 of the convention. The Home Secretary's power was removed by the Criminal Justice Act 2003. In 2003, the courts held that a section of the Matrimonial Causes Act 1973 was incompatible with the convention. Parliament then passed the Gender Recognition Act – conferring rights on those who changed gender, including the right to a new birth certificate – to bring the law into line with the court's interpretation. In 2010, provisions of the Safeguarding Vulnerable Groups Act 2006 were held to be incompatible with the convention. The courts held that they did not enable someone barred from working with children or vulnerable adults to make representations as to why they should not be included on a barred list. The government included an amendment to the Protection of Freedoms Bill to amend the 2006 Act.

The courts, in particular, are concerned to ensure that powers granted by Parliament or exercised by ministers are 'proportionate'. A policy goal may be desirable, but the powers vested may be excessive in order to achieve it and may conflict with the provisions of the convention. In 2004, for instance, section 23 of the Anti-terrorism, Crime and Security Act 2001 was held to be disproportionate and permitted the detention of suspected international terrorists in a way that discriminated on the ground of nationality or immigration status. The provision was repealed by the Prevention of Terrorism Act 2005. A provision of the 2005 Act was later subject to a declaration of incompatibility by the Administrative Court, but the declaration was overturned by the Court of Appeal and the Appeal Court's decision was upheld by the House of Lords.

The courts have thus variously utilized their power to issue declarations of incompatibility, including in some notably high-profile cases. Its decision in 2004 on the Anti-Terrorism Act attracted particular criticism, not least from ministers. However, two qualifications have to be noted. First, the cases in which declarations of incompatibility are made and upheld are few in number, averaging fewer than two a year. Second, the courts recognize that Parliament is democratically elected and may give it the benefit of the doubt (see Edwards 2002; Clayton 2004). There is thus a margin of appreciation for what Parliament enacts.

The courts fulfil their judicial role as interpreters of an Act of Parliament. The broad scope of convention rights has given them greater scope for interpretation (determining, for example, what is encompassed within the right to privacy) than is usually the case with statutes that are drawn in specific terms. The challenge to Parliament has been how to cope with the new constitutional framework created by the Act. One option would be to *do nothing* and simply leave it to the courts to determine cases brought before them under the Act. Another would be to see the role in relation to the courts as *competing*, effectively challenging or seeking to amend the law when the courts deliver judgments that are unpalatable to parliamentarians. A third is to the see the role as *complementary* and, in effect, fulfilling a distinct role of scrutiny in relation to human rights. Whereas the courts are confined to adjudicating on cases brought before them, Parliament has scope to fulfil a wider remit. It not only examines bills to determine whether they comply with convention rights – in effect reducing the likely pressure on the courts – but also keep under review the scope and effectiveness of human rights protection in the UK. As such, it may be seen principally as a partner with the courts in keeping in check attempts by government or other public bodies to encroach on human rights. Indeed, according to Alison Young, the Act facilitates a 'democratic dialogue' between courts and Parliament (Young 2009). Together, they may serve to create a culture shift in the sphere of human rights.

It is largely this third route that has been adopted by Parliament. At times, the government has given the impression of going down the second route, the adversarial route, with ministers on occasion attacking judges for some of the decisions they have reached. Indeed, at one point, Tony Blair as Prime Minister dropped heavy hints that it may be time to consider amending the Act. Conservative leader David Cameron spoke of crafting a specific English Bill of Rights and Responsibilities. The coalition government formed in 2010 agreed to establish a commission to examine the case for an English Bill of Rights.

At times the courts have rendered judgments that have been opposed by parliamentarians. This has been most notably the case with prisoners' voting rights. The European Court on Human Rights has held the UK's blanket ban on prisoners being able to vote to be incompatible with the convention. Ministers in successive government have not moved with any haste to rectify the situation and MPs have voted overwhelmingly against prisoners being given the vote. However, the stance of Parliament following passage of the 1998 Act has been primarily a proactive and rights-based one. This has been shown most evidently in the creation of the Joint Committee on Human Rights.

The Joint Committee on Human Rights

The Joint Committee on Human Rights (JCHR) was established at the beginning of 2001 (see Evans 2004). It has 12 members, six from each House, and is aided by a legal adviser; it has the powers of a select committee, and can thus examine witnesses as well as meet at places outside Westminster. As a joint committee, it has been able to utilize the skills of members of both Houses. A number of senior MPs and peers have been appointed. The first chair of the committee, Jean Corston MP, was also chair of the parliamentary Labour Party. The House of Lords has normally appointed some senior lawyers. Indeed, of the members of the joint committee in the 2012–13 Session (see Table 9.1) four of the six peers were leading barristers. One – Lord Lester of Herne Hill – is generally acknowledged as being one of people principally responsible for achieving the introduction and passage of the Human Rights Act.

The JCHR was created in order to consider 'matters relating to human rights in the United Kingdom (but excluding consideration of individual cases)' and remedial orders introduced under the Human Rights Act. In practice, the committee has utilized its broad terms of reference to consider each government bill brought before Parliament for compatibility with the Human Rights Act. It announced its intention so to do in its First Special Report: 'Where appropriate our Chairman will put written questions to the relevant Minister in charge of the bill and we may, in the light of the answers we receive, decide to conduct a detailed inquiry of the bill' (Joint Committee on Human Rights 2001, para. 1). Since then, it has

Table 9.1   Members of the Joint Committee on Human Rights, Session
2012–13

Member	Party	Background
Dr Hywel Francis MP (Chair)	Labour	Former professor of adult continuing education
Rheman Chisti MP	Conservative	Barrister
Mike Crockart MP	Lib Dem	Former police constable and IT Project manager
Dominic Raab MP	Conservative	Lawyer; also served in Foreign and Commonwealth Office
Virendra Sharma MP	Labour	Former council day services manager
Richard Shepherd MP	Conservative	Former company director
Baroness Berridge	Conservative	Barrister
Lord Faulks QC	Conservative	Barrister; Recorder
Baroness Kennedy of the Shaws QC	Labour	Barrister
Lord Lester of Herne Hill QC	Lib Dem	Barrister
Baroness Lister of Burtersett	Labour	Former professor of social policy
Baroness O'Loan	Cross-bencher	Former law lecturer and Police Ombudsman for Northern Ireland

extended its coverage to private members' bills and private bills, and begun to consider the extent to which bills comply with obligations and guarantees contained in international human rights instruments, other than the ECHR, to which the UK is a party (Corston 2004, p. 164). The result has been a significant correspondence with ministers, all of which has been published. Each government bill is examined by the committee's legal adviser, who reports to the committee on whether it has implications for human rights. The committee normally, though not always, accepts that advice.

The joint committee has proved to be an active one. In the first five years of its existence, up to the end of the 2001–5 Parliament, it issued 90 reports. In the 2005–10 Parliament, it published 129 (Hunt *et al.* 2012, p. 22). Its first report was on the implementation of the Human Rights Act. The committee examined the extent to which government departments had prepared for the implementation of the Act and begun to build a 'human rights culture'. It has been especially vigilant in reporting on anti-terrorism legislation and has variously challenged government over its use of control orders, arguing that their use was bound to lead to breaches of the ECHR. Most of its work comprises scrutinizing legislation. Table 9.2 lists the reports issued by the JCHR in the long 2010–12 Session,

Table 9.2 Reports from the Joint Committee on Human Rights, Session 2010–12

First Report *Work of the Committee in 2009–10*
Second Report *Legislative Scrutiny: Identity Documents Bill*
Third Report *Legislative Scrutiny: Terrorist Asset-Freezing etc. Bill (Preliminary Report)*
Fourth Report *Terrorist Asset-Freezing etc Bill (Second Report); and other Bills*
Fifth Report *Proposal for the Asylum and Immigration (Treatment of Claimants, etc) Act 2004 (Remedial) Order 2010*
Sixth Report *Legislative Scrutiny: (1) Superannuation Bill; (2) Parliamentary Voting System and Constituencies Bill*
Seventh Report *Legislative Scrutiny: Public Bodies Bill; other Bills*
Eighth Report *Renewal of Control Orders Legislation*
Ninth Report *Draft Asylum and Immigration (Treatment of Claimants, etc) Act 2004 (Remedial) Order 2010 — second Report*
Tenth Report *Facilitating Peaceful Protest*
Eleventh Report *Legislative Scrutiny: Police Reform and Social Responsibility Bill*
Twelfth Report *Legislative Scrutiny: Armed Forces Bill*
Thirteenth Report *Legislative Scrutiny: Education Bill*
Fourteenth Report *Terrorism Act 2000 (Remedial) Order 2011*
Fifteenth Report *The Human Rights Implications of UK Extradition Policy*
Sixteenth Report Legislative *Scrutiny: Terrorism Prevention and Investigation Measures Bill*
Seventeenth Report *The Terrorism Act 2000 (Remedial) Order 2011: Stop and Search without Reasonable Suspicion (second Report)*
Eighteenth Report *Legislative Scrutiny: Protection of Freedoms Bill*
Nineteenth Report *Proposal for the Sexual Offences Act 2003 (Remedial) Order 2011*
Twentieth Report *Legislative Scrutiny: Terrorism Prevention and Investigation Measures Bill (Second Report)*
Twenty-first Report *Legislative Scrutiny: Welfare Reform Bill*
Twenty-second Report *Legislative Scrutiny: Legal Aid, Sentencing and Punishment of Offenders Bill*
Twenty-third Report *Implementation of the Right of Disabled People to Independent Living*

reflecting both the scale of its activities as well as the focus on legislation. However, it also reports on wider issues. Thus, for example, it has reported on matters such as deaths in custody and the meaning of 'public authority' under the Human Rights Act. The committee, after a two-year investigation, advocated the creation of a Human Rights Commission and the government subsequently established a Commission for Equality and Human Rights, largely in line with the committee's recommendation.

The JCHR represents Parliament's way of dealing with a situation that it has itself sanctioned. Parliament has enacted a measure to protect rights, in effect limiting its own capacity to determine rights, and then established a body to ensure that bills comply with those provisions. Despite occasional controversy, the committee has established itself as a significant element of Parliament's scrutiny powers. Apart from influencing particular decisions, it has persuaded departments to place more information in the public domain, especially material underpinning claims that a bill is compliant with the ECHR (Corston 2004; Hazell 2004, p. 498). As a consequence, it has helped to build up in government what Jean Corston termed 'a culture of justification' rather than one of assertion (Corston 2004).

Though the committee has continued to press government to enhance its leadership in using the Act to its full potential, it has prompted a more co-ordinated approach within government. Following a review of the implementation of the Act, a Senior Human Rights Champions Network was established. In a 2010 response to a JCHR report, the government reported that the network met every three months 'to share good practice and information across Whitehall and is an important vehicle to maintain human rights momentum within Departments' (Joint Committee on Human Rights 2010, p. 8). Each department, it reported, was taking steps to implement a human rights framework, including within its agencies and sponsored bodies. The Ministry of Justice was also working with the UK's inspectorates and regulatory bodies to provide leadership for the implementation of a human rights approach within these bodies.

The JCHR has also served to affect the culture of both Houses. As we have seen in respect of both the European Scrutiny Committee and the departmental select committees on Scottish, Welsh and Northern Ireland Affairs in the Commons, there has been a problem in achieving a link with the chamber. The JCHR appears to have been more successful than the foregoing committees in developing such links. However, as with both European and devolution issues, the link appears to be greater in the House of Lords than in the House of Commons.

The extent to which the JCHR has increased awareness of its activities in the two chambers was demonstrated by research published in 2012 on the extent to which MPs and peers refer to the committee. It found that from the inception of the committee through to the end of the 2005–10 Parliament, there had been 1,029 substantive references to the joint committee (and 1,754 mentions of it). However, there were three striking features. First, and most remarkable, was the sharp increase in substantive references in the 2005–10 Parliament compared with the preceding Parliament. In the 2001–5 Parliament, there were 23 substantive mentions and in the 2005–10 Parliament there were 1,006 (Hunt *et al.* 2012, p. 19). Secondly, the same period also saw a significant increase in references to human rights (of 23,328 mentions, over 17,000 were in the 2005–10 Parliament). As the authors note, there may be several explanations for this sharp increase in references to the JCHR and to human rights. One may be the practice of the joint committee encouraging members to move amendments to bills to give effect to committee recommendations, thus highlighting the work of the committee. Another may be the fact that following the bombings in London in July 2005 and the extent to which Parliament debated anti-terrorism legislation, there was a greater awareness and certainly greater opportunities to debate issues affecting human rights (Hunt *et al.* 2012, p. 22). Of the references, 60 per cent were in the context of legislative scrutiny (Hunt *et al.* 2012, pp. 30–1).

These data may support the view that Parliament was developing a culture of discussing human rights. In so far as it was – the third feature – it was more notably so in the House of Lords than in the House of Commons. Approximately two-thirds of all references (66 per cent) to JCHR reports were made in the House of Lords (and hence only 34 per cent in the House of Commons). It could also be described as something of a specific sub-culture in that the references tended to be made by the same members. Seven parliamentarians were described as high frequency users, each making 30 or more references to the reports. These comprised two MPs and five peers; all bar one were members of the JCHR (Hunt *et al.* 2012, pp. 24–6). There were 43 parliamentarians who made at least 5 references and, perhaps more relevantly in developing a human rights culture, 241 who made at least one substantive reference. Furthermore, as the report noted:

> The great majority of substantive references supported or reflected the position of the JCHR, but, not surprisingly, some references were opposed to the position of the JCHR. In either case it is clear that the

work of the JCHR has provoked debate in Parliament about human rights. (Hunt *et al.* 2012, p. 24)

The work of the JCHR has thus not only provided a specialized means of examining human rights – not least ensuring that the government complies with the ECHR and develops a human rights culture – but also had some impact on both Houses. It has not been a case of members leaving it to the JCHR and not paying attention to its work. Rather, as we have seen, recent years have seen a remarkable increase in references to it by name in the two chambers as well as a notable increase in references to human rights. It has fulfilled an important role in advising each House of the human rights implications of legislation being brought forward by government. It is perhaps in this respect that it has the advantage over the committees dealing with EU and devolution legislation in that these committees do not get the same opportunity to report on legislation (because there is relatively little of it) being brought before the House.

Parliamentary adaptation

How successful has Parliament been in adapting to the situation created by the Human Rights Act? The Act is formally the same as any other Act of Parliament, but in practice – rather like the Bill of Rights 1689 – it is treated as a statute of great constitutional significance. In terms of the pluralist view of power, the courts have been vested with what amounts to an enhanced persuasive capacity. Though Parliament is not bound by decisions of the courts, the UK is bound by the ECHR. Decisions of UK courts may be appealed to the European Court at Strasbourg. Given that, the likelihood of Parliament exercising its coercive capacity is low. The fact that it exists is important, but the political reality is that it is not going to be exercised other than in the most exceptional circumstances. What is important, therefore, is how Parliament has developed its extant persuasive capacity. As we have seen, it has sought to do so alongside, rather than in competition with, that of the courts. Parliament may seek to influence the courts in terms of how human rights are interpreted, but it has a more consistent role in scrutinizing government in how it deals with human rights. It has the advantage over the courts in that it examines bills. The courts interpret Acts. The Joint Committee on Human Rights checks that a bill is compatible with the ECHR as soon as it is introduced into Parliament; there is, therefore, time for it to influence government and achieve changes to the measure.

Given the constraints within which Parliament operates, it could be argued that it has adapted as well as it can in relation to the Human Rights Act.

The persuasive capacity of Parliament is essentially exercised jointly through the JCHR and each chamber. The government engages in a dialogue with the JCHR and amendments may be made to a bill. That is an important aspect of its work. However, the work of each House, and that of the JCHR in particular, is seen in a somewhat different light when viewed from the other perspectives of power. In terms of agenda-setting, or non-decision-making, then the deterrent effect becomes important. Ministers and officials know that all their bills will be checked for compatibility with the ECHR. Though ministers are required to certify that a bill is compatible with the ECHR, Parliament does not take that certificate to be conclusive, and the JCHR may take a different view. The result has been expressed well by the first chair of the Committee. Jean Corston, identified 'the *threat* of parliamentary scrutiny' and an adverse opinion from the Joint Committee as the key to influencing ministers and officials. As she said:

> the growing awareness that within government departments that each and every bill will be examined by us means, I believe, that the human rights implications of proposed legislation are subject to specially anxious scrutiny by departmental lawyers and draftsmen, and where there are problems, it is more likely that they will be drawn to the attention of Ministers before bills are published. (Corston 2004, p. 165)

This is a view reinforced by a former legal adviser to the Joint Committee, Professor David Feldman, who concluded that fewer government bills in the 2002–3 session gave rise to serious rights concerns than had been the case in the two preceding sessions: 'Fewer provisions are drafted in ways that leave rights subject, in my view, to inadequate safeguards' (quoted in Hazell 2004, p. 498). This has occurred at the same time, as we have seen, as the reports of the JCHR and references to human rights are becoming more pronounced in the two Houses, especially the House of Lords. The deterrent effect may be seen especially in the case of the House of Lords. This may be attributed to the number of peers who are senior lawyers (some, like Lord Lester of Herne Hill, being prominent in the field of human rights) and the fact that the government lacks a majority in the House. The House has a reputation for being especially vigilant in respect of measures that may encroach on human rights. The reports of the JCHR thus provide useful material for it. As we have seen, references to the committee are more pronounced in the Lords than in the Commons.

Viewed from the institutional perspective, we can see what has happened in two different lights. On the one hand, the Human Rights Act has accorded new powers, certainly an enhanced prominence, to the courts, representing a transfer of some competence from Parliament to the judiciary. On the other hand, Parliament has created its own institutional arrangements and the committee process in respect of measures affecting human rights is now well established and accepted by government.

The JCHR is not in a position to say no to government, but government accepts the institutional process: all bills are considered by the JCHR. The *process* is important and limiting, especially in a deterrent sense. It may limit the flow of bills – government may decide not to bring a bill forward because of its implications for human rights. It may so decide (consciously or subconsciously) because it anticipates the reaction of the Joint Committee on Human Rights or, for that matter, the courts (or both). Government prefers to avoid a negative response from either.

Conclusion

The passage of the Human Rights Act 1998 has arguably had a paradoxical consequence. At one level, Parliament has handed over a role that it previously held, that of guardian of human rights, to the courts. Yet at another, the consequence has been to create within Parliament a more consistent focus on, and greater awareness of, issues of human rights than was previously the case. Whereas prior to 1998, attention to human rights in Parliament was essentially sporadic, since then – and more especially since 2005 – there has been far more notice taken of human rights issues. As we have seen, the stance taken by Parliament has essentially been one complementary to, rather than competing with, the courts. The principal means of achieving this has been the creation of the JCHR. The commitment of members of the joint committee (as well as the background of several of them) ensures that it works as well as it can within the boundaries within which it operates.

There thus exist within Parliament the two levels of debate that are observable in respect of the EU and devolution. There is a high level constitutional debate. Should the UK remain a member of the EU? Should England have its own Parliament? Should Scotland be granted independence? In the case of human rights, should there be a distinct

British Bill of Rights? These issues attract significant media and public attention, with views tapped by opinion polls. There is then the second level, essentially the consistent scrutiny that takes place of what is occurring within the context of membership of the EU, devolution, and the Human Rights Act. There is a major debate as to what *should* be, but Parliament has proved willing to address what *is*. So long as the Human Rights Act is in place, then there is a role for Parliament in examining its implications and indeed generating a human rights culture within both government and Parliament. As such, Parliament and its committees – in other words, institutions – matter.

Part III
Parliament and Citizen

10

Representing the People

The history of Parliament, as we have seen, has largely been shaped by its relationship to the executive. Yet there is another relationship that is important, that of Parliament to the people. Each relationship has had an impact on the other, though the distinction between the two is especially important in the context of Parliament's longevity. Parliament is the national representative assembly. However, the nature of its relationship to the people, like its relationship to the executive, has changed substantially over time.

Fundamental to understanding Parliament is the concept of representation (see Loewenberg 2011, Chapter 2). The term itself post-dates the development of Parliament and has been accorded several meanings. The word itself has come into the English language through French derivatives of the Latin *repraesentare* (meaning 'to make present or manifest or to present again') and did not assume a political meaning until the sixteenth century (Beard and Lewis 1959, pp. 22–3; Pitkin 1967, pp. 241–52). The term has come to be used in different ways. It is possible to identify four separate usages (see Pitkin 1967):

(i)   acting on behalf of some individual or group (that is, defending or promoting the interests of the person or body 'represented');
(ii)   being freely elected;
(iii) replicating the typical characteristics of a group or class (as in socioeconomic background or, as in a survey, a sample group); and
(iv)   acting as a symbol ('standing for' something: for example, a monarch or flag 'representing' the unity of the nation).

All four usages are relevant for analysing Parliament. However, because of Parliament's longevity, pre-dating the emergence of a mass electorate in the nineteenth century, none is problem free.

Acting on behalf of some individual or group

The use of the term as denoting acting on behalf of some individual or group has been common in Britain from at least the beginning of the seventeenth century (Beard and Lewis 1959, p. 23) and is the key to understanding Parliament's contemporary role and its popular legitimacy. However, the way in which it has served as a representative body has changed fundamentally over time.

Parliament existed initially to fulfil a form of functional representation. Those summoned to give assent to the monarch's demand for more money attended in order to give assent on behalf of the clergy, barons and different communities (counties and boroughs). As we have seen (Chapter 2), what emerged over time were two Houses, with the Lords comprising the Lords spiritual (the senior clergy) and the Lords temporal (the senior barons). The Commons has its origins in the summoning of knights, and then burgesses, to the king's court. They were summoned from particular *communes*, or organized communities, hence the emergence of the name Commons.

There has thus been a long-standing link between particular communities and members of Parliament. The perception that MPs are 'representatives' of local communities, or constituencies, is well entrenched. However, what has changed over time has been the nature of that link. For most of Parliament's history, the nature of representation by MPs has been what Edmund Burke termed 'virtual representation' (Pitkin 1967, ch. 8). By that, he meant that MPs could speak on behalf of particular interests (such as agriculture and trade), and that what was best for those interests could be discerned without the members necessarily being chosen by popular election. As long as there was at least one constituency defined by a particular interest (say, agriculture) returning an MP, then that member was able to represent the interest as a whole. Indeed, by not being dependent on a popular vote, it was possible to argue that MPs could act in their better interests rather than in response to their immediate opinions. The representative owed the people 'devotion to their interest' rather than 'submission to their will' (quoted in Pitkin 1967, p. 176).

This interpretation thus justified a detachment of Members of Parliament from the people. MPs represented the interests of the people but they were neither elected by the people nor subservient to their views. There was a highly restricted franchise, dictated by custom and statute. From the fifteenth century to the seventeenth, the standard qualification to be an elector in a county seat was ownership of a freehold valued at 40 shillings a year. In the boroughs, the franchise was remarkably varied.

The electorate comprised a small body of electors, normally amenable to patronage or bribery. Many seats were, in effect, owned by local landowners, often members of the House of Lords. Politics were largely conducted 'within parliamentary circles and the drawing rooms connected with them' (Ostrogorski 1902, p. 15). There was a link between MPs and the shires and boroughs, but it was arguably no stronger than that of the landowning aristocrats who had a territorial base.

This Burkean view of representation gave way eventually to a liberal conception. Under this conception, which already held sway in the USA, representation was generally seen in terms of individuals rather than of interests or classes (Pitkin 1967, pp. 190–1). With the country being too large to sustain a system of direct representation (citizens meeting to make decisions) then representatives have to be chosen to act on behalf of citizens. However, the general acceptance of a liberal view of representation did not equate initially to all the people having the vote. There were concerns that not everyone had the capacity to exercise an informed choice and act for the public good rather than for personal benefit. Hence, rather than extending the vote to all – seen in preceding centuries as a dangerously radical view (Birch 1964, ch. 3) – a property franchise was employed, property owners being thought to be better able to exercise a sound judgement than those without property.

The move towards a view of representation encompassing all the adult population was a gradual one. The nineteenth century, as we have seen, was the crucial transitional period. Burkean and liberal views clashed over parliamentary reform. During debate on the 1832 Reform Bill, Sir Robert Peel stuck to the concept of virtual representation, arguing that 'we are here to consult the interests, not to obey the will of the people, if we honestly believe that will conflicts with those interests' (Birch 1964, p. 49). However, the liberal view came to dominate (Birch 1964, ch. 4), supported by the growing clamour for political reform.

The emergence of a mass, though not universal, franchise had major constitutional consequences. At the beginning of the nineteenth century, the government was chosen by the monarch, who was often able to use patronage and position to ensure a favourable House of Commons, but by the end of that century, the government was chosen by most of the adult male population. As we have seen (in Chapter 2), the 1832 and 1867 Reform Acts enlarged the electorate, and other measures ensured greater equity in constituency boundaries. By 1884, a majority of adult males, albeit a bare majority, had the vote (Butler 2004, p. 737). Other Acts, not least the Parliamentary and Municipal Elections Act 1872, more popularly known as the Ballot Act, helped largely to eliminate corrupt practices.

The transformation was reflected not only in the transfer of the capacity to choose the government, but also in the relationship between the two Houses. The Commons could then claim to be the chamber elected by the people. We have already quoted the observation of Lord Shaftesbury on the effect of the change (see Chapter 2). It is worth recording his opening comments:

> So long as the other House of Parliament was elected upon a restricted principle, I can understand that it would submit to a check from a House such as this. But in the presence of this great democratic power and the advance of this great democratic wave ... it passes my comprehension to understand how a hereditary House like this can hold its own. (Quoted in Norton 1981, p. 21)

As we have seen, it was not able to hold its own, and the country witnessed a shift from a form of co-equal bicameralism to one of asymmetrical bicameralism, a position confirmed in statute by the Parliament Act of 1911 (Ballinger 2011, Norton 2012d). The Commons thus came to be the dominant chamber by virtue of its claim to be the representative chamber, elected to act on behalf of the people.

The House of Commons has thus established its claim to be the representative chamber of the nation. It is popularly elected – a point to which we shall return – to defend and act on behalf of the people of the United Kingdom. However, a number of problems arise from the nature of Parliament's adjustment to the changing conceptions of representation. It is in this context that Parliament's longevity is crucial. Parliament existed long before the liberal view of representation took hold. Though Parliament has adapted to the political pressures resulting in a mass franchise, it has not necessarily discarded the views that predated the emergence and acceptance of this franchise. The liberal view has dominated but has not displaced other views of representation. As a result, we can identify certain tensions within the political system.

The first is between the role of government and the electorate. Anthony Birch has identified Tory and Whig attitudes to representation (Birch 1964, ch. 2) which clashed in the seventeenth and eighteenth centuries. The former emphasized the need for government by the monarch; the latter saw the need for Parliament to have a greater role, limiting royal power. However, both saw government as an essentially elite activity. The Whig view embraced some concept of representation but it was essentially Burkean: that of virtual representation and with the Members of Parliament exercising their own judgement. These views gave way in the nineteenth century to the liberal view, but this view essentially married acceptance of popular election with existing views of the role of Parliament. Parliament had asserted its dominance over the monarch in the Glorious Revolution of 1688. The Glorious Revolution served to confirm the doctrine of parliamentary supremacy. The doctrine had been asserted before but not necessarily accepted by leading lawyers. Now that the monarch was subject to the will of Parliament, then so too were the monarch's courts; they were thus bound to accept the outputs of Parliament and could not set them aside as being contrary to some superior body of law. The doctrine of parliamentary supremacy thus pre-dated the emergence of popular election. However, the effect of popular election was not to displace but rather to sustain the doctrine. The House of Commons was now elected by the people. A. V. Dicey, the leading nineteenth-century law professor, argued that the legal sovereignty of Parliament was underpinned by the political supremacy of the electorate (Dicey 1959).

As Birch has noted, Dicey was expressing an idealized view: 'It assumed that the political power flowed exclusively in one direction, from the electors to Parliament and from Parliament to the government, and never in the opposite way' (Birch 1964, p. 74). As Birch noted, the view did not take into account party management and the political reality that the cabinet could control Parliament. The view may have been idealized, but it is a view that has held sway and dictated the constitutional framework within which government operates. Parliamentary sovereignty may be a political fiction, but it continues to dictate the formal structures of the British constitution. Recent decades, as already discussed (see Chapter 7), have seen major constitutional changes. Yet, as David Judge (2004, p. 696) has noted: 'Each constitutional reform ... has been accompanied by a ritual reaffirmation of the continuing centrality of parliamentary sovereignty to the legitimation of the state and government.' The doctrine of parliamentary sovereignty has been written into the devolution legislation and the Human Rights Act. The outputs of Parliament remain supreme; Parliament can override the devolved bodies and is not bound by declarations of incompatibility made by the courts; it could repeal the 1972 European Communities Act. The result, paradoxically, as Judge (2004, pp. 696–7) observes, is that representative government in the UK continues to be conceived as a means of legitimating executive power. Through popular election, the people are, in effect, sustaining executive dominance.

A second tension is between party and constituency. One can identify two types of parliamentary representation: the general and the specific

(Norton 1981, pp. 56–62). The former, representing broad interests within the population, is fulfilled through the medium of political parties. Parties serve to aggregate opinions, to express them and seek to give effect to them in public policy. Party government is sustained by the doctrine of the mandate. This developed in the nineteenth century and has underpinned the political process since then. One can distinguish mandates as being permissive or prescriptive. A permissive mandate is one in which a party, by virtue of enjoying a majority of seats in the House of Commons, is deemed to have legitimacy to govern: 'we have the people's mandate'. The prescriptive mandate is one in which a party is elected to fulfil particular promises laid before the electorate in a general election. These promises are embodied in a party manifesto. A government can thus claim that in carrying out its manifesto promises it is carrying out its electoral mandate. Both forms of the mandate have currency, usually employed by the governing party as appropriate to justify its actions. The party in government can, and does, utilize the claim to have a mandate as the basis for requiring the loyal support of its MPs. The MPs were elected because of the party label and as such are expected to support the manifesto on which the party stood for election.

The other form, specific representation, constitutes acting on behalf of individuals or particular groups. It is fulfilled principally, though not exclusively, through MPs acting as constituency members. There is substantial empirical evidence for the claim that MPs are elected on the basis of the party label. There is some evidence of a personal vote (Norton and Wood 1993) but it is not usually sufficient to affect the electoral outcome in a constituency. However, the long-standing link between an MP and a particular geographic constituency remains important. That link pre-dates the emergence of popular election and the mandate. The MP is elected as the member for a particular constituency. In the Commons, MPs address one another not by name but by constituency (the Honourable Member for such-and-such a constituency). There are survey data to show that constituents expect the Member to accord priority to speaking and acting on behalf of the constituency over that of the collective function of calling government to account. Equally, MPs themselves accord priority to their constituency role (Norton 2002a, pp. 29–34).

Normally, MPs perceive party policy as being congruent with the interests of their constituencies and vote accordingly. On occasion, however, a perceived constituency interest clashes with government policy. The government may decide that there is a need for cuts in the defence budget and – to take actual examples – earmark some dockyards for closure or merge army regiments based in constituencies represented by some of its MPs. Those MPs then have to resolve an apparent conflict between loyalty to party and standing up for the interests of constituents. Such occasions are infrequent but notable for the intensity of the tensions experienced by MPs. Bodies lobbying for a change in public policy sometimes encourage supporters to put pressure on MPs at the constituency level. The defeat of the Shops Bill in 1986 (see Chapter 2) is attributable in part to effective constituency lobbying. That was an exceptional event, but illustrates the clash that MPs sometimes face between party and constituency.

A third tension is between constituency (or party) and conscience. An MP, as we have just seen, represents both constituency *and* party. On some issues, though, the MP may be influenced by a personal philosophy or religious beliefs that clash with the preference of the party *or* of constituents. On occasion, a party may recognize that it is split on an issue and allow MPs a free vote, though justifying it on the moral high ground that it is an 'issue of conscience' (see Cowley 1998a). However, if the party stands aside from an issue, constituents do not necessarily do so. An MP may decide to follow what is perceived as a constituency view – there is rarely any systematic polling of constituents in a specific seat to determine what in fact constituents *do* think – or decide to follow their own view. When they take their own line, this is usually justified in Burkean terms: that is, that they are trustees rather than delegates, offering constituents their judgement rather than a slavish capacity to follow whatever it is that constituents or the local party want. There are various instances of this in recent years, not least on the issue of capital punishment and European integration. Judge (1999b, p. 22) quotes Tony Blair arguing in 1994 against the restoration of the death penalty. He said he understood why a majority of his constituents favoured a return of the death penalty, but Parliament had at various times voted against it:

> Such a large majority of Members did not vote against the restoration of the death penalty on each occasion because they were unaware of their constituents' views but because, on reflection and after considered debate, they could not support those views ... I certainly do not believe that my understanding is superior to that of my constituents, but ... we are representatives, not delegates, and we must act according to our conscience.

In practice, MPs generally adhere to the party line, or vote along party lines even where there is a free vote (Cowley and Stuart 1997; 2010; 2011; Cowley 1998a). They none the less like to reserve to themselves the discretion to follow their consciences should a conflict occur, an approach that appears to have a wider resonance. Judge (1999b, pp. 31–2) quotes one observer as writing: 'We expect them [MPs] to exercise their own judgement, not simply to reflect ours'. As Judge notes, what is noteworthy about the statement is that it was made at the end of the twentieth century, not the end of the eighteenth: 'The ghost of Burke continues to haunt British parliamentary politics!' (Judge 1999b, p. 32).

Freely elected

We have already seen how the House of Commons has moved from being elected by a narrow band of electors to being elected by the adult population. The nineteenth century saw the widening of the franchise and the introduction of the secret ballot. (Before 1872, an open ballot was employed: the list of how electors had voted was published.) The 1880s also saw single-member constituencies, and the first-past-the-post method of election (the candidate with a plurality of votes being declared elected), become the norm. Neither, however, became universal: some two-member constituencies survived, as did a system of proportional representation in university seats (seats where the constituencies were not geographic but functional: the electors were graduates). The 1918 Representation of the People Act provided for universal suffrage for men based on residence rather than rates, though a 'business vote' survived based on occupancy of business premises worth £10 a year. (Defence of the business vote reflected a residual attachment to the concept of functional representation.) The 1948 Representation of the People Act abolished two-member constituencies as well as university seats (and hence the only surviving use of a system of proportional representation) and the business vote (see Butler 1963, pt II). The effects of the Act were seen for the first time in the general election of 1950.

The 1950 election thus saw the realization in large measure of the principle of 'one man, one vote', to which Jeremy Bentham had added 'one value' (Norton 1981, p. 53). MPs were elected in single-member constituencies in which every adult (with very few exceptions, such as convicted criminals) had one vote and one vote only. They were able to cast their votes in general elections that were regulated by statute in order to ensure fairness and secrecy. Electors cast their ballots in the privacy of the polling booths. Only electoral officials were permitted in the room where voting took place. Accusations of fraud by individual electors or by party officials were rare.

Boundary Commissions had been established in 1944 to review regularly constituency boundaries in order to try to ensure equity. As a result of demographic changes, the size of constituencies varied substantially – there was no boundary review between 1918 and 1944 – and the Commissions (one for each part of the United Kingdom) were designed to make sure that the electoral quota (the average size of the electorate per constituency) did not deviate too dramatically. The greater the equity in the size of constituency electorates, the closer it was possible to achieve what Bentham meant by 'one value', since a vote cast in one constituency would carry the same weight, proportionately, as one cast in another.

The achievement of one person, one vote served to underpin the popular legitimacy of the political system. As Birch (1964, p. 65) observed, the liberal view of the constitution 'amounted to a theory of legitimate power'. It did not derive from some mythical social contract, as advocated by John Locke and Jean-Jacques Rousseau, and had the advantage that it was tied to existing institutions: 'Partly because it was a local rather than a universal theory, it could readily be accepted by the man-in-the-street' (Birch 1964, p. 66). There was a willingness to accept the outputs of a Parliament freely elected by the people. Electors demonstrated a willingness to exercise the vote. In the 1950 election, 84 per cent of electors turned out to cast a ballot.

However, various criticisms have been levelled at the means by which MPs are elected. Three principal criticisms can be identified. The liberal view of the constitution has been challenged as being incomplete. The electoral system is undermined by the fact that 'one person, one vote' is not the same as saying that each vote is equal. The first-past-the-post system, it is pointed out, can produce 'wasted' votes (votes cast for losing candidates have no effect) and, given that it is difficult to ensure constituency electorates of precisely equal size, a vote in a constituency with a small electorate will count for more than one cast in a large constituency. Population movement (as well as tactical voting and differential turnout) can have a distorting effect. Since 1987, when there was a level playing field, '[T]he electoral system appears to have developed a spectacular bias in favour of Labour' (Butler and Butt 2004, p. 169). As Johnston and Pattie (2011, p. 237) recorded, 'The British electoral system remains biased against the Conservatives … largely because of the geography of turnout that favours Labour and, to a lesser extent, differentials in electorate size'. Following the 2010 general election, Curtice *et al.* (2010) estimated that if the Conservatives and Labour were to secure the same overall share of the vote, Labour would have as many as 51 more seats than the Conservatives. 'The Conservatives need to be four points ahead of Labour in votes before they emerge ahead in seats. And whereas Labour would win an overall majority ... with a lead of a little under three points, the Conservatives would require one of over 11 points' (Curtice *et al.* 2010, p. 416). Furthermore, the system is non-proportional, in that it can – and usually does – result in a party winning an absolute majority of seats on the basis of less than 50 per cent of the votes cast. In the 2005 general election, for example, the Labour government was returned to office with 356 seats – 56 per cent of the total – with just over 35 per cent of the votes cast nationally.

Conservatives argue the case for some adjustment to the electoral arrangements to address this disparity but are against a change of electoral system. They want to see constituencies more equal in size and in 2011 the coalition government achieved passage of the Parliamentary Voting System and Constituencies Act, designed to ensure constituencies more equal in electoral size (as well as reduce the number of MPs from 650 to 600). However, the Liberal Democrat leader, Nick Clegg, announced in 2012 that his party would vote against the orders to give effect to the boundary changes.

Opponents of the existing electoral system argue the case for a new electoral system, claiming that a system of proportional representation (PR) – the percentage of seats equalling the percentage of votes cast – would be a fairer system and hence more legitimate, serving to bolster support for the political system (Norton 1982a, pp. 231–2). They also claim that a consequence would be greater continuity in public policy, since a stable coalition government is likely to achieve enduring support and thus be able to engage in long-term planning, hence resulting in a more stable system.

Supporters of the existing arrangements counter that a system of proportional representation would be likely to break the link between MP and constituency (depending on the type of PR system chosen) as well as result in no overall majority for any one party, necessitating either coalition or minority government and thus jeopardizing the coherence of the existing system. There is also an allied argument based on the one value' argument, namely that 10 per cent of votes equalling 10 per cent of the seats will not then equal 10 per cent of the negotiating power in the House of Commons. Instead, a minority party or parties holding the balance of power will exercise disproportionate negotiating power (Norton 1998b). There is also a likelihood that coalition governments will be the product of post-election bargaining. That, it is argued, would constitute a greater threat to the legitimacy of the political system than any flaws in the existing arrangements. When a coalition government was formed in 2010, the result of post-election bargaining between the Conservatives and Liberal

Democrats, producing a coalition agreement that was not placed before the electors, supporters of the existing electoral system argued that such an outcome would be the norm under a PR system, whereas it was the exception in the UK under first-past-the-post.

Attempts to move to a new electoral system were made in 1997: the Labour party's election manifesto promised a review of the electoral system and a referendum on an alternative to the existing system. In the event, there was a review (chaired by Liberal Democrat peer, Lord Jenkins of Hillhead), published in 1998 and advocating the use of what was termed AV+: most MPs elected by the Alternative Vote plus some additional (top-up) members (Independent Commission on the Voting System, 1998). The proposed system, however, was not widely supported and was not pursued: there was no referendum.

The issue returned as a major issue during negotiations in 2010 to form a coalition government. The Conservatives wanted to retain the existing first-past-the-post method of voting, whereas the Liberal Democrats favoured a system of PR. The deadlock was broken by agreeing to hold a referendum on replacing the existing method with the Alternative Vote, a non-proportional preferential method of voting. The referendum was held in May 2011 and the Alternative Vote rejected by a decisive margin, two-thirds of those voting casting a 'no' vote.

The contending views reflect different perspectives of what elections are for. Supporters of PR tend to argue the case on grounds of equity, or fairness, while opponents tend to embrace the older view of elections as confirming a government in office in order to ensure that government is carried on. The conflict means that the legitimacy of the existing system is thus contested. In this, there is nothing particularly startling. The electoral system has frequently been the subject of political dispute (Norton 1982a, p. 227). Nor is the United Kingdom exceptional in this regard. When a political system is under pressure, there are often demands for a change in the electoral system. The essential point, though, for our purposes is that the legitimacy of the existing system in the United Kingdom does not go unchallenged. The critical voices are much louder now than in post-war decades. The 2011 referendum meant that a change to the existing system was unlikely in the near future, but critics remain vocal in their demands for a new method of electing MPs. They are able to point out that first-past-the-post is now exceptional within the UK, other methods being employed to elect members of devolved bodies and of the European Parliament.

A second criticism of the electoral system is not only the disparity between constituency sizes but also the disproportionate distribution between the different parts of the United Kingdom. Both Scotland and Wales have had a larger number of seats than their population justifies. The electoral quota in both has been significantly lower than that for England. As we have seen (Chapter 8), when Northern Ireland had its own Parliament at Stormont, the number of seats was lower than its population justified. After the Stormont Parliament was abolished, the number of Westminster seats was increased (in 1978) from 12 to 17. With devolution, it was argued that the smaller electoral quota in Scotland and Wales, relative to England, could not be justified (in so far as it ever was justified). The point was conceded by government in respect of Scotland. At the 2005 election, as we have seen (Chapter 8), the number of seats was reduced from 72 to 59 to bring the electoral quota into line with England. However, there are no proposals to reduce the number of seats in Wales. The issue is not as politically divisive as that of proportional representation but remains a contested one, especially given that one party (Labour) has benefited substantially from the over-representation of Scotland and Wales. Even with the number of seats in Scotland reduced, the electoral quota in Scotland is the same as that in England, even though Scotland has its own Parliament and England does not: hence there is the argument, detailed in Chapter 8, that the precedent of Northern Ireland should be followed, with the number of constituencies in Scotland being reduced even further to compensate for the existence of its own legislature.

A third criticism that has arisen is more recent. In the twenty-first century, there have been various experiments with all-postal voting in elections. Initially, these were confined to local elections, but in 2004 it was extended to four of the ten regional constituencies for elections to the European Parliament. The justification for all-postal voting was principally because of its potential to increase voter turnout: it was more convenient for electors to vote by post than to go to a polling booth on a specified day. There was an increase in voter turnout, by 5 per cent on average, but the elections were marred by some allegations of fraud. More pervasively, one of the criticisms was that the effect of all-postal voting undermined the Ballot Act of 1872. The Act, as we have noted, introduced the secret ballot and helped to reduce the potential for fraud and undue influence. This was overturned by all-postal voting. Whereas the polling booth guarantees secrecy, the family home does not. The Electoral Commission, the official independent body created to advise on electoral matters, urged a change in the law to deal with issues of secrecy and undue influence (Electoral Commission 2004, pp. 75–80). In 2012, the government introduced a bill to provide for individual voter registration, as a means of tackling fraud, but such a move did not address the issue of the secrecy of the ballot.

The popular legitimacy of the electoral process thus underpins the acceptance of the political system and the outputs of Parliament. If the electoral process is contested, then it undermines the legitimacy of the parliamentary process. The most contested element is the first-past-the-post method of election.

Socially typical

Seen in terms of representation denoting a body that is socially typical, Parliament is not a representative body. Members of both Houses of Parliament are predominantly white, male and middle-class. There is no formal requirement that the membership of either House should be socially typical, and it would be almost impossible to achieve a precise cross section of the population. This is partly because of constraints on who can sit in Parliament (only those aged 18 and over) and the nature of the job.

Being an MP is essentially a middle-class job and its time demands mean that most do not wish to sit for too long beyond retirement age. Indeed, the introduction of a pension has ensured that MPs are more likely now to choose to retire in their sixties, resulting in a more middle-aged House. There are – by virtue of appointment for life – more elderly members in the Lords than in the Commons. Also, as people tend to be elevated to the peerage in middle age, after achieving prominent positions, there are few peers under the age of 40. The removal of most hereditary peers in 1999 took away one mechanism for bringing in young members, since some peers succeeded to their titles while in their twenties and thirties. Lord Freyberg (b. 1970), for example (who remains in the Lords as one of the 92 hereditary peers chosen to stay on), entered the House at the age of 23. In 2010, the median age of MPs was just under 50, and the average age of members of the Lords was 69.

The House of Lords is predominantly middle and upper class in economic terms. In terms of occupational background, it is notably professional, with a preponderance of members drawn from 'representative politics' (especially ex-MPs), lawyers, academics, and people with backgrounds in business and finance (Russell 2010a, p. 5). As we have seen (in Chapter 2), the House of Commons is now a notably middle-class body. However, the biggest disparity, relative to the population as a whole, is in terms of ethnicity and gender.

For much of the twentieth century, there were few female MPs or Members drawn from ethnic minority backgrounds. Recent decades have seen changes, though most notably so in the case of the House of Lords. The fact that members of the second chamber are appointed has meant that it has been possible to give peerages to people who otherwise might have difficulty being selected by local party associations.

In 1975, Dr David Pitt, a West Indian, was elevated to the peerage. Two years later he was joined by Pratap Chitnis, an Indian, and they have since been joined by other non-white members. More than 6 per cent of the membership is drawn from ethnic minority backgrounds. This also has had consequences for the religious diversity of the House; in addition to the principal Christian religions, it has members who belong to the Jewish, Muslim, Hindu, Sikh and Bhuddist faiths. One peer is a Parsi Zoroastrian. There is also a significant Humanist group in the House.

Although women were only admitted to the House of Lords in 1958, there has been a growing number appointed, especially in the twenty-first century. By 2012, 21 per cent of members were women, the same proportion as in the Commons, though more in absolute terms. What has been noteworthy has been the number of women holding leadership positions in the House. Of the six Leaders of the House in the period since 1997, four have been women. The first Lord Speaker to be elected, in 2006, was a woman (Baroness Hayman); she was succeeded, in 2011, by another woman (Baroness D'Souza). Baroness Amos became the first black woman to sit in the cabinet when she was appointed Secretary of State for International Development in 2003. Baroness Warsi, co-chair of the Conservative party 2010–12, became the first Muslim member of the cabinet when she was appointed minister without portfolio in 2010.

The first woman elected to the House of Commons was Countess Markiewicz in 1918. However, she was a Sinn Fein candidate and refused to take her seat. Nancy (Lady) Astor became the first woman to sit in the House after she was elected as Conservative MP for Plymouth in 1919 (in succession to her husband, who had been raised to the peerage); she sat until 1945. The number of women MPs increased only gradually. In the 1983 general election, only 23 were elected, by 1987 the number had increased to 41 – just over 6 per cent of the total – and in 1997 it had reached 120, still less than 20 per cent of the membership, even though women comprise just over half of the population. The number fell to 118 in 2001 but reached 127 in 2005 and a record 143 in 2010.

Gradually, women have come to occupy leadership positions in the Commons. Margaret Thatcher was the first female Prime Minister (1979–90) and Betty Boothroyd the first woman Speaker of the House of Commons (1992–2000). Women have also been appointed to some of the most senior cabinet positions, including those of Foreign Secretary

(Margaret Beckett 2006–7) and Home Secretary (Jacqui Smith 2007–9, Theresa May 2010–).

The first non-white MP was elected in 1892: Dadabhai Naoroji, an Indian, was returned as Liberal member for Finsbury Central with a majority of five. (As some electors found it difficult to pronounce his name, he was dubbed 'Mr Narrow Majority'; Gifford 1992, p. 33.) Mancherjee Bhownagree became the second Indian to sit in Parliament when he was elected as Conservative MP for Bethnal Green in 1895; he was knighted two years later. A third – Shapurji Saklatvala – was elected as member for Battersea North in 1922, sitting initially as a Labour member; after the 1924 election, he sat as a Communist (Gifford 1992, p. 40). He lost his seat in 1929.

There was then a gap of 58 years before the return of another non-white member. In 1987, four MPs were elected (Diane Abbott, Paul Boateng, Bernie Grant, and Keith Vaz), all representing Labour. Though the number was small – less than 1 per cent of the House – it constituted the largest number of non-white MPs ever to sit in the House of Commons. The number increased in later elections (including in two by-elections in 2000), and in the general election of 2001, 12 MPs from ethnic backgrounds were elected (Criddle 2002, p. 197), two of whom were Muslims. Paul Boateng became the first black MP to enter the cabinet, in 2002 as chief secretary to the Treasury. The 2005 election saw a further increase, with 15 MPs elected from ethic backgrounds. Of these, 13 were Labour (four of them Muslims) and two Conservative. In 2010, the number increased to 27, of which 16 were Labour and 11 were Conservative, including the first Conservative female Asian MP, Priti Patel. Labour provided the first three female Muslim MPs (Criddle 2010, pp. 320–1).

Other members from different groups have also been returned. The House has had MPs with various disabilities. Of current MPs, one is wheelchair-bound (the Lords has several such members) and another, former cabinet minister David Blunkett, is blind. Both Houses have members drawn from a variety of religions. We have already noted the range in the Lords. In the Commons, Michael Howard, Conservative leader from 2003 to 2005, was the first practising Jew to be elected party leader. (Nineteenth-century leader Benjamin Disraeli was of Jewish descent but converted to the Anglican faith.) Chris Smith, the Labour MP for Islington South and Finsbury, was the first MP to declare publicly in the 1980s that he was gay. By the end of the 2001–5 Parliament, there were 11 openly gay MPs, mainly on the Labour benches. The 2010 election saw a notable influx of gay MPs on the Conservative benches, producing more gay MPs on the Tory than the Labour benches (McManus 2011, p. 302). At one point under the Labour government there were three gay cabinet members; a number of gay MPs were promoted to office under the coalition government in 2010. The House of Lords also saw the number of gay members increase as a result of new appointments.

The calls for MPs to be socially typical reflect a particular, but not an uncontested, view of representation. In many respects, it can be seen to hark back to the early view of MPs as representing particular interests. By being drawn from a certain section of society, an MP can speak for that section. S/he, it is argued, will have an understanding of the needs and expectations of that section in a way that someone who is outside it cannot have. Such representation, it is argued, is also important for maintaining the legitimacy of the institution. If particular sections of society do not see some of their own number in Parliament, they feel that their interests are not represented. It was a view with which Burke would have had some sympathy. He argued the case for some sections of society (such as Irish Catholics) that had no MPs to express their interests, to at least have the franchise extended to some of their number (Pitkin 1967, pp. 177–80). However, as we have seen, he did not see the need for popular election in order to achieve such representation.

This somewhat functional view is in conflict with the liberal view. An MP is elected to represent the individuals who reside in the constituency. An MP does not necessarily have to be drawn from a particular background in order to grasp the needs and interests of constituents. An MP does not have to be tied to particular interests any more than s/he should be a delegate rather than a trustee, and is freely elected. Electors have freedom of choice in voting for whichever candidate they wish: however desirable it may be for MPs to be drawn from particular backgrounds, electors cannot necessarily be relied upon to elect candidates from those backgrounds to Parliament. In some seats, the main party candidates have been women, and in some they have been drawn from ethnic backgrounds, but such cases are in the minority. The maintenance of single-member constituencies, with some degree of local autonomy in candidate selection, makes it difficult to ensure that MPs are socially typical. In the 1990s, the Labour Party introduced provision for all-women short lists in certain constituencies; the result was the increase in the number of female Labour MPs in 1997. (The use of such short lists fell foul of sex discrimination legislation in an employment tribunal, and an Act of Parliament had to be passed to enable parties that wished to utilize such short lists to be able to do so.) Conservative leader David Cameron introduced a candidates' A-list in 2006, designed to boost the number of female candidates, as well as candidates drawn from ethnic minority backgrounds.

The conflict between the liberal view of representation and that favouring a socially typical House can be argued to be a false dichotomy. If the typically white, male, middle-class MP can act on behalf of all the diverse 70,000 constituents in the constituency, then so can MPs drawn from other backgrounds. As one leading female MP argued, it is a myth 'that women are in Parliament to represent women. Every MP is elected represent all of their constituents, male and female, young and old, and of all political affiliations' (May 2004, p. 845). They may have a particular affinity with the concerns of a particular section of society, and on rare occasions that might cause the sort of conflict we have already identified between party and conscience, but it is going to be exceptional rather than the norm.

Though such members will normally seek to avoid being single-issue members – not confining themselves to women's issues, black issues and so on – their presence provides the basis for some resonance with members of society with similar characteristics. By being seen to be in Parliament, and in a position to serve some safety-valve function, they can work to enhance the legitimacy of Parliament among groups that otherwise may feel alienated from it.

Symbolic

Parliament fulfils a symbolic role. As with many other parliaments, it has a clear physical presence that is instantly recognizable, in the same way that the Capitol in Washington DC is also instantly recognizable. Some parliaments, such as the European Parliament (lacking a clear single site), have no such presence.

In this respect, the institution of Parliament is important in a physical sense. There is one part of the Palace of Westminster – Westminster Hall – that dates back several centuries, originating in the Norman period, though remodelled at various times since (Field 2002). However, Westminster Hall aside, the Palace of Westminster is a relatively new building. The old Palace – something of a melange of buildings, set back a little from the Thames – was destroyed by fire in 1834. A grand, mock-Gothic building replaced it; the Lords occupied their new chamber in 1847 and the Commons in 1850. (The chamber of the House of Commons was destroyed by enemy bombing on 10 May 1941. It was rebuilt along the lines of the old chamber.) Despite the addition of various outlying buildings, such as Portcullis House (see Chapter 2), Parliament is still seen solely in terms of the Palace of Westminster, running alongside the Thames, with the Clock Tower, renamed the Elizabeth Tower in 2012 (housing the Big Ben bell), at one end and Victoria Tower at the other. The building is iconic. It symbolizes the nation's law-effecting body and, with its mock-Gothic façade, is suggestive of Parliament's long history.

The interior echoes the grandeur of the exterior, with long corridors and high ceilings, and with rooms – particularly in the House of Lords – that are crammed with elaborate fittings and pictures. The chamber of the House of Commons is itself iconic, captured in numerous paintings and now accessible to the public through the medium of television. It has a claim to be the best known debating chamber in the world.

However, there is a potential tension between what it does and what it appears to be. The building exudes grandeur. It conveys a sense of the nation's history. This tends to be reinforced when people visit the Palace, especially on guided tours. Westminster Hall has a plaque to commemorate the fact that Charles I was tried there; other plaques commemorate other historical events. There is the danger of seeing the Palace principally in terms of its history rather than as a working institution, and there is a particular danger of people seeing an incongruence if they perceive a great building housing a politically insignificant Parliament. For Parliament, achieving a balance between the two – conveying that it is entrenched in the nation's history, yet remains relevant through fulfilling important representative functions – arguably constitutes the ideal state for maintaining popular legitimacy.

The challenge to legitimacy

Parliament has had to adapt to the changing political environment. Before the nineteenth century, Parliament's principal relationship was with the executive. There was little direct contact with the people. Since then, it has developed a direct relationship with the expanding electorate, and that relationship has affected, but has also had to accommodate, the pre-existing relationship with the executive. How well, then, has Parliament adapted?

From a pluralist perspective, the expansion of the franchise has weakened Parliament but made the people powerful. The growth of party has enabled the cabinet to dominate Parliament. The cabinet is powerful because it can claim an electoral mandate. The people now exercise a coercive capacity through parliamentary elections: they can decide who sits in the House of Commons and, through those elections, will normally determine which party forms the government. If they do not like the performance of a party in government, they can turn it out at the next election. Election day is, in the words of the late philosopher, Sir Karl Popper, 'judgement day'. The people also exercise a persuasive capacity, through making their views known, through contacting MPs, being polled in surveys, through mass lobbies and marches, by submitting petitions, and through the mass media. As we shall see, they are contacting MPs (and peers) on an ever-increasing and unprecedented scale. MPs – and the government – are driven by the need to be re-elected, and so are responsive to shifts in popular opinion.

However, the coercive power exercised by the people is essentially a blunt weapon. The electorate is not so much a positive driving force as an endorsing body. The electorate assents (or withholds it assent) to the party in government. The relationship between Parliament and government continues to be shaped by the constitutional norms that pre-dated the growth of the franchise. As we have seen, through popular election, the people are endorsing executive dominance and do so through Parliament.

The institutional perspective helps us to identify a problem of legitimacy. If the parliamentary process is to be accepted as legitimate, and the exclusive process for determining issues of public policy, then people have to accept that the House of Commons is a representative body. However, as we have seen, there are inherent tensions within the representative system.

On the one hand, by meeting regularly, by debating, by requiring ministers to justify their actions, by allowing members to express conflicting views, by allowing members to make representations to ministers on behalf of constituents and different groups in society, and by operating generally in a public session – observable by visitors and, now via television cameras – Parliament provides an outlet for tensions, grievances and demands that otherwise might find no outlet. By providing such an outlet – and by being seen to do so – Parliament enhances its own legitimacy in the eyes of the citizenry as well as the legitimacy of the body drawn from it: the government. By engaging in such activity, it is not making policy. It is, however, serving to bolster support for the political system of which it is a core institution. Arguably, it is more active as a representative body than ever before.

On the other hand, the tensions we have identified convey that Parliament's claims to be a representative body are contested. As we have seen, the pre-eminence of the House of Commons derives from the fact that it is the elected chamber. This underpins its legitimacy as the principal assent-giving body. However, perceptions of its legitimacy are affected by the *method* by which it is elected, *who* is elected, and *how* it behaves in defending and pursuing the interests of those who elected it. Since people cannot usually make their views known, regularly and in a structured manner, to government, they rely on Parliament, primarily the House of Commons, to do it for them. Parliament is thus fundamental to making the views of the people known to government. The method of election and who serves in Parliament can be seen to figure in producing a Parliament able to speak for the people. There are, as we have seen, perceived problems with respect to both. This limits the acceptance by some of Parliament as a representative body.

Can it, then, still fulfil a representative role in the first sense of the term? How well have the links between Parliament and people developed, facilitating the capacity of MPs to speak for the people? That is the question we explore in Chapter 11.

11

The Voice of Constituents

Members of Parliament have a dual but not necessarily incompatible existence. They are in most cases elected under a party label. As we saw in Chapter 10, parties fulfil the role of general representation, aggregating the views of large sections of the population. As such, this form of representation transcends individual constituencies. MPs, as party members, are part of a body that links them with like-minded members, and they generally operate as a collective entity. However, each MP is also elected to represent a particular constituency. Members thus fulfil the role of specific representation, defending and pursuing the interests of individuals and groups within their constituencies. (They may, and do, promote the interests of groups unconnected with, or not confined to, their constituencies, and we shall address this in the next chapter.) Our concern in this chapter is the representation of constituents, which is generally an individual rather than a collective exercise, though MPs from constituencies with a shared interest may work together to defend and promote that interest. Over the years, demands made of members by constituents have changed in nature and increased in volume. Members have sought to meet those demands and have done so in various ways.

The changing nature of constituency demands

There is no formal or definitive job description for a Member of Parliament: it depends in large measure on what the MP makes of it, and it also depends to a large extent on what constituents expect of the MP. Constituents have generally called on 'their' MP to fulfil a range of tasks, or functions. It is possible to identify seven constituency roles fulfilled by MPs (Norton 1994b, pp. 705–8):

(i)   *safety valve*, allowing constituents to express their views, usually through writing or sometimes having a meeting with the MP;

(ii)   *information provider*, giving information, or advice, to those constituents who seek it;

(iii)   *local dignitary*, being seen in the constituency and attending civic and other events;

(iv)   *advocate*, giving support to a particular cause, either through lending the MP's name to the cause or being active in its support;

(v)   *benefactor*, providing benefits to particular constituents who seek them, usually those who are needy or greedy;

(vi)   *powerful friend*, intervening with government or other bodies to achieve a redress of grievance for a constituent or constituents; and

(vii) *promoter of constituency interests*, advancing the case for collective interests (such as employment) in the constituency.

The first three are primarily, though not exclusively, internal to the constituency. The rest normally involve action beyond the borders of the constituency, with the MP pursuing some action in relation to other bodies, frequently public bodies, on behalf of constituents. Most are usually pursued as a consequence of approaches made to the MP, though the MP may act as an information provider to constituents collectively (through newsletters, newspaper articles, websites, blogs and tweets), and may also act in pursuit of constituency interests without specific prompting. MPs may also solicit invitations to local events in order to raise their public profile. However, the demands made of MPs are now such, both in quantity and quality, that members have little time to adopt a proactive approach in handling constituency matters.

There are two generalizations that can be drawn about the nature of constituency service over the past century. The first is the shift in emphasis from certain roles to others (Rush 2001, pp. 199–211); and the second is the quantity of demands made of MPs by constituents in fulfilling those roles.

In the nineteenth century and the early decades of the twentieth, the benefactor role was an important one. The MP was frequently invited to support local interests, often financially, and to act to acquire jobs and benefits for constituents. Rush (2001, p. 203) quotes Liberal MP Richard Cobden complaining in 1846, 'I am teased to death by place-hunters of every degree.' Civil service reform helped to reduce the potential for patronage, but other demands continued to be made. The new MP for Ashton-under-Lyne in 1910 – the millionaire Canadian, Max Aitken – faced a daunting array of pleadings from constituents. These included requests to join societies, or to support local bodies in their activities. According to his biographers:

Nearly always a donation or subscription was involved ... There was also a stream of begging letters from individuals. All were looked in to; Aitken was prepared to be generous, but hated being taken for granted ... Often he would ask his agents to give a needy family food or clothes rather than cash. (Chisholm and Davie 1993, p. 85)

The benefactor role remained important for some years but declined as the twentieth century progressed. In part, this reflected the rise of the Labour Party, with MPs who did not have independent financial means. After 1945, it reflected the demise of wealthy members on the Conservative benches (the result of internal party reforms) and, more pervasively, the growth of the welfare state. Citizens could now in certain circumstances obtain, as of right, support from the state, and no longer needed to turn to local benefactors, at least not to the same extent as before.

However, just as the benefactor role declined, many of the others increased in significance, including those of powerful friend and information provider. Public bodies grew in the twentieth century and became a central feature of the state after 1945. The greater the number, and the greater the scope, of public bodies, the greater was the potential for citizens to feel aggrieved by the actions of public officials. When individuals felt they had not received some benefit due to them, or been discriminated against by a public body, they would contact the local MP to intercede on their behalf. Similarly, if they were not sure why they had been treated in a particular way, or needed help in pursing an issue, they would contact the MP. The MP was 'their' MP, and was in a position to act on their behalf in a way that no other body was. There was a limited number of grievance-chasing agencies to approach and none, other than the MP, had direct access to government departments.

The latter half of the twentieth century also saw a growing significance of the MP acting as safety valve and advocate. Post-war years saw an expansion of secondary education and the growth of the mass media. People became more aware of particular issues and were increasingly willing to express themselves (see Inglehart 1977). They were more likely to join pressure groups; the number of groups increased dramatically in the last four decades of the century. An outlet for their views was the local MP. A British Social Attitudes survey in 1984 found that, in response to an unjust or harmful law being considered by Parliament, most respondents (55 per cent) would contact an MP (Jowell and Witherspoon 1985, p. 12). This was the most popular course of personal action. The Hansard Society *Audit of Political Engagement* 2012 Report found that on the specific issue of local health services, constituents who were unhappy with the service would contact their doctor or GP (44 per cent), but the second choice – the most popular outside the health service itself – was the local MP (or MSP or AM) (25 per cent), way ahead of friends and family and other bodies such as the local council or citizens' advice bureau (Hansard Society 2012, p. 53). As the Report noted, 'Only 1% would seek assistance from Parliament directly, confirming that MPs individually rather than the institution of Parliament itself is seen as the conduit for grievances' (Hansard Society 2012, p. 52).

The role of local dignitary has remained a prominent one. Some MPs in the nineteenth and early twentieth centuries were drawn from the locality they represented (Rush 2001, p. 204) and were already local figures of some standing. Others had no connection with the constituency but were accorded status by virtue of their position and this may have been enhanced by infrequent, rather than regular, visits to the constituency. Visits by the local MP were often something of an occasion. When Duff Cooper was elected Conservative MP for Oldham in 1924, he rarely visited the town: 'Although Duff may not have spent long in Oldham, when he was there there was scarcely a Chamber of Commerce dinner or a mothers' meeting which was not graced by a speech from the senior burgess' (Charmley 1997, p. 48). The role remains important, though now imposing different demands. For reasons we shall explore, MPs spend more time in their constituencies and are keen to be seen locally; they have moved from being Olympian figures, descending occasionally from London, to being local worthies. Their contribution to the constituency has shifted from one of material beneficence to one of time.

The other development has been the increase in the demands made of the local MP. There has been a marked increased in the sheer volume of representations made to MPs, especially by constituents. At the beginning of the twentieth century, it was not unknown for members to raise personal constituency cases with ministers (see Chester and Bowring 1962, pp. 104–5). Requests for action by constituents with problems – war disabilities, unemployment and tax problems, for example – increased as the century progressed. This was reflected in a notable increase in the number of letters that flowed between MPs and ministers. In 1938, for example, the Financial Secretary to the Treasury wrote 610 letters to members. In 1954, the number was 3,349 (Couzens 1956). There was also a marked increase in the number concerning the Post Office (Phillips 1949).

However, pursuing cases with departments and other public bodies on behalf of constituents was not extensive. Relatively few problems were brought to an MP's attention. Peter Richards (1959) estimated that a typical MP received between 12 and 20 letters a week; in other words, about two or three a day, though other studies suggest the number may have been higher. By the last quarter of the twentieth century, the burden of constituency correspondence had increased substantially. In 1967 most MPs estimated that they received between 25 and 75 letters a week from constituency sources (Barker and Rush 1970, p. 174), but a survey in 1986 found that a typical MP received between 20 and 50 letters *a day*, with more than half coming from constituents (Griffith and Ryle 1989, p. 72).

The quantitative increase is indicated by the number of letters and e-mails that flow into the Palace of Westminster. The number of letters arriving in the Palace of Westminster each year runs into the millions, though the number has decreased in recent years, apparently as constituents have begun utilizing e-mail on a major scale. In 2008, in excess of 4 million items of mail were delivered to Parliament. (Earlier estimates by the post office put the figure much higher, but the figure was reduced when a more precise count was introduced.) The figure in 2009 and in 2010 exceeded 3 million. In 2011, the figure was just over 2.6 million (*Lords Hansard,* 25 January 2012, col. *242W*). Of this mail, approximately 75 per cent went to the Commons; the rest (just over 670,000 items) went to the Lords.

Almost all MPs now use e-mail (see Chapter 14) and, for constituents and pressure groups, it constitutes an easy and cheap way of making contact with MPs. In 2002, the Information Committee of the Commons noted that, typically, '10 to 20 per cent of a Member's correspondence might be received electronically', adding: 'but this figure seems set to climb' (Information Committee 2002, p. 9). By 2012, it appeared to have climbed exponentially and constitutes now a major means of correspondence, increasingly supplanting ordinary mail, the ease and cheapness of contact facilitating if not encouraging multiple contacts.

Not all e-mails and letters are from constituents. The volume of correspondence is a product of increased lobbying by organized groups (see Chapter 10) as well as representations from constituents. None the less, it does indicate the change in the demands made of MPs in the twenty-first century compared with those a century before. The volume varies from one MP to another. The 1986 survey found that MPs from seats in the South-West of England received the largest number of letters. This finding was reinforced by the Hansard Society 2012 Report which found that people living in the South-West were more likely than people elsewhere to contact the local MP if they were not happy with the local health services

(Hansard Society 2012, p. 54). It is also generally accepted by MPs that those representing inner-city seats tend to receive more correspondence than those representing seats in suburban areas. The former face particularly problems of housing (though not a responsibility of central government), urban deprivation and social problems. In some, immigration is also a significant problem that generates substantial casework.

Nor are letters and e-mails the only means by which constituents make contact with their MPs. The traditional method of contact has not only been by letter but also through attendance at an MP's constituency 'surgery', where the MP is available at a particular time in the constituency to see constituents wishing to discuss problems or issues. One study of just over 1,000 cases dealt with by seven MPs in the 1980s found that 556 had originated from letters and 366 from surgeries. Just over 100 had derived from telephone calls (Rawlings 1990, p. 29). Surgeries are seen as valuable means through which constituents, who may be unwilling or even unable to put pen to paper, to see the MP to make their case in their own words.

MPs' responsiveness

MPs have responded to the demands made of them in two principal ways: one is pursuing constituency casework in the Commons and through contact with ministers, and the other is by spending more time in the constituency.

Some of the mail received by MPs falls into the 'safety valve' category, where the important thing for the writer is simply to have written. As one MP put it, 'The main satisfaction is to the constituent who feels he has gone as far as he can in getting his grievance aired' (Norton 1982b, p. 65). More frequently, the constituent is contacting the MP as a powerful friend, information provider or advocate. In these roles – especially as powerful friend or information provider – the MP will normally pursue the matter on behalf of the constituents. This may be with a body in the constituency (most often the local authority) or, if concerned with central government, with the relevant government minister. Writing to a minister on behalf of a constituent is a well-established and, as may be inferred from the demands made of MPs by constituents, a growing part of MPs' parliamentary work.

MPs themselves have a fairly standard procedure for dealing with constituents' letters. Those that express an opinion normally receive a standard response, usually acknowledging receipt and thanking the correspondent for passing on their views, and some may provide a substantive answer. Where constituents ask the MP to intercede, as a powerful friend, in a dispute with a government department (or, usually, some agency of the department, such as a local social security office), the constituent's letter is forwarded to the relevant minister for a response. This practice is so standard, and extensive, that printed cards exist for MPs to attach to the letter, absolving them of the need to dictate a covering letter. The ministers' replies are normally then forwarded to constituents. In many cases, MPs thus act essentially as transmission belts for constituents' letters. Only if the minister's response is unsatisfactory, or if the constituent complains further about the response, is the MP likely to pursue the matter. This is done either by writing again to the minister or (especially if correspondence fails to resolve the issue) by a meeting with the minister or by raising the matter on the floor of the House.

MPs will sometimes seek meetings with ministers, on a formal or an informal basis. A formal meeting is one that is scheduled and may take place in the department. This is especially likely to be held where MPs are pursuing their role as protectors of constituency interests, taking up issues such as the closure of a naval dockyard or a hazard affecting the health of local inhabitants. Informal meetings frequently take place in the Palace of Westminster. MPs, as we have noted previously, often make use of the opportunity to speak to ministers when votes are taking place.

Raising a constituent's case or, more generally, a constituency interest, on the floor of the House is something undertaken only if earlier attempts by correspondence or private meetings have failed to resolve the matter satisfactorily. A member may table a parliamentary question for written or oral answer or, if requiring a more detailed response, raise it during the daily half-hour adjournment debate (see Chapter 6). Such debates provide an opportunity for back bench MPs to raise non-partisan issues, either of a general nature or one affecting their constituencies, or, sometimes, particular constituents. A study of adjournment debates in the 1995–6 session found that 43 per cent (61 out of 142) were on constituency issues; and a further 15 per cent were on regional issues (Russell 1998, p. 29). Debates in Westminster Hall have extended the opportunity to raise constituency issues. The advantage of such debates, whether in the chamber or Westminster Hall, is that the minister's response is on the public record and is more detailed than an answer to a parliamentary question.

Using the floor of the House to pursue constituency issues is something usually kept in reserve. Corresponding with a minister is usually sufficient, and this is the most extensive form of contact between MPs and those of their number who are ministers. Anything between 200,000 and 250,000 items of correspondence (some now electronic) flow from MPs to ministers each year (and a similar number from ministers to MPs) (Elms and Terry 1990; *Lords Hansard* 17 February 1999, col. 746). The number varies from department to department. Some, like the Foreign Office, receive relatively little correspondence, but other have a large mailbag. To take one department, the Department for Environment, Food and Rural Affairs (DEFRA), it received between 12,000 and 16,700 letters or e-mails from MPs in each of the five years 2007 to 2011 (*Lords Hansard,* 16 July 2012, *WA6*), a total of 73,566 items of correspondence over the period.

MPs are thus busy dealing with constituency casework, especially through correspondence with ministers. They have also responded to the changing nature of constituency demands by spending more time in their constituencies, a tendency reinforced by greater electoral volatility (and hence instability for incumbents), local party pressure, and by the change in the nature of the work of MPs. The growth of the career politician (see Chapter 2) has increased the dependence on re-election as a necessary condition for career fulfilment.

Responding to pressure from their local parties, new MPs from the 1960s onwards increasingly took up residence in their constituencies. In the 1980s, newly-elected MPs were far more likely than longer-serving MPs to record addresses in or near their constituencies (Norton and Wood 1993, p. 35). They also spent more time there. Donald Searing (1994, p. 136), in his survey of MPs in the early 1970s, found that recently elected backbenchers were more likely to claim to spend more time in their constituencies than did their longer-serving colleagues. Surveys by the Review Body of Top Salaries revealed that the amount of time MPs claimed to spend on constituency work increased from 11 hours a week in 1971 to 16 hours a week in 1984 (Norton and Wood 1990, p. 199), and time spent in the constituency appeared to be even more time consuming. In 1996, MPs estimated that, when the House was sitting, around 40 per cent of their time each week was devoted to constituency work (and over 60 per cent when the House was in recess; Review Body on Senior Salaries 1996, p. 30). In 2006, MPs newly-elected the previous year put the figure at 49 per cent (Rosenblatt 2006, p. 32) and in 2011 those newly-elected in 2010 put it at 59 per cent (Hansard Society 2011, p. 6).

Effects

What, then, are the effects of the changing nature and demands of constituency work? We can see important effects for government, MPs, and for constituents.

Government

Letters from MPs are given priority within departments. By convention, a letter from an MP must receive a reply from a minister. (There are occasional exceptions, as when ministers authorize the chief executives of executive agencies to reply.) As one former minister recalled, 'I became acutely aware that, whoever had drafted the reply, the responsibility for it lay with me' (Lord Glenarthur, *Lords Hansard*, 17 February. 1999, col. 740). The Cabinet Office has a 15-page guidance note on best practice (Cabinet Office 2005), but it is up to ministers as to how they in fact handle the correspondence.

For government, there are benefits as well as costs. The principal benefit is that correspondence from members helps to raise awareness of particular problems, which otherwise might not emerge publicly until much later. By writing, an MP can ensure that a matter, which otherwise might not reach a minister, is brought to that minister's attention. On occasion, this can be helpful to ministers in identifying issues, not least those that civil servants may prefer not to see raised. Correspondence also serves as something of a barometer of parliamentary opinion, though this is most likely to be the case in respect of policy issues (Norton 1982b, p. 65). In short, the effect of letter-writing by MPs is to ensure that ministers are better-informed about issues affecting their departments.

There are also costs to government. One is the financial cost of replying. Many letters will require some research or the calling in of files in order to draft a reply. There may be various exchanges between civil servants in a department, including with regional or local offices, before a draft is agreed, and if the minister is not satisfied with the draft, further work may be necessary. Given the scale of the correspondence, there is a burden on departmental budgets, not least on those being forced to handle the greatest volume of correspondence. There is also a cost in terms of time. Checking, sometimes dictating, and signing letters takes up ministers' time. There is an opportunity cost: the ministers could be engaged in more strategic work, or be devoting themselves to more pressing parliamentary and departmental concerns, such as working on bills before Parliament.

There is also a more personal cost to ministers in terms of sheer work-load. Those elevated to ministerial office remain MPs and, as such, have constituency responsibilities (see Chapter 3). The fact that they have been, and remain, MPs, is of benefit to members engaging in correspondence with ministers. As parliamentarians themselves, ministers appreciate the importance of constituency correspondence. They can therefore empathize with the MPs writing to them. As constituency members, they may also write to fellow ministers in pursuit of a constituency case. Some find constituency work a relief from departmental pressures, and it may also serve a useful political purpose: 'To work in the constituency obliged one to keep up to date with all the issues being dealt with by ministerial colleagues and served as a useful discipline' (Shephard 2000, p. 154). However, it adds to their burden of work: 'Ministers who have constituencies to look after don't stop and can't hand over the work to someone else: it just has to be fitted in somehow' (Currie 1989, p. 233). They have to deal with constituency issues as well as attend to ministerial, parliamentary and party duties. Backbenchers also have parliamentary and party duties, but the pressure on ministers to address party gatherings is normally far greater. The constituency work is ever-present. Seeing Foreign Secretary Douglas Hurd signing constituency letters at an international meeting, a German minister exclaimed that 'Mrs Smith's plumbing problems' could not be the proper responsibility of a minister (Hurd 2003, p. 312). Hurd took a different view, but the effect of constituency work is demanding. Cabinet ministers not only have to find time to reply to constituency correspondence; they also frequently maintain constituency surgeries. The effect can be exhausting as well as distracting. One cabinet minister (Nott 2002, p. 123) recalled: 'When I became a Cabinet Minister, these surgeries became something of a burden because I returned to London with a voluminous correspondence about a host of personal problems – sorting them out had to take priority over such insignificant issues as modernisation of the nuclear deterrent!' One minister, in his memoirs (Fowler 1991, p. 322), outlined a fairly typical week when his 'weekend' did not begin until four o'clock on Sunday. The process, he thought, 'had become dangerously all-devouring. It pushed out everything else'.

MPs

For MPs, whether ministers or backbenchers, there are also benefits as well as costs. It provides them with some self-esteem. The individual backbencher is not likely to have much success in changing public policy.

Getting hold of some information for constituents is much easier and can carry with it a significant element of delivering a service. Generally, what constituents want is not so much a changed decision as for the MP to act as a safety valve or information provider. Of the responses to MPs' enquiries in just over 700 cases studied by Rawlings (1990, p. 42), 44 per cent involved the provision of further information and 18 per cent confirmation that the matter was in hand. On other occasions, the MP is able to act as a powerful friend. Some decisions may be – and are – changed as a result of an MP's intervention, especially in such areas as welfare payments and immigration where ministers or officials have some discretion to vary decisions (Rawlings 1990, p. 168). MPs appear to gain some job satisfaction from their work (see Norris 1997). It is not uncommon for MPs about to retire to express regret at giving up constituency work. It serves also to bolster their esteem as a local dignitary. In the House of Commons, one is a single member in a 650-member body. In the constituency, one is *the* Member of Parliament.

Constituency work may also have a more political reward. MPs may work hard in order to bolster their electoral base, with the need to do so being seen as more significant in recent decades as a consequence of greater electoral volatility. Even supposedly safe seats can be lost in an electoral landslide, as many Tory MPs discovered in 1997 and some Labour MPs in 2010. Constituency work is not thought to persuade many voters to switch their votes, but may serve to retain support that might otherwise drift away. If both the MP's party and the MP are unpopular, this provides little incentive for former supporters, disillusioned with the party, to continue supporting the MP. If the MP's party is unpopular but the MP is popular because of the work done in the constituency, supporters may think twice before switching their vote to another party. There is some evidence that first-time incumbents in some recent elections have managed to achieve a better performance in maintaining their share of the vote than longer-serving members or challengers. The explanation offered for this has been the greater level of constituency activity undertaken by the new MP compared with that undertaken by the MP's predecessor (Norton and Wood 1993, ch. 7; see also Norris 1997). Data are not available that would allow us to know whether this is an intergenerational or a life-cycle phenomenon, and it may be a combination of both: new MPs may generally work harder than their predecessors in their first Parliament but nowadays, because of external pressures, may work even harder than previous first-termers.

Constituency work might not only help MPs at election time; it might also serve to fulfil an educative role in between elections. As one put it, it sensitizes MPs 'to the concerns that are pressing on at least a portion of our fellow citizens' (Brandreth 1992, p. 24). It can help to keep MPs informed about specific local issues or about issues affecting a wide body of citizens. It is a valuable way of connecting with citizens and stops MPs from feeling detached from the rest of the populace. There is a general perception, not least on the part of MPs, that it keeps them in touch with 'real people'.

However, there are also costs. MPs see constituency work as being to the fore in determining their role as representatives (see Table 11.1). However, while MPs tend to extol the value of constituency service, the public stance is not always consistent with the private one. Though MPs recognize that constituents take priority when it comes to serving as representatives in Parliament, they do not necessarily consider protecting constituency interests to be their most important role in Westminster. They have a collective Westminster role as well as an individual constituency role and, as Table 11.2 reveals, the collective role of holding the government to account is regarded as the most important role by almost twice as many MPs as regard protecting constituency interests as most important.

MPs thus face cross-pressures between their constituency and their Westminster roles (Norton and Wood 1993). The time-consuming aspect

Table 11.1   Influences on MPs' roles as representatives: MPs' evaluations

Q. MPs are expected to represent a number of different interests in Parliament. How important are the following interests in determining your role as a representative?

Answering very important/quite important

	%
My political party	71.5
My geographical constituency	92.7
Individual constituents	91.0
Constituency party	33.0
The nation as a whole	89.4
Sectional interests	33.0
A particular cause	48.0

$N = 179$.
Source: Derived from Hansard Society Commission on Parliamentary Scrutiny (2001, pp. 138–9).

Table 11.2   The most important role of MPs: MPs' evaluations

Q. Which of these is the most important role (for an MP)?

	%
Holding the government to account	33.0
Examining legislation	12.8
Speaking in chamber	0.6
Dealing with constituents' grievances	15.1
Voting with political party	2.2
Informing constituents about government activity	0.6
Protecting interests of constituency	18.4
Writing/giving speeches	0.6
Working on departmental select committees	2.2
Appearing on TV	0.6
No reply	14.0

$N = 179$.

Source: Hansard Society Commission on Parliamentary Scrutiny (2001, p. 142); by permission of Dod's Parliamentary Communications.

of constituency work has been a concern for many MPs in recent years. Resources available to members have increased (see Chapter 2), enabling them to cope more efficiently with constituency correspondence, but the sheer volume of letters and e-mails, and demands to attend constituency functions, means that the overall burden has increased. As we have seen, MPs newly elected in 2010 estimated that they devoted more than half their time to constituency work when the House was sitting. Much of this time was devoted to dealing with constituency casework that could be dealt with by other bodies or grievance-chasing agencies. It limits the time available to spend on those collective tasks that MPs alone can fulfil. Recent years have seen a decline in attendance at meetings of select committees and back-bench party committees. One possible explanation (but not necessarily the only one) is the amount of time MPs have to devote to the growing volume of constituency work. Indeed, the House has changed its own procedures in order to accommodate this burgeoning constituency activity. Ten Fridays in each session are designated as non-sitting Fridays, to enable MPs to devote more time to their constituencies, and, as part of the change in sitting hours, the rising time on Thursdays has gradually been brought forward, initially to 6.00 p.m. and then, from October 2012, to 5.00 p.m. to allow MPs to return to their constituencies that evening. The House has moved from a five-day week to what amounts, in effect, to a three-day week (lasting from Monday evening to

Thursday evening), if that. Most important business is now concentrated on Tuesdays and Wednesdays.

The challenge faced by MPs in juggling constituency work with other responsibilities was summed up by Peter Hain, Labour MP for Neath:

> The pressures on new MPs are enormous, not just from constituents but from the daily, unfamiliar, whirl of duties and meetings in Westminster. Some are simply overwhelmed and never really find their feet. Others get buffeted around by competing demands. Even though I had pre-planned considerably, I felt as if I was on a constant treadmill, keen to do my best for Neath and to make my mark in Parliament. (Hain 2012, pp. 161–2)

MPs devote, then, considerable time to constituency work, but much of that time is occupied by the concerns of a limited number of constituents who may not be typical of constituents as a whole. As Labour MP Paul Flynn recorded:

> A tiny number of constituents and campaigners can hi-jack the attention of the office with a relentless flow of letters and calls. Often they have genuine grievances or are pushing fine causes. Sooner rather than later they must be told firmly that they are destroying goodwill and exasperating staff. Often they have a single all-consuming problem and fail to understand the mass of daily demands on a MP's time. (Flynn 2012, p. 143)

An MP may draw generalizations on the basis of a few letters or e-mails from constituents. In some cases, this may suit the MP's purpose, but it may also distort the input the MP has in the political process. Letters tend to be from more literate constituents. In some cases, MPs are well aware that certain constituents who contact them are not representative of others but, as Flynn noted, are simply using the MP to pursue a burning and sometimes irrational grievance. MPs have to cope with what are generally deemed 'crank' cases. These can be time-consuming and, on rare occasions, dangerous. (In 2010, one MP was stabbed twice, suffering life-threatening injuries, at his constituency surgery; ten years earlier, another MP was seriously injured, and his assistant killed, by a mentally disturbed constituent who turned up at the constituency surgery wielding a sword.) MPs can find themselves fulfilling a social welfare role that could, and probably should, be fulfilled by professional agencies.

Constituents

Constituents accord priority to the MP's constituency role. Survey data drawn on by Cain *et al.* (1987, p. 38) show that a plurality of respondents identified the protection of the district, or constituency, as the most important representative role. ('Keeping in touch' came second.) Dealing with policy and engaging in oversight was bottom of the list. The attachment to protecting the constituency was even more highly rated by people in Britain than in the USA: 'The constituency service roles, protecting the district and helping people, were ranked highest by one-quarter of the American respondents and by nearly half of the British. Indeed, protecting the district was the highest-ranking role in Britain' (Cain *et al.* 1987, p. 39). This finding was reinforced by a later survey, undertaken for a study for a House of Commons committee, which found that two-thirds of respondents thought that MPs ought to be 'working on behalf of individual constituents' (Select Committee on Televising the Proceedings of the House 1990, p. 85).

MPs generally appear to achieve what constituents expect of them. In many cases, this is an authoritative explanation of why some action has been taken. A letter from a minister, or an agency chief executive, forwarded by the MP, demonstrates not only action by the MP on the constituent's behalf but also usually provides a substantive response to the constituent's concerns.

Constituents not only expect their MP to be active on behalf of the constituency but they also appear to have some knowledge of the MP and, in the case of a substantial minority, call on the services of the MP. One survey found that almost two-thirds of respondents could name their MP; this compares with just over 30 per cent of Americans who could name their member of Congress (Cain *et al.* 1987, p. 28; though see Modernisation Committee 2004, p. 9). In the 1985 Social Attitudes Survey, 11 per cent of respondents claimed to have contacted their MP, a figure that is 1 per cent to 3 per cent higher than earlier estimates. The Hansard Society *Audit of Political Engagement* found that approximately 16 per cent of respondents had contacted an MP (or MSP or AM) or local councillor, the figure not varying much over the years of the audit (Hansard Society 2010, p. 82).

The work that is undertaken by MPs appears to attract a positive evaluation, and that response appears to be most positive in the event of contact. One survey in the 1970s found that, the closer the contact, the greater the belief that the MP was doing a good job. As Ivor Crewe (1975, p. 322) memorably put it, on reviewing the data: 'familiarity appears to

Table 11.3   Evaluations of local MPs

Q. On balance, are you satisfied or dissatisfied with the job the local MP is doing for this constituency?

	1991	*1995*	*2001**
Satisfied	43	43	42
Dissatisfied	23	23	19
Don't know/no opinion	34	34	39

Note: * Satisfied combines 'very/fairly satisfied', dissatisfied combines 'fairly/very dissatisfied', don't know/no opinion combines 'neither satisfied nor dissatisfied' and 'don't know'.
Sources: MORI, *State of the Nation, 1995* (London: MORI, 1995) for 1991 and 1995; MORI, 'Polls and survey archive 2001' accessed at www.mori.com for 2001.

breed content'. Members' responsiveness may also have encouraged more constituents to make contact. One survey found that, of those who contacted their MP, 75 per cent reported a 'good' or 'very good' response (Cain *et al.* 1979, pp. 6–7). More generally, constituents believe that the local MP is doing a good job. The State of the Nation surveys undertaken for the Joseph Rowntree Trust show that roughly twice as many people think the local MP is doing a good job as those believing the s/he is doing a bad job. Table 11.3 suggests that this evaluation remains fairly stable. As the Commons Modernisation Committee reported in 2004, the evidence it had received showed that individual MPs 'remain fairly credible in the public eye' (Modernisation Committee 2004, p. 9).

Furthermore, as reported in the Hansard Society 2010 *Audit of Political Engagement*, constituents tend to have a much more positive view of the work of the local MP compared with Parliament and MPs in general (Figure 11.1). The MPs' expenses scandal in 2009 (see Chapter 2) badly affected MPs generally and some Members in particular, resulting in some being deselected by their local parties or effectively being forced to retire (see Criddle 2010, pp. 310–13). However, constituents continued to distinguish between MPs in general and their local MP. Figure 11.1 reflects the distinction, but it is even more marked in the data shown in Figure 11.2, showing the results of a poll conducted at the end of May 2009, just after the expenses' scandal erupted. Constituents trusted the local MP to tell the truth in a way they did not expect of MPs generally. As the pollsters noted, 'Although the public have consistently for many years distrusted, and been dissatisfied with the performance of, politicians in general and MPs in particular, we have always found a sharp

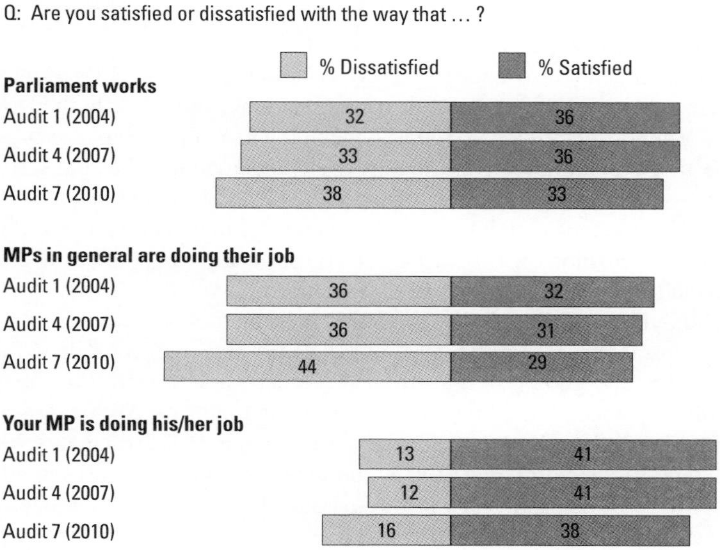

Q: Are you satisfied or dissatisfied with the way that … ?

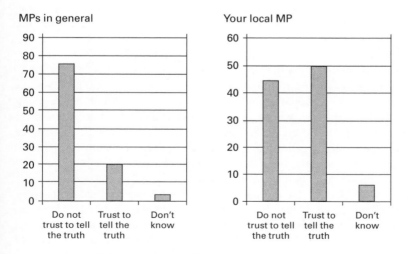

Source: Hansard Society 2010, p. 88.

Figure 11.1   Satisfaction with Parliament and MPs

MPs in general   **Your local MP**

Source: Worcester, Mortimore, Baines and Gill 2011, p. 140

Figure 11.2   Trust in MPs

distinction in their views when asked about their own MP' (Worcester *et al.* 2011, p. 139).

Constituents also appear to have benefited more recently from the changes made to how they collectively can make their case to the House of Commons. Until the 2010 Parliament, the use of petitions was mostly inefficient and ineffective. Citizens could spend hours, even days, soliciting signatures for a petition to be presented to Parliament. It was sent to an MP – the local MP where it affected a local interest (as, for example, with the closure of a local hospital) – who then presented it, either formally on the floor of the House, or informally, by placing it in a bag behind the Speaker's chair. The formal presentation was very short, with no substantive speech being allowed. Petitions were not debated and were largely ignored by government. Perhaps not surprisingly, citizens with grievances started favouring petitioning the Prime Minister instead of Parliament. In the two-year period from January 1999 to January 2001, 492 petitions with over 200 signatures in each were presented to Downing Street: citizens were by-passing Parliament in favour of the head of government.

The situation changed significantly in the Parliament returned in 2010. As we have noted (Chapter 6), the government introduced e-petitions, enabling citizens to sign petitions electronically. If a petition achieves more than 100,000 signatures, the government forwards it to the Backbench Business Committee in the Commons. It is then up to the committee to determine whether a debate should take place. It has not confined itself to considering petitions which have met the 100,000 threshold, but has considered petitions championed by MPs which may, for example, be of particular local interest. Thus, for example, when an e-petition was started in Hull on potential job losses at a local BAE aircraft factory, it was supported by local MPs and, even though not reaching 100,000 signatures, was accepted by the Backbench Business Committee for debate. The difference between petitions reaching 100,000 signatures and those falling below that figure is that most falling in the former category have, to date, been accepted for debate, whereas only a small number of the latter have been accepted.

On the face of it, constituents thus seem to be well served (and appear to regard themselves as being well served) by their local MP. However, there are problems. As we have seen, only a minority of constituents make contact with their MP. This could reflect contentment (or a lack of discontent) on the part of those who do not make contact. As we have seen, more think the local MP is doing a good job than those who think s/he is doing a bad job. The proportion expressing satisfaction, however, is a minority. More than a third of constituents do not have an opinion on the work of their MP (see Table 11.3).

Levels of satisfaction also appear to vary, depending on the nature of the constituency. By parliamentary tradition, constituency cases are dealt with by the local MP. If a constituent writes to another MP, that MP will pass the letter on to the constituency MP. The constituent is thus dependent on the quality of the local MP in pursuing casework. Some are more competent, persistent and interested than others. Though MPs generally accord significance to casework, not all treat it in the same way. There is anecdotal (and some hard) evidence that some MPs are fairly disdainful of constituency work (see Searing 1994, pp. 137–8): Labour MP Tony Banks, for example, when announcing in 2004 his decision to retire from the Commons, declared that he had found constituency work 'tedious in the extreme' (BBC News Online, 27 November 2004).

Also, MPs are not trained in grievance-chasing roles; they are essentially amateurs in the task. In the words of one MP, they are 'unspecialised, ill-equipped, amateurish and over-worked' (Alan Beith, cited in Norton 1982b, p. 66). They are expected to pursue grievances in a wide range of areas, many of which will not fall within their field of specialization or interest. They are also expected to pursue grievances with bodies, most notably local authorities, for which they have no responsibility. The number of such bodies is, if anything, growing: 'The number of government functions and services privatised, contracted-out or deregulated has further reduced the scope for the MP to exert direct influence. They may apply pressure by dint of their position, but only to get access to the people who do make the decisions' (Power 1996, p. 15).

Conclusion

The link between Parliament and citizen, in terms of direct contact, is through the individual Member of Parliament. That link historically is well established and is reinforced by the nature of the electoral system. Research by Bowler and Farrell (1993) shows election by geographic constituencies is more likely to encourage constituency service than election by list systems of proportional representation. Constituents expect 'their' Member of Parliament to take action on their behalf, independent of the MP's collective and party roles. MPs, as we have seen, have fulfilled a number of roles as constituency MPs, and those roles have changed as the nature of MPs has changed, and as constituents' expectations have grown. Constituents contact their local MP in increasing numbers to take action on their behalf, typically by requesting information or confirmation that a matter is being investigated. A growing number also write to express opinions on issues of public policy. MPs have sought to meet constituents' expectations and have devoted more time to constituency service.

Constituency activity is an intrinsic part, then, of the work of the MP. However, as we have seen, it is not problem-free. From a pluralist perspective, it is possible to identify what may be considered as the principal concern. The emphasis on constituency work reinforces the realization that MPs are not able to utilize their coercive capacity, or, for that matter, much persuasion, in affecting outcomes of public policy. Members therefore absorb themselves in constituency work, which may engender a degree of satisfaction and occasionally result in a changed decision, but which none the less constitutes a distraction from the collective task of members. This view is best encapsulated by the observation of Greg Power that

> there are many MPs who work assiduously on behalf of their constituents and achieve much success in doing so. But such work largely fails to call on the expertise or skills of the MP and almost totally fails to utilise their role in Parliament. At a time when Parliament is failing to act as a check on the power of the Executive, there is a serious question as to whether this role is the best use of an MP's time and resources. (Power 1996, p. 15)

The institutional approach enables us to look at constituency work from a different perspective: it stresses the extent and institutionalization of the process by which MPs pursue constituents' concerns. There is a well-established process by which MPs take up issues on behalf of constituents. It is highly institutionalized, encompassing an acceptance by ministers as well as backbenchers that it is legitimate and should therefore be undertaken. As we have seen, despite the time-consuming nature of the work, MPs accept it is as a necessary part of their work, and equally important, so too do ministers. As we have seen, they abide by the convention that letters from parliamentarians to ministers must receive a reply from a minister, and not from a civil servant. Much of this activity does not result in changed decisions; it absorbs a great deal of time of ministers and officials and it potentially detracts MPs from other, collective, activities. None the less, it delivers a service to citizens, one that they expect and appear to appreciate. Citizens attach importance to the constituency role and rate it above the collective, or Westminster, role of MPs.

The evaluation of the work undertaken by the MP as a constituency member exists independently of citizens' evaluation of the collective role undertaken by MPs. As we have seen from Table 11.3 and Figure 11.1, evaluations of the work done by the local MP have tended to remain stable, as well as positive, certainly relative to MPs in general. Though MPs collectively are usually deemed to do a good job, evaluations of their work can swing markedly. Voters appear able to distinguish the service provided by the local MP from the institution of the House of Commons.

The institutional approach also alerts us to the complexity of addressing the demands imposed nowadays by constituency work. To expect MPs to devote more time to work in Westminster requires reducing the demands of constituency work, ignoring it or providing more resources to cope with it. There is little obvious scope for reducing the demand, other than through a widespread educative process. Ignoring it has the potential to build up tension within the political system. Expanding resources may, but not necessarily, enable MPs to keep pace with the demands made of them. Some MPs have been able to deploy their staff and office resources in such a way as to enable them to concentrate on their role in Westminster. However, there is a challenge in that resources are finite. There is limited opportunity to increase them at a time of economic stringency, yet this is the very time when one might expect demands on MPs to be even greater than before, as many of their constituents struggle to hold jobs or keep their businesses afloat.

Demands on MPs also come from organized interests and these, as we shall see in the next chapter, are also adding considerably to the workload of MPs. For MPs, the challenge is one of balance, ensuring that the MP–constituency link is maintained effectively, while not jeopardizing their Westminster responsibilities. Whereas there are alternative agencies to MPs grievance chasers, only MPs collectively can fulfil the tasks accorded to the House of Commons in relation to government.

12

Speaking for Different Interests

Members of Parliament are elected for defined constituencies. As we saw in Chapter 9, constituents expect them to give priority to local concerns and an increasing amount of time is devoted by members to constituency casework. However, members also devote considerable time to listening to, and expressing the demands of, different interests in society. Citizens with shared interests have increasingly come together to form organized bodies – interest groups – to defend or advance their policy preferences (Grant 2000; Coxall 2001; Watts 2007; see also Jordan and Maloney 2007). Some groups may be composed of a member's constituents: a local charity or the local chamber of commerce, for example. Others may have no direct constituency connection but believe they have a case that will engage the MP's attention.

Like constituency casework, the task of pursuing the demands of different groups is a growing one. However, unlike constituency work, it is not confined to the House of Commons. Peers are also important targets for groups seeking to have some influence on the content of public policy. By expressing the views of different interests in society, members of both Houses fulfil a number of functions, not unlike to those carried out by the MP as a constituency member. They act as safety valves, advocates and powerful friends.

The role of party

For more than a century, the most important organized interest has been that of party (see Chapter 2). MPs are elected on the basis of their party label; parties serve to aggregate interests, and candidates stand on the basis of their party's manifesto and are expected, if elected, to support the party in implementing the promises made to the electorate. The result of this, as we have seen, has been party cohesion in Parliament. Within Parliament, and especially the House of Commons, parties dominate not only voting but also most other aspects of parliamentary behaviour. Debate is frequently, though not always, partisan, and members are called to speak on the presumption that it *is* (hence they are called from alternate sides of the chamber). Question Time is seen increasingly as representing a partisan tussle between government and opposition front benches (see Franklin and Norton 1993), especially on Wednesdays when there is a gladiatorial contest between the Prime Minister and the Leader of the Opposition. Public bill committees, as we have seen, are essentially the chamber in miniature, with proceedings dominated by the party clash and the operation of the whips.

This domination by party has advantages for the political system. It ensures some degree of coherence, and electors know what they are voting for. The names of individual candidates may not mean much to them, but they understand the party label. Parties compete essentially for the all-or-nothing gains of electoral victory. Once returned with a majority of seats, a party can implement a particular programme of public policy and is then answerable to the electorate at the next general election. Electors are offered a choice, and they can turn a government out.

A number of problems have been identified in this system. Some critics have queried whether there is much to choose between the parties. The more they resemble 'catch-all' parties (Kirchheimer 1966), the less differentiated a choice they offer. Other critics have contended that at various points the choice has been far too stark, with little point of contact between the main parties – as, for example, in the 1983 general election. As we have seen in Chapter 10, some critics of the political system have also challenged the basic legitimacy of an electoral system that can produce an absolute majority of seats on the basis of less than 50 per cent of the votes cast. There is also an important question of legitimacy stemming from popular perceptions of party domination.

The stance of electors towards Parliament and its members presents a conundrum. On the one hand, voters elect MPs on the basis of the party label, but on the other, they expect the MP to do far more than merely support the party in Parliament, and greater emphasis is given to a local than to a national role. For MPs, there is thus an important balance to be maintained, loyally supporting the party on whose label they were elected, while at the same time carving out a role independent of party, not least in order to pursue constituency demands. At times, the roles may conflict, as when local interests are threatened by government policy and the local MP is a member of the governing party.

In post-war decades, the balance has been tipped predominantly, if not overwhelmingly, in favour of party. Party cohesiveness reached its peak in the 1950s (Norton 1975). Independent activity by members was extremely limited and the stranglehold of party rendered Parliament essentially a closed institution, with no means of independent access (Norton 1991a). Though party was essential for ensuring a coherent system, its hegemony conveyed the appearance of MPs as 'lobby fodder' and the institution as a body for little more than rubber-stamping decisions taken elsewhere. The consequence was frustration for MPs wanting to have some effect on the political system, and a tendency for organized groups to ignore Parliament and to concentrate their efforts on government. Government neglected Parliament in favour of pressure groups, generating what Richardson and Jordan (1979) dubbed 'a post-parliamentary democracy'. There were few opportunities for members of the public to follow what was going on, and little point in making the effort (Norton 1991a, pp. 223–4).

However, the situation was to change in the last quarter of the twentieth century. As discussed in Chapter 2, the stranglehold of party was relaxed. The change was relative, but significant. The demands made of MPs by constituents increased, and so too did the demands made by organized interests. Increasingly, MPs – and peers – found themselves the targets of representations, better known as lobbying (a phrase deriving from those who used to hover in the lobby of the New York state capitol to seek special favours: Congressional Quarterly 1987, p. 2) from a vast range of organized interests. The most important organized interest, still largely determining their parliamentary behaviour, was that of party. But it was no longer the exclusive interest determining their actions. Parliament became a more open institution.

As the Political and Constitutional Reform Committee of the House of Commons noted in 2012, 'The right of citizens to lobby their Government and elected representatives is fundamental to a healthy, vibrant democracy' (Political and Constitutional Reform Committee 2012, p. 3). Such contact, it recorded, could be beneficial to government and parliament. However, it went on, 'when there are concerns, as published widely in the media of late, that some lobbyists may have undue access and influence over the policy-making process it threatens to reduce public confidence in the wider political system'. These concerns affected principally the lobbying of government rather than of Parliament (Public Administration Committee 2009). Lobbying of Parliament, though, has also been affected. Such lobbying has increased in recent decades, mostly to the benefit of Parliament and to those making representations, but the activity has been far from problem free. For MPs, the challenge has been one of pursuing causes on the basis of merit rather than self-interest.

The impact of groups

Lobbying of members of both Houses by organized interests, such interests including large companies, professional bodies, charities, unions, consumer groups and a vast array of pressure groups seeking a change in public policy, is now a pervasive feature of Westminster life.

Lobbying by such interests is not new. As early as 1910, for example, the National Farmers' Union appointed a 'Parliamentary Lobbyist' (Wootton 1975, p. 216). The presence of lobbyists was noted in the 1950s and 1960s (Finer 1958, p. 23; Walkland 1968). What has changed is the extent and the visibility of such lobbying. Organized interests now impinge massively on the time and consciousness of members of both Houses. This was demonstrated towards the end of twentieth century by a survey carried out of more than 250 organizations – encompassing the range just noted (companies, charities, consumer groups and the like) – which found that three-quarters maintained 'regular or frequent contact with one or more Members of Parliament' (Rush 1990, p. 280).

That contact is sometimes in person, not least during the committee stage of bills. The representatives of groups with a particular interest in a bill will normally be present during sittings, and committee members will sometimes be seen leaving the room for a quick discussion in the corridor with a lobbyist for a group on whose behalf the member is speaking. Such lobbyists are frequently in evidence in the public gallery during the report stage of bills and on occasion fill the public seating during select committee hearings.

More frequently, the contact is by letter or e-mail. The increase in constituency mail has been supplemented by mail from organized groups of one type or another. The survey of organizations found that 34 per cent of them sent information or briefings regularly or often to MPs, and almost 60 per cent did so occasionally. Only 6 per cent of them did not send such material (Rush 1990, p. 280).

For members, then, the burden lies in more than simply being the recipients of straightforward information. The material often involves the member being invited to take some action. Of the 189 organizations found in the survey to maintain contact with MPs, 83 per cent had asked an MP to table a parliamentary question. Most had also asked an MP to arrange a meeting at the Commons (78 per cent), to table an amendment to a bill (62 per cent) and to table a motion (51 per cent). Approximately half of the groups had also asked MPs to arrange meetings with ministers. More than a third had asked a member to sponsor a private member's bill (Rush 1990, p. 281).

Group contact with parliamentarians was thus substantial by the ninth decade of the twentieth century and since then lobbying has become more prominent. The change has been qualitative as well as quantitative. The burden is not just in the number of e-mails or letters written to members. The issues are often complex and technically demanding. Groups interested in a particular clause of a bill will write to explain why it needs amending. Finance bills and those that impose regulatory regimes can be highly detailed, requiring knowledge of the subject in order to grasp the arguments being advanced by those seeking changes to the measures.

During the passage of a bill, members will draw on material supplied by groups in order to question provisions and to propose amendments. The extent of group activity is frequently apparent from explicit references to their briefing material. Thus, for example, during second reading of the Welfare Reform Bill in the Commons in March 2011, there were various references to ideas, briefings or comments from bodies such as Capability Scotland, Centre for Social Justice, CLIC Sargent, Enable (Scotland), Family Action, Federation of Small Businesses, Haringey Phoenix Group, Institute for Fiscal Studies, Mencap, Mindwise, Multiple Sclerosis Society, Muscular Dystrophy Campaign, Rethink, Scope, Social Market Foundation, and the Zacchaeus 2000 Trust. The most frequent references were made by those speaking for the opposition. Indeed a good example of the use made of input from such groups is found in the intervention made by one Labour MP during the speech of the Secretary of State, Iain Duncan Smith:

> **Kate Green (Stretford and Urmston) (Lab):** Can the right hon. Gentleman confirm that as a result of that further consideration, there will be no circumstances in which, as a result of child care costs, a parent could be faced with a marginal deduction rate of more than 100%, as some models prepared for us by Family Action have suggested?

However, the most intensive lobbying tends to take place at committee stage. The names of members of the committee are published, and organizations seeking changes direct their efforts towards those members. Committee members will often be swamped with letters and briefings. Such lobbying is not confined to government bills. Private members' bills can be the subject of even more intense pressures. Bills on abortion, assisted dying and animal welfare, for example, elicit extensive lobbying by pressure groups and their supporters.

Nor is such lobbying confined to MPs:

the House of Lords offers fruitful ground for inserting relatively technical amendments which may be important to a pressure group's
members. Even if the amendment is not pressed to a vote, it may be
used to extract further assurances from the government. (Grant 2000,
p. 158)

A survey by Baggott found that half of the groups surveyed were in touch
with peers at least once a month, and almost one in five were in contact
on a weekly basis (see Baggott 1995, pp. 93, 164). Groups utilizing regular contact with the House, and understanding the legislative process, will
not only identify particular problems with a bill but also offer the text of
amendments. The House is valuable also for raising issues through
debates and questions, thus ensuring that the issues are on the public
record and elicit a ministerial response. One survey of active peers found
that almost all of them had asked written questions on behalf of pressure
groups. More than 60 per cent had tabled oral questions, and a similar
proportion had raised a point in debate (Baldwin 1990, pp. 162–3).

The extent of lobbying of the House of Lords is indicated by the data
reported in Chapter 11 regarding the volume of mail received in the
Palace of Westminster. In 2011, more than half-a-million items of post
flowed into the House of Lords: given that peers do not have constituents,
the bulk of this was from outside organizations. This total does not
include e-mails, a form of communication that is now pervasive and,
when a bill is going through the House, usually more extensive than letter
writing (other than when a group has encouraged supporters to write
personally to peers). Correspondence will peak when a contentious bill is
going through; otherwise, correspondence will tend to be of the sort keeping the target member informed of activities; it is common to receive
newsletters and magazines.

Members of both Houses are thus subject to extensive lobbying by
organized groups, and not simply through occasional letter writing or the
submission of briefing material. Many organizations will have a degree of
contact that is semi-institutionalized, not least through the burgeoning all-
party groups (see Chapter 6) and through having staff permanently
employed to deal with parliamentary affairs. As we noted in Chapter 6, one
study in 2012 found that more than 300 all-party groups had received funding or support from outside groups; some provide the administrative
support for groups. More than 80 groups issued parliamentary passes to
staff with outside interests, including members of lobbying firms and think
thanks. A number of organizations made contributions in order to enjoy
associate membership of an all-party group (Ball and Beleaga 2012).

The result is extensive contact between organized groups and parliamentarians. Despite the realization that policy originates with government – and that measures brought forward by government will pass – groups none the less perceive some utility in lobbying Parliament and engage in such lobbying on an ever-increasing scale.

Explanations of change

As with the growth of constituency demands, there is no single explanation for the increase in parliamentary lobbying by organized interests. There are several independent developments that appear to have coincided, producing this phenomenon (Norton 1991b, pp. 65–9). Changes in the nature of groups, of government and of Parliament have contributed to the change.

Interest groups

The most significant changes in organized groups are, firstly, the greater utilization of lobbying by existing groups – especially since 1979, groups appear to have 'discovered' Parliament – and, secondly, the growth in the number of groups, previously unorganized sections of society coming together to form bodies to make their case both to government and to Parliament, sometimes with notable success.

Making use of Parliament

Interest groups are well established, but for much of the twentieth century did not make much use of Parliament. They either provided services to their members (especially so in the case of sectional interest groups) and were not much involved in seeking to influence public policy, or else did seek to influence public policy but sought to do so primarily through contact with ministers and civil servants. Contacting MPs or going on a demonstration in Parliament Square was seen as a mark of failure, of not being able to get one's view over to government. It was the recourse of 'outsider' groups; 'insider' groups had the inside track to government departments (Grant 2000; Heffernan 2011, pp. 177–8) and often formed with other groups and civil servants to form policy networks (Marsh and Rhodes 1992; Smith 1993). It was only as a result of changes within both government and Parliament, discussed below, that groups were encouraged to see Parliament in a new light and make more effort to connect with MPs and peers. Though the target remained the executive, Parliament assumed greater significance than before as a channel to the executive. Groups now sought to go through Parliament rather than round it.

The changes in government and Parliament provided an impetus for groups to lobby Parliament more than before, but the motivation to do so has been allied with enhanced facilities for doing so. These have included the facility of new technology, providing the means of more rapid communication. Much of the material received by MPs and peers is now through e-mail and desktop publishing facilities. E-mail, as we have noted (Chapter 11), is an efficient and cheap way of making contact, enabling all parliamentarians with e-mail addresses to be contacted at the press of a button. The value to groups is one especially of speed. Briefing material can be e-mailed quickly, if necessary the day before a particular amendment is being discussed. MPs and peers are more likely to see an e-mail sent the day before a particular debate. A letter sent the day before may arrive in the Palace of Westminster, but it may not reach the member's desk, or may not be opened, before the debate. The preferred means of contact by groups is now an e-mail with a briefing document attached. When a second reading debate is imminent, the e-mail in-boxes of members will start to fill with briefing material. Hefty documents, which would be expensive to send by mail to a large number of parliamentarians, can be sent electronically without having to stuff envelopes and pay postage. E-mails and text messages can be sent in response to developments in the chamber or in committee.

The other change has been in the professional bodies available to undertake such lobbying activities. Some employ lobbying firms, known formally as political consultancies. The last quarter of the twentieth century was the growth period for such bodies (see Grantham 1989; Grantham and Seymour-Ure 1990). Such firms, often composed of former civil servants, parliamentary officials, party officials and ex-MPs offer a range of services, including the monitoring of activities in Westminster – and Whitehall – for clients, advising on how to lobby effectively, and lobbying politicians and civil servants on behalf of clients. The range of bodies using their services grew and their use soon became widespread among organizations seeking to influence public policy (see Grantham and Seymour-Ure 1990, pp. 50–6). Not only do such consultancy firms facilitate lobbying, it is also in their commercial interest to encourage it. The more they engage in such activity, especially if it appears to have some effect, the more it encourages other organizations to use their services. However, as we shall see, their activities have proved to be controversial.

Many organizations have also enhanced their lobbying capacity by appointing their own in-house parliamentary affairs officers, with responsibility for developing relations with MPs and peers. Most leading charities, consumer groups and public bodies such as English Heritage, as well as firms and other commercial organizations, have such officers.

The result of this growth of lobbying firms and in-house lobbyists is that there are estimated to be 3,500 to 4,000 full-time lobbyists in the UK (Political and Constitutional Reform Committee 2012, p. 13).

Getting organized

Established groups have sought to influence public policy through Parliament and have had to do so in an increasingly crowded lobbying environment. More groups have come into existence not least as previously unorganized sections of society have started to find a voice.

As we saw in Chapter 2, interests began to organize during the nineteenth century more extensively than before. That trend continued into the twentieth century and has been pronounced in the period since 1960. With increased education and political awareness – what Inglehart (1977) has termed cognitive mobilization – more and more people have been willing to join together to seek some change in public policy. 'To some extent, the 1980s and 1990s have been a period of increased pluralism. More groups are involved in politics and more people are involved in pressure groups' (Smith 1995, p. 110). Groups are now notable both for their number, their different forms, and the support that they enjoy. The National Trust and the Royal Society for the Protection of Birds (RSPB) have memberships that far exceed the membership of any political party.

A good illustration of a section of society previously unorganized is to be found in the case of disabled people, of whom there are nearly 10 million in Britain. Despite post-war decades seeing some organizations being formed to make demands on behalf of disabled people, this group was still an under-represented and ill-organized sector of society, and the problems suffered were only dimly perceived by the public and by politicians:

> Before ... 1964 disablement had simply not figured on the parliamentary agenda at all. There had been no mention of the problems of the disabled in either of the major party manifestos, and there had been no debate on disablement in the whole of the parliamentary term from 1959 to 1964. (Topliss and Gould 1981, p. 4)

Another example is that of homosexuals. Though there were organizations such as the Homosexual Law Reform Society, founded in 1958 (see Grey 1992), the voice of those who were gay was hardly heard in the corridors of Whitehall or Westminster. There were other groups, formed in the 1970s, campaigning for homosexual equality, and some support from bodies such as the National Council for Civil Liberties, but, as Read and Marsh (1998, p. 26) noted, 'this growth in institutional support for homosexual equality was not universal, with conservative views remaining prevalent both in society and (especially) at Westminster'. Others not well organized included – to take just a few examples – students, the homeless, retired people, the unemployed, travellers, and prisoners. For such people in society, there was a danger of seeing Parliament as having little to offer them. MPs represented parties and could use party as a cloak to protect them from having to deal with issues that did not engage the support of their party or constituents.

What has been notable has been the extent to which this situation has changed. In the field of disablement, for example, existing charities were joined in the latter half of the twentieth century by a raft of campaigning organizations. The poverty lobby gained a powerful voice through the Child Poverty Action Group (Field 1982, pp. 42–4). The range as well as the volume has been extensive, and by the beginning of twenty-first century, the interests of the disabled were well represented, and found a parliamentary voice through an active all-party group on disability – with a secretariat provided by the charity Disabilities Rights UK – and complemented by other all-party groups covering particular disabilities (such as chronic pain, dementia, and diabetes) as well as through various champions in both Houses. In June 2012, for example, Lord Touhig initiated a question for short debate on the steps being taken by government to provide support for people with dementia. This followed earlier debates on the subject, including one in 2009, and another in 2004 initiated by Lord Sutherland of Houndwood (president of Alzheimer's Scotland – Action on Dementia) on the needs of those suffering from Alzheimer's disease and other forms of dementia. Relevant to our foregoing discussion, he noted that it was the twenty-fifth anniversary of the foundation of the Alzheimer's Society. Success for the lobby on disabilities has been reflected both in legislation (the Disability Discrimination Acts of 1995, 2005 and 2010) and in the formation of an Office for Disability Issues to co-ordinate within government the development and delivery of services for the disabled.

Similarly, the period since the late 1980s has seen a remarkable growth in bodies promoting gay rights. The most prominent has been the campaign group Stonewall (www.stonewall.org.uk), formed in 1989 in reaction to the enactment of Section 28 of the Local Government Act 1988 which prohibited the 'promotion' of homosexuality by local authorities (see McManus 2011, Chapters 9 and 10). Stonewall soon developed as a highly organized political lobbying organization, with professional staff, and was to the fore in lobbying MPs and peers in order to achieve a reduction in the age of consent for homosexual sex and the repeal of Section 28, both of which were eventually achieved. It campaigned, successfully, for gay couples to adopt children, and for civil partnerships. Its annual fundraising dinner became a high profile event, attracting media celebrities and cabinet ministers. By 2012, it employed more than 60 staff in England, Wales and Scotland, engaged in research and education as well as lobbying. Other gay rights organizations also came into being or established a greater prominence, including within each of the main political parties.

Such newly-formed groups also benefited from the facility of the internet and e-mail to contact parliamentarians and ensure that their voice was heard. They thus added to what was becoming an extremely active phenomenon of parliamentary lobbying.

Government

In the years from 1945 to 1979, government drew on organized interests in developing public policy. There was co-operation between government, labour and business; in essence, the post-parliamentary democracy identified by Richardson and Jordan (1979). That co-operation came under pressure as economic conditions worsened and government had to move from distributive to redistributive policies. Groups were forced to compete for a share of resources that were not expanding. The relationship then changed substantially during the era of Conservative government from 1979 to 1997: 'The election of Mrs Thatcher heralded a new approach to pressure group relationships' (Grant 2000, p. 3). The government sought greater autonomy in policy-making (Gamble 1994), resulting in more distant relationships with organized interests, especially at the level of high policy (such as economic policy). Bodies such as the Trades Union Congress were virtually frozen out of policy discussions. The more groups perceived that they lacked the access they previously enjoyed to government, the more they turned to Parliament as a means of achieving some input into the deliberations on public policy. Though the perception that government distanced itself from organized interests was greater than the reality (extensive contact was maintained between departments and outside bodies), this perception affected behaviour, and the lobbying of Parliament continued under a Labour government that also exhibited some autonomy in policy-making. Despite developing relationships with various organizations, 'there was no reversion to the old style corporatism of the 1970s' (Grant 2000, p. 4; see Heffernan 2011, p. 179). Economic recession after 2008 also exacerbated the competition between groups for limited resources, especially in the form of public funding. MPs and peers were recruited as allies in the attempt to maintain existing support or to stave off government encroachment.

Parliament

Groups thus turned to Parliament in various ways. At the same time, there were developments internal to the institution that increased its attractiveness. The greater behavioural independence of MPs (see Chapter 2) meant that changes to public policy, in particular to the detail of bills, might be achievable as a result of back-bench pressure. The change has been marked in the twenty-first century, and especially among Conservative MPs newly elected in 2010. Following the removal of most hereditary peers from the second chamber in 1999, the House of Lords has appeared to be more self-confident in challenging government (Russell 2010b, pp. 866–85) and been active in achieving changes to a range of bills.

The introduction of the departmental select committees in the Commons has also provided groups with a very clear focus for their activities. Select committees determine their own agendas, the evidence they take is published, and the government responds in writing to a committee's recommendations. For groups, select committees are a valuable conduit for getting their views on the public record and before government. As one Labour member of the Trade and Industry Committee once observed, 'trade unions are delighted with the committee ... the main benefit is to put into the "public domain" information that otherwise might not be available' (Judge 1990, p. 192). They may also serve to influence the recommendations.

The attractiveness has increased as the committees have achieved a high profile. That profile has been enhanced by the reforms implemented in the 2010 Parliament. The election of committee chairs and the members has contributed to a perception of greater independence. Media coverage of some high profile hearings has also raised the profile of the committees. For the leaders of interest groups, appearing before a select committee is an opportunity to make one's case (not least in relation to others who may be appearing) as well as a challenge: witnesses take such appearances seriously and in some cases may seek coaching from their in-house parliamentary advisers or from political consultants.

The degree of committee attractiveness to groups is reflected not just in the oral evidence provided by the representatives of groups – they attend by invitation of the committee – but also in the volume of written evidence submitted. Anyone may submit written evidence and committees routinely put out calls for evidence once an enquiry begins. Many groups ensure that they are on committees' mailing lists, and once an enquiry in their area of interest is announced they prepare and submit written evidence. Committees are often inundated with memoranda.

The same consideration applies to committees in the Lords. There has been a growth in the number of committees in the twenty-first century (Chapter 6) and inquiries, including by *ad hoc* committees, can attract a flurry of written evidence. The Constitution Committee, for example, has examined topics, ranging from regulators (Constitution Committee 2004a) to judicial appointments (Constitution Committee 2012b), which have attracted extensive submissions from interested groups.

The attraction of the House of Commons to interest groups has been enhanced in the 2010 Parliament not only by the reforms made to extant select committees, but also by the creation of the Backbench Business Committee and by the introduction of an e-petition system. Groups can now encourage supporters to sign an e-petition in the hope that it will attract sufficient signatures, and support from MPs, for the committee to schedule a debate.

In terms of the legislative process, the growth of pre-legislative scrutiny since 1997 also offers a particular opportunity to pressure groups. As we have seen in Chapter 4, input at the formulation stage of legislation enhances the opportunity to influence the content of bills. Consultation on bills has enabled the views of interested organizations to be given to the sponsoring department, but scrutiny of draft bills by a parliamentary committee provides a particular focus for group lobbying in order to influence the committee's recommendations. With the growth in pre-legislative scrutiny, parliamentary lobbying by pressure groups is likely to become even more pronounced.

Parliament may also have increased its attractiveness to organized groups as a result of the televising of proceedings. Since cameras were introduced in the Commons, it has achieved more public prominence. A particular feature of the twenty-first century is the use of cameras to interview members within the Palace of Westminster. This, and the growth of

24-hour news coverage, has meant that back-bench MPs are now more likely than before to be interviewed by the media. They are therefore more attractive to groups seeking a public outlet for their views.

These various developments have coalesced to produce the increase in parliamentary lobbying. The volume of such lobbying shows no sign of receding; quite the reverse, in fact. But what effect has it had?

Consequences

As with the increase in constituency casework, the burgeoning of lobbying by pressure groups has had several consequences for the political system. Such lobbying has served to strengthen members of both Houses in carrying out a number of tasks; and it has served to enhance the legitimacy of Parliament among organized groups. In addition, it appears to have contributed towards some changes in public policy. Against this must be set the fact that there are problems of popular legitimacy as a result of perceived inequities in group influence and, as with constituency casework, problems for parliamentarians in trying to cope with all the demands made of them.

Benefits

Much of the material that is sent to MPs and peers is of little use to most of the recipients. Some is outside the members' areas of interest, and some is so badly prepared and argued, and sometimes too late, to have any effect. Much, if not most, of the material is discarded, often unread. As one MP wrote: 'Throughout the year the brown tide of letters pours in. The basic weapons for mail warfare are a paper knife and a large waste paper basket – known in the trade as "the circular file"' (Flynn 1997, p. 61). His advice to new members: 'Be ruthless'.

However, what is more important is the fact that not all the material sent is discarded. The material supplied by organizations outside Parliament ensures that members, and committees, of both Houses have a source of information independent of government and party. This material adds to the members' store of knowledge and provides the basis for questioning the detail of provisions laid before them. Such is the value of the material supplied by interested organizations that members will sometimes actively solicit it (Norton 1990b, p. 197). Within the context of their particular enquiries, departmental select committees do so on a regular basis.

Given their own limited resources, MPs and – especially – peers use outside groups almost as substitutes for research assistants, their own areas of interest and political predispositions serving as a filter for the material they are sent. Information likely to be of use is read and retained; the rest is discarded. For members who may be critical of a particular measure, or may have been unaware of inherent problems with it, the information supplied by groups can be invaluable. As a result, it adds to their critical capacity and ensures that Parliament is a more effective body of scrutiny than it otherwise would be.

Well-briefed members are in a stronger position to press amendments and to challenge government than would be the case if they were reliant on government for information. Pressure from members, especially government backbenchers, and the quality of argument may be sufficient to persuade ministers to accept changes to their bills. The House of Lords offers particular scope to pursue amendments. Government is less in control of proceedings – and the outcome of votes – in the Lords than in the Commons, and peers with a particular knowledge of a subject can pursue it in order to elicit a response from government. The capacity of members to have a significant impact on the legislative process remains limited (see Chapter 5), but the link with outside groups ensures that it is not quite so limited as it once was.

Similarly, well-informed select committees have had some impact on public policy, or rather, as was noted in Chapter 6, the *detail* of policy. Outside organizations have ensured that the committees have material that supplements or challenges that provided by ministers and officials. Knowing that committees may obtain information from other sources can have an effect on departmental thinking and intentions. Again, the impact of departmental select committees may be limited, but their existence – and their extensive use of evidence from organizations independent of government – has provided a new dimension to parliamentary scrutiny. That dimension has increased as a result of the greater number of bills published in draft and subject to pre-legislative scrutiny. As we have seen (in Chapter 4), most bills subject to pre-legislative scrutiny have been scrutinized by departmental select committees.

The pursuit of group demands by members of both Houses (and the effect it sometimes has) has also helped to enhance the legitimacy of Parliament among such groups. The perception of groups is generally a positive one. The 1986 survey found that, of those groups that had sought to have some influence on legislation, more than half claimed to have been successful (Rush 1990, p. 285). Lobbying is often inefficient (see Norton 1990b, pp. 193–6), but none the less the perception of groups involved in the exercise is that it has some effect. Less than 6 per cent of the groups questioned in 1986 deemed their efforts to have been unsuccessful.

The value of Parliament extends to agenda setting. By giving evidence to committees, groups can place their views on the public record and influence the committee's recommendations. Even if the recommendations are not accepted, the fact of their publication can help to place the issue on the public agenda: 'Coupled with pressure through other channels, this raises the possibility of a more positive outcome in the longer term' (Baggott 1995, p. 148). This may be especially important in the context of sections of society that are not organized and which may not be that popular, but whose cause deserves a hearing. MPs and peers are able to exploit the procedures available to them (Chapter 6) to get their case on the record. Peers, lacking constituents, can sometimes be better placed than MPs to raise the concerns of marginalized or unpopular groups.

For many groups, getting their views on the record in an authoritative forum is an end in itself; they have had an opportunity to express themselves. Parliament thus serves as an important safety valve for groups as well as for individuals. The possibility of actually influencing some change in public policy is an added attraction, enhancing the legitimacy of the institution.

Furthermore, they have been able to do so in what they perceive as a fair setting. By listening to the different groups, Parliament may enhance its own legitimacy as an arbiter between them. Ian Marsh studied the link between select committees and external groups when the committees were first established: he found that 70 per cent of those who gave evidence to committees regarded the select committee process as fairer than departmental procedures, and more than 40 per cent regarded MPs as more legitimate arbitrators of an issue than departmental officers (Marsh 1986, pp. 173–4).

And the legitimacy of the institution, in the eyes of pressure groups, is also enhanced by the fact that it serves as an important transmission belt between groups and government. As we have seen, this role has acquired greater significance since 1979. Parliament offers not only an opportunity to give a public airing to group demands, but it can also help to channel those demands to government, both publicly and privately. Through arranging such meetings, through tabling questions, and through tabling amendments to bills, members in both Houses can ensure that group demands are considered by government.

The significance of these activities should not be exaggerated. Public policy is determined by government (see Chapter 4). For the purposes of groups, ministers and senior civil servants remain the principal targets of their lobbying activities. Despite the arm's-length relationship of government to many economic groups since 1979, the contact between departmental ministers and organized interests remains extensive and continuous (Norton 1999c, pp. 19–21). Parliament remains a supplementary rather than a primary point of contact.

None the less, Parliament occupies the time and attention of organized interests on a more extensive basis than before. While persuading government remains the essential and normally sufficient task for most groups seeking some change in policy, Parliament fulfils an important role in providing groups with a safety valve and another opportunity to fight a battle that may have been lost in Whitehall. Their activity also adds to the store of members' knowledge, thus providing them with the means to adopt a more critical stance and, in so doing, reinforce the legitimacy of the institution in the eyes of citizens.

Limitations

Though the increased activity of groups may have helped to bolster perceptions of Parliament's legitimacy among such groups, there are problems of popular legitimacy arising from the access that such groups enjoy. There are perceived inequalities of access between groups, and between groups and the individual citizen.

There remains the problem that not all interests are organized. Unorganized sections of society still often go unnoticed or the full extent of their problems goes unrecognized. There are various explanations for this, many not particular to the United Kingdom. Some may have a culture that militates against seeking to express themselves politically (such as Jehovah's Witnesses). Some may not feel that their needs are such as to require a remedy through the political process. Some may be formed of individuals with little knowledge of the existence or location of others with the same characteristics (individuals with extraordinarily rare medical conditions, for example). Some may not know how to get organized and may not feel that there is much point in organizing for political purposes. Gangs of inner-city youngsters may have some form of organization, but not one geared to making demands of elected representatives. The problems of such sections of society may thus go unarticulated in Parliament, at least until a major problem arises or unless individual Members recognize they have a case and are prepared to raise it, sometimes at the risk of ridicule or unpopularity.

Even where groups are organized, there are perceptions of privileged access on the part of the better resourced ones. There is a perception on the part of smaller groups or those with limited resources that they are squeezed out. As the representative of one voluntary organization put it, 'those like us with little money, staff and resources can't mount such a good show and tend to be overlooked' (Grantham and Seymour-Ure 1990, p. 76). Wealthy groups are believed to be able to buy influence. This perception was compounded in the 1980s and 1990s by the fact that a significant proportion of parliamentarians were themselves consultants or retained by consultancy firms. Influence-buying had been alleged in earlier decades (Norton 1999a, p. 34) but claims of MPs being in the pay of outside groups reached new heights during this period. In 1989, 180 MPs – 137 of them Conservatives – were retained by outside groups as parliamentary consultants or advisers (Grantham and Seymour-Ure 1990, p. 67).

Stories about links between MPs and organized interests attracted critical press stories and a number of books appeared, their titles reflecting the critical content: for example, *Corruption and Misconduct in Contemporary British Politics* (Doig 1984), *Westminster Babylon* (Doig 1990) and *MPs for Hire* (Hollingsworth 1991). The links also attracted a growing body of academic literature (see Rush 1990; Jordan 1991). Investigation of lobbying by the Select Committee on Members' Interests in the Commons tapped unease about the activities of lobbyists among some MPs, some of whom gave voice to perceived misuse of Commons facilities by lobbyists (Select Committee on Members' Interests 1990). Allegations of abuse were common, though rarely substantiated. Stories about links between MPs and lobbying organizations affected the public perception of members. A MORI poll in 1985 found that 46 per cent of respondents agreed with the statement that 'most MPs make a lot of money by using public office improperly', against only 31 per cent who disagreed. Just over two-thirds of those questioned (67 per cent) agreed with the statement that 'most MPs care more about special interests than they care about people like you'. Less than one in five (19 per cent) disagreed with the statement.

The issue of MPs' links with outside bodies attracted particular media attention in 1994 as a result of allegations that MPs were being paid in return for tabling parliamentary questions. The 'cash for questions' scandal led to the than prime minister, John Major, setting up a Committee on Standards in Public Life (the Nolan Committee) to make recommendations. Against a background of growing public disapproval, and a marked increase in the number of people (64 per cent in 1995) believing that most

MPs make a lot of money by using public office improperly, the Commons agreed to a number of recommendations emanating from the Nolan Committee. Despite some opposition, the House voted to ban paid advocacy by MPs (members could still advise outside interests for payment, but could not raise an issue on their behalf in Parliament); to require disclosure of income derived from activities relating to their work as an MP (in effect, tightening up the rules on its existing register of members' interests); to establish a code of conduct; to create a Parliamentary Commissioner for Standards (to maintain the register of interests, to advise MPs, and to investigate complaints of breaches of the rules); and to create a Select Committee on Standards (the new committee succeeded the Select Committee on Members' Interests and was then merged with the long-standing Select Committee on Privileges) (Rush 1998, pp. 106–10; Norton 1999a, pp. 35–6; Riddell 2000, pp. 144–8). The House of Lords subsequently tightened its rules of disclosure, making them even more rigorous than those of the Commons.

Allegations of misconduct – subsumed under the term 'sleaze' – continued to be made (Riddell 2000, pp. 149–51). The changes made by the House helped address the issue in large measure (adverse findings by the Standards and Privileges Committee peaked in the 1997–2001 Parliament; Allen 2011, p. 225), but the public perception of self-interest by MPs was reinforced in 2009 by the expenses' scandal (see Chapters 2 and 11). MPs were perceived as bolstering their income through misuse of public funds rather than, as before, through offering their services to outside groups, though claims of misuse of their positions through links with outside organizations continue to be made. In 2010, three ex-cabinet ministers were caught on camera by undercover journalists offering their services to lobby on a paid consultancy basis. (One described himself as the equivalent of a 'cab for hire' and was available to lobby for £3,000 to £5,000 a day.) The Independent Parliamentary Standards Authority (IPSA) was created to deal with MPs' salaries and expenses, and to investigate any misuse of expenses, whereas claims of Members selling their services in breach of the parliamentary code continued to be investigated by the Parliamentary Commissioner for Standards.

There is also a negative consequence – the impact on members' workloads. The more they are lobbied, the less time they have to devote to other activities, sifting the unsolicited material received into useful and useless material is itself a time-consuming exercise. Office staff can carry some, but not all, of the burden, and the qualitative as well as the quantitative change adds to the burden. The fact that members have limited research resources means that they often rely on the material they are sent by outside groups. However, those limited resources also mean that the members have difficulty in evaluating its significance.

Lobbying by groups extends beyond corresponding with members. Meetings will be sought. A good portion of material from groups is in the form of invitations, usually to presentations or receptions. MPs often accept such invitations in order to demonstrate support or to find out more. Attending such events eats into the members' time. Meeting rooms, and especially dining rooms, are booked well in advance. Most lunchtimes and evenings, the private dining rooms in the Palace of Westminster are full, with members hosting events for outside groups or constituency bodies.

Lobbying by outside groups adds considerably to the burden of parliamentarians, forcing them to establish priorities in terms of their parliamentary activities and the demands made of them. As a consequence, some activities may be abandoned. Lobbying contributes significantly to the potential of parliamentary overload.

Conclusion

Members of both Houses of Parliament are lobbied heavily by organized interests and on an ever-increasing scale. From a pluralist perspective, the activity appears to be somewhat perplexing. Parliament is essentially a body for approving legislation, not making it. Anyone seeking to change public policy should address their attention to ministers and civil servants, and not to Parliament. Parliament may use its coercive capacity to change a measure, but it is extremely rare that it does so. The House of Commons in 1986 defeated the Shops Bill (see Chapter 5) but that was an exceptional event; so too was the decision by the government in 2012 to drop the House of Lords Reform Bill when most Conservative MPs not part of the payroll failed to vote for it. Members may more often use their persuasive capacity to affect outcomes. Ministers may be influenced by the arguments put before them or may feel it unwise to antagonize their backbenchers on a particular issue. Such occasions, though, are not easily quantifiable, and do not appear to be extensive. On the face of it, the impact of Parliament on legislation appears to be sporadic and minor. Furthermore, from a pluralist perspective, what influence that groups have through Parliament is not only limited but also distorted. In pure pluralist theory, groups should enjoy equality of access to the policy-making process, including to Parliament, but in practice, some groups are seen to have better access than others.

The pluralist conundrum is well summarized by Baggott (1995, p. 142):

> Although MPs can in certain circumstances have a direct impact on government policy and legislation, the scope for achieving even a modification of the government's position is fairly limited on the vast majority of issues. As long as the government has a majority its view will generally prevail on the key issues. Indeed, if the direct impact of Parliament upon legislation were the sole reason why groups lobbied MPs, it is doubtful that the scale of parliamentary lobbying would be at its present level.

It is possible that groups have misunderstood the role of Parliament, assuming it to be more powerful than it is, and being overawed by the very institution of Parliament itself, nestling in the iconic Palace of Westminster. However, there is arguably more to it than that. Here, the other approaches to power provide some useful insights.

Why do a great many groups send their newsletters and other publications to members of both Houses, and why do they hold receptions or exhibitions for the benefit of MPs and peers? Lobbying takes two basic forms. One is what is known as 'fire brigade' lobbying, in essence having to respond quickly to a piece of legislation that affects one's interests adversely. The other is essentially that of building goodwill among parliamentarians. This is long-term and it can benefit groups in two ways. One is in terms of building support among parliamentarians who may one day be ministers (or, indeed, may already be – ministers attend various parliamentary receptions) and hence in a position to determine public policy. The other is in terms of developing, and demonstrating, such strong support in Parliament that it would be a foolhardy government that decided to legislate against the interests of the group.

The fact that ministers are drawn from, and remain within, Parliament (see Chapter 3) is important in this context. MPs may become ministers. Backbenchers mix with ministers, enjoying a proximity that is not available to most outside organizations. The head of a major company may be invited to meetings with ministers at the Department of Business, Innovation and Skills (BIS) more often than a back-bench MP, but s/he is unlikely to bump into BIS ministers in the division lobby of the Commons or in the tea room and dining rooms in the Palace of Westminster. Junior ministers want to be senior ministers, and support from parliamentary colleagues may help one's reputation. Perhaps more importantly, hostility from one's parliamentary colleagues may destroy prospects of advancement. Ministers therefore have good reason to listen to backbenchers. Nor should it be forgotten that partisanship in the chamber is not necessarily replicated outside. Friendships exist across parties as well as within them; in the Lords, party is often irrelevant in terms of social relationships. Members may thus serve to convey a particular view, but one that is not necessarily on the public record nor one that has an immediate or perceptible impact on public policy.

MPs and peers thus serve to articulate the views of outside groups to government. As such, they have helped to open the process more to groups in society. From an institutional perspective, Parliament is important because of the processes that exist for views to be expressed. It provides not only the mechanisms for those views to be conveyed, but also provides a structured, and public, forum in which competing views can be pitted against one another. Groups involved on the two sides of an argument make representations to MPs and peers. The groups may not talk directly to one another, but they talk indirectly through Parliament. Both Houses provide a forum in which each side can be heard and assessed, including by government and by the media. If one side is going to be expressed, the other is likely to organize and lobby MPs and peers.

Parliament thus has an appeal, a necessary appeal, to organized groups. Its continued relevance, in terms of popular perception, is shown in the number of mass lobbies that occur. It is shown in the fact that demonstrations against particular measures are held, not outside a particular ministry, but outside Parliament. Mass lobbies are held in Parliament Square; smaller demonstrations take place by the King George V statute opposite the House of Lords. In 2004, for example, thousands of supporters of hunting filled Parliament Square to oppose the Hunting Bill, then going through Parliament; in 2009, an estimated 10,000 Tamil Tiger supporters filled the square to call for a ceasefire in Sri Lanka. Even if MPs and peers do not act in the way the demonstrators want, Parliament is still the focus for activity and, through that attention, is the means of sending out a message to government and the wider public.

Parliament thus constitutes an important body for organized interests. It can serve to articulate their interests to government; and MPs and peers can serve as advocates, sometimes even powerful friends (or at least friends) in seeking a change to a bill going through Parliament. Groups consider it legitimate to lobby Parliament to achieve change, not necessarily seeing Parliament as the target but rather as a channel for reaching their ultimate target – the government. Their activities, and the failure of some MPs to distinguish their public duty from private gain, have undermined the standing of MPs in popular perception. Both Houses have sought to address the problem, and have necessarily done so through regulating the conduct of members rather than seeking to prevent groups making representations to members. Party may limit the capacity of MPs to determine outcomes, but it also serves as a protective shield against undue influence by special interests. By getting the processes right, Parliament can serve as the basic – and legitimate – link between organized interests (which, in many cases, are organized groups of citizens) and government. If they get them wrong, the effect on the perceptions, by the public or particular sections of society, of the legitimacy of the political system in the UK can be profound.

13

Reaching the Public

Individual citizens, and a vast array of groups in society, both organized and unorganized, make demands of Members of Parliament. MPs raise the concerns of constituents, groups and different sections of the public in Parliament, and can ensure that the government takes note. The flow of communication in this relationship is essentially from those outside Parliament to those inside; but what about the communication from Parliament to those outside?

One of the functions ascribed to Parliament by Walter Bagehot (1867) was that of 'teaching' – 'to teach the nation what it does not know' (see Chapter 1). A century later, Samuel Beer identified the potential of legislators to mobilize popular support for policies. He had in mind policies approved by Parliament that imposed often complex requirements on citizens. Such policies, he contended, were numerous and a consequence of having a welfare state and a managed economy:

> A great deal is expected of the citizen in the form of new necessities that oblige him to conform his behaviour to the complex requirements of economic and social policy ... To win both the mind and the heart of the citizen to an acceptance of these coercions is a major necessity, but a severe problem. (Beer 1966)

If the policies were explained to citizens, then support would more be likely to be forthcoming, thus facilitating the desired effect. However, Beer argued, the potential was not one that had been fulfilled by the British Parliament.

To what extent, then, does Parliament in the twenty-first century educate and raise support for measures to which it has given its approval? Are citizens better-informed and more supportive of policies as a result of the activities of parliamentarians?

Lack of contact

The developments of the nineteenth century have resulted in party domination of Parliament and an increase in both the volume and complexity
of legislation. As was shown in Chapter 2, Parliament failed to keep pace
with these developments. Successive governments were prepared to use
their party majorities to prevent detailed and critical scrutiny by
Parliament. They were prepared to rely on the mandate of a general election victory and the resulting party majority as sufficient to legitimize
their measures.

The consequence was a Parliament that was able and prepared to
debate policy on a partisan basis but denied the resources (and largely
lacking the political will) to subject that policy to informed and detailed
scrutiny. Lacking information about the detail and the case for particular
provisions of the bills they were approving, Members of Parliament were
in no position to mobilize popular support for those provisions.

The position was exacerbated in post-war decades, with the realization
of the 'closed' institution outlined earlier. Legislation became more
specific and reached more than ever before into the economic and social
lives of the citizenry. Far from being in a position to inform and mobilize
support among citizens, parliamentarians appeared increasingly to have
little scope for action independent of assenting to what government
placed before them. MPs and peers were generalists struggling to cope
with a mass of highly detailed legislation. They had no mechanism for
specialized enquiry. Their inability to engage in independent action
appeared to lessen interest in their activities and hence their capacity to
influence those affected by the measures they were approving.

During the 1950s and 1960s, there was little opportunity for individuals to find out what Parliament was doing. Continuous daily reporting of
Parliament was confined to the serious press. Television and radio coverage was limited, and the BBC had a self-imposed rule prohibiting the
broadcasting of any statement or discussion on matters to be debated in
Parliament within a period of 14 days. The '14-day rule' was not removed
until 1957. For those interested in knowing what was being said throughout an entire debate, it was a case either of sitting in the public gallery or
consulting *Hansard*, the official report of proceedings. Sales of *Hansard*
of both Commons and Lords were small.

For individuals, there was little incentive to find out what was being
said in debate. For pressure groups and all bodies affected by legislation,
there was some reason to follow what was going on, but attempts to do so
do not appear to have been extensive. Occasions when either House

debated matters of interest to a particular group would, in any event, be few and far between.

Individuals and groups were thus faced with an institution that was essentially enveloped by party and which appeared to offer little of relevance to them. Parliamentarians had limited contact with constituents (see Chapter 11) and what they said in the chamber had a very small audience. The communication from members of the two Houses to the outside world could thus be described as extremely muted, making little contribution to understanding on the part of individuals and organizations.

This was the position recognized and sketched by Samuel Beer, but it was to change soon after his words were published.

Developing links

In his analysis of Parliament, Beer contended that there were two obstacles that clearly stood in the way of Parliament being able to mobilize support in the period between general elections. One was secrecy, both in government and in Parliament itself. The other was the lack of specialized committees for investigating what government was doing: 'If the public is to be given a greater sense of participation, not only must secrecy be reduced, but MPs must be given better instruments for understanding, explaining, and – inevitably – criticizing what the government is doing' (Beer 1966). Both obstacles have been tackled. If they have not been removed totally, they have at least been substantially eroded. They have been supplemented by another fundamental change that has constituted a further instrument for communicating with citizens: the growth of the Internet.

More openness

Parliament itself has moved towards greater openness in its proceedings. There is long-standing openness in terms of voting behaviour, and division lists are published the day following the vote. Both Houses retain absolute power to determine whether proceedings should be open or closed to the public. The public are granted access to watch the proceedings in each chamber unless the House votes to go into secret session, as occasionally happened during the Second World War. In the Commons, select committees often sat in public in the nineteenth and early twentieth centuries. However, private sittings became the norm after the Second World War. This only changed in the latter half of the 1960s. Today, public sessions for evidence-taking are the norm among select committees.

Exceptionally, a departmental select committee will go into closed session, the most obvious example being the Defence Committee when hearing sensitive details affecting national security. (The published proceedings appear with the sensitive information 'sidelined' – that is, omitted.) Some of the domestic committees, such as the Privileges Committee, used to hold closed meetings, but generally no longer do so. Meetings of public bill committees are open to the public unless the committee votes otherwise. Consequently, the position now is one where closed committee hearings are rare.

However, meeting in public session is necessary but not sufficient to ensure that parliamentary activities are widely known about. Media coverage was limited, but this changed dramatically in the 1980s, with the admission of television cameras to the chamber and the committee rooms of both Houses.

An early attempt by the BBC in the 1920s to be allowed to broadcast special occasions in Parliament came to nothing (Griffith and Ryle 1989, p. 81). Little then happened until 1966, when a select committee in the Commons recommended a closed-circuit experiment, on the basis of which the House could decide whether limited public broadcasting should be permitted. The recommendation was defeated by 131 votes to 130. The House of Lords was less reticent and passed a motion declaring that it 'would welcome the televising of some of its proceedings for an experimental period as an additional means of demonstrating its usefulness in giving a lead to public opinion'. The reason given reveals sensitivity to Bagehot's teaching function. The experiment duly took place, in 1968, but was not pursued, partly for technical reasons, partly because of the expense, and partly because the Lords did not wish to be out of line with the practice of the Commons (Wheeler-Booth 1989, pp. 511–12).

In 1975, the Commons approved an experiment in sound broadcasting and, following the experiment, both Houses approved the principle of proceedings being broadcast on radio. The decision was taken in principle in 1976, and sound broadcasting began in both Houses in April 1978.

Pressure for proceedings to be televised continued. In 1983, the Lords voted to endorse its earlier decision of 1966 and take steps to implement it. An experiment began in 1985 and it was agreed in 1986 that broadcasting be made permanent. The Commons, as in 1966, was more reticent. In 1985, the House voted by 275 to 263 against the idea. Three years later, by 318 votes to 264, it reached a different conclusion, approving in principle the conducting of an experiment in television broadcasting. After some delay, the cameras eventually started transmitting proceedings on 21 November 1989. The following year, the House agreed that broadcasting was to be made a permanent feature.

During the period of broadcasting solely from the Lords, coverage of the Upper House was more extensive – and more popular – than had generally been expected by either broadcasters or parliamentarians. The same proved true initially of Commons coverage from November 1989 onwards, though the extent of coverage declined after the first decade or so of broadcasting. Since then, developments in digital technology have greater expanded the opportunities for the public to watch proceedings.

Parliamentary proceedings are broadcast now on a dedicated channel, BBC Parliament, enabling viewers to follow proceedings live in the Commons and to see the recorded broadcasts of proceedings in the Lords and in select committees. In 2010 the channel has a monthly viewing audience of 1.9 million (Norton 2012b, p. 411). There is also a website, *BBC Democracy Live* (http://news.bbc.co.uk/democracylive/hi/), that provides live feeds from both chambers, as well as the European, Scottish, Welsh, and Northern Irish legislatures.

Though the focus of media coverage, especially the principal television channels, tends to be Prime Minister's Question Time, some select committee hearings have also proved attractive to the broadcasters. This has been especially the case when high profile and controversial figures have appeared to give evidence. These have included the media magnate Rupert Murdoch appearing before the Culture, Media and Sport Committee in 2011 to discuss 'phone hacking and Barclays Bank former chief executive, Bob Diamond, appearing before the Treasury Committee in 2012 to discuss the LIBOR – the inter-bank lending rate – scandal.

Both Houses have also proved more willing to give access to the media in order to report proceedings and to provide interviews with both MPs and peers. Broadcasting companies have their Westminster headquarters at 4 Millbank, just across the road from the Palace of Westminster. There has also been a relaxation of the restrictions on where the media can broadcast from within the Palace. Initially, permission was given for filming in an alcove off the Central Lobby. Now, reporters can broadcast from Central Lobby – an attractive venue because of its convenience for parliamentarians and because of the backdrop for the cameras. The extent to which Parliament is relevant to the broadcast media is reflected in the number of parliamentary passes held by representatives of the broadcasting companies. In October 2004, 111 security passes were held by people employed by or contracted to the BBC, and 78 passes were held by representatives of other broadcasting organizations (*Lords Hansard*, 14 October 2004, WA 65). Parliament now attracts the media in a way that it did not do, and could not do, at the time that Beer was writing.

Specialization

By the end of the twentieth century, Parliament was a far more open institution than at any time in its history. It was also a far more specialized institution. The most significant change occurred, as we have seen already, in 1979 with the creation of the departmental select committees. This specialization has had two consequences. One has been to render government more open, and the other has been to provide a more precise and extensive link between Parliament and outside groups.

By taking evidence from ministers and civil servants, the departmental select committees have elicited information that otherwise would not be on the public record. The committees (see Chapter 6), have proved to be prolific in taking evidence and producing reports. During the lifetime of a Parliament, the committees will usually interview at least 200 ministers and more than 1,000 civil servants (see Norton 1991b, p. 73). The committees have become more experienced (though, as we shall see, not necessarily expert) at questioning witnesses and teasing details from them.

Obtaining such information benefits the committees: they are better informed than they would otherwise be. By virtue of each committee's concentration on a particular sector, and by each acquiring information and issuing reports, usually with recommendations for particular action, committee activity has also attracted the attention of a wide array of interested organizations. As we have seen, the committees provide groups with a clear parliamentary target for lobbying activities.

Select committees, then, have acted as magnets for such groups. However, groups are not simply providers of inputs to committees. They are also consumers of the outputs. Through their reports, committees thus reach an important audience. However, though the reports reach particular audiences on a regular basis, for example through trade publications, they also on occasion reach the wider public. Press coverage of committee reports has to some degree compensated for a decline in coverage of what happens in the chamber (Kubala 2011, pp. 698–9), with coverage of committees increasing in the period from 1987 to 2007 (Kubala 2011, pp. 703–4). Whereas interest groups are likely to be most interested in committee reports, newspapers have tended to cover evidence sessions more than the reports, with coverage of sessions increasing over time

(Kubala 2011, pp. 708–9). This, as Kubala notes, could be the result of a more concerted effort by the Commons to attract journalists to sessions, of more sessions being held, and an interest on the part of journalists to cover what ministers say, but 'it also suggests that the media increasingly consider select committees to be of news value when performing their function of publicly scrutinising, and holding to account, the Government and others – whilst their other main function of proposing policy change, via their reports, has perhaps diminished in importance'(Kubala 2011, p. 711).

The House of Lords, as we have seen, has given a lead in terms of greater openness; it has also now developed its use of specialized committees. As we have seen, the number has expanded notably in recent years (see Chapter 6). As with reports from Commons committees, reports from Lords committees also serve to engage with affected sections of the public.

The importance of the output side of committee work has also been recognized by both Houses, with the appointment of staff responsible for arranging the publication date of reports and press releases. Press conferences are arranged to launch the publication of the more significant reports. This may be seen as possibly a cause and/or consequence of the media coverage of committees. Both Houses invest resources to draw attention to committee reports. As media coverage continues or increases, the more each House recognizes the value of engaging with television and the press.

Use of the Internet

The Internet is also now crucial to the relationship between Parliament and public. As Andrew Chadwick observed, 'In the developed world, the Internet is now ubiquitous. The issue is no longer *whether* politics is online, but *in what form* and *with what consequences?*' (Chadwick 2006, p. 1). The development of the Internet has facilitated communication between Parliament and the public at both collective and the individual levels.

At the collective level, Parliament has introduced its own website (www.parliament.uk). It has been expanded and variously redesigned since its inception. It was initially criticized, the Modernisation Committee reporting 'widespread dissatisfaction' with it, working for the few who knew how to navigate it, but not for the majority (Modernisation Committee, 2004, p. 18). Since then, it has been enhanced and redesigned to cater for those with an interest in what Parliament discusses rather than with how it is structured. It embodies a mass of data and provides access to *Hansard* as well as to committee reports and proceedings. The transcripts of committee hearings are now put on the website shortly after the hearings take place. Bills before Parliament, as well as explanatory notes to them, are available on the site. There is also a large volume of information about Parliament and its work, and data on members and details of how to contact them.

Anyone with Internet access can examine material immediately in a way that previously was either impossible or very time-consuming – and expensive. Committee reports, which in paper form may cost £20 or £30 each, and sometimes considerably more, can be accessed at no charge on the website. The same applies to copies of *Hansard*; an annual subscription for the daily edition of the *Commons Hansard* in 2012 cost £865 and for the weekly edition £440. (The cost for *Lords Hansard* was £525 and £255 respectively.) The Internet has thus enabled Parliament to put a great deal of information in the public domain in a more accessible manner than ever before.

The Internet has also made possible greater access to committee proceedings. Meetings are televised on a selective basis – only a limited number of committee rooms are equipped for television coverage – but all chamber and committee proceedings are now webcast, so anyone wanting to listen to proceedings can do so via the Internet. The web-casting began on an experimental basis in January 2002 and was made permanent in October 2003 (Parry 2004, p. 2). All committee proceedings are available in audio format. During the first year of the experimental period of webcasting, more than 200,000 visits to the site were recorded and, in the run-up to the war in Iraq, up to 600 users were logged on at any one time (House of Commons Commission 2003, p. 38).

Some committees also use the Internet not only for dissemination of their evidence and reports but also for consultation. There have been online consultations on such topics as family tax credit, credit searches, electronic democracy, the Constitutional Reform Bill, the draft Communications Bill, the role of prison officers, and hate crimes in Northern Ireland. The Modernisation Committee commissioned an online consultation for its inquiry into connecting Parliament and the public. Online consultations have also been employed by the Parliamentary Office of Science and Technology, on flood management, and by the all-party group on domestic violence, the latter encouraging input from people who otherwise might not have been able or willing to contribute to a parliamentary inquiry.

These consultations have often involved connecting with other online sites. The Treasury Committee invited Martin Lewis at Moneysavingexpert.com to ask his 3.7 million subscribers for their experiences and difficulties in seeking to locate and obtain credit.

The nature and value of the exercise was recorded by the Liaison Committee in reporting on such web-based consultations:

> The Justice Committee's e-consultation on justice reinvestment was so successful that it held a second e-consultation, this time on the role of the prison officer. By the time the e-consultation was closed, it had received nearly 18,000 hits and had 357 registered users. At one point during the session there were no fewer than five on-line forums being run by departmental select committees. (Liaison Committee 2010, p. 45)

Professor Stephen Coleman of the Oxford Internet Institute told the Modernisation Committee:

> On-line consultations are something that you [Parliament] have in fact pioneered, and have done better than any other parliament in the world. There is quite a lot of data suggesting that these consultations have had an effect on the fairly small minority of people who have engaged in them – because they have been deliberative, because they have been expansive over a period of a month, and because you have taken people seriously. (Modernisation Committee 2004, pp. 20–1)

Nor has the use of the web been confined to online consultations. As the Liaison Committee recorded:

> The Science and Technology Committee experimented with the use that might be made of Twitter in committee work. During a seminar with leading members of the scientific community, the Chair of the Committee posted the questions under discussion on Twitter and invited responses. Members of the Speaker's Conference made a video for YouTube about their motivation for entering politics in support of its online forum, in order to encourage participation by individuals from under-represented groups. Advances in communication technology are changing the way in which people communicate with each other at a seemingly ever-increasing pace. (Liaison Committee 2010, p. 45)

Parliament also uses the Internet as an integral part of its outreach programme, designed to inform people about Parliament. The programme encompasses dedicated outreach officers in different parts of the UK. In the Lords it encompasses a 'Peers in Schools' programme (peers visiting schools to talk about the work of the House) as well as *Lords of the Blog*, the only collaborative blog in the world drawing on members from different parties in a legislative chamber. Parliament also has its own Education Service, with a dedicated site on the Parliament website. It also uses Twitter, Flickr and Facebook, as well as uploading interviews and other material on YouTube. By August 2012, Parliament's YouTube channel had achieved over 2 million views.

The Internet has thus opened Parliament to a much wider audience than previously existed. Professor Coleman pointed out to the Modernisation Committee that more people now visit Parliament virtually than physically. The Committee also received evidence that more people access *Hansard* online than receive the printed edition. Peter Riddell of *The Times* told the MPs that the Internet was now the principal means by which Parliament as an institution communicates with voters, significantly reducing the importance of press reporting of Parliament (Modernisation Committee 2004, p. 16).

At the individual level, MPs are also making great use of the Internet to communicate with citizens: the use of e-mail and websites is now pervasive (though not quite universal) among MPs. By 2009, 92 per cent of MPs used e-mail and 83 per cent had a personal website (Williamson 2009, p. 8). There has also been a notable increase in the number of MPs using blogs, Twitter and Facebook. Labour MP Tom Watson was the first MP to start blogging, in 2003, and Alan Johnson the first politician to claim to use Twitter (Jackson and Lilleker 2011, p. 86). The use of such means soon became popular with parliamentarians. By 2009 23 per cent of MPs were employing social networking and 11 per cent had blogs (Williamson 2009, p. 8). By 2011, over 40 per cent were using Twitter (Harrison 2011). Some MPs use e-newsletters as a means of keeping constituents informed of what they are doing.

The Internet has thus provided the means for Parliament and for MPs individually to reach citizens in a way that was not previously possible, and for a greater degree of interaction than was possible before. Parliament is now more open to citizens than it has ever been in its long history.

Consequences

Since the time that Beer was writing, both Houses have thus moved to dismantle the obstacles he identified, to achieve the capacity to mobilize support for measures of public policy. But have greater openness, specialization and the use of new technologies served as teachers and mobilizers of popular support?

The positive impact

The effect of a more open Parliament, particularly through the medium of television and the Internet, would appear to be a more informed public. The reaction to televised proceedings has generally been positive (Negrine 1998, p. 69). Televised proceedings, which mean essentially televised extracts, reach a large audience, especially through news and regional programmes. Once televising began, dedicated programmes attracted audiences of between 200,000 and over 1 million (Select Committee on the Televising of Proceedings of the House 1990, p. xxix). Not surprisingly, coverage of the chamber increased significantly compared with the period before 1989. Negrine compared coverage in 1996 with that of 1986. The number of items, including audio or audio-visual material from the chamber, increased by 188 per cent, and within these items the total number of seconds recorded in the chamber increased by 127 per cent: 'The percentages indicate a dramatic increase in the time for which politicians are seen in the chamber and illustrate the importance of the introduction of television cameras for news producers' (Negrine 1998, p. 79). The use of the Internet has also facilitated Parliament reaching a wide audience and, unlike television coverage, has provided the means for more direct contact between MPs and citizens; it has also provided the means for some interaction between committees and citizens, and between individual MPs and citizens.

Contact between members and constituents is growing rapidly (see Chapter 11). The Internet provides the means for direct, in effect unmediated, contact between MP and constituents. E-bulletins can be sent at regular intervals to those requesting them. Blogs provides a means for constituents to provide feedback to MPs' comments.

As we saw in Chapter 12, contact between individual backbenchers – in both Houses – and organized groups is also more extensive than before. The contact is two way. The Internet has been a boon for those responsible for monitoring parliamentary proceedings, providing not only immediate access but also the capacity to track down specific material through search engines.

Similarly, among the unorganized public, members are playing a greater – though not such an extensive – role. By utilizing local media and the Internet, MPs inform as well as learn. The greater the number of MPs – and, indeed, select committees – utilizing the Internet to connect with the public, the more they may benefit in terms of information and in building links between citizens and Parliament. The Internet has facilitated contact that might otherwise have proved impossible. We have already referred to the online consultation on domestic violence. Nearly 1,000 messages of evidence were received from women survivors of domestic violence, some of whom were 'voices largely unheard by hon. Members, including Irish women travellers and Bangladeshi women' (*Commons Hansard*, 6 November 2001, col. 108). The potential value to MPs of such contact was emphasized by Graham Allen, MP:

> The more voices that are allowed to be heard, the more likely we are to get the ideas to make good legislation even better. Many of the legislative disasters that Governments have imposed on Parliament ... could probably have been avoided. To refer to my own experience, I led for my party in opposition on the Child Support Act 1991, which had to be re-written about five times. I have no doubt that had we had a sensible process of pre-legislative scrutiny – either online or offline – and had we listened to the practitioners and to those whom it affected, we would have been able to make that law far better, far earlier. (*Commons Hansard*, 6 January 2004, col. 3WH)

Allen's comments bring together two recent developments – pre-legislative scrutiny and online consultation – in a manner that demonstrates the capacity of Parliament to have a greater influence on legislation. The forum in which he was speaking – Westminster Hall – also emphasizes the utility of another recent innovation.

The greater the capacity Parliament has to reach people, then the greater the capacity it has to inform and educate. The capacity of Parliament to hear the views of those outside may also help in the legislative process and in bringing issues on to the political agenda. The more groups and individuals are involved, the greater the likelihood of them being supportive of the resulting legislation and of the parliamentary process. In combination, then, this increase in contact between parliamentarians and those outside Westminster provides a greater capacity for teaching and for mobilizing the support of the public for particular measures of public policy. What evidence we have suggests that, to a small extent, that capacity is being realized.

Limitations

The capacity of parliamentarians to teach and to mobilize is none the less limited. Coverage of proceedings in news broadcasts and other programmes is in the form of extracts rather than an extended coverage or continuous feed. Coverage of a large part of a debate is exceptionally rare. There is a particular concentration on Prime Minister's Question Time, which may generate heat but very little light. Hence opportunities for increasing knowledge on the substance of issues are limited. Viewers may gain some understanding of Parliament, but increased knowledge of particular issues will tend to be confined to major issues that are already the focus of public discussion.

Negrine has also drawn attention to the focus on the chamber. Televising proceedings has resulted in coverage of the chamber to the detriment of other locations:

> This greater attention to the institutional political arena provides the audience with a visual taste of the world inhabited by the politician, but it could also be argued that it offers a restricted register of work-places. Other institutional locations are neglected – committees, departments, overseas, and so on. It is arguable, therefore, whether this concentration on the chamber is a positive thing. (Negrine 1998, p. 82)

The Commons Information Committee (2002) also recorded problems with e-mails. It noted that MPs considered e-mails both an opportunity and a threat, fearing that such communication might generate demands they could not meet, and e-mail could add to paper mail rather than be a substitute for it. There was particular concern that interest groups would utilize e-mail addresses for mass campaigns. As the committee noted, some members therefore declined to publish their e-mail address. The committee cautioned against this approach:

> Our view is that the demand for Members to adapt to e-mail and other communication technologies is so great that a more pro-active strategy is required. The reputation of Members – and of the House – could be damaged by a refusal to embrace such technologies at a time when they are becoming standard in most other organisations. (Information Committee 2002, p. 9)

MPs have, in practice, combined a belief that use of the Internet is necessary but not something that they necessarily welcome. As we have seen, they have made increasing use of websites. However, they have tended to do so because other have done so – it is the product of a bandwagon effect (Ward and Lusoli 2005; Jackson and Lilleker 2011). Though it is an innovative technology, they have not used it innovatively. We can identify four models of political representation: the *traditional* (rejecting the use of ICT for communicating with citizens), *party* (using ICT to bolster the position of the party), *representative* (using ICT to disseminate and mobilize support for members' views) and *tribune* (using ICT to enable the MP to be the voice of the people). A few MPs hold to the traditional model, but MPs predominantly operate in the party mode, using websites for essentially one-way communication, saying what they are doing in Parliament and for the constituency (Norton 2008, p. 24). MPs use the Internet:

> to promote their own causes and that of their parties, essentially as an extension of what they already do: it is used as a medium for making speeches, press releases and details of the MPs' activities available to constituents. Few MPs reject it, or seek to use it to bolster an independent status or to discover the collective view of their constituents. Perhaps for these reasons few people appear to be interested in Members' websites. (Norton 2008, pp. 25–6)

This conclusion was reinforced by a Hansard Society study. 'MPs' focus', it recorded, 'remains largely on promoting themselves through reportage of their efforts in the House or constituency and by linking to ideologically similar commentators or websites' (Williamson 2009, p. 3). As the report noted, this was unsurprising given the tribal nature of British politics.

Members are often wary of using blogs. 'Although one MP was overwhelmingly positive, seeing blogs as a way of raising and sustaining debate around local issues, others were sceptical and, in some cases, critical of them, seeing blogs as time-consuming and of limited value' (Williamson 2009, p. 18). Where blogs are used, they have not always elicited a positive evaluation. The Hansard Society used a citizen jury to monitor some political blogs. Though jurors tended to like the presentation, they were not impressed with the content. Although they were optimistic about the capacity of blogs to enhance political participation, the vast majority said they would not return to the blog they were monitoring. 'More worryingly still, not a single juror felt that his or her political participation and awareness had been enhanced by the blogs' (Ferguson and Howell 2004, p. 2). Twitter is increasingly used, though not necessarily to inform constituents about an MP's constituency or parliamentary work (Harrison 2011).

Some MPs, then, do embrace the Internet and utilize e-newsletters and blogs as a means of engaging with constituents, but more see it is a means of supplementing existing modes of contact, essentially conveying what the MP is doing rather than inviting a response. As one long-serving MP observed:

> The drip feed of blog, tweets, early morning radio interviews that are repeated throughout the day, widely advertised surgeries, and attendance in the Chamber in a camera-exposed position, all propagate the message 'Busy MP'. (Flynn 2012, p. 142)

The capacity to educate and mobilize support among particular groups is also limited. The bi-partisanship of select committees is a strength but also a weakness, as it discourages committees from addressing some central issues that are the subject of party conflict. Of the impact that committee reports have on group attitudes, most of those identified by Marsh took the form of clarifying attitudes. Less than one in five mentioned developing attitudes towards other issues as an important or very important outcome (Marsh 1986, p. 172).

Though contact between committees and groups, and between individual members and constituents, has increased, and members have displayed a relatively greater willingness to act independently of their party leaders, party none the less continues to act as the principal barrier to mobilizing support behind a particular policy. Where there is cross-party agreement, the potential is considerable. Where the parties take opposing stances, the opportunity to inform and mobilize support behind particular provisions is limited. As we saw in Chapter 5, the partisan conflict in public bill committees results in much of the detail being neglected in favour of argument over the contentious clauses. Individual members often find it difficult to avoid giving their communications with constituents – particularly speeches and press articles – a partisan slant, but once this practice has been recognized, constituents tend to discount it accordingly.

Nor is the problem confined to partisanship. Committee sessions do not always go the way the members intended. The appearance of Rupert Murdoch before the Culture, Media and Sport Committee in 2011 was remembered as much for a protestor attacking the witness with a plate of shaving foam as for the incisiveness of the questioning. (It was also to attract negative comment when the committee's report was published, with the members failing to agree a unanimous report; see Culture, Media and Sport Committee 2012.) The session of Bob Diamond with the Treasury Committee in 2012 attracted negative coverage because of the failure of the members to pursue consistent lines of questioning and their failure to elicit anything useful from the witness. So much so, that some commentators suggested that there should instead be a judge-led inquiry, with counsel questioning witnesses under oath, rather than leaving it to a disparate array of members, often unskilled in forensic questioning (Prince 2012).

There is also a problem from the perspective of the media in respect of the televised coverage of proceedings. Though the rules have been relaxed over the years, there are still restrictions on how footage can be used. UK media have been prohibited from editing extracts of video from parliamentary proceedings. This has not only limited UK media from doing that which overseas media are able to do (the satirical US show, *Daily Show,* carried an edited extract of a debate, which Channel 4 was then not able to show), but has also limited MPs who want to show clips of themselves on their blogs or websites.

The capacity for parliamentarians to educate and, more particularly, to mobilize support for particular provisions of public policy thus remains restricted. For members of either House to engage in a teaching role, they have first to be informed on the issue and be prepared to communicate with individuals, groups and less organized sections of the public to inform them. Limited time and resources restricts the opportunity to obtain the information. Partisanship also acts as a barrier to both obtaining and disseminating information, and more particularly to offering a united front to the public.

Conclusion

In recent decades, both Houses of Parliament have acquired a greater potential to educate the public, and particular groups, and to mobilize support for specific provisions of public policy. Relative to past practice, both Houses are more open than before and, indeed, more open than some other legislatures. Both Houses have utilized new media of communication to reach the public. There is much greater contact between parliamentarians and those outside Westminster – individuals, organized groups and the unorganized public.

From a pluralist perspective, there are clearly significant limitations. The affect of such communication between Parliament and people on policy outcomes is limited. Party principally dictates what happens. Most people who see parliamentary proceedings on television are essentially passive recipients. They have not actively sought to watch or listen to what is happening in Parliament, and are not likely to be influenced to take any particular action as a result. MPs themselves have been wary of the Internet, recognizing they need to exploit it, but worrying that it may create unmanageable demands.

However, from an institutional perspective, channels of communication are expanding and being embedded in the political system. Newspaper coverage of select committees has increased. The number of people seeking information from and about Parliament has increased significantly. Educating citizens is sometimes achieved by Parliament, and on occasion – primarily where there is cross-party agreement – members are able to assist in mobilizing popular support behind a particular policy. The development of such channels has the capacity to strengthen the linkage between Parliament and people. Partisanship, though, continues to limit what the institution can achieve and the means for informing people are not as fully exploited as they could be. The opportunity exists to engage in a more extensive dialogue with the public; it is an opportunity that both Houses, as well as individual members, seek to exploit, but it is an opportunity not yet fully realized.

14
The Reform of Parliament

Parliament does not exist in a vacuum. It has developed as a highly institutionalized body, but not one that operates wholly detached from other actors within the political system. As a legislature, it has proved to be a multifunctional and functionally adaptable body. It has acquired a range of functions and it has developed or shed functions as it has adapted to the political environment within which it operates.

Parliament, as we have seen (Chapter 2), has been shaped by its relationship to the executive. However, to focus solely on that relationship, and within that to treat Parliament's role exclusively as one of 'law making', is to misunderstand Parliament's place in the political system. It is nonetheless a focus, as we have seen (Chapter 1), that has shaped much of the literature on Parliament for more than a century. That has skewed popular perceptions of Parliament and generated narrow or flawed prescriptions for change.

Those legislatures that have survived and sometimes flourished are those that have adapted to the political environment, generating and fulfilling tasks that ensure they remain relevant both to the political elite and to the public – what Michael Mezey (1979) would class as 'more supported' legislatures. Identifying the reasons why and how support is or could be maintained entails addressing not just the relationship to the executive, but also to the people. Indeed, it could be argued that the several waves of democracy in the twentieth century (Huntington 1991; Norton 2012e, p. 73) have rendered legislatures more, not less relevant, to the people. At times of popular dissatisfaction with government or widespread apathy, then the role of legislatures may be crucial in maintaining or reinforcing political stability. Political authority, and hence stability, rests as we have noted (Chapter 1) on a government being able to raise resources to meet its commitments of public policy and maintain the consent of the people (Rose 1979, pp. 351–70). The legislature is crucial to the maintenance of that consent. It constitutes the buckle that links the executive and the people.

The different views of power that we have identified have provided a valuable analytical tool, but also provide the basis for prescribing the means by which Parliament can be strengthened as a means of sustaining political authority and carrying out the tasks expected of it. Focusing on the pluralist perspective of power is necessary, but it is not sufficient. The institutional approach sensitizes us to what may prove to be the most crucial dimension of Parliament's role, that of ensuring the voices of the people are heard. That may be of even greater importance at a time of globalization and a perception that decisions are being taken elsewhere.

Explaining reform

Calls for parliamentary reform have been heard throughout Parliament's history. These calls have been louder at certain times than others. At times, Parliament has been a player in national unrest, such as the English Civil War and Glorious Revolution, but these occasions have been exceptional. Parliament has normally managed to adapt, willingly or otherwise, within the limits of the existing constitutional arrangements. However, it has never been free of calls for change that would bestow upon it new tasks or enhance its capacity to fulfil those tasks that it has acquired or had ascribed to it.

There have been calls, sometimes strident, for parliamentary reform in recent decades and especially so in the period since the 1960s. Various reforms, detailed in the preceding chapters, have been implemented, but others remain on the political agenda. The debate over reform, though, has often lacked clarity and coherence. There is agreement among many politicians that parliamentary reform is desirable, but there the agreement ends. There is reform and there is reform.

We can distinguish between reform *within* Parliament and reform *of* Parliament. The former is essentially internal to the institution, encompassing changes – such as the appointment of new committees or the election of committee members – which can be achieved by a decision of the House. The latter is external to Parliament, though will be achievable usually only through legislation (which requires the assent of both Houses, as distinct from change carried out within a single chamber) and entails a major change to the constitution, with significant implications for Parliament. Sometimes the implications are incidental (in other words, not the purpose of the legislation), as with membership of the European Community; on other occasions, they may be intended: a good example is the introduction of fixed-term parliaments. The Fixed-term

Parliaments Act 2011 was designed to remove the Prime Minister's capacity to encourage party discipline through calling an early election.

We can also distinguish between the two chambers. Though it is common to hear reference to parliamentary reform, in practice it is very rarely reform of Parliament *qua* Parliament, but rather one chamber of Parliament. The term usually refers to reform of the Commons, with reform of the second chamber more frequently being referred to specifically as Lords reform. Reform of the Commons usually encompasses powers, procedures and changes designed to affect behaviour, whereas Lords reform generally addresses composition.

There is thus a problem with referring to *parliamentary* reform. However, we also encounter problems with terminology in referring to *reform*. It is not necessarily a generic term for any change to Parliament, but rather has on occasion acquired a very specific meaning. At the time of debate over the Parliament Bill in 1911, for example, reform did not mean limiting the powers of the House, but rather changing the composition of the House. It was thus possible to oppose the Bill (which limited the powers) and to be a supporter of Lords reform (Norton 2012d, p. 474). In the twenty-first century, debate over the future of the second chamber has also led to terminological confusion. Supporters of an elected second chamber have tended to refer to Lords reform as the term encompassing their proposals. Opponents have used the term to refer to changes to the existing House (such as creating a statutory appointments commission and removing members who do not attend), regarding proposals for election as amounting to proposals for the abolition, and not the reform, of the House. One does not re-form something by destroying it.

There is also a lack of clarity as to *why* reform should be pursued. As the Commission to Strengthen Parliament (2000, p. 7) observed, reform can be pursued for different reasons. It may be undertaken to enable the government to get its business more expeditiously. It may be undertaken for the convenience of members, enabling them to get away earlier or have a better working environment. It may be carried out in order to get rid of archaic or obscure practices that no longer serve much purpose or which may have little meaning to those outside (or even inside) Parliament. It may also be pursued for the purpose of strengthening Parliament as a body of scrutiny and to call government to account for its actions. 'These purposes may be described as attempts to provide for, respectively, efficiency, convenience, appearance and effectiveness' (Commission to Strengthen Parliament 2000, p. 7). Given the need to address the public as well as the Westminster face of Parliament, we may also add the purpose of enabling the voices of citizens to be heard.

Given this, we can briefly sketch the demands for change to the Commons and the Lords, utilizing the distinction that we have drawn between reform *of* (internal) and reform *to* (external) before addressing the case for reforming Parliament.

Reforming the Commons

Calls for reform of the House of Commons are frequently heard and the House has undergone a number of changes over the course of the past century (Hansard Society 1967; Kelso 2009). These calls have been fairly constant over the past half-century following the publication of Bernard Crick's seminal *Reform of Parliament* in 1964 (Crick 1964; see Norton 1981, pp. 203–8). They have variously borne fruit, most notably in the creation of the departmental select committees (1979), public bill committees (2006) and the election of committee chairs and appointment of the Backbench Business Committee (2010) (see Riddell 2011, pp. 86–7). They have also encompassed innovations such as debates in Westminster Hall.

Such calls have, for most of the century, fallen within the internal approach. They are premised on an acceptance that the existing relationship between the executive and the legislature is sound and that what is required primarily is a strengthening of the capacity of MPs to scrutinize and challenge government.

The approach, however, has been muddled as well as narrow. The muddle has derived from the fact that proposals have not been confined to that particular goal. The House of Commons established a Modernisation Committee in 1997 to advance proposals for reform. Though it initially brought forward proposals for strengthening the Commons in the legislative process, it moved on to address proposals that were designed for some of the other purposes identified by the Commission to Strengthen Parliament, such as changes for the convenience of members (issues such as sitting hours).

In so far as the approach has been concerned with the relationship of the House to other parts of the political system, it has focused on the relationship to the executive. It is only in recent years that some attention has been directed at the relationship of Parliament to the people. The Modernisation Committee in 2004 published a report on *Connecting Parliament with the Public* acknowledging that it 'serves no-one if we make it difficult for voters to understand what their elected representatives are doing'. It produced recommendations designed to 'reconcile the necessary purpose of Parliament with the reasonable expectation of the people to have access to the processes by which we govern ourselves' (Modernisation Committee 2004, p. 3). These included greater use of on-line consultations, a radical upgrade of the Parliament website, changes to the process of petitioning the House, and the provision of dedicated educational resources.

These recommendations were essentially modest and well within the gift of the House. The only recommendation reaching beyond it was for the government to re-examine the balance in the citizenship curriculum in schools, given that 'an understanding of the country's democratic institutions is also of fundamental importance to today's young people, and to the engaged voters of tomorrow'.

For those embracing the external approach, such proposals may be necessary, but they are not sufficient. Advocates of the external approach begin from the premise that changes within the House will not destroy the stranglehold of the executive. For them, the existing system is essentially broken and requires radical surgery, not the sticking plaster of internal reform. Modest changes may enhance the capacity of MPs to challenge government, but they will not affect fundamentally the relationship between the House and the government. Indeed, internal reform is itself normally dependent on government support, or at least acquiescence, in order to be achieved. Government may not be too keen on supporting change that may limit its capacity to govern or may make its life more difficult.

Given that, more radical reformers argue the case for constitutional surgery. The most notable reform advocated is a new system of electing MPs. Advocates of a system of proportional representation for parliamentary elections justify reform in terms of fairness for political parties (the proportion of parliamentary seats equalling the proportion of votes cast). However, it is also seen in terms of affecting both the effectiveness of the House of Commons (the parliament–executive relationship) and the representativeness of the House (the parliament–citizen link), though the extent to which either or both are achievable depends on the PR system. Under a PR system, it is argued, no one party (on current voting trends) would have an overall majority, thus making coalitions likely and making the House of Commons more important as the site of political deliberation. PR systems can also have the effect of producing more women members than under first-past-the-post. Under the single-transferable-vote (STV), voters can choose between candidates within the same party, thus enhancing choice.

These claims are contested by defenders of the present system, arguing that coalitions can undermine the accountability of government to the people (given post-election bargaining and coalition parties fighting the next election as separate entities) and that the proposal does not even meet the criterion of fairness, at least in terms of bargaining power: 10 per cent of the vote may produce 10 per cent of the seats in the House of Commons, but 10 per cent of the seats may (if holding the balance of power) produce far more than 10 per cent of the bargaining power in the House of Commons (see Johnston 1998; Norton 1998b). Some PR systems have also not facilitated greater independence on the part of Members, but rather reinforced the need for unity in order to deliver policies that have been negotiated and agreed between parties.

The key point for our purpose is that reform of the House of Commons is a generic term for a range of changes. The prescriptions derive from different perceptions of the role of the House of Commons, or at least the capacity of the current House to utilize its coercive and persuasive capacity to the extent that the House is able to fulfil the tasks expected of it. We can thus distinguish between internal and external approaches. What both have in common is a focus on executive–legislative relationships. It is not an exclusive focus and both can make some claim to recognizing the need to bolster the link between Parliament and the citizen, though – as we have seen in the case of internal reformers – it has been accorded importance only in recent years.

Reforming the Lords

Calls to reform the House of Lords have littered the political landscape for more than 150 years. They became marked in the nineteenth century as the franchise was extended, the House of Commons having a strengthened claim to be the voice of (most of) the people. The twentieth century, as we have seen (Chapter 1), saw changes to both the powers (Parliament Acts 1911 and 1949) and to the composition (Life Peerages Act 1958, House of Lords Act 1999) of the House, transforming the nature of the institution. It moved from being a largely atrophying aristocratic body mid-century to a more active, self-confident and meritocratic institution by the start of the new century (see Russell and Sciara 2007; 2008; Russell 2010b; Dorey and Kelso 2011, p. 217).

The House itself has adapted to major change (Chapter 2), but the change that has taken place – both *to* it and *within* it – have not stilled calls for further change. Some, as we have seen, have come to fruition. Others have fallen by the wayside, most recently in 2012, when the government decided not to proceed with a bill to replace the existing House with one that has 80 per cent of its members elected. As Dorey and Kelso have noted, 'The story of House of Lords reform over the last 100 years or so has been characterised both by remarkable institutional change as well as by frequently stalled political processes' (Dorey and Kelso 2011, p. 217). Achieving one set of changes does not still demands for more radical reform. The House of Lords Act 1999 was characterized as stage one of a two-stage process, the second stage involving attempts to achieve a partially, largely or wholly elected House. Proposals by the Labour government between 2000 and 2010 for a partially or largely elected House failed to achieve all-party support (see Norton 2010c, pp. 368–70; Dorey and Kelso 2011, ch. 6).

The principal reason for the failure of the various proposals for an elected or part-elected House is a fundamental disagreement over the basis of legitimacy of the second chamber. For those who advocate an elected House, legitimacy derives from being elected: they focus, therefore, on input legitimacy (see Kelso 2006). Those who wish to retain the existing appointed chamber view it as legitimate because of the work that it does (a revising chamber, not challenging the hegemony of the elected chamber): they therefore focus on output legitimacy. There has thus been a tendency for those engaged in the debate to argue from different premises.

There have been exceptions, some supporters of the existing chamber making a democratic argument for an appointed second chamber (Norton 2011d; Tyler 2012). If democracy is about how people choose to govern themselves, then in a representative democracy, the choice of government – and its accountability to the people – is fundamental. Government is chosen through elections to the House of Commons and is accountable to the people through the House of Commons. There is thus what has been termed core accountability. That accountability is threatened if it is divided (not necessarily evenly but divided nonetheless) between two elected chambers, the second being able to affect outcomes of public policy. This results in policy not put forward to the people at an election and denies the electorate a body that can be held collectively accountable for the outputs of public policy (Norton 2011c; see also Norton 2007d). As one specialist in democratic theory put it to the Joint Committee on the Draft House of Lords Reform Bill, 'democratising one part of Parliament (the Lords) will reduce the democratic character of the whole (Parliament). And ultimately it is the democratic character of Parliament that matters, not the democratic character of its constituent parts considered in isolation from each other.' (Tyler 2012, p. 200)

Supporters of election believe that input legitimacy is paramount and that there is no case for an appointed chamber, however distinguished. Others seek in essence to square the circle by retaining some element of appointment (to help maintain the independence and merit of the existing house) while introducing electoral legitimacy through some members being elected. The Labour government (1997–2010) moved from favouring having 20 per cent of the members elected to having 50 per cent elected and, then following a vote of the House of Commons in 2007, to having 80 per cent elected. The coalition government formed in 2010 pursued, as we have noted, a bill making provision for 80 per cent of the members to be elected. It was dropped after most Conservative MPs not part of the payroll failed to support the bill on second reading in July 2012. Offered the option of pursuing instead reform, in the sense of changes within the House (such as reducing the number of members), the minister in charge of constitutional reform, Deputy Prime Minister Nick Clegg, declined it.

These different stances mean that no approach has garnered majority support. We can discern four basic stances, what have been termed the four R's: retain, reform, replace and remove altogether (Norton 1982a; 2010c, pp. 370–3). The *retain* approach entails maintaining an appointed chamber, though admitting of reform within the existing framework. The *reform* approach entails taking the existing House and introducing an elected element (the stance taken by the Labour government until 2007). The *replace* approach involves removing the existing House and replacing it with a largely or wholly elected second chamber (the stance of the Labour government after 2007 and of the coalition government). The option of *remove altogether* is to get rid of the existing House and not replace it, moving from bicameralism to unicameralism. More than 100 MPs voted for the abolition option in 2007. By dint of government failing to mobilize sufficient support for any option involving change, the retain option has succeeded by default.

What is crucial for our purposes is not so much the division of opinion but rather the unity in terms of focus: the debate, as it has since the passage of the Parliament Acts, has focused primarily on composition. The starting point has been *who* is in the Lords and *how* they got there. It has not been to ask what is the purpose of Parliament and then, having established the purpose, to determine, as a consequence, the role within it of the second chamber. As various commentators observed, form should follow function. Successive governments have tended to approach the issue the other way round.

Reforming Parliament

Reforming Parliament entails, or should entail, having an appreciation of the role expected of the institution. There has been little thought given to how Parliament fits within the nation's constitutional arrangements. As legal specialist and former Liberal Democrat MP, David Howarth, told the House of Lords Constitution Committee:

> We have no structural thinking going on about the interaction between the composition of the Houses [of Parliament], the electoral systems, the courts and so on. We have no thinking about how all this fits together into a system of government. (Constitution Committee 2011, p. 13).

One could extend the observation to encompass the relationship between these institutions and the people. Howarth's criticism also informed his criticism of the government's House of Lords Reform Bill. In giving evidence to the joint committee on the bill, he observed:

> If ... you want it [the Lords] to be complementary ... something has to be done that has not been done yet. I know that this will cause some distress among Members of the House of Commons, but in order for the second Chamber to be complementary to the first Chamber, you have got to say what is wrong with the first Chamber. Since no one seems to be able to admit that there is anything wrong at all with the first Chamber, we do not get that debate off the ground. (Joint Committee on the Draft House of Lords Reform Bill, Vol. 2, 2012, p. 109)

Although the United Kingdom has undergone major constitutional change over the past half-century, it has been essentially disparate and discrete, deriving from no coherent view of constitutional change (Norton 2007b; see also Flinders 2010). Parliament has authorized the particular measures, and sought to adapt to them (Chapters 7–9), but it has had little time, or not attempted, to address the wider context and how it as a parliament relates to it.

This provides the basis for the first of our two concluding points. That is, that there is a need to look at Parliament holistically. The pluralist focus on observable decision-making is relevant, but arguably dangerous in so far it focuses exclusively or largely on the coercive capacity of the legislature. That capacity in a formal sense is not in doubt. We shall come on to the will to exercise it in due course. For the moment, our focus is the scope rather than the means for realizing change. By looking at Parliament from different perspectives of power, and the range of functions fulfilled by members, we can appreciate that Parliament is more significant in the political process than that conceded by a narrow pluralist approach.

A holistic approach encompasses the relationship of Parliament to the people. This, as we have seen, has always been important – MPs have always had a territorial base – but has grown in significance with the expansion of the franchise. Representation at the collective level (general representation, through parties) has been complemented by the growing importance of representation of constituents (specific representation, through individual MPs). The workload of MPs has increased as they have sought to fulfil the demands made of them. We have addressed these demands seriatim, but Figure 14.1 enables us to see the richness of the demands made of parliamentarians. The figure identifies the various functions, or consequences, identified by Packenham (1970) (Chapter 1) but distinguishes between the two faces of Parliament (to the executive and to the public) and ranks the functions in order of significance. It draws together what has been covered in this volume and estimates their importance relative to one another.

Identifying the range of functions, and in particular those fulfilled in linking the citizen with the political process, is central to identifying the

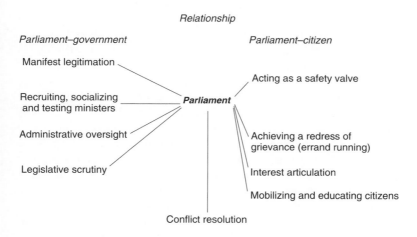

Figure 14.1   The functions of the UK Parliament

potential of Parliament. There is distrust of politicians and of politics, a feature not specific to the United Kingdom. Citizens, according to Russell Dalton, have grown 'distrustful of politicians, sceptical about democratic institutions, and disillusioned about how the democratic process functions' (Dalton 2004, p. 1). The more government has sought to deal with more complex and incompatible issues, the more it has failed to deliver what the people want (Dalton 2004, pp. 152–3). 'Top down pressures from economic and political globalisation may come up against bottom-up demands for maintaining the benefits of the welfare state' (Norton 2012e, p. 82). As distrust increases, political participation tends to decrease, leading instead to protest movements and calls for constitutional reform (Dalton 2004, pp. 173–7, 184–7).

For some critics, Parliament is part of the problem rather than part of the solution. Some advocate by-passing or supplementing Parliament through more participatory democracy. The Power Report (2006) wanted both reform within Parliament and a more participatory democracy, not least through such mechanisms as citizens' juries and 'democracy hubs'. Some advocates of giving the people a greater say have essentially ignored Parliament (see, for example, Hind 2010).

As Riddell has noted, there is little evidence that political disengagement is a response to political structures (Riddell 2011, p. 99). That is a useful corrective in that Parliament should not be seen as a cause, or at least not *the* cause, of the problem nor written off as a potential answer to it. Indeed, Parliament can be seen as part of the solution. Although people will espouse the need for more participatory democracy, and for greater use, for example, of referendums, they are usually not then prepared to get involved. Whereas a large majority will normally support the idea of referendums, only a minority will usually turn out to vote when one is held (turnout also tends to be lower than in elections of candidates; Butler and Ranney 1994, pp. 5–6). As the 2012 Hansard Society *Audit of Political Engagement* recorded, 'An increasing proportion of the population now believe that their participation can make a difference to the way their area is run. However, as yet, there has been no apparent growth in the public's appetite for greater involvement in decision-making at the local level' (Hansard Society 2012, p. 57). This is not an argument against greater engagement, but rather a recognition of the limitation of seeing participatory democracy as the answer to ensuring the voice of the people is heard. Nor can most of the mechanisms of participatory democracy be seen as a substitute for a dedicated, institutionalized process of deliberation, one that ensures that different voices are heard within a neutral arena. That is why Parliament is crucial in constituting that arena.

Parliament is the core institutionalized means through which the voice of citizens can be heard. We have identified the problems with the process, hence the need for reform. But in order to pursue reform we need to have a clear view of Parliament within the political system and what we expect of it. The institution has adapted over time to the demands made of it. That adaptation may not have been as successful as it might, but Parliament has shown a capacity to respond to the demands made of it. Taking a holistic view provides a necessary starting point. Rather than isolating one particular relationship or function, looking at the range of functions fulfilled by Parliament (Figure 14.1) – recognizing that we define functions as consequences – provides the basis both for analysis and prescription. There has been a greater recognition of the importance of the Parliament–citizen link. Developing that link is arguably crucial to Parliament's future.

At times of austerity and a growing recognition that decisions are being taken at a multi-national or global level, through bodies such as the IMF and the World Bank, there is the danger of people feeling distant or isolated from decision making. That could be taken as a basis for asserting the growing irrelevance of legislatures (Norton 1981, p. 218). It could also be taken as identifying their potential, some may say necessity, for fulfilling the functions, especially the expressive functions, identified in Figure 14.1. Legislatures, as we have seen, are the institutions through which the people speak to the executive (and, in parliamentary systems, through which the executive is chosen) and the executive speaks to the people. They are the means by which the voice of the people can be heard in between elections. The need for them to do that is arguably greater at times of national or international crisis; without the legislature fulfilling that role, and being seen to do so, the greater the danger of the people ignoring the legislature and taking to the streets.

There is thus a challenge for legislatures at a national level; beyond that, there is a case for greater collaboration between national legislatures. There is some collaboration between national legislatures within the European Union (Chapter 7) as well as between legislatures at a global level, through bodies such as the Inter-Parliamentary Union (IPU). There is a growing recognition of the need to address the representative role of legislatures. As the 2012 Global Parliamentary Report of the IPU and United Nations Development Programme (UNDP), on *The Changing Nature of Parliamentary Representation*, recorded, citizens' expectations have increased as the number of parliaments has expanded, and legislatures are having to compete with a variety of ways in which citizens can express their views. But, as it went on:

Yet parliaments have never been more vital. Parliaments remain the only bodies that exist specifically to collate and articulate the interests of the nation as a whole ... The challenge facing parliaments in all parts of the world is one of continuous evolution, ensuring that they respond strategically and effectively to changing public demands for representation. (IPU/UNDP 2012, p. 5)

Parliament in the UK may enjoy a longevity not matched by others, but the challenge it faces is the same as other legislatures. Addressing that entails looking at Parliament in terms of the totality of its functions. As economic and other pressures faced by the nation increase, the function of educating and mobilizing citizens may assume a much greater significance.

Our second concluding point is that reform does not happen by itself: there has to be the political will to achieve it (Norton 1983, pp. 54–69). The history of Parliament has been littered with schemes for reform. Think tanks, commentators and academics advance proposals for strengthening Parliament. What they often omit is how they expect to get from the current position to their ideal. Parliamentary reform, as with wider constitutional change, does not just happen. The impetus has usually come from government. The executive brings forward legislation and utilizes its majority to get it enacted. Even with internal reform, where resolutions of the House are sufficient, it is ministers, usually the Leader of the House, who brings forward the relevant motions. This has generally meant that parliamentary reform has not done great damage to the government's ability to get its business. Attempts in the 1960s to achieve a series of investigative select committees were essentially undermined by ministers and their officials (Norton 1981, pp. 221–2). When there have been reforms, they have tended to be modest, sometimes anaemic.

If significant change is to be achieved, then it is dependent on the political will of MPs to achieve it. They have to be willing to vote for it, even in the face of executive reluctance or hostility. The introduction of the departmental select committees in 1979 was the product of pressure from MPs on both sides of the House, achieved against a reluctant Cabinet (the prime minister, Margaret Thatcher, was hostile to the proposals) as were essentially the reforms introduced at the start of the 2010 Parliament. The changes of 2010 bore out the analysis of the 1979 reforms, namely that the chances of achieving reform are greatest at the start of a new parliament under a new government (creating a particular window of opportunity), when there is a clear reform agenda (a report from the Procedure Committee in the case of the 1979 reforms and the Wright Committee report in 2010), and some degree of leadership (be it from the Leader of the House, as with Norman St John-Stevas in 1979, or from a backbencher, as with Tony Wright in the 2005–10 Parliament). However, these count for nought without political will on the part of Members. That will may not exist; the point is that without it significant reform will not be achieved.

The impetus for MPs being willing to act may come from within Parliament (as with the select committees in 1979; see Norton 1981, pp. 231–2) or it may come from the public. The public reaction to the expenses scandal in 2009 provided the key for reform. The scandal did not fundamentally change people's views, but rather 'confirmed and hardened the public's widely held scepticism about politicians' (Hansard Society 2010, p. 3). Daily revelations about expenses claims buffeted the House of Commons. Prime Minister Gordon Brown was to describe it as 'the biggest parliamentary scandal for two centuries' (Winnett and Rayner 2009, p. 349). The impact on MPs was marked; the daily revelations of MPs' claims undermined morale and fuelled a recognition that something had to be done to restore public trust. There was already pressure from some Members for change designed to strengthen the House in calling government to account and in ensuring a greater connection with the public. The reaction to the scandal swept away any government reluctance to consider change. The result was the appointment of the House of Commons Reform Committee, under the chairmanship of a leading reformer, Labour MP Tony Wright. The report of the Wright Committee, entitled *Rebuilding the House* (House of Commons Reform Committee 2009), constituted the reform agenda and the incoming coalition was neither inclined nor arguably able to resist the implementation of the recommendations, with the effects that we have seen.

Reform thus requires not only a clear basis in terms of what is intended – and why – but also necessitates mobilizing support for its achievement. Parliamentarians cannot disclaim responsibility for what is done, or equally for what is not done. At the end of the day, reform – be it internal or external – requires their approval. Ensuring that Parliament fulfils the roles expected of it requires the exercise of political will on their part. Others may come up with the analysis and the proposals but ultimately parliamentarians have to act to achieve change.

Conclusion

The pluralist focus on Parliament conveys a narrow and hence misleading view of Parliament. The institution has a much broader array of functions than is apparent from this perspective. Parliament fulfils tasks that are crucial in the British polity, not least in ensuring that the views of the people – expressed through parties, groups and individual constituents – are heard and if possible acted upon. Both Houses are active in scrutinizing the legislation and actions of the executive as well as adapting to major constitutional change. Neither is necessarily as efficient and effective as it could be in fulfilling the functions ascribed to it, nor necessarily in prioritizing its tasks. Both increasingly recognize the need not only to be more effective in calling government to account, but also to build their links with the people. Parliament has moved from being a closed to a far more open institution than ever before. It is also becoming more specialized, through committees, and more independent in behaviour. The government is normally assured of getting its measures through each House, but it can no longer take it as given that it will.

Our conclusion is best summed up in the words of Peter Riddell, in his work, *In Defence of Politicians:* 'MPs, and peers, need to address three areas: first, their own conduct; second, their own effectiveness; and, third, their connection with the public' (Riddell 2011, p. 151). This not only identifies what needs to be done but by whom. We have addressed these in the foregoing chapters. Responsibility for reforming Parliament should not rest with the executive – the equivalent of giving prisoners the key to the cells – but with those who form Parliament. The positive feature of the Parliament returned in 2010 is, as Riddell has argued, that Members have shown themselves willing to act, both in achieving reform and in acting independently of the executive. 'The overall picture is of a more vigorous and lively Parliament than is commonly assumed' (Riddell 2011, p. 91). As we have seen (Chapter 11), MPs have also devoted more time to constituency work. The potential is there. Whether it is realized or not, especially in relation to ensuring that the voice of citizens is heard, is in the hands of those very parliamentarians.

Further Reading

Facts and figures

Valuable quantitative material about the House of Commons is to be found in the *Sessional Information Digest,* produced after the conclusion of each session by the House of Commons Information Office. This contains sections covering sittings of the House and dates of session, legislation, the work of committees, documentation, and membership of the House. It is published on the Parliament website at: www.publications.parliament.uk/pa/cm/cmsid.htm. Some useful data on the House of Lords are published each year in the House of Lords *Annual Report,* including statistics on sittings and membership. The report is available at: www.publications.parliament.uk/pa/ld/ldlordsrep.htm. There are useful research briefings produced by the libraries of the two Houses on a range of topics related to Parliament. These can be accessed at: www.parliament.uk/briefing-papers/parliament-government-and-politics/.

The rules, precedents, practices and law of Parliament are detailed in the 24th edition of *Erskine May's Treatise on The Law, Privileges, Proceedings and Usage of Parliament* (Jack 2011). The first edition first appeared in 1844. Though essentially for the parliamentary specialist (and, for reasons of cost, the library), it contains some useful historical material and information on both Houses of Parliament.

Parliament and government

The most useful recent analysis of the legislative process, and the problems associated with it, are to be found in Fox and Korris (2010). On public bill committees, see Levy (2010). On pre-legislative scrutiny see Snookler (2006) and, for the period since 2010, the note prepared by the House of Commons Library, *Pre-legislative Scrutiny under the Coalition Government* (2011) – www.parliament.uk/documents/commons/lib/research/briefings/snpc-05859.pdf – and, for post-legislative scrutiny, the Library note, *Post-legislative Scrutiny* (2010), www.parliament.uk/

documents/commons/lib/research/briefings/snpc-05232.pdf. On attempts to improve how Parliament scrutinizes legislation, see the outcome of the 2012 inquiry into legislative standards by the Political and Constitutional Reform Committee of the House of Commons.

The most recent comprehensive study of Question Time remains Franklin and Norton (1993), though for a comparative perspective see Martin and Rozenberg (2012). On select committees, see the article on committee influence by Hindmoor *et al.* (2009). There is also valuable material in the evidence submitted to the House of Commons Liaison Committee as part of its 2012 inquiry into the powers and effectiveness of select committees: www.publications.parliament.uk/pa/cm201213/cmselect/cmliaisn/writev/scp/contents.htm.

On the powers of select committees, see the report by the Clerk of the House, www.publications.parliament.uk/pa/cm201213/cmselect/cmliaisn/writev/scp/scp36.htm. Much useful data are included in reports of the Liaison Committee, comprising select committee chairs; see, for example, its report on *The Work of Committees in 2008–09* (2010): www.publications.parliament.uk/pa/cm200910/cmselect/cmliaisn/426/426.pdf. On media coverage of select committees, see Kubala (2011). On the changes implemented in the House of Commons in 2010 (the election of committee chairs and creation of the Backbench Business Committee), see Russell (2011) and chapter 5 of Riddell (2011).

On Parliament and the European Union, see the outcome of the 2012 inquiry into parliamentary scrutiny of EU legislation by the European Scrutiny Committee in the House of Commons. See also Giddings and Drewry (2004). For a comparative perspective, see Winzen (2012) and Cooper (2012). On Parliament and devolution, see Trench (2010), Bogdanor (2010), Norton (2011b) and House of Commons Library, 'The West Lothian Question' (2012) www.parliament.uk/documents/commons/lib/research/briefings/snpc-02586.pdf. On Parliament and human rights, see Young (2009) – primarily for the specialist reader – and Hunt *et al.* (2012).

On MPs, see Searing (1994) and Rush (2001). Rush and Giddings (2011) look at the socialization of MPs. See also the Hansard Society (2011). Data on members' backgrounds are to be found in Byron Criddle's chapter in the Nuffield study covering each general election (see Criddle 2010), in *The Times Guide to the House of Commons*, published after each general election, and in the annual *Dod's Parliamentary Companion*. On parliamentary behaviour, see especially Cowley (2002a; 2005; 2007), Norton (2012a) and Cowley and Stuart (2012). On the role of the backbench MP, see the House of Commons

Modernisation Committee, *Revitalising the Chamber: the role of the back bench Member* (2007): www.publications.parliament.uk/pa/ cm200607/cmselect/cmmodern/337/337.pdf On the 2009 MPs' expenses scandal see Winnett and Rayner (2009).

On the House of Lords, the principal text is Shell (2007). For a fascinating anthropological study, see Crewe (2005) – a similar study of the Commons is expected to be published in 2013. See also Russell (2000) and Norton (2007d).

Parliament and citizen

On the concept of representation, the classic work is that of Hanna Pitkin (1967). See also Mansbridge (2011). For recent scholarship in the context of the United Kingdom, see Judge (1999a; 1999b). On the relationship of MP and constituent, see Cain *et al.* (1987), Norton and Wood (1993), Norris (1997), Power (1998) and Norton (2002c; 2012b). On the relationship in a comparative context, see the special issue of *The Journal of Legislative Studies* on 'Parliaments and Citizens', vol. 18, nos.3/4, 2012, and the IPU/UNDC (2012) *Parliamentary Report: The Changing Nature of Parliamentary Representation*, available at: www.ipu.org/pdf/publications/gpr2012-full-e.pdf. Flynn (2012) offers an entertaining insight into the work of the constituency MP. The most substantial academic study of the relationship between Parliament and pressure groups remains the volume edited by Rush (1990). On lobbying, see the useful note prepared by the House of Commons Library, *Lobbying* (2012), www.parliament. uk/briefing-papers/SN04633. On Parliament and the media, see Negrine (1998), and on Parliament and the Internet, Ward and Lusoli (2005), Norton (2008), Williamson (2009), and Jackson and Lilleker (2011). See also, in a comparative context, Williamson and Fallon (2011).

Attitudes towards Parliament are variously covered in the annual *Audit of Political Engagement* published by the Hansard Society.

Parliament and reform

On the history of parliamentary reform, see Kelso (2009). On the history of House of Lords reform, see Dorey and Kelso (2011) and Ballinger (2012). For a chronology, see House of Lords Library Note, *House of Lords Reform 1997-2010: A* Chronology (2011) www.parliament.uk/ briefing-papers/LLN-2011-025. For the contemporary debate, see

Fitzpatrick (2011), Norton (2011c), the report of the Joint Committee on the Draft House of Lords Bill – www.publications.parliament.uk/pa/jt201012/jtselect/jtdraftref/284/284i.pdf – and the oral and written evidence submitted to the Joint Committee:

> Oral: www.publications.parliament.uk/pa/jt201012/jtselect/jtdraftref/284/284ii.pdf.
> Written:www.publications.parliament.uk/pa/jt201012/jtselect/jtdraftref/284/284iii.pdf.

Parliamentary publications

Parliamentary publications are accessible on the Parliament website (www.parliament.uk). The website includes *Hansard*, the text of bills before Parliament (as well as the explanatory notes), reports from select committees (as well as the transcripts of hearings held as part of current inquiries), details of business, information on members, and a host of archival and educational material. Paper copies of publications can be ordered from the Stationery Office. For a comparative study, the websites of other parliaments can be reached through the website of the Inter-Parliamentary Union (www.ipu.org).

Journals

Articles on Parliament are variously carried in journals, most notably *The Journal of Legislative Studies* and *Parliamentary Affairs*. Both are published quarterly.

Bibliography

Allen, Graham (2001) *The Last Prime Minister* (London: Graham Allen).

Allen, Nicholas (2011) 'Dishonourable Members? Exploring Patterns of Misconduct in the Contemporary House if Commons', *British Politics*, vol. 6, pp. 210–40.

Allmark, Liam (2012) 'More than Rubber Stamps: The Consequences Produced by Legislatures in Non-Democratic States beyond Latent Legitimation', *Journal of Legislative Studies*, vol. 18, pp. 184–202.

Arter, David (2004a) 'The Scottish Committees and the Goal of a 'New Politics': A Verdict on the First Four Years of the Devolved Scottish Parliament', *Journal of Contemporary European Studies*, vol. 12, pp. 71–91.

Arter, David (2004b) *The Scottish Parliament: A Scandinavia-Style Assembly?* (London: Frank Cass).

Bachrach, P. and Baratz, M. (1962) 'Two Faces of Power', *American Political Science Review*, vol. 56, pp. 947–52.

Bagehot, Walter (1867) *The English Constitution* (London: Chapman & Hall).

Baggott, Rob (1995) *Pressure Groups Today* (Manchester: Manchester University Press).

Baldwin, Nicholas D. J. (1985) 'The House of Lords: Behavioural Changes', in P. Norton (ed.), *Parliament in the 1980s* (Oxford: Basil Blackwell).

Baldwin, Nicholas D. J. (1995) 'The House of Lords and the Labour Government 1974–79', *Journal of Legislative Studies*, vol. 1, pp. 218–42.

Baldwin, Nicholas D. J. and Shell, D. (eds) (2001) *Second Chambers* (London: Frank Cass).

Ball, James and Beleaga, Teodora (2012) 'MPs' £1.8m in Perks Revealed', *The Guardian*, 10 April.

Ballinger, Chris (2011) 'Hedging and Ditching: The Parliament Act 1911', *Parliamentary History*, vol. 30, pp. 19–32.

Ballinger, Chris (2012) *House of Lords 1911–2011: A Century of Non-Reform* (Oxford: Hart Publishing)

Barker, Anthony and Rush, M. (1970) *The Member of Parliament and His Information* (London: George Allen & Unwin).

Beard, Charles A. and Lewis, J. D. (1959) 'Representative Government in Evolution', in J. C. Wahlke and H. Eulau (eds), *Legislative Behavior: A Reader in Theory and Research* (New York: The Free Press of Glencoe).

Beer, Samuel H. (1966) 'The British Legislature and the Problem of Mobilising

Consent', in E. Frank (ed.), *Lawmakers in a Changing World* (Englewood Cliffs, NJ: Prentice-Hall).

Beer, Samuel H. (1969) *Modern British Politics*, revd edn (London: Faber).

Beetham, David, Byrne, I., Ngan, P. and Weir, S. (2002) *Democracy Under Blair: A Democratic Audit of the United Kingdom* (London: Politico's).

Berry, Roger (1996) 'A Case Study in Parliamentary Influence: The Civil Rights (Disabled Persons) Bill', *Journal of Legislative Studies*, vol. 2, pp. 135-44.

Birch, Anthony H. (1964) *Representative and Responsible Government* (London: George Allen & Unwin).

Birch, Anthony H. (1977) *Integration and Disintegration in the British Isles* (London: Allen & Unwin).

Blackburn, Robert and Kennon, A. (2003) *Griffith and Ryle on Parliament: Functions, Practice and Procedures*, 2nd edn (London: Sweet & Maxwell).

Blondel, Jean, Gillespie, P., Herman, V., Kaati, P. and Leonard, R. (1970) 'Legislative Behaviour: Some Steps towards a Cross-National Measurement', *Government and Opposition*, vol. 5, pp. 67–85.

Bogdanor, Vernon (2009) *The New British Constitution* (Oxford: Hart Publishing).

Bogdanor, Vernon (2011) *The Coalition and the Constitution* (Oxford: Hart Publishing).

Bowler, Shaun and Farrell, D. (1993) 'Legislator Shirking and Voter Monitoring: Impacts of European Parliament Electoral Systems upon Legislator-Voter Relationships', *Journal of Common Market Studies*, vol. 31, pp. 45–69.

Bowman, Sir Geoffrey (2004) Evidence, *Parliament and the Legislative Process*, Select Committee on the Constitution, House of Lords. 14th Report, Session 2003-4. HL Paper 173-11; pp. 96–109.

Bown, Francis A. (1990) 'The Shops Bill', in M. Rush (ed.), *Parliament and Pressure Politics* (Oxford: Clarendon Press).

Bradley, Anthony W. and Ewing, K. D. (2007) *Constitutional and Administrative Law*, 14th edn (London: Pearson Longman).

Brandreth, Gyles (1992) 'Post Haste', *The House Magazine*, 5 October.

Brandreth, Gyles (1999) *Breaking the Code* (London: Phoenix).

Brazier, Alex, Flinders, M. and McHugh, D. (2005) *New Politics, New Parliament?* (London: The Hansard Society).

Brazier, Rodney (1997) *Ministers of the Crown* (Oxford: Clarendon Press).

Bromhead, Peter (1958) *The House of Lords and Contemporary Politics 1911–1957* (London: Routledge & Kegan Paul).

Bruyneel, Gaston (1978) *Interpellations, Questions and Analogous Procedures for the Control of Government Actions and Challenging the Responsibility of Government* (Geneva: Association of Secretaries General of Parliaments).

Bryce, Lord (1921) *Modern Democracies* (London: Macmillan).

Buck, Philip W. (1963) *Amateurs and Professionals in British Politics* (Chicago, IL: University of Chicago Press).

Butler, David (1963) *The Electoral System in Britain Since 1918*, 2nd edn (Oxford: Clarendon Press).

Butler, David (2004) 'Electoral Reform', *Parliamentary Affairs*, vol. 57, pp. 734–43.

Butler, David and Butt, S. (2004) 'Seats and Votes: A Comment', *Representation*, vol. 40, pp. 169–72.

Butler, David and Ranney, A. (1994) 'Practice', in D. Butler and A. Ranney (eds), *Referendums around the World* (Washington DC: The AEI Press).

Cabinet Office (2004) *The Government's Response to the Report of the Joint Committee on the Draft Civil Contingencies Bill*, Cm 6078 (London: Cabinet Office).

Cabinet Office (2005) *Handling Correspondence from Members of Parliament, Members of the House of Lords, MEPs and Members of Devolved Assemblies* (London: The Cabinet Office).

Cain, Bruce E., Ferejohn, J. and Fiorina, M. (1979) 'Popular Evaluations of Representatives in Great Britain and the United States', California Institute of Technology Working Paper No. 288 (Passadena. CA: California Institute of Technology).

Cain, Bruce E., Ferejohn, J. and Fiorina, M. (1987) *The Personal Vote* (Cambridge, MA: Harvard University Press).

Campion, Lord (1952) 'Parliament and Democracy', in Lord Campion (ed.), *Parliament: A Survey* (London: George Allen & Unwin).

Cannon, John and Griffiths, R. (1988) *The Oxford Illustrated History of the British Monarchy* (Oxford: Oxford University Press).

Carmichael, Paul and Dickson, B. (1999) *The House of Lords* (Oxford: Hart Publishing).

Cazalet-Keir, Thelma (1967) *From the Wings* (London: Bodley Head).

Chadwick, Andrew (2006) *Internet Politics* (Oxford: Oxford University Press).

Charmley, John (1997) *Duff Cooper: The Authorised Biography*, paperback edn (London: Phoenix).

Chester, Norman and Bowring, N. (1962) *Questions in Parliament* (Oxford: Oxford University Press).

Child, Susan (2002) *Politico's Guide to Parliament*, 2nd edn (London: Politico's).

Chisholm, Anne and Davie, M. (1993) *Beaverbrook: A Life* (London: Pimlico).

Clayton, Richard (2004) 'Judicial Deference and "Democratic Dialogue": The Legitimacy of Judicial Intervention under the Human Rights Act 1998', *Public Law*, Spring, pp. 33–47.

Coleman, Stephen and Van De Donk, W. (1999) *Parliament in the Age of the Internet* (Oxford: Oxford University Press).

Commission to Strengthen Parliament (2000) *Strengthening Parliament* (London: The Conservative Party).

Committee on Standards in Public Life (2004) *Survey of Public Attitudes Towards Conduct in Public Life* (London: Committee on Standards in Public Life).

Congleton, Roger D. (2011) *Perfecting Parliament* (Cambridge: Cambridge University Press).

Congressional Quarterly (1987) *The Washington Lobby*, 5th edn (Washington DC: Congressional Quarterly Inc).

Constitution Committee, House of Lords (2003) *Devolution: Inter-Institutional Relations in the United Kingdom*, 2nd Report, Session 2002-3, HL Paper 28 (London: The Stationery Office).

Constitution Committee, House of Lords (2004a) *The Regulatory State: Ensuring Its Accountability*, 6th Report, Session 2003-4, HL Paper 68-I, 68-II, 68-III (London: The Stationery Office).

Constitution Committee, House of Lords (2004b) *Parliament and the Legislative Process*, 14th Report, Session 2003-4, HL Paper 173-I (London: The Stationery Office).

Constitution Committee, House of Lords (2010) *Pre-Legislative Scrutiny in the 2008-09 and 2009-10 Sessions*, 8th Report, Session 2009-10, HL Paper 78 (London: The Stationery Office).

Constitution Committee, House of Lords (2011) *The Process of Constitutional Change*, 15th Report, Session 2010-12, HL Paper 177 (London: The Stationery Office).

Constitution Committee, House of Lords (2012a) *Referendum on Scottish Independence*, 24th Report, Session 2010-12, HL Paper 263 (London: The Stationery Office).

Constitution Committee, House of Lords (2012b) *Judicial Appointments*, 25th Report, Session 2010-12, HL 272 (London: The Stationery Office).

Cook, Robin (2003) *The Point of Departure* (London: Simon & Schuster).

Cooper, Ian (2012) 'A "Virtual Third Chamber" for the EU: National Parliaments after the Treaty of Lisbon', *West European Politics*, vol. 35, pp.441–65

Corston, Jean (2004) Written Evidence, *Parliament and the Legislative Process*, Select Committee on the Constitution, House of Lords, 14th Report, Session 2003-4, HL Paper 173-II, pp. 164–7.

Couzens, K. (1956) 'A Minister's Correspondence', *Public Administration*, vol. 34. pp. 237–44.

Cowley, Philip (1998a) 'Unbridled Passions? Free Votes, Issues of Conscience, and the Accountability of Members of Parliament', *Journal of Legislative Studies*, vol. 4, pp. 70–88.

Cowley, Philip (ed.) (1998b) *Conscience and Parliament* (London: Frank Cass).

Cowley, Philip (2002a) *Revolts and Rebellions* (London: Politico's).

Cowley, Philip (2002b) 'Legislatures and Assemblies', in P. Dunleavy, A. Gamble, R. Heffernan, I. Holliday and G. Peele (eds), *Developments in British Politics* 6 (Basingstoke: Palgrave).

Cowley, Philip (2005) *The Rebels* (London: Politico's).

Cowley, Philip (2007) 'Parliament', in A. Seldon (ed), *Blair's Britain 1997–2007* (Cambridge: Cambridge University Press).

Cowley, Philip and Norton, P. (1999) 'Rebels and Rebellions: Conservative MPs in the 1992 Parliament', *The British Journal of Politics and International Relations*, vol. 1, pp. 84–105.

Cowley, Philip and Stuart, M. (1997) 'Sodomy, Slaughter, Sunday Shopping and Seatbelts', *Party Politics*, vol. 3, pp. 19–30.

Cowley, Philip and Stuart, M. (2004a) 'The Mother of all Rebellions: Iraq and the PLP', Paper presented at the Political Studies Association Annual Conference, University of Lincoln, April (accessible on www.revolts.co.uk).

Cowley, Philip and Stuart, M. (2004b) 'Parliament: More Bleak House than Great Expectations', *Parliamentary Affairs*, vol. 57, pp. 301–14.

Cowley, Philip and Stuart, M. (2010) 'Party Rules OK: Voting in the House of Commons on the Human Fertilisation and Embryology Bill', *Parliamentary Affairs*, vol. 63, pp. 173–81.

Cowley, Philip and Stuart, M. (2011), 'Response to Alison Plumb and David Marsh', *Parliamentary Affairs*, vol. 64, pp. 777–80.

Cowley, Philip and Stuart, M. (2012) 'A Coalition with Two Wobbly Wings: Backbench Dissent in the House of Commons', *Political Insight*, vol. 3, pp. 8–11.

Cox, Gary W. and Morgenstern, S. (2002) 'Epilogue: Latin America's Assemblies and Proactive Presidents', in S. Morgenstern and B. Nacif (eds), *Legislative Politics in Latin America* (Cambridge: Cambridge University Press).

Coxall, Bill (2001) *Pressure Groups in British Politics* (Harlow: Longman).

Crewe, Emma (2005) *Lords of Parliament* (Manchester: Manchester University Press).

Crewe, Ivor (1975) 'Electoral Reform and the Local MP', in S. E. Finer (ed.), *Adversary Politics and Electoral Reform* (London: Anthony Wigram).

Crick, Bernard (1964) *The Reform of Parliament* (London: Weidenfeld & Nicolson).

Criddle, Byron (2002) 'MPs and Candidates', in D. Butler and D. Kavanagh, *The British General Election of 2001* (Basingstoke: Palgrave).

Criddle, Byron (2010) 'More Diverse, Yet More Uniform: MPs and Candidates', in D. Kavanagh and P. Cowley, *The British General Election of 2010* (Basingstoke: Palgrave Macmillan).

Criddle, Byron, Childs, S. and Norton, P. (2005) 'The Make-Up of Parliament', in P. Giddings (ed), *The Future of Parliament: Issues for a New Century* (Basingstoke: Palgrave Macmillan).

Crossman, Richard H. S. (1963) 'Introduction' to W. Bagehot, *The English Constitution* (London: Fontana).

Crowe, Edward (1986) 'The Web of Authority: Party Loyalty and Social Control in the British House of Commons', *Legislative Studies Quarterly* vol. 11, pp. 161–85.

Culture Media and Sport Committee, House of Commons (2012) *News International and Phone-hacking*, Eleventh Report, Session 2010-12, HC 903-I (London: The Stationery Office).

Currie, Edwina (1989) *Lifelines* (London: Sidgwick & Jackson).

Curtice, John, Fisher, S. and Ford, R. (2010) 'Appendix 2: An analysis of the Results', in D. Kavanagh and P. Cowley, *The British General Election of 2010* (Basingstoke: Palgrave Macmillan).

Dalton, Russell M. (2004) *Democratic Challenges Democratic Choices* (Oxford: Oxford University Press).

Dicey, A. V. (1959) *An Introduction to the Study of the Law of the Constitution* (first published 1885), 10th edn (London: Macmillan).

Dod's Parliament Companion (annual) (London: Dod's Parliamentary Communications).

Doig, Alan (1984) *Corruption and Misconduct in Contemporary British Politics* (Harmondsworth: Penguin).

Doig, Alan (1990) *Westminster Babylon* (London: Allison & Busby).

Dorey, Peter and Kelso, A. (2011) *House of Lords Reform Since 1911* (Basingstoke: Palgrave Macmillan).

Double, Paul (2004) 'The Impact of European Community Law on the British Legislative Process', in A. Brazier (ed.), *Parliament, Politics and Law Making* (London: The Hansard Society).

Drewry, Gavin (1985) 'Public General Acts – Now and a Hundred Years Ago', *Statute Law Review*, Autumn, pp. 152–61.

Drewry, Gavin (ed.) (1989) *The New Select Committees*, rev. edn (Oxford: Clarendon Press).

Dunleavy, Patrick and Jones, G. W. (1995) 'Leaders, Politics and Institutional Change: The Decline of Prime Ministerial Accountability to the House of Commons, 1868–1990', in R. A. W. Rhodes and P. Dunleavy (eds), *Prime Ministers, Cabinets and Core Executives* (London: Macmillan).

Dunleavy, Patrick, Margetts, H., Smith, T. and Weir, S. (2001) *Voices of the People* (London: Politico's).

Edwards, Richard A. (2002) 'Judicial Deference under the Human Rights Act', *The Modern Law Review*, vol. 65, pp. 859–82.

Electoral Commission (2004) *Delivering Democracy?* (London: The Electoral Commission).

Elms, Tim and Terry, T. (1990) *Scrutiny of Ministerial Correspondence* (London: Cabinet Office Efficiency Unit).

Engle, George (1983) "Bills are Made to Pass as Razors are Made to Sell": Practical Constraints in the Preparation of Legislation', *Statute Law Review*, Spring, pp. 7–23.

European Scrutiny Committee, House of Commons (2010) *The Work of the Committee in 2008-09*, Sixth Report, Session 2009-10, HC 267 (London: The Stationery Office).

European Scrutiny Committee, House of Commons (2011) *Opting into International Agreements and Enhanced Parliamentary Scrutiny of Opt-In Decisions*, Thirtieth Report, Session 2010-12, HC 955-I (London: The Stationery Office).

European Scrutiny Committee, House of Commons (2012) *Treaties on Stability, Coordination and Governance: Impact on the Eurozone and the Rule of Law*, 62nd Report, Session 2010-12, HC 1817 (London: The Stationery Office).

European Union Committee, House of Lords (2010) *Annual Report 2010*, 3rd Report, Session 2010-11, HL Paper 70 (London: The Stationery Office).

Evans, Paul (2004) 'The Human Rights Act and Westminster's Legislative Process', in A. Brazier (ed.) *Parliament, Politics and Law Making* (London: The Hansard Society).

Ferguson, Ross and Howell, M. (2004) *Political Blogs – Craze or Convention?* (London: The Hansard Society).

Field, Frank (1982) 'Backbenchers, the Executive and Theories of Representation', in Royal Institute of Public Administration, *Parliament and the Executive* (London: RIPA).

Field, John (2002) *The Story of Parliament* (London: Politico's/James & James).

Finer, Samuel E. (1958) *Anonymous Empire* (London: Pall Mall).

Fisher, Mark (2004) *Parliament and the Legislative Process*, Select Committee on the Constitution, House of Lords, 14th Report, Session 2003-4, HL Paper 173-II, pp. 83–95.

Fitzpatrick, Alexandra (2011) *The End of the Peer Show?* (London: The Constitution Society).

Flinders, Matthew (2010) *Democratic Drift* (Oxford: Oxford University Press).

Flynn, Paul (1997) *Commons Knowledge: How to Be a Backbencher* (Bridgend: Seren).

Flynn, Paul (2012) *How to be an MP* (London: Biteback Publishing).

Foley, Michael (1993) *The Rise of the British Presidency* (Manchester: Manchester University Press).

Fowler, Norman (1991) *Ministers Decide* (London: Chapman).

Fox, Ruth and Korris, Matt (2010) *Making Better Law* (London: Hansard Society).

Franklin, Mark and Norton, P. (1993) *Parliamentary Questions* (Oxford: Clarendon Press).

Franklin, Mark, Baxter, A. and Jordan, M. (1986) 'Who Were the Rebels? Dissent in the House of Commons 1970–1974', *Legislative Studies Quarterly*, vol. 11, pp. 143–59.

Friedrich, Carl (1963) *Man and his Government: An Empirical Theory of Politics* (New York: McGraw-Hill).

Gamble, Andrew (1994) *The Free Economy and the Strong State*, 2nd edn (Basingstoke: Macmillan).

George, Bruce and Morgan, J. D. (1999) 'Parliamentary Scrutiny of Defence', *Journal of Legislative Studies*, vol. 5, pp. 1–11.

Giddings, Philip (1998) 'The Parliamentary Ombudsman: A Successful Alternative?', in D. Oliver and G. Drewry (eds), *The Law and Parliament* (London: Butterworth).

Giddings, Philip and Drewry, G. (eds) (2004) *Britain in the European Union* (Basingstoke: Palgrave).

Gifford, D. J. and Salter, J. (1996) *How to Understand an Act of Parliament* (London: Cavendish).

Gifford, Zerbanoo (1992) *Dadabhai Naoroji: Britain's First Asian MP* (London: Mantra).

Gilmour, Ian (1971) *The Body Politic*, rev. edn (London: Hutchinson).

Golding, John (2003) *Hammer of the Left* (London: Politico's).

Gordon, Strathearn (1948) *Our Parliament*, 3rd edn (London: Hansard Society).

Grant, Wyn (2000) *Pressure Groups and British Politics* (Basingstoke: Macmillan).

Grantham, Cliff (1989) 'Parliament and Political Consultants', *Parliamentary Affairs*, vol. 42, pp. 503–18.

Grantham, Cliff and Moore Hodgson, C. (1985) 'The House of Lords: Structural Changes', in P. Norton (ed.), *Parliament in the 1980s* (Oxford: Basil Blackwell).

Grantham, Cliff and Seymour-Ure, C. (1990) 'Political Consultants', in M. Rush (ed.), *Parliament and Pressure Politics* (Oxford: Clarendon Press).

Greenway, John (2004) Evidence, *Parliament and the Legislative Process*, Select Committee on the Constitution, House of Lords, 14th Report, Session 2003-4, HL, Paper 173-II; pp. 112–25.

Grey, Anthony (1992) *Quest for Justice: Towards Homosexual Emancipation* (London: Sinclair-Stevenson).

Griffith, John A. G. and Ryle, M. (1989) *Parliament: Functions, Practice and Procedure* (London: Sweet & Maxwell).

Hain, Peter (2004) Evidence, *Parliament and the Legislative Process*, Select Committee on the Constitution, House of Lords, 14th Report, Session 2003-4, HL Paper 173-II, pp. 1–16.

Hain, Peter (2012) *Outside In* (London: Biteback Publishing).

Hansard Society (1967) *Parliamentary Reform 1933–60*, 2nd rev. edn (London: Cassell).

Hansard Society (1992) *Making the Law: Report of the Hansard Society Commission on the Legislative Process* (London: The Hansard Society).

Hansard Society (2004) *Issues in Lawmaking: 5. Pre-Legislative Scrutiny* Hansard Society Briefing Paper (London: Hansard Society).

Hansard Society (2010) *Audit of Political Engagement 7: The 2010 Report* (London: Hansard Society).

Hansard Society (2011) *A Year in the Life: From Members of Public to Members of Parliament* (London: Hansard Society).

Hansard Society (2012) *Audit of Political Engagement 9: The 2012 Report: Part One* (London: Hansard Society).

Hansard Society Commission on Parliamentary Scrutiny (2001) *The Challenge for Parliament: Making Government Accountable* (London: Vacher Dod).

Harrison, David (2011) 'OMG! MPs spend 1,000 hours a year on Twitter', *Sunday Telegraph*, 31 July.

Hawes, Derek (1993) *Power on the Back Benches? The Growth of Select Committee Influence* (Bristol: SAUS Publications).

Hazell, Robert (2004) 'Who Is the Guardian of Legal Values in the Legislative Process: Parliament or the Executive?', *Public Law*, Autumn, pp. 495–500.

Hedlund, Ronald D. and Friesema, H. R (1972) 'Representatives' Perceptions of Constituency Opinion', *Journal of Politics*, vol. 34, pp. 730–52.

Heffernan, Richard (2011) 'Pressure Group Politics', in R. Heffernan, P. Cowley and C. Hay (eds), *Developments in British Politics Nine* (Basingstoke: Palgrave Macmillan).

Hibbing, John R. (2002) 'Legislative Careers: Why and How We Should Study Them', in G. Loewenberg, P. Squire and D. R. Kiewiet (eds), *Legislatures: Comparative Perspectives on Representative Assemblies* (Ann Arbor, MI: University of Michigan Press).

Hind, Dan (2010) *The Return of the Public* (London: Verso).

Hindmoor, Andrew, Larkin, P. and Kennon, A. (2009) 'Assessing the Influence of Select Committees in the UK: The Education and Skills Committee, 1997–2005', *Journal of Legislative Studies*, vol. 15, pp. 71–89.

Hofferbert, R. I. and Budge, I. (1992) 'The Party Mandate and the Westminster Model: Election Programmes and Government Spending in Britain, 1945–85', *British Journal of Political Science*, vol. 22, pp. 151–82.

Hogg, Douglas (2004) Evidence, *Parliament and the Legislative Process*, Select Committee on the Constitution, House of Lords, 14th Report, Session 2003-4, HL Paper 173-II, pp. 83–95.

Hollingsworth, Mark (1991) *MPs for Hire* (London: Bloomsbury).

House of Commons Commission (2003) *25th Annual Report*, Session 2002–3, HC 806 (London: The Stationery Office).

House of Commons Information Office (2003) *Sessional Information Digest 2002–2003* (London: House of Commons).

House of Commons Library (2011a) *House of Lords Statistics*, Standard Note SN/SG/3900, 26 April (London: House of Commons Library).

House of Commons Library (2011b) *Parliamentary Private Secretaries*, Standard Note SN/PC/04942, 9 May (London: House of Commons Library).

House of Commons Library (2012) *The West Lothian Question*, Standard Note SN/PC/2586, 18 Jan. (London: House of Commons Library).

House of Commons Reform Committee (2009) *Rebuilding the House*, First Report, Session 2008–09, HC 1117 (London: The Stationery Office).

House of Commons Reform Committee (2010), *Rebuilding the House: Implementation*, First Report, Session 2009–10, HC 372 (London: The Stationery Office).

House of Lords (2002) *Annual Report 2001–2002*, HL Paper 153 (London: The Stationery Office).

House of Lords (2003) *Annual Report 2002–2003*, HL Paper 146 (London: The Stationery Office).

House of Lords Information Committee (2009) *Are the Lords Listening? Creating Connections between People and Parliament*, Vol. 1: Report, 1st Report, Session 2008–09, HL Paper 138-I (London: The Stationery Office).

Hunt, Murray, Hooper, H. and Yowell, P. (2012) *Parliament and Human Rights: Redressing the Democratic Deficit* (Swindon: Arts and Humanities Research Council).

Huntington, Samuel P. (1991) 'Democracy's Third Wave', *Journal of Democracy*, vol. 2, pp. 12–34.

Hurd, Douglas (2003) *Memoirs* (London: Little, Brown).

Independent Commission on the Voting System (1998) *The Report of the Independent Commission on the Voting System*, Cm 4090-1 (London: The Stationery Office).

Information Committee, House of Commons (2002) *Digital Technology: Working for Parliament and the Public*, First Report, Session 2001–2, HC 1065 (London: The Stationery Office).

Inglehart, Ronald (1977) *The Silent Revolution* (Princeton, NJ: Princeton University Press.)

IPU/UNDP (2012) *Global Parliamentary Report: The Changing Nature of Parliamentary Representation* (Geneva and New York: Inter-Parliamentary Union, United Nations Development Programme).

Jack, Malcolm (ed.) (2011) *Erskine May's Treatise on The Law, Privileges, Proceedings and Usage of Parliament*, 24th edn (London: LexisNexus UK).

Jackson, Nigel and Lilleker, D. (2011) 'Microblogging, Constituency Service and Impression Management: UK MPs and the Use of Twitter', *Journal of Legislative Studies*, vol. 17, pp. 86–105.

James, Simon (1992) *British Cabinet Government* (London: Routledge).

Jefferson, Kurt W. (2011) *Celtic Politics* (Lanham, MD: University Press of America).

Jogerst, Michael (1993) *Reform in the House of Commons* (Lexington, KY: University Press of Kentucky).

Johnson, Nevil (1988) 'Departmental Select Committees', in M. Ryle and P. G. Richards (eds), *The Commons Under Scrutiny* (London: Routledge).

Johnston, Ron (1998) 'Proportional Representation and a "Fair Electoral System" for the United Kingdom', *Journal of Legislative Studies*, vol. 4, pp. 128–48.

Johnston, Ron, and Pattie, C. (2011) 'The Local Campaigns and the Outcome', in N. Allen and J. Bartle (eds), *Britain at the Polls 2010* (London: Sage).

Joint Committee on the Draft House of Lords Reform Bill (2012) *Draft House of Lords Reform Bill, Report, Vol. 2: Oral and Associated Written Evidence*, Session 2010–12, HL Paper 284-II, HC 1313-II (London: The Stationery Office).

Joint Committee on Human Rights (2001) *Criminal Justice and Police Bill*, First

Special Report, Session 2000–1, HL Paper 42, HC 296 (London: The Stationery Office).

Joint Committee on Human Rights (2010) *Work of the Committee in 2008–09: Government Response to the Committee's Second Report of Session 2009–10; Legislative Scrutiny (Finance Bills and Academies Bills)*, First Report, Session 2010–11, HL Paper 32, HC 459 (London: The Stationery Office).

Jones, J. Barry (1990) 'Party Committees and All-Party Groups', in M. Rush (ed.), *Parliament and Pressure Politics* (Oxford: Clarendon Press).

Jordan, Grant (1991) *The Commercial Lobbyists* (Aberdeen: Aberdeen University Press).

Jordan, Grant and Maloney, W. A. (2007) *Democracy and Interest Groups: Enhancing Participation?* (Basingstoke: Palgrave Macmillan).

Jordan, Grant and Richardson, J. (1982) 'The British Policy Style or the Logic of Negotiation', in J. J. Richardson (ed.), *Policy Styles in Western Europe* (London: George Allen & Unwin).

Joseph Rowntree Reform Trust (2004) *The State of British Democracy* (York: Joseph Rowntree Reform Trust).

Jowell, Roger and Witherspoon, S. (1985) *British Social Attitudes: The 1985 Report* (Aldershot: Gower).

Jowell, Roger, Witherspoon, S. and Brook, L. (1987) *British Social Attitudes: The 1987 Report* (Aldershot: Gower).

Judge, David (1990) *Parliament and Industry* (Aldershot: Dartmouth).

Judge, David (1999a) *Representation: Theory and Practice in Britain* (London: Routledge).

Judge, David (1999b) 'Representation in Westminster in the 1990s: The Ghost of Edmund Burke', *Journal of Legislative Studies*, vol. 5, pp. 12–34.

Judge, David (2004) 'Whatever Happened to Parliamentary Democracy in the United Kingdom?', *Parliamentary Affairs*, vol. 57, pp. 682–701.

Kelly, Richard, Gay, O. and Cowley, P. (2006) 'Parliament: The House of Commons', in M. Rush and P. Giddings (eds), *The Palgrave Review of British Politics 2005* (Basingstoke: Palgrave Macmillan).

Kelso, Alexandra (2006) 'Reforming the House of Lords: Navigating Representation, Democracy and Legitimacy at Westminster', *Parliamentary Affairs*, vol. 59, pp. 563–81.

Kelso, Alexandra (2009) *Parliamentary Reform at Westminster* (Manchester: Manchester University Press).

Kennon, Andrew (2004) 'Pre-Legislative Scrutiny of Draft Bills', *Public Law*, Autumn, pp. 477–94.

King, Anthony (1981) 'The Rise of the Career Politician in Britain – and Its Consequences', *British Journal of Political Science*, vol. 11, pp. 249–85.

King, Anthony (2007) *The British Constitution* (Oxford: Oxford University Press).

Kirchheimer, Otto (1966) 'The Transformation of the Western European Party

Systems', in J. LaPolombara, and M. Weiner (eds), *Political Parties and Political Development* (Princeton, NJ: Princeton University Press).

Klug, Francesca and O'Brien, C. (2002) 'The First Two Years of the Human Rights Act', *Public Law*, Winter, pp. 649–62.

Kubala, Marek (2011) 'Select Committees in the House of Commons and the Media', *Parliamentary Affairs*, vol. 64, pp. 694–711.

Lambert, David and Navarro, M. (2004) 'Law Making for Wales', in A. Brazier (ed.), *Parliament, Politics and Law Making* (London: Hansard Society).

Lang, Ian (2002) *Blue Remembered Years* (London: Politico's).

Laugharne, Peter (1994) *Parliament and Specialist Advice* (Liverpool: Manutius Press).

Laws, David (2010) *22 Days in May* (London: Biteback Publishing).

Leston-Bandeira, C. (2005) (ed) *Southern European Parliaments in Democracy* (London: Routledge).

Levy, Jessica (2010) 'Public Bill Committees: An Assessment. Scrutiny Sought; Scrutiny Gained', *Parliamentary Affairs*, vol. 63, pp. 534–44.

Liaison Committee, House of Commons (2000) *Shifting the Balance: Select Committees and the Executive*, First Report, Session 1999–2000, HC 300 (London: The Stationery Office).

Liaison Committee, House of Commons (2004) *Annual Report for 2003–04*, First Report, Session 2003–4, HC 446 (London: The Stationery Office).

Liaison Committee, House of Commons (2010) *The Work of Committees in Session 2008–09*, Second Report, Session 2009–10, HC 426 (London: The Stationery Office).

Lipset, S. M. (1997) *American Exceptionalism* (New York: W. W. Norton).

Locke, John (1960) *Second Treatise on Government*, first published 1689; with an introduction by Peter Laslett (Cambridge: Cambridge University Press).

Loewenberg, Gerhard (1971) (ed.) *Modern Parliaments: Change or Decline?* (Chicago, IL: Aldine-Atherton).

Loewenberg, Gerhard (2011) *On Legislatures* (Boulder, CO: Paradigm Publishers)

Lowell, A. Lawrence (1896) *Government and Parties in Continental Europe* (Cambridge, MA: Harvard University Press).

Lowell, A. Lawrence (1924) *The Government of England, Vol. II* (New York: Macmillan).

Lukes, Steven (2004) *Power: A Radical View*, 2nd rev. edn (Basingstoke: Palgrave Macmillan).

Mackintosh, John P. (1977) *The British Cabinet*, 3rd edn (London: Methuen).

Maer, Lucinda and Sandford, M. (2004) *Select Committees Under Scrutiny* (London: The Constitution Unit).

Major, John (1999) *The Autobiography* (London: HarperCollins).

Mansbridge, Jane (2011) 'Identifying the Concept of Representation', *American Political Science Review*, vol. 105, pp. 621–30.

Marsh, David and Read, M. (1988) *Private Members' Bills* (Cambridge: Cambridge University Press).

Marsh David and Rhodes, R. (1992) *Policy Networks in British Government* (Oxford: Oxford University Press).

Marsh, Ian (1986) *Policy-Making in a Three-Party System* (London: Methuen).

Martin, Shane (2011) 'Parliamentary Questions, the Behaviour of Legislators, and the Function of Legislatures: An Introduction', *Journal of Legislative Studies*, vol. 17, pp. 259–70.

Martin, Shane and Rozenberg, O. (2012) (eds) *The Role and Function of Parliamentary Questions* (London: Routledge).

Matthews, Donald R. (1985) 'Legislative Recruitment and Legislative Careers', in G. Loewenberg, S. C. Patterson and M. E. Jewell (eds), *Handbook of Legislative Research* (Cambridge, MA: Harvard University Press).

Maxwell, Patricia (1999) 'The House of Lords as a Constitutional Court: The Implications of *Ex p. EOC*', in P. Carmichael and B. Dickson (eds), *The House of Lords: Its Parliamentary and Judicial Roles* (Oxford: Hart Publishing).

May, Theresa (2004) 'Women in the House: The Continuing Challenge', *Parliamentary Affairs*, no. 57, pp. 844–51.

McKenzie, Kenneth (1968) *The English Parliament* (London: Penguin).

McManus, Michael (2011) *Tory Pride and Prejudice* (London: Biteback Publishing).

Melhuish, David and Cowley, P. (1995) 'Whither the New Role in Policy Making? Conservative MPs in Standing Committees 1979 to 1992', *Journal of Legislative Studies*, vol. 1, pp. 54–75.

Mezey, Michael (1979) *Comparative Legislatures* (Durham, NC: Duke University Press).

Miers, David and Brock, J. (1993) 'Government Legislation: Case Studies', in D. Shell and D. Beamish (eds), *The House of Lords at Work* (Oxford: Clarendon Press).

Miller, Charles (1990) *Lobbying: Understanding and Influencing the Corridors of Power*, 2nd edn (Oxford: Basil Blackwell).

Miller, Warren E. and Stokes, D. E. (1963) 'Constituency Influence in Congress', *American Political Science Review*, vol. 57, pp. 45–56.

Ministry of Justice (2011) *Responding to Human Rights Judgments*, Cm 8162 (London: Ministry of Justice).

Mitchell, Neil J. (1997) *The Conspicuous Corporation* (Ann Arbor, MI: University of Michigan Press).

Modernisation Committee, House of Commons (1997) *The Legislative Process*, 1st Report, Session 1997–98, HC 190 (London: The Stationery Office).

Modernisation Committee, House of Commons (2002) *Modernisation of the House of Commons: A Reform Programme*, Second Report, Session 2001–2, HC 1168-I (London: The Stationery Office).

Modernisation Committee, House of Commons (2004) *Connecting Parliament with the Public*, First Report, Session 2003–4, HC 368 (London: The Stationery Office).

Modernisation Committee, House of Commons (2007) *Revitalising the Chamber: the role of the back bench Member*, First Report, Session 2006–07, HC 337 (London: The Stationery Office).

Montesquieu, Charles de Secondat, Baron de (1949) *The Spirit of the Laws* [*De L'esprit des lois*], first published 1748 (New York: Hafner).

Moonie, Lewis (2004) Evidence, *Parliament and the Legislative Process*, Select Committee on the Constitution, House of Lords, 14th Report, Session 2003–4, HL Paper 173-II, pp. 111–25.

Moyes, Jonathan (2004) 'What Do All-Party Groups Need to Have in Place to Be an Influential Lobbying Voice?', Undergraduate Dissertation (Hull: Hull University Department of Politics and International Studies).

Mullin, Chris (2011) *A Walk-On Part* (London: Profile Books).

Natzler, David and Hutton, M. (2005) 'Select Committees: Scrutiny à la Carte', in P. Giddings (ed), *The Future of Parliament: Issues for a New Century* (Basingstoke: Palgrave Macmillan).

Negrine, Ralph (1992) 'Reporting Parliamentary Committees: The Investigation of the Rover Group Sale to British Aerospace', *Parliamentary Affairs*, vol. 45, pp. 399–408.

Negrine, Ralph (1998) *Parliament and the Media: A Study of Britain, Germany and France* (London: The Royal Institute of International Affairs).

Nixon, Jaqi (1986) 'Evaluating Select Committees and Proposals for an Alternative Perspective', *Policy and Politics*, vol. 14, pp. 415–38.

Norris, Pippa (1997) 'The Puzzle of Constituency Service', *Journal of Legislative Studies*, vol. 3, pp. 29–49.

Norris, Steven (1996) *Changing Trains* (London: Hutchinson).

Northern Ireland Affairs Committee, House of Commons (2010) *Progress Towards Devolution in Northern Ireland During the 2005 Parliament*, 7th Report, Session 2009–10, HC 319 (London: The Stationery Office).

Norton, Philip (1975) *Dissension in the House of Commons 1945–74* (London: Macmillan).

Norton, Philip (1978a) *Conservative Dissidents* (London: Temple Smith).

Norton, Philip (1978b) 'Government Defeats in the House of Commons: Myth and Reality', *Public Law*, Winter, pp. 360–78.

Norton, Philip (1979) 'The Organisation of Parliamentary Parties', in S. A. Walkland (ed.), *The House of Commons in the Twentieth Century* (Oxford: Clarendon Press).

Norton, Philip (1980) *Dissension in the House of Commons 1974–1979* (Oxford: Clarendon Press).

Norton, Philip (1981) *The Commons in Perspective* (Oxford: Basil Blackwell).

Norton, Philip (1982a) *The Constitution in Flux* (Oxford: Martin Robertson).

Norton, Philip (1982b) '"Dear Minister...". The Importance of MP-to-Minister Correspondence', *Parliamentary Affairs*, vol. 35, pp. 59–72.

Norton, Philip (1983) 'The Norton View', in D. Judge (ed), *The Politics of Parliamentary Reform* (London: Heinemann Educational Books).

Norton, Philip (1985) 'The House of Commons: Behavioural Changes', in P. Norton (ed.), *Parliament in the 1980s* (Oxford: Basil Blackwell).

Norton, Philip (1986) 'Independence, Scrutiny and Rationalisation: A Decade of Changes in the House of Commons', *Teaching Politics*, vol. 15, pp. 69–98.

Norton, Philip (1987), 'Dissent in the House of Commons: Rejoinder to Franklin, Baxter, Jordan', *Legislative Studies Quarterly*, vol. 12, pp. 143–52.

Norton, Philip (1989a) 'The Constitutional Position of Parliamentary Private Secretaries', *Public Law*, Summer, pp. 232–6.

Norton, Philip (1989b) 'Collective Ministerial Responsibility', *Social Studies Review*, vol. 5, pp. 33–6.

Norton, Philip (1990a) 'Introduction', in P. Norton (ed.), *Legislatures* (Oxford: Oxford University Press).

Norton, Philip (1990b) 'Public Legislation', in M. Rush (ed.), *Parliament and Pressure Politics* (Oxford: Clarendon Press).

Norton, Philip (1990c) *Parliaments in Western Europe* (London: Frank Cass).

Norton, Philip (1991a) 'Parliament Since 1945: A More Open Institution?', *Contemporary Record*, vol. 5, pp. 217–34.

Norton, Philip (1991b) 'The Changing Face of Parliament: Lobbying and its Consequences', in P. Norton (ed.), *New Directions in British Politics?* (Aldershot: Edward Elgar).

Norton, Philip (1993a) 'Congress: Comparative Perspectives', in D. C. Bacon, R. H. Davidson and M. Keller (eds), *The Encylopedia of the United States Congress* (New York: Simon & Schuster).

Norton, Philip (1993b) 'Questions and the Role of Parliament', in M. Franklin and P. Norton (eds), *Parliamentary Questions* (Oxford: Clarendon Press).

Norton, Philip (1994a) 'The Party in Parliament', in A. Seldon and S. Ball (eds), *Conservative Century* (Oxford: Oxford University Press).

Norton, Philip (1994b) 'The Growth of the Constituency Role of the MP'. *Parliamentary Affairs*, vol. 47, pp. 705–20.

Norton, Philip (1994c) 'Parliament in the United Kingdom: The Incumbency Paradox', in A. Somit, R. Wildenmann, B. Boll and A. Rommele (eds), *The Victorious Incumbent: A Threat to Democracy?* (Aldershot: Dartmouth).

Norton, Philip (1994d) 'The Legislative Power of Parliament', in C. Flinterman, A. W. Heringa and L. Waddington (eds), *The Evolving Role of Parliaments in Europe* (Antwerp: Maklu/Nomos).

Norton, Philip (1996a) 'The United Kingdom: Political Conflict, Parliamentary Scrutiny', in P. Norton (ed.), *National Parliaments and the European Union* (London: Frank Cass).

Norton, Philip (1996b), 'Conservative Politics and the Abolition of Stormont', in P. Catterall and S. McDougall (eds), *The Northern Ireland Question in British Politics* (Basingstoke: Macmillan).

314   *Bibliography*

Norton, Philip (ed.) (1998a) *Parliaments and Governments in Western Europe* (London: Frank Cass).
Norton, Philip (1998b) *Power to the People* (London: Conservative Policy Forum).
Norton, Philip (ed.) (1999a) *Parliaments and Pressure Groups in Western Europe* (London: Frank Cass).
Norton, Philip (1999b) 'The United Kingdom: Parliament under Pressure', in P. Norton (ed.), *Parliaments and Pressure Groups in Western Europe* (London: Frank Cass).
Norton, Philip (1999c) *The New Barons? Senior Ministers in British Government*, Goldsmiths College Public Policy Paper (London: Goldsmiths College).
Norton, Philip (2001a) *The British Polity*, 4th edn (New York: Longman).
Norton, Philip (2001b) 'Playing by the Rules: The Constraining Hand of Parliamentary Procedure', *Journal of Legislative Studies*, vol. 7, pp. 13–33.
Norton, Philip (ed.) (2002a) *Parliaments and Citizens in Western Europe* (London: Frank Cass).
Norton, Philip (2002b) 'The Conservative Party: Is There Anyone Out There?', in A. King (ed.), *Britain at the Polls, 2001* (New York: Chatham House).
Norton, Philip (2002c) 'The United Kingdom: Building the Link between Constituent and MP', in P. Norton (ed.), *Parliaments and Citizens in Western Europe* (London: Frank Cass).
Norton, Philip (2003a) 'Cohesion without Discipline: Party Voting in the House of Lords', *Journal of Legislative Studies*, vol. 9, pp. 57–72.
Norton, Philip (2003b) 'Governing Alone', *Parliamentary Affairs*, vol. 56. pp. 543–59.
Norton, Philip (2004a) 'The Power of Parliament', *Politics Review*, vol. 14 (2), pp. 24–7.
Norton, Philip (2004b) 'Parliament', in A. Seldon and K. Hickson (eds). *New Labour, Old Labour* (London: Routledge).
Norton, Philip (2004c) 'Reforming the House of Lords: A View from the Parapets', *Representation*, vol. 40, pp. 185–99.
Norton, Philip (2005) 'Parliament and the Courts', in N. D. J. Baldwin (ed.), *Parliament in the 21st Century* (London: Politico's).
Norton, Philip (2007a) 'The Constitution', in A. Seldon (ed), *Blair's Britain, 1997–2007* (Cambridge: Cambridge University Press).
Norton, Philip (2007b) 'Tony Blair and the Constitution', *British Politics* vol. 2, pp. 269–81.
Norton, Philip (2007c) 'National Parliaments in Europe: Recent Developments', in J. Th. J. van den Berg, L. M. F. Verhey, and J. L. W. Broeksteeg (eds), *Het Parlement* (Nijmegen: WLP).
Norton, Philip (2007d) 'Adding Value? The Role of Second Chambers', *Asia Pacific Law Review*, vol. 15, pp. 3–18.
Norton, Philip (2008) 'Four Models of Political Representation: British MPs and

the Use of ICT', in X. Dai and P. Norton (eds), *The Internet and Parliamentary Democracy in Europe* (London: Routledge).

Norton, Philip (2010a) 'The Crown', in B. Jones and P. Norton, *Politics UK*, 7th edn (Harlow Longman).

Norton, Philip (2010b) 'The Politics of Coalition', in N. Allen and J. Bartle (eds), *Britain at the Polls 2010* (London: Sage).

Norton, Philip (2010c) 'The House of Lords', in B. Jones and P. Norton, *Politics UK*, 7th edn (Harlow: Longman).

Norton, Philip (2010d) *The British Polity*, 5th edn (New York: Longman).

Norton, Philip (2011a) 'Divided Loyalties: The European Communities Act 1972', *Parliamentary History*, vol. 30, pp. 53–64.

Norton, Philip (2011b) 'The Englishness of Westminster', in A. Aughey and C. Berberich (eds), *These Englands* (Manchester: Manchester University Press).

Norton, Philip (2011c) 'Reform of the House of Lords?' The Stevenson Lecture, University of Glasgow http://www.effectivesecondchamber.com/d/ Stevenson.pdf.

Norton, Philip (2012a) 'Coalition Cohesion', in T. Heppell and D. Seawright (eds), *Cameron and the Conservatives* (Basingstoke: Palgrave Macmillan).

Norton, Philip (2012b) 'Parliament and Citizens in the United Kingdom', *Journal of Legislative Studies*, vol. 18, pp. 402–17.

Norton, Philip (2012c) 'Opt Out: Britain's Unsplendid Isolation', in J. Hayward and R. Wurzel (eds), *European Disunion: Between Sovereignty and Solidarity* (Basingstoke: Palgrave Macmillan).

Norton, Philip (2012d) 'Resisting the Inevitable? The Parliament Act 1911,' *Parliamentary History*, vol. 31, pp. 473–88.

Norton, Philip (2012e) 'Constitutional Change and the Tensions of Liberal Democracy', in J. Connelly and J. Hayward (eds), *The Withering of the Welfare State: Regression* (Basingstoke: Palgrave Macmillan).

Norton, Philip and Wood, D. M. (1990) 'Constituency Service by Members of Parliament: Does it Contribute to a Personal Vote?', *Parliamentary Affairs*, vol. 43, pp. 196–208.

Norton, Philip and Wood, D. M. (1993) *Back from Westminster* (Lexington, KY: University of Kentucky Press).

Nott, John (2002) *Here Today, Gone Tomorrow* (London: Politico's).

Oliver, Dawn and Drewry, G. (eds) (1998) *The Law and Parliament* (London: Butterworth).

Olson, David M. and Mezey, M. (1991) *Legislatures in the Policy Process* (Cambridge: Cambridge University Press).

Olson, David M. and Norton. P. (eds) (1996) *The New Parliaments of Central and Eastern Europe* (London: Frank Cass).

Olson, D. M. and Norton, P. (2008) *Post-Communist and Post-Soviet Parliaments: The Initial Decade* (London: Routledge).

O'Neill, Aidan (2001) 'Judicial Politics and the Judicial Committee: The

Devolution Jurisprudence of the Privy Council'. *The Modern Law Review*; vol. 64, pp. 603–18.

O'Neill, Michael (2004), 'Challenging the Centre: Home Rule Movements', in M. O'Neill (ed), *Devolution and British Politics* (Harlow: Longman).

Ostrogorski, Moisei (1902) *Democracy and the Organisation of Political Parties*, Vol. I (London: Macmillan).

Packenham, Robert (1970) 'Legislatures and Political Development', in A. Kornberg and L. D. Musolf (eds), *Legislatures in Developmental Perspective* (Durham, NC: Duke University Press).

Page, Alan and Batey, A. (2002) 'Scotland's Other Parliament: Westminster Legislation about Devolved Matters in Scotland since Devolution', *Public Law*, Autumn, pp. 501–23.

Parry, Keith (2004) *Webcasting of Parliament*, Standard Note, SN/PC/1761 (London: House of Commons Library).

Paxman, Jeremy (2002) *The Political Animal* (London: Michael Joseph).

Phillips, A. (1949) 'Post Office Parliamentary Questions', *Public Administration*, vol. 27, pp. 91–9.

Pitkin, Hanna (1967) *The Concept of Representation* (Berkeley, CA: University of California Press).

Political and Constitutional Reform Committee, House of Commons (2012) *Introducing a Statutory Register of Lobbyists*, Second Report, Session 2012–13, HC 153 (London: The Stationery Office).

Powell, Christopher (1980) *The Parliamentary and Scientific Committee. The First Forty Years 1939–1979* (London: Croom Helm).

Powell, Enoch (1982) 'Parliament and the Question of Reform', *Teaching Politics*, vol. 11 (2), pp. 167–76.

Power, Greg (1996) *Reinventing Westminster* (London: Charter88).

Power, Greg (1998) *Representing the People: MPs and their Constituents* (London: The Fabian Society).

Power Report (2006) *Power to the People: An Independent Inquiry into Britain's Democracy* (London: Joseph Rowntree Reform Trust).

Prince, Rosa (2012) 'MPs Admit They Let Diamond Slip Away Ahead of Inquiry Vote', *Daily Telegraph*, 5 July.

Privy Counsellor Review Committee (2003) *Anti-Terrorism, Crime and Security Act 2001 Review: Report*, Session 2003–4, HC 100 (London: The Stationery Office).

Public Administration Committee, House of Commons (2009) *Lobbying: Access and Influence in Whitehall*, First Report, Session 2008–09, HC 36-I (London: The Stationery Office).

Rawlings, Richard (1990) 'The MP's Complaints Service', *The Modern Law Review*, vol. 53, pp. 22–42, 149–69.

Read, Melvyn D. and Marsh, D. (1998) 'Homosexuality', in P. Cowley (ed.), *Conscience and Parliament* (London: Frank Cass).

Read, Melvyn D., Marsh, D. and Richards, D. (1994) 'Homosexual and Capital Punishment Votes', *Parliamentary Affairs*, vol. 47, pp. 374–86.

Reform Group, All-Party House of Commons (1984) 'Findings of the Survey of MPs' Attitudes to Reform and the Role of the MP', Mimeo (London: House of Commons Reform Group).

Regan, Paul (1987) 'The 1986 Shops Bill', *Parliamentary Affairs*, vol. 41, pp. 218–35.

Renton, Tim (2004) *Chief Whip* (London: Politico's).

Review Body on Senior Salaries (1996) *Review of Parliamentary Pay and Allowances*, Report No. 38, Vol. 2: Surveys and studies, Cm 3330-II (London: Her Majesty's Stationery Office).

Review Body on Senior Salaries (2004) *Review of Parliamentary Pay and Allowances 2004*. Report No. 57, Cm 6354-1 (London: The Stationery Office).

Richard Commission (2004) *The Report of the Richard Commission* (Cardiff: National Assembly for Wales).

Rhodes, R. A. W. (1994) 'The Hollowing Out of the State: The Changing Nature of the Public Service in Britain', *Political Quarterly*, vol. 65, pp. 138–51.

Richards, Peter G. (1959) *Honourable Members* (London: Faber & Faber).

Richards, Peter G. (1970) *Parliament and Conscience* (London: George Allen & Unwin).

Richardson, Jeremy and Jordan, A. G. (1979) *Governing Under Pressure* (Oxford: Martin Robertson).

Riddell, Peter (1993) *Honest Opportunism* (London: Hamish Hamilton).

Riddell, Peter (1995) 'The Impact of the Rise of the Career Politician', *Journal of Legislative Studies*, vol. 1, pp. 186–91.

Riddell, Peter (2000) *Parliament Under Blair* (London: Politico's).

Riddell, Peter (2011) *In Defence of Politicians* (London: Biteback Publishing).

Robinson, Geoffrey (2000) *The Unconventional Minister* (London: Michael Joseph).

Rogers, Robert and Walters, R. (2004) *How Parliament Works*, 5th edn (London: Pearson Education).

Rogers, Robert and Walters, R. (2006) *How Parliament Works*, 6th edn (London: Pearson Education).

Rose, Richard (1979) 'Ungovernability: Is There Fire Behind the Smoke?', *Political Studies*, vol. 27, pp. 351–70.

Rose, Richard (1984) *Do Parties Make a Difference?* (London: Macmillan).

Rose, Richard (2001) *The Prime Minister in a Shrinking World* (Cambridge: Polity).

Rosenblatt, Gemma (2006) *A Year in the Life* (London: The Hansard Society).

Roskell, John S. (1993) *The House of Commons 1386–1421. 1: Introductory Survey, Appendices, Constituencies* (Stroud: Alan Sutton).

Royal Commission on the Reform of the House of Lords (2000) *A House for the Future*, Cm 4534 (London: The Stationery Office).

Rush, Michael (1979) 'The Member of Parliament', in S. A. Walkland (ed.), *The House of Commons in the Twentieth Century* (Oxford: Clarendon Press).

Rush, Michael (ed.) (1990) *Parliament and Pressure Politics* (Oxford: Clarendon Press).

Rush, Michael (1998) 'The Law Relating to Members' Conduct', in D. Oliver and G. Drewry (eds), *The Law and Parliament* (London: Butterworth).

Rush, Michael (2001) *The Role of the Member of Parliament Since 1868* (Oxford: Oxford University Press).

Rush, Michael (2005) 'Career Patterns and Professionalisation', in P. Giddings (ed), *The Future of Parliament: Issues for a New Century* (Basingstoke: Palgrave Macmillan).

Rush, Michael and Giddings, Philip (2011) *Parliamentary Socialisation* (Basingstoke: Palgrave Macmillan).

Russell, David J. T. (1998) 'The Nocturnal Habits of MPs', Unpublished Undergraduate Dissertation (Hull: Hull University Politics Department).

Russell, Meg (2000) *Reforming the House of Lords* (Oxford: Oxford University Press).

Russell, Meg (2010a) *Analysis of Existing Data on the Breadth of Expertise and Experience in the House of Lords* (London: UCL Constitution Unit).

Russell, Meg (2010b), 'A Stronger Second Chamber? Assessing the Impact of the House of Lords Reform in 1999, and the Lessons for Bicameralism', *Political Studies*, vol. 58, pp. 866–85.

Russell, Meg (2011) '"Never Allow a Crisis to Go to Waste": The Wright Committee Reforms to Strengthen the House of Commons', *Parliamentary Affairs*, vol. 64, pp. 612–33.

Russell, Meg and Sciara, M. (2007) 'Why does the Government get Defeated in the House of Lords? The Lords, the Party System and British Politics', *British Politics*, vol. 2, pp. 299–322.

Russell, Meg and Sciara, M. (2008) 'The Policy Impact of Defeats in the House of Lords', *British Journal of Politics and International Relations*, vol. 10, pp. 571–89.

Schwarz, John E. (1980) 'Exploring a New Role in Policy Making: The British House of Commons in the 1970s', *American Political Science Review*, vol. 74, pp. 23–37.

Scottish Affairs Committee, House of Commons (2009) *The work of the Committee in 2008–09*, First Report, Session 2009–10, HC 71 (London: The Stationery Office).

Scottish Affairs Committee, House of Commons (2010) *Commission on Scottish Devolution*, Third Report, Session 2009–10, HC 255 (London: The Stationery Office).

Scottish Affairs Committee, House of Commons (2012) *The Referendum on Separation for Scotland: Making the Process Legal*, Second Report, Session 2012–13, HC 542 (London: The Stationery Office).

Searing, Donald (1994) *Westminster's World* (Cambridge, MA: Harvard University Press).

Seaton, Janet and Winetrobe, B. (1998) 'The Passage of Constitutional Bills in Parliament', *Journal of Legislative Studies*, vol. 4, pp. 33–52.

Select Committee on Members' Interests (1990) *Parliamentary Lobbying*, HC 283 (London: Her Majesty's Stationery Office).

Select Committee on Procedure (1992) *Petitions*, Fourth Report, Session 1991–92, HC 286 (London: Her Majesty's Stationery Office).

Select Committee on Televising the Proceedings of the House (1990) *Review of the Experiment in Televising the Proceedings of the House*, First Report, Session 1989–90, HC 265-I (London: Her Majesty's Stationery Office).

Select Committee on the Sittings of the House, House of Commons (1992) *Report from the Select Committee on the Sittings of the House*, Session 1991–92, HC 20 (London: Her Majesty's Stationery Office).

Seyd, Patrick and Whiteley, P. (2001) 'New Labour and the Party: Members and Organisation', in S. Ludlam and M. J. Smith (eds), *New Labour in Government* (London: Macmillan).

Shell, Donald (1988) *The House of Lords* (Deddington: Philip Allan).

Shell, Donald (2007) *The House of Lords* (Manchester: Manchester University Press).

Shephard, Gillian (2000) *Shephard's Watch* (London: Politico's).

Shepherd, Robert (1991) *The Power Brokers* (London: Hutchinson).

Silk, Paul (1987) *How Parliament Works* (London: Longman).

Smith, Martin J. (1993) *Pressure, Power and Policy: State Autonomy and Policy Networks* (Hemel Hempstead: Harvester Wheatsheaf).

Smith, Martin J. (1995) *Pressure Politics* (Manchester: Baseline Book Company).

Snookler, J. (2006) 'Making a Difference? The Effectiveness of Pre-Legislative Scrutiny', *Parliamentary Affairs*, vol. 59, pp. 522–35

Sontheimer, Kurt (1984) 'Parliamentarianism in Modern Times – a Political Science Perspective', *Universitas*, no. 26.

Speakers' Working Group on All-Party Groups (2012) *Speakers' Working Group on All-Party Groups: Report to the Speaker and Lord Speaker* (London: Speakers' Working Group).

Stevens, Robert (2002) *The English Judges* (Oxford: Hart Publishing).

Supreme Court, United Kingdom (2012) *Scottish Criminal Cases and the UK Supreme Court* (London: Supreme Court of the United Kingdom).

Teeling, William (1970) *Corridors of Frustration* (London: Bodley Head).

Theakston, Kevin (1987) *Junior Ministers in British Government* (Oxford: Basil Blackwell).

Topliss, Eda and Gould, B. (1981) *A Charter for the Disabled* (Oxford: Basil Blackwell).

Tordoff, Lord (2000) 'The Conference of European Affairs Committees: A Collective Voice for National Parliaments in the European Union', *Journal of Legislative Studies*, vol. 6, pp. 1–8.

Trench, Alan (2004a) 'Devolution: The Withering Away of the Joint Ministerial Committee?', *Public Law*, Autumn, pp. 513–17.

Trench, Alan (ed.) (2004b) *Has Devolution Made a Difference?* (London: Imprint Academic).

Trench, Alan (2010) 'Devolution since 2007', *Politics Review*, vol. 17 (2), pp. 2–5.

Trevelyan, George M. (1938) *The English Revolution* (London: Thornton Butterworth).

Tsebelis, George (2002) *Veto Players: How Political Institutions Work* (New York: Russell Sage Foundation/Princeton University Press).

Tyler, Colin (2012) Submission, Joint Committee on the Draft House of Lords Reform Bill, *Draft House of Lords Reform Bill, Report, Vol. 3: Other Written Evidence*, Session 2010–12, HL Paper 284-III, HC 1313-III (London: The Stationery Office).

Tyrie, Andrew (2000) *Mr Blair's Poodle* (London: Centre for Policy Studies).

Wakefield of Kendal, Lord (1980) 'Memoir', in C. Powell, *The Parliamentary and Scientific Committee. The First Forty Years 1939–1979* (London: Croom Helm).

Walker, Brian M. (2012) *A Political History of the Two Irelands* (Basingstoke: Palgrave Macmillan).

Walkland, Stuart A. (1968) *The Legislative Process in Great Britain* (London: George Allen & Unwin).

Walters, Rhodri (2004) 'The House of Lords', in V. Bogdanor (ed.), *The British Constitution in the Twentieth Century* (Oxford University Press).

Ward, Stephen and Lusoli, W. (2005) 'From Weird to Wired: the Internet and Representative Politics in the UK', *Journal of Legislative Studies*, vol.11, pp. 57–81.

Watts, Duncan (2007) *Pressure Groups* (Edinburgh: Edinburgh University Press).

Welsh Affairs Committee, House of Commons (2010) *Work of the Committee 2008–09*, Third Report, Session 2009–10, HC 154 (London: The Stationery Office).

Westlake, Martin (1994) *Britain's Emerging Euro-Elite?* (Aldershot: Dartmouth).

Wheeler-Booth, Michael (1989) 'The Lords', in J. A. G. Griffith and M. Ryle (eds), *Parliament: Functions, Practices and Procedures* (London: Sweet & Maxwell).

White, Albert B. (1908) *The Making of the English Constitution 449–1485* (London: G. B. Putnam's Sons).

Whiteley, Paul F. and Winyard S. J. (1987) *Pressure for the Poor* (London: Methuen).

Williamson, Andy (2009) *MPs Online: Connecting with Constituents* (London: Hansard Society).

Williamson, Andy and Fallon, F. (2011) 'Transforming the Future Parliament through the Effective Use of Digital Media', *Parliamentary Affairs*, vol. 64, pp. 781–92.

Wilson, Robert (2010) *5 Days to Power* (London: Biteback Publishing).

Winetrobe, Barry K. (2002) 'Scottish Devolved Legislation and the Courts', *Public Law*, Spring, pp. 31–8.

Winetrobe, Barry K. (2004) 'Making the Law in Devolved Scotland', in A. Brazier (ed.), *Parliament, Politics and Law Making* (London: The Hansard Society).

Winnett, Robert and Rayner, G. (2009) *No Expenses Spared* (London: Bantam Press).

Winzen, Thomas (2012) 'National Parliamentary Control of European Union Affairs', *West European Politics*, vol. 35, pp.657–72.

Wiseman, H. Victor (1966) (ed.) *Parliament and the Executive* (London: Routledge & Kegan Paul).

Woodhouse, Diana (1994) *Ministers and Parliament* (Oxford: Clarendon Press).

Woodhouse, Diana (2002) 'The Law and Politics: In the Shadow of the Human Rights Act', *Parliamentary Affairs*, vol. 55, pp. 254–70.

Wootton, Graham (1975) *Pressure Groups in Britain 1720–1970* (London: Allen Lane).

Worcester, Robert, Mortimore, R., Baines, P. and Gill, M. (2011), *Explaining Cameron's Coalition* (London: Biteback Publishing).

Young, Alison L. (2009) *Parliamentary Sovereignty and Human Rights* (Oxford: Hart Publishing).

Young, Ross, Cracknell, R., Tetteh, E., Griffin, G. and Brown, D. (2003) *Parliamentary Questions, Debate Contributions and Participation in Commons Divisions.* House of Commons Library, Research Paper 03/32 (London: House of Commons Library).

Index